GREAT
BATTLEFIELDS
OF THE WORLD

GREAT
BATTLEFIELDS
OF THE WORLD

John Macdonald

Foreword by General Sir John Hackett

CHARTWELL
BOOKS, INC.

This edition first published in 2002 by
Chartwell Books, Inc.
A Division of Book Sales, Inc.
114 Northfield Avenue
Edison, New Jersey 08837

Conceived, edited and designed by Marshall Editions
The Old Brewery
6 Blundell Street
London N7 9BH
UK

Copyright © 1984 Marshall Editions

ISBN–10: 0-7858-1719-0
ISBN–13: 978-0-7858-1719-2

Printed and bound in China by 1010 Printing Limited

10 9 8 7 6 5 4 3 2

Editors	Anthony Livesey
	Patrick Harpur
Text Editor	Gwen Rigby
Assistant Editors	Louise Tucker
	Clare Badham
Editorial Assistant	Randal Gray
Art Director	Vivienne Quay
Consultant	Dr Brian Holden Reid
	(Lecturer in War Studies,
	King's College, London)
Art Director	Paul Wilkinson
Chief Illustrator	Harry Clow
Picture Research	John and Diana Moore
	(Military Archive and
	Research Services)
Production	Barry Baker
	Janice Storr

Contents

"Take the high ground" is the best-known infantry order. Why? ask the uninitiated. Because from the high ground the low ground can be observed and fired upon. It is not easy to interpret a contour map to find the high ground and for this reason the army uses sand tables to reproduce the hills and valleys so that bored subalterns can be subjected to those tedious exercises that used to be called TEWTs, Tactical Exercises Without Troops.

Throughout history soldiers have admired commanders who could read and understand the landscape over which they must fight. And afterwards historians gain new insights from visiting such battlefields. During my long years of researching *Blitzkrieg* (a book about the battles of the Panzer divisions in May 1940), I made a point of visiting all the terrain through which the Germans fought. Then, a year or so later, I went back again, when it became clear that the weather, the water levels, the 'going', the land, and the visibility in May is quite different from the cold leafless days of the winter. It was instructive to read some history books of this fighting while actually on the site, for it proved beyond doubt that most writers had worked entirely from maps and some had been led into reckless suppositions.

Until computers evolved there was no simple way of interpreting a map. One could, of course, join up common elevations and perhaps colour them to indicate height. More artistic map makers would darken the shadows of hills – as does low-angled sunlight – to give a bird's eye view. But such colouring and shading made any map more difficult to read and for the sake of clarity some other information had to be omitted.

For the computer it is a simple task to superimpose a grid upon a contour map and build a three-dimensional sketch of any piece of landscape.

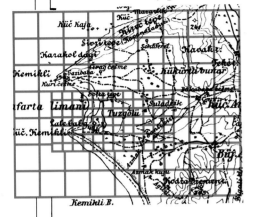

It is one of the marvels of computer graphics that a three-dimensional shape can be turned and twisted into any position, north, south, east or west. And the perspective can be changed to provide a view from anywhere to anywhere. After that came the artist, that neglected and despised figure whose contribution to books of any sort is (for good or bad) more important than any other single factor.

But given the intelligence and skills of the illustrator, it is this employment of computer graphics that makes *Great Battlefields of the World* a brilliant new concept, quite different from any other treatment of this subject. And it is this fresh look at battle sites that provides an opportunity for the armchair historian to look anew at some classic accounts of old wars. Who will be the first to find some glaring errors in 'the memoirs of the victors'?

Len Deighton

Foreword by General Sir John Hackett

Warfare is one of the oldest occupations known to man. It is as ancient and enduring as song or measurement and is likely to persist as long as man remains what he is—contentious, tribal, acquisitive and prone to impose solutions by force. Man's nature has changed little over the millennia. The surface of the earth over the millennia has not changed much either. Warfare in all this time has been conducted on, or near, the surface of the earth, first on land and then at sea, and subsequently in the airspace immediately above both. A new chapter is now opening as operations of war have tended to move not only into upper airspace but beyond that into outer space as well. We do not yet know where we are going in this new dimension. What we know, or should know, is where we are now and how we got here.

Warlike operations confined to the surface of the earth have inevitably been constrained by characteristics and features which have changed little in man's time upon it. The climate, the season of the year, contour and terrain, mountain ridges and ravines, peaks and precipices, snow and ice, sea coast, sandy beach or cliff, marsh or river (whether broad and gently flowing or in a swift and narrow torrent), the places with no water at all and the places with too much, desert, defile and delta—the constraints these have imposed upon military operations in the past have been virtually constant. This theme of the dependence of the pattern of military operations on land upon the unchanging natural environment could be enlarged upon at great length. A short exemplification must suffice here.

The Levant, the coastal strip with sea on one side and desert on the other, which forms a bridge between Asia and Africa, has remained unchanged in essentials since the beginning of recorded history. Over the centuries there has been military movement across this land bridge between two continents of an intensity unmatched anywhere else in the world. Armies moving from north to south (like that of Cambyses, from Persia into Egypt in 525 BC) or from south to north (like Napoleon's, from Egypt into Syria in 1799, or the British Imperial Forces in 1917, or the British Commonwealth Forces and Free French in 1941) could use any or all of three routes. There was the road running north and south along the sea coast. There were the valleys of the Great Rift, from the Gulf of Aqaba up through the Dead Sea and along the Jordan and then the Orontes valleys,

up toward the Taurus mountains, with its passes into Asia Minor. There was also, farther to the east, open desert.

There have never been more than a very few lateral routes available for the movement of military forces across these main axes, and what there are have often been secured at strong points in their turn by Greeks, Romans, Byzantines, Arabs, Franks and Turks. The remains of places they fortified are still to be seen. So is much other evidence of the continuity with which the routes, from east to west or from north to south, have been used.

One of the most spectacular examples of this is to be found on the coast road, at the little gorge where the Nahr el Kalb, the Dog River, near Beirut, tumbles down into the Mediterranean. There is a rock face here, the only place on the road at which the gorge can be crossed without a rough scramble. This rock face carries graffiti, ranging from inscriptions by Persian soldiers long before Christ to those by Australian Light Horse and British Yeomanry in our own time. There is abundant other evidence of the canalization of military movement in the Levant.

In 1187, Jerusalem fell to Saladin, and the Frankish, or Latin, kingdom of the Crusaders was destroyed. Reinforcement of the remnant of the Franks, overland from Europe, was seen to be inevitable and Saladin hurried north to secure the routes, and their strong places, along which what we now call the Third Crusade would have to come—although much of it in the end was to be brought in by sea. I wrote a thesis on this for an Oxford research degree in the thirties.

In 1941, we on the Allied side in the Middle East awaited a powerful German onslaught down through the Caucasus toward the Suez Canal, to coincide with the thrust of the Afrika Corps out of the Western Desert toward the Nile. Wounded in some earlier fighting, I was myself having a lighter time just then as an operations staff major in the British Ninth Army in the Lebanon. We were to prepare divisional defensive positions in the few lateral approaches from the desert over the coast. 'Go out', I was told, 'and reconnoitre suitable places.' 'No need,' I had to reply, 'there is no choice.' You could put your defensive positions only

where Roman, Byzantine, Saracen, Crusader and Turk had put theirs these 2,000 years and more.

That was, in the event, where we put them. The German onslaught through the Caucasus never came: Stalingrad prevented that. During our preparations to meet it, however, reminders of the undeviating pressure of terrain, over the centuries, on military operations were not infrequent. The north–south coastal road between Tripoli and Antioch, for example, runs at one place along a cliff face. In 1188, the galleys of King William II of Sicily came close inshore, to harass Saladin's troops on the march with volleys of arrows fired from the sea. In 1941, the security of that road was vital to us too. There was a real danger that German submarines could interrupt it by torpedo attacks, for a well-directed salvo of torpedoes could bring the cliff down. We had to put out nets, I seem to recall, to protect it.

It is hard to avoid here another personal reminiscence. In 1943, I was training a parachute brigade in Galilee, the brigade I had later to take on to its destruction at Arnhem. The Horns of Hattin, looking down the Sea of Galilee, where Saladin routed the Frankish armies of King Guy of Lusignan in the summer of 1187, were not far away. There was much of interest to be found in that battle. I held a tactical exercise without troops—a TEWT—for officers of 4 Parachute Brigade on it, at the place where it was fought, not forgetting to mention that King Guy was presented with the identical problem over water that faced the British and Anzac forces in the battles for Gaza in 1917—and chose the wrong answer.

Perhaps one more example of the continuity of pattern in Levantine warfare may be permitted. One of the best armoured commanders Britain has ever had was King Richard I, the Lionheart. What does it matter if the armoured weapons platform is powered by one horse or a thousand? It is used in much the same way. Richard's victory at Arsuf in the Third Crusade, in September 1191, was based on tactics for movement (armoured protection on the periphery of lighter and more vulnerable forces moving in the centre) which were also

used in 7th Armoured Division, the Desert Rats, in the Western Desert in 1941. Richard fought his way to a position commanding Jerusalem. Should he go on and take it? His discussion with senior officers near Ramleh in January 1192, as recorded in sources like the Itinerarian Regis Ricardi, strikes twentieth-century echoes. 'We are strong in armour,' the arguments ran, 'and so we could take it. We are not strong in infantry and so could not hold it.' You could have heard Corps commanders talking like that in the 1940s.

Colossal changes in weapons and battlefield techniques over the centuries have done little to reduce the constraints of the natural environment upon operations in war. Nor have they swept into oblivion the methods evolved when techniques and weapons were simple. The turning attack, which is at the heart of the Soviet land-fighting method today—derived by Tukachevsky from Tsarist practice, disregarded after Stalin's purges and now rehabilitated and revered again—goes back to Epaminondas and the victory of the Thebans over Sparta at Leuctra in 371 BC.

The thirty battles analysed in *Great Battlefields of the World*, with the use of advanced techniques hitherto hardly applied at all in this way, will do much to illustrate the dependence of battle-fighting on environment and to open up new and fascinating prospects of further exploration in this and contiguous areas of enquiry. This book marks an important step forward.

General Sir John Hackett, soldier and scholar, with Oxford degrees in Classics and in Medieval History, ended a military career (three times wounded and with three decorations for gallantry in the Second World War) as Commander of NATO's Northern Army Group before returning to university life. A devoted supporter of the Atlantic Alliance, he has particularly close affinities with U.S. forces. His two books on a Third World War have sold more than two million copies worldwide.

Cannae/*August, 216 B.C.*

After the Second Punic War had erupted between Carthage and Rome in Spain in 218 BC, Hannibal and his mixed force of Carthaginians, Numidians, Spaniards and Gauls fought their way northward and, to the amazement of Rome, crossed the Alps in the middle of winter to invade Italy. Hannibal's need to secure plentiful supplies for the Carthaginian army brought him to Cannae in southern Italy in 216 BC. There, in the centre of the corn-growing province of Apulia, was a vast granary from which the Roman Legions were being replenished. Hannibal camped on the right bank of the river some way south of Cannae.

Hannibal had already defeated the Romans twice and, now that their grain supplies were threatened, the people of the Republic clamoured for the overthrow of the invaders. Accordingly the Senate mustered the greatest army that Rome had ever put into the field. Comprising Romans and allies in equal numbers, it was despatched to Cannae under two Consuls, Paulus and Varro, who exercised supreme command on alternate days.

For three days, the armies faced each other across the plain, skirmishing intermittently under a blazing August sun. All the while, Paulus, a much more experienced soldier than Varro, was counselling caution against tackling Hannibal head-on in the open. His sound advice went unheeded on the fourth and fateful day, when Varro resolved to force battle for the honour of Rome, confident that his overwhelming superiority in numbers would guarantee victory. The heat was intense, and a strong wind from the southwest was whipping up columns of dust as the opposing armies arranged themselves for combat.

Outnumbering the Carthaginians by almost two to one, Varro disposed his 80,000 infantry and 6,000 cavalry in the traditional Roman manner—a skirmish line thrown out before a huge, tightly packed phalanx of foot soldiers, flanked by Roman horse on the right and allied horse on the left.

Hannibal, undaunted by this imposing display of military might, deployed the Spaniards and Gauls in a half-moon formation, pointing in convex shape toward the enemy. At each end of the crescent he positioned reserve columns of crack Carthaginian infantry. His left flank was protected by his heavy cavalry, under Hasdrubal, while the magnificent Numidian light horsemen were free to operate on the open ground on Hannibal's right, away from the river.

There was no real clash until Hannibal ordered the heavy cavalry on his left to engage the opposing Roman horse, led by

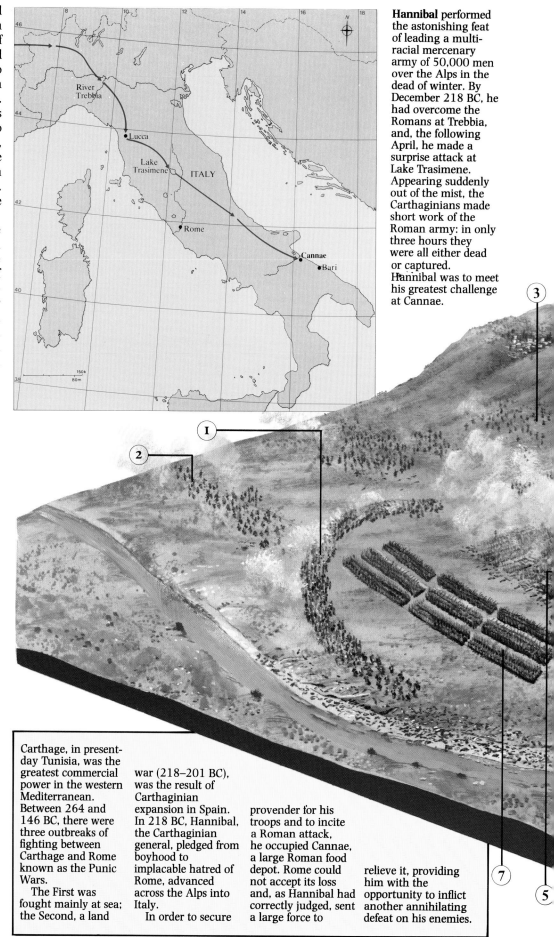

Hannibal performed the astonishing feat of leading a multi-racial mercenary army of 50,000 men over the Alps in the dead of winter. By December 218 BC, he had overcome the Romans at Trebbia, and, the following April, he made a surprise attack at Lake Trasimene. Appearing suddenly out of the mist, the Carthaginians made short work of the Roman army: in only three hours they were all either dead or captured. Hannibal was to meet his greatest challenge at Cannae.

Carthage, in present-day Tunisia, was the greatest commercial power in the western Mediterranean. Between 264 and 146 BC, there were three outbreaks of fighting between Carthage and Rome known as the Punic Wars.

The First was fought mainly at sea; the Second, a land war (218–201 BC), was the result of Carthaginian expansion in Spain. In 218 BC, Hannibal, the Carthaginian general, pledged from boyhood to implacable hatred of Rome, advanced across the Alps into Italy.

In order to secure provender for his troops and to incite a Roman attack, he occupied Cannae, a large Roman food depot. Rome could not accept its loss and, as Hannibal had correctly judged, sent a large force to relieve it, providing him with the opportunity to inflict another annihilating defeat on his enemies.

The battlefield at Cannae, where as many as 70,000 Romans may have perished.

This silver coin—a triple shekel—is thought to portray the great Carthaginian general himself. Coins were minted in Spain in huge numbers in order to pay Hannibal's formidable army of mercenaries.

In August, 216 BC, Hannibal's army (on the right), numbering about 40,000 men and 10,000 cavalry, confronted a Roman army of some 86,000 men, the largest legionary force ever deployed. The battle was fought in an area 1.75 km by 1.5 km (1.1 mls by 0.9 mls).

Spanish and Gaulish horsemen, 1, commanded by the Carthaginian general, Hasdrubal, drove off Paulus's Roman cavalry, 2, from the banks of the River Aufidus.

Varro's allied cavalry, 3, attacked the Numidians, 4, under the command of Maharbal. But after fierce fighting, they were forced to flee to the hilltop town of Cannae.

Varro's Legions, 5, advanced on the Spanish and Gaulish infantry, 6, commanded by Hannibal himself.

The Romans' superior strength pushed them back so that their original formation, a convex crescent, became concave.

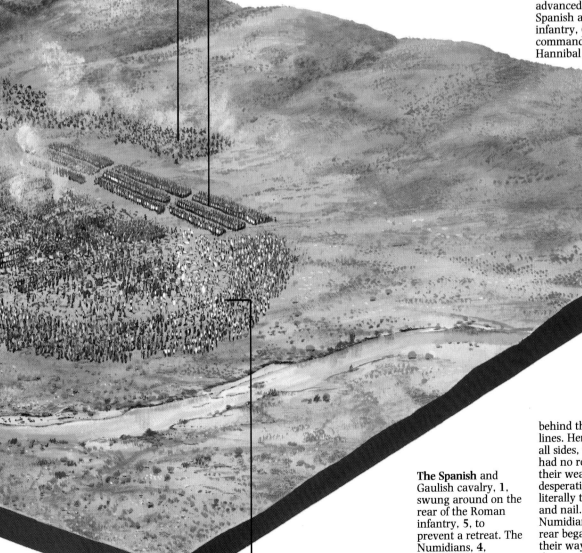

The heavily-armed African infantry, 7, were deployed in a solid block on each flank. Holding their position as the Spaniards and Gauls fell back, they began to close in on the Roman infantry, 5. With every quarter turn they made, the enemy was squeezed tighter.

The Spanish and Gaulish cavalry, 1, swung around on the rear of the Roman infantry, 5, to prevent a retreat. The Numidians, 4, returned from pursuing Varro's cavalry to close in behind the Roman lines. Hemmed in on all sides, the Romans had no room to wield their weapons and, in desperation, began literally to fight tooth and nail. The Numidians at the rear began to work their way through the Roman ranks, hamstringing the men from behind.

Cannae/2

Consul Paulus. They met in violent conflict along the banks of the Aufidus (now the Ofanto); soon the élite of the Roman army was overcome and driven from the field.

Paulus then led the Legions toward the enemy. With choking dust blowing in their faces, the Roman and allied infantry advanced shoulder to shoulder behind a wall of shields, slowly pushing back the outthrust line of Spaniards and Gauls. By sheer weight of numbers they turned Hannibal's half-moon deployment inside out and, scenting easy victory, rushed into the apparently disintegrating centre.

Meanwhile, the Numidian horsemen on the Carthaginian right galloped into action against the allied cavalry under Varro, who may have wished he had listened to his fellow general's advice, for he and his command were mauled and put to flight.

Hannibal waited until the Legions were deep inside his now U-shaped line. He then signalled his uncommitted Carthaginian infantry to swing inward and crush the Romans in a manoeuvre that has come to be known as double envelopment. To the front of the hapless Romans, the retreating Spaniards and Gauls now turned and stood their ground. In their rear, encirclement was completed by the arrival of the enemy's cavalry under Hasdrubal; it had ridden around from its station on the left flank to block the Romans' only avenue of escape.

Hannibal succeeded in wrapping his 40,000 foot and 10,000 horse so tightly around the close-packed Legion ranks that the enemy soldiers had no room to swing their swords. Assailed on all sides by stabbing, hacking Carthaginians, the Romans and their allies suffered fearful slaughter. Both Livy (59 BC – AD 17) and Plutarch (c.AD 46 – c.120) estimated 50,000 dead, while Polybius (c.203 – c.120 BC) set the grim total as high as 70,000.

For the loss of just 6,000 men, Hannibal had inflicted a crushing defeat on Roman arms and had robbed the Republic of a large proportion of its ruling class. Paulus was among those who fell but, ironically, Varro, the instigator of the disaster, escaped.

Hannibal remained in Italy for another 13 years until he was summoned back to Carthage to combat a Roman invasion. There he was defeated by Scipio at the Battle of Zama, in 202 BC. He spent the remainder of his life in the Kingdoms of Asia Minor, resisting the encroaching tide of Imperial Rome. When the fortunes of war once more turned against him, Hannibal took poison rather than fall into the hands of his enemies. A brilliant general, Hannibal's greatest memorial has been the constant emulation of his tactics by commanders down the ages.

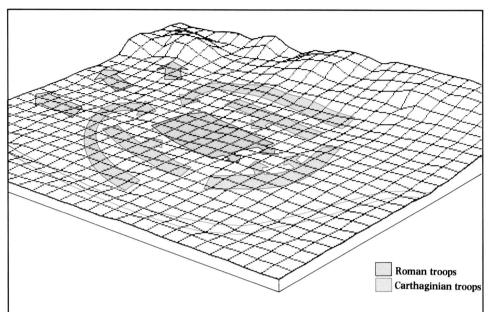

Roman troops
Carthaginian troops

The double envelopment was not only the finest tactical achievement in the whole of Hannibal's career but also an inspiration to many generations of generals, and a recurring feature of warfare—it was used again at the Battle of Tannenberg, in 1914.

Initially, both armies were drawn up in traditional formation with the infantry centrally placed and flanked by the cavalry. Hannibal showed his cunning by deploying his weakest forces, the Spanish and Gaulish infantry, in a convex crescent to meet the brunt of the Roman attack. The crescent soon gave way, and the Romans were drawn forward, only to find themselves encircled by Hannibal's infantry and cut off in the rear by cavalry. Thus trapped, the Romans were crushed as their huge numerical advantage was turned against them.

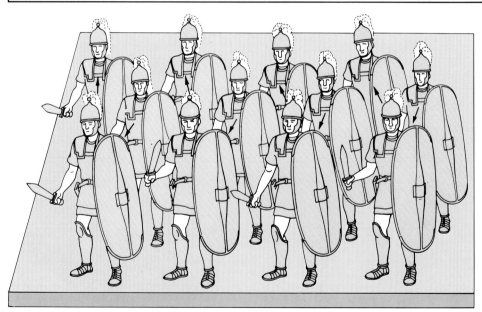

At the time of Cannae, Roman methods of warfare had hardly changed for nearly a century: skirmishers went ahead of the heavy infantry, who followed in maniples or, literally, 'handfuls'. The maniples were staggered so that the men in the second rank could cover the intervals in the first, and those of the third, the intervals in the second.

When attacking, the maniples advanced in an open formation, which allowed the men room to hurl their *pila* and to wield their swords. An attacking position could be changed into a defensive one almost immediately as each rank stepped forward to fill the spaces in the rank in front.

Another advantage was that troops could be withdrawn, and fresh men brought forward through the lines. This way of attacking in relays could be highly effective in wearing down the enemy's front lines.

This frieze at the Temple of Neptune in Rome shows the type of uniform worn by Roman infantry. Helmets were made of bronze, and tunics, weighing over 9 kg (20 lb), were of mail, with leather backing on the vulnerable shoulders. Shields were convex rectangles, made of two layers of wood and covered with leather and canvas; the upper and lower edges were rimmed with iron.

Hannibal's victory over the Romans at Cannae was absolute, but his political objectives were largely unfulfilled. His intention had been as much to break up the confederation of Rome and her dependent states as it had been to destroy her army. In this he failed, however, for the confederation, though dismayed, remained largely intact.

Rome revised her military strategy. So that the army should not risk another direct confrontation with Hannibal's forces, it resorted to guerrilla-type attacks.

In 202 BC, Hannibal fought the last great battle of the Second Punic War at Zama in North Africa. He faced the Roman general, Scipio, who had fought in the ranks at Cannae and had witnessed the superiority of cavalry over heavy infantry. For the first time, Hannibal found his cavalry outnumbered by two to one, and he was defeated.

Some 50 years later, the Third Punic War broke out: Rome destroyed Carthage itself and thereby became the undisputed mistress of the Mediterranean.

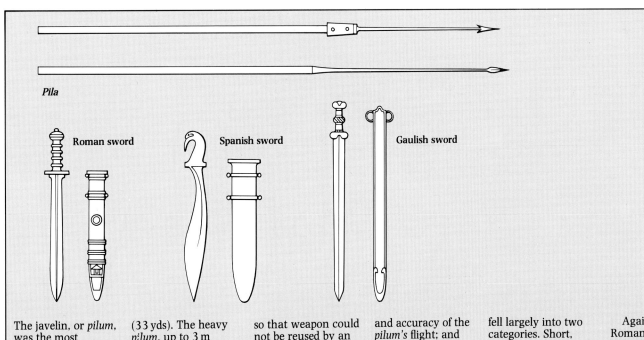

Pila

Roman sword   Spanish sword   Gaulish sword

The javelin, or *pilum*, was the most important Roman weapon and came in two types. The lighter version had a socketed head and, when it was well thrown, could travel about 30 m (33 yds). The heavy *pilum*, up to 3 m (10 ft) long, was thrown just before the infantry charged forward to engage the enemy with swords.

The barbed head was designed to bend so that weapon could not be reused by an opponent. A leather thong, attached to the shaft of the *pilum*, was pulled as it was thrown. This produced a rifling effect, which increased the range and accuracy of the *pilum's* flight; and once it had penetrated a shield, it was extremely difficult to dislodge, so hampering the enemy's movement.

The swords used by Hannibal's forces fell largely into two categories. Short, sharp swords, most effective for stabbing, were favoured by the Spanish; longer swords were chosen by the Gauls for wider sweeping and slashing movements.

Against these, the Romans pitted their pointed, double-edged swords, about 0.6 m (2 ft) long, which were derived from Spanish models and were worn on the right-hand side in the Greek manner.

Hastings/*14 October, 1066*

On his deathbed, Edward the Confessor is reputed to have bequeathed his kingdom to Harold Godwin, then aged about 44 and the most powerful nobleman in the land. Although Harold had no English royal blood, the Witan—the council of the day —ratified his elevation to the throne.

Harold's chief rival for the English crown was William, Duke of Normandy, a distant kinsman of Edward the Confessor. The Duke claimed that, during a visit to England in 1051, the King had bequeathed him the realm should he die without a direct successor. This was the basis of William's claim and in Europe it was widely regarded as being legitimate.

While William was preparing an invasion fleet, another claimant to the throne landed with his troops in the northeast of England—King Harald Hardrada of Norway. The landing caught Harold off balance and with an insufficient force. Since early summer, he had been expecting an invasion from Normandy and had taken the precaution of calling out the fyrd, or local militia, to stand ready to repel it. Several weeks passed but no invasion materialized, so at the end of their two-month term of enlistment—8 September—the militia had to be disbanded and they began to return to their homes.

Harold went north with his bodyguard of housecarles and part of the fyrd which had not yet dispersed. Mounted on ponies, they rode hard toward the enemy and surprised them at Stamford Bridge in Yorkshire on 25 September. Harald Hardrada was killed in the encounter, from which Harold's troops emerged victorious.

Less than a week later, while still at York, Harold learned that, on 28 September, Duke William had landed at Pevensey Bay. He immediately led his depleted force southward on another fast ride, reaching London on about 6 October. He remained there for merely five days, to gather as many men as he could muster at such short notice. Then he marched to the coast to confront the Normans.

On Friday, 13 October, Harold deployed his army on Senlac Hill. It was an ideal defensive position, dominating the Hastings to London road 11 km (7 mls) inland from the Channel coast. The front was only about 550 m (600 yds) long, and his flanks were secured by steep slopes cut with gullies. The Asten stream, running through the western end of the open ground below the heights, created a further obstacle for the invaders.

News of Harold's sudden appearance on Senlac Hill surprised, but did not dismay, William, who was at his fortified camp at Hastings. Then aged 38 and the veteran of

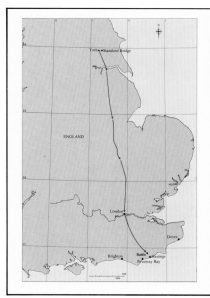

Duke William of Normandy had maintained cordial relations with the English court, but the King, Edward the Confessor, was near to death in 1065 and childless. William had some claim to the throne, but there was a powerful rival: Harold Godwin, Earl of Wessex, Edward's lieutenant and virtual ruler of England.

On Edward's death, Harold, quickly accepted by London and the south where his power lay, was crowned King. Duke William resolved to take by force the kingdom he claimed was his. Support for his cause in Normandy and farther afield was immediate and generous, for all knew that, if William prevailed, rewards in land and plunder would be bountiful.

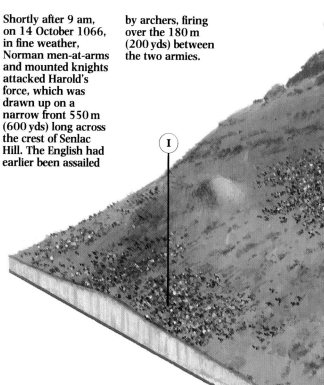

Shortly after 9 am, on 14 October 1066, in fine weather, Norman men-at-arms and mounted knights attacked Harold's force, which was drawn up on a narrow front 550 m (600 yds) long across the crest of Senlac Hill. The English had earlier been assailed by archers, firing over the 180 m (200 yds) between the two armies.

Pevensey Bay, where William's army landed, was unsuitable as a permanent base because it was surrounded by marshy land. Duke William, unmolested by Harold's army, which was still in the north, had leisure to transfer his troops and fleet to the securer position of Hastings. There he ordered the building of an earth and timber castle, to serve him as a base.

A **scene** from the Bayeux Tapestry, *above*, shows Normans carrying chain mail to William's ships.

William's inferior Breton troops, on his left, **1**, were repulsed and then pursued down the hill by the troops of Harold's right wing, **2**.

William saved the situation by sending Norman knights, **3**, to encircle and destroy the pursuing Anglo-Saxons.

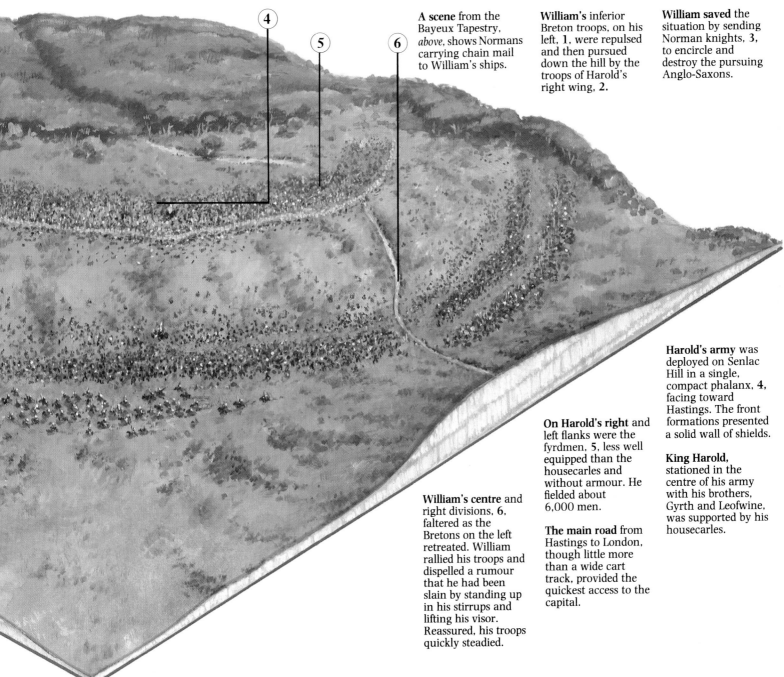

William's centre and right divisions, **6**, faltered as the Bretons on the left retreated. William rallied his troops and dispelled a rumour that he had been slain by standing up in his stirrups and lifting his visor. Reassured, his troops quickly steadied.

On Harold's right and left flanks were the fyrdmen, **5**, less well equipped than the housecarles and without armour. He fielded about 6,000 men.

The main road from Hastings to London, though little more than a wide cart track, provided the quickest access to the capital.

Harold's army was deployed on Senlac Hill in a single, compact phalanx, **4**, facing toward Hastings. The front formations presented a solid wall of shields.

King Harold, stationed in the centre of his army with his brothers, Gyrth and Leofwine, was supported by his housecarles.

many battles, he swiftly gathered in his 6,000 or so troops and marched them north to Senlac at dawn on the 14th.

Across the rising open ground in front of the Anglo-Saxons' hilltop position, William organized his well-rested force into three divisions: on the right, he deployed the French and his mercenaries under Count Eustace of Boulogne; on the left, a predominately Breton contingent led by Count Alan of Brittany, while in the centre, he positioned the strongest element, the Norman formation, which he himself commanded.

It would appear that battle was joined some time after 9am, when William's trumpeters sounded the order for the bowmen to advance and bombard the Anglo-Saxons. This they did with impunity, for Harold had few archers to retaliate. When their quivers were empty, the Norman bowmen moved aside and let the men-at-arms pass through to engage in a grim hand-to-hand trial of strength. After a mêlée of cutting, hacking, stabbing and bludgeoning with swords, axes, spears and clubs, the infantry withdrew to make way for the mounted knights. They fared no better against the Anglo-Saxon line.

Not long after the battle began, it seems that William's inferior Breton troops on his left flank began to flee, chased by a party of ill-disciplined fyrdmen who broke ranks on Harold's right wing. The Bretons' panic began to infect William's other two divisions, but he managed to rally them and sent some of his Norman knights to encircle and cut down the Anglo-Saxons.

After prodding at the Anglo-Saxons with attack after attack, the Duke, mindful of what had happened when his Breton force had retreated earlier, pretended to retreat so as to draw Harold's men off the ridge. The ruse succeeded, for more of the undisciplined fyrdmen rushed in pursuit of what they thought was a fleeing army, only to be surrounded and slaughtered.

The day of the ceaseless conflict was drawing to an end when, if the Bayeux Tapestry is to be believed, William ordered his archers to advance and aim high in the air, so that their arrows would rain down directly on the enemy. This stratagem obliged the Anglo-Saxons to raise their shields above their heads to protect themselves, thus leaving them vulnerable to an assault by men-at-arms and knights.

As the arrows fell, close combat was furiously renewed. In the fierce cut and thrust, the Normans made deep inroads into the fraying Anglo-Saxon ranks. King Harold was hacked to death by a knight; his brothers Gyrth and Leofwine had already been killed, and the leaderless English army began to disintegrate.

The Bayeux Tapestry is an embroidery 68.5 m (75 yds) long, depicting the Conquest and what came immediately before and afterward. This panel shows that the Normans, unlike the Anglo-Saxons, relied heavily on men-at-arms and mailed knights mounted on strong horses. Of William's force, which comprised about 6,000 men, a third were mounted. The principal feature of Norman tactics was the impact of charging cavalry. The horsemen carried lances and, for close combat, swords or axes. At Hastings, cavalry saved the day for the Normans after the retreat of the Bretons on their left, but failed effectively to pursue the enemy at the end of the battle because, in failing light and ignorant of the terrain, many horsemen crashed into a steep valley where, encumbered by their armour, they were immobilized.

The housecarles were specialized, heavily armed soldiers, who formed the backbone of Anglo-Saxon armies. They were united not so much by loyalty to their king as to each other and adhered to a code of conduct whereby each man respected the honour of his fellows. At Hastings, they were stationed in the centre, around King Harold, as a matter not only of military sense but of prestige and traditional right.

Fyrdmen were a local militia which could be summoned by the king, but only for a limited number of days at a time. They had been disbanded immediately prior to the Battle of Hastings, and Harold has been much criticized for not reassembling them in force, despite the delay entailed, before advancing on Duke William.

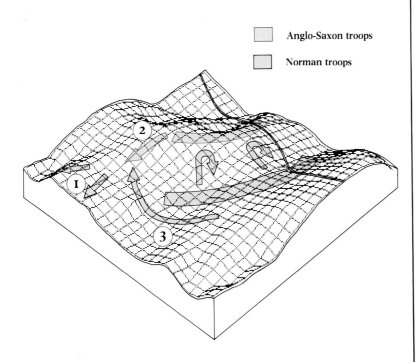

Harold, King of England (*r.* 1066), had been proclaimed as his heir by Edward the Confessor. A brave man and kindly by the standards of the time, on hearing of the Normans' landing and William's brutality he did not delay in seeking battle. He would have been better advised to have recruited his full army before engaging in the decisive battle.

William of Normandy (*r.* 1066–87), an astute politician, had also an unrivalled reputation as a soldier, one familiar with every aspect of warfare. It was his proven ability, rather than his alleged right to the throne of England, that enabled him to raise a force sufficiently large to invade England.

Early in the battle, the attacking Breton contingent, **1,** on William's left was repulsed and withdrew, to be pursued by Harold's fyrdmen, **2,** on his right flank. William saved the day by sending in cavalry, **3,** in a wide sweep well behind the Anglo-Saxons and cutting them down. As a *ruse de guerre,* William's right flank withdrew later in the day and was likewise pursued when he repeated the earlier tactic, with equal success. The Normans always included a sizeable body of cavalry in their armies; the Anglo-Saxons were always unmounted, a decisive factor at Hastings.

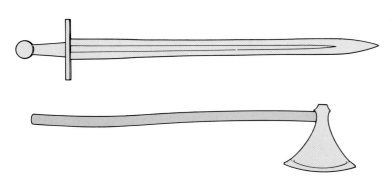

Swords in the 11th century and for many years later were made principally for cutting and so were long and had broad blades. They were heavy and required both strength and dexterity for effective use. Axes, with either single or double heads, were the main Anglo-Saxon weapon. Soldiers would stick the point of their shields into the ground so as to have freedom to use their axes. Most of Harold's army was equipped with them, although some men were armed only with spears or clubs.

The Battle of Hastings was decisive and, ten weeks later, on Christmas Day 1066, 'William the Conqueror', as he has come to be known, was crowned King of England in Westminster Abbey, the great seventh-century church that had been refounded by Edward the Confessor. For some years there was sporadic resistance by the Anglo-Saxons, by such heroes of folklore as Hereward the Wake in the fen country of East Anglia, but all uprisings were doomed, for the Anglo-Saxon army was broken and the Normans, well equipped and organized, were ruthless in their suppression of revolt.

The consequences of Duke William's overwhelming victory at Hastings were profound, diverse and long-lasting. He quickly portioned out vast tracts of his new territory, rewarding his followers in varying degree by dispossessing Anglo-Saxon landowners. Moreover, since only clerics and clerks had skill in writing, he replaced them with Normans, and the language soon became infused with Norman-French. New laws were quickly introduced, as strange as they were objectionable to the Anglo-Saxons; the feudal system was enforced and a major building programme for castles, cathedrals and churches begun. Perhaps most important of all, England became tied to France. A century later, the Norman Empire under Henry II would be the strongest power in Europe, embracing Scotland, Ireland and England in the north and western France to the Pyrenees in the south. Much of Europe's unfolding history would be affected by that mighty and bellicose conglomerate.

Arsuf/7 September, 1191

When Richard I ultimately reached Palestine, on 8 June 1191, he found the Franks divided over who should rule them, even though most of their colony, known as Outremer (beyond the sea), was in enemy hands. Richard backed the faction supporting Guy of Lusignan, whose family were his vassals in the English-occupied part of France. Guy was ineffectual as the King of Jerusalem, as Outremer rulers were titled, and had forfeited his realm after losing the Battle of Hattin in 1187.

King Philip, on the other hand, supported followers of his cousin, Count Conrad of Monferrat, who had emerged as the natural leader of those Franks who survived the disaster of Hattin. Conrad's followers claimed that Guy, who had acquired the crown through marriage, had no right to be restored as King after his crushing defeat and subsequent captivity.

The power struggle continued while siege was laid to a Muslim force in the prosperous Mediterranean port of Acre. All efforts by Saladin, the Muslim leader, to relieve the defenders were thwarted, and, on 12 July 1191, the city capitulated. Terms stipulated the return of the True Cross, payment of a ransom to the Franks and the release of 1,500 Christian prisoners in return for the lives of the garrison.

Richard, Philip, their European Crusaders and local Frankish barons then entered Acre, where they met in conference to settle the question of sovereignty over the Kingdom of Jerusalem. The compromise reached was that Guy was to remain King until his death, when Conrad would succeed him. Now that his kinsman's future was secured, the ailing King Philip relinquished command of his army to the Duke of Burgundy and set sail for France.

Richard the Lionheart, England's warrior king, remained to lead the Third Crusade. His first order was to put the luckless garrison of Acre to the sword. Negotiations with Saladin concerning the fulfilment of the surrender terms had broken down and the King was anxious to begin the march on Jerusalem without being encumbered by some 2,500 prisoners, including women and children. It was a barbarous act that shocked even the Saracens. Richard ordered that the move south should begin on 22 August.

The Crusaders set off along the hot, dusty coastal road toward Jaffa, 96 km (60 mls) away. The army probably numbered some 14,000, and was accompanied by a large baggage train. As the long column of heavily armed men moved slowly on in the fiery heat, it was shadowed by Saladin's army, drawn from a number of Muslim countries. There was constant skirmishing,

Jerusalem was captured by the Muslims in 1187 and the True Cross, Christendom's most sacred relic, fell into heathen hands. The clergy were outraged and Pope Clement III called for the Third Crusade to regain it.

Frederick Barbarossa, the Holy Roman Emperor, was the first monarch to answer the call. He set out for Palestine in 1189 at the head of a huge army. Frederick, however, died on the way to Jerusalem, and this so demoralized his force that little more than 1,000 continued with their journey to the Holy Land.

The Franks, as the European colonists in the eastern Mediterranean were called, then looked to King Richard I of England and the French King, Philip II, to help them recover their lands and pious relics from Sultan Saladin's invading army. Richard was actually at war with Philip at the time, but the two monarchs hastily concluded a peace treaty and set out together on 4 July 1190. It was a long, eventful journey, punctuated by quarrels, although the English and French armies did not always follow the same route. Philip in fact reached the Holy Land seven weeks before Richard, who conquered Messina and the island of Cyprus before turning his attention to Jerusalem.

On 7 September 1191, the Crusaders were a short distance north of Arsuf when Saladin brought them to battle. It was a day of bright sunshine and intense heat. To the Crusaders' rear was the sea; to their front, 3.2 km (2 mls) inland, lay the forest of Arsuf.

Throughout the march south along the coast, the Crusaders had been harassed by attacks from Saladin's force. Richard, however, had so organized his march that, on alternate days, one column of infantry marched in defensive order while another marched 'at ease', so that half of his force was always rested. When the battle began, Richard stationed his baggage

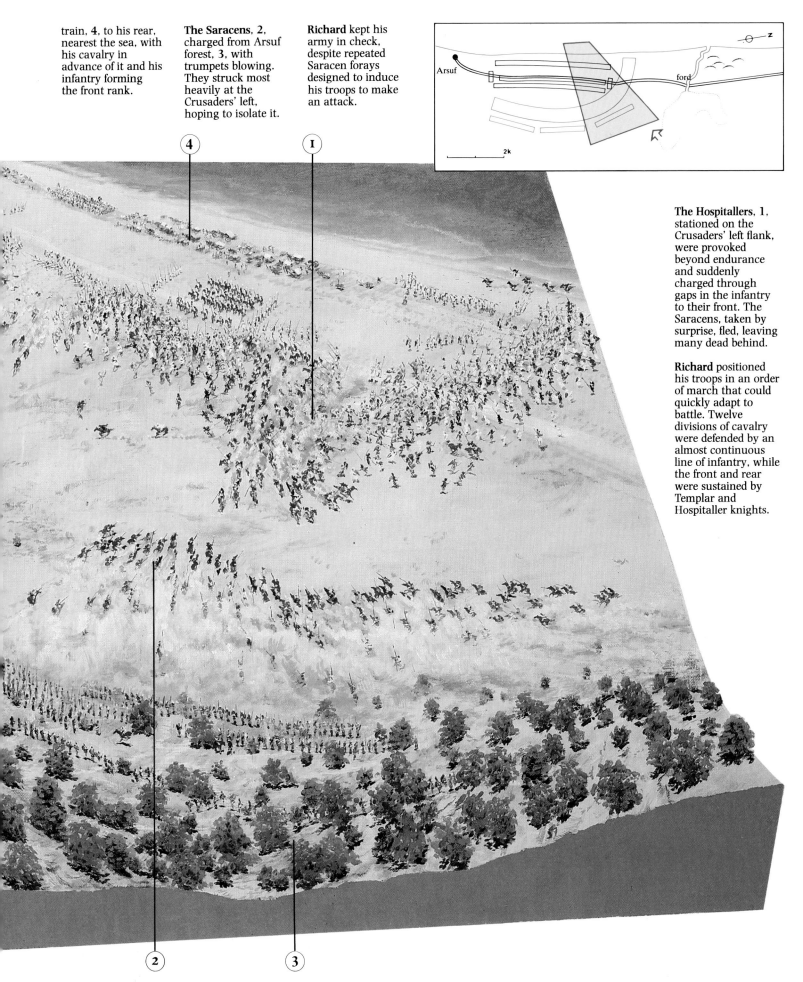

train, **4**, to his rear, nearest the sea, with his cavalry in advance of it and his infantry forming the front rank.

The Saracens, **2**, charged from Arsuf forest, **3**, with trumpets blowing. They struck most heavily at the Crusaders' left, hoping to isolate it.

Richard kept his army in check, despite repeated Saracen forays designed to induce his troops to make an attack.

The Hospitallers, **1**, stationed on the Crusaders' left flank, were provoked beyond endurance and suddenly charged through gaps in the infantry to their front. The Saracens, taken by surprise, fled, leaving many dead behind.

Richard positioned his troops in an order of march that could quickly adapt to battle. Twelve divisions of cavalry were defended by an almost continuous line of infantry, while the front and rear were sustained by Templar and Hospitaller knights.

and harrying attacks were made on Richard's rearguard. Any unfortunate Christian who succumbed to sunstroke and fell behind the main body was butchered in reprisal for the massacre of Acre. Saladin was all the while searching for a site at which to bring Richard to battle.

The English King, however, was not eager to seek a confrontation. His knights in armour and infantry in chain mail and thick felt jerkins were suffering in the unaccustomed heat and were exhausted from the march and from fending off repeated attacks by Muslim archers. Richard called a truce, on 5 September, to conduct peace talks, but these came to nothing.

Two days later, Saladin resolved to force a major trial of strength a few kilometres north of Arsuf on a plain 3.2 km (2 mls) wide, flanked by forest to the east and the Mediterranean to the west.

Richard had no alternative that Saturday morning except to prepare to meet the onslaught he knew would soon be directed against him. He halted his baggage train and detached some infantry to guard it, then drew up his army in battle array with their backs to the sea. He placed a line of archers and infantry in front of the mounted knights, who were his main striking force. On the right of the line of horsemen were the Knights Templar and, on the left, the Hospitallers, two military orders of monks. French, Flemish, Frankish and English chevaliers took position between them, commanded in the centre by King Richard. Time and again Saracen archers and spearmen, operating well ahead of Saladin's main body, tempted the Crusaders into a precipitate charge. The King, an experienced soldier, anticipated this tactic and had ordered his knights not to advance until his trumpet sounded.

It is a tribute to his leadership that he managed to hold so many men of different nationalities in check for so long, for his front line was continually breaking and reforming under the Saracens' attacks, and the knights were anxious to strike back at their enemy. Even when Saladin sent in a cavalry assault on the left flank, and the commander of the Hospitallers sent message after message to Richard appealing for permission to retaliate, the King bade him have patience.

But suddenly two Hospitallers spurred forward, and all along the line other knights followed. Richard quickly took command of the advance which, as it happened, was at almost the time he wanted it. The Saracen army disintegrated as the Crusaders rode through its ranks, skewering Muslims on their lance points and driving the rest from the field.

Richard the Lionheart hard pressed by Saracens.

Two of the most famous military orders took part in the Battle of Arsuf—the Hospitallers and the Knights Templar. Both orders had originally been founded to help pilgrims, the Knights Templar by giving them protection on the road to Jerusalem, and the Hospitallers by providing inns and hospitals. During the 12th century, they developed into an élite military force, committed to fighting anywhere in the defence of Christendom. Hospitallers wore a black mantle with a white cross, while the Templars had a white, hooded mantle, like that worn by Cistercian monks. They replaced this when preparing for battle with a white cloak, with a red cross, *right*.

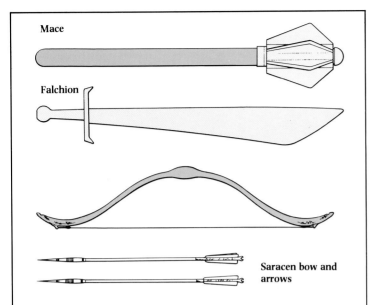

Mace

Falchion

Saracen bow and arrows

In trained hands the iron mace was a formidable weapon: it could crush a skull or break a limb, even through armour. Mace heads, which weighed 1.8–2.7 kg (4–6 lb), were about 14 cm (5½ in) in length.

The English falchion was a short, heavy sword, generally used by infantry. The sword always had a curved cutting edge, but the back of the blade might be straight or curved. Saracen bows

were made from strips of horn, wood and sinew, covered with bark or animal skin. These materials provided elasticity. Arrows had clips of horn to hold them in place on the bowstring.

Richard I (1157–1199) spent almost all his life fighting, not only his enemy, Philip II of France, but also his father and his brothers. On the way home from the Third Crusade, Richard was captured by Leopold V of Austria and held to ransom; an enormous sum was raised by his English subjects.

Saladin (*c.* 1137–1193), declared himself Sultan of Egypt, and made conquests along the North African coast and in Syria and Palestine. His capture of Jerusalem seemed to presage the collapse of Christendom. A patron of the arts, Saladin was also renowned for his chivalry.

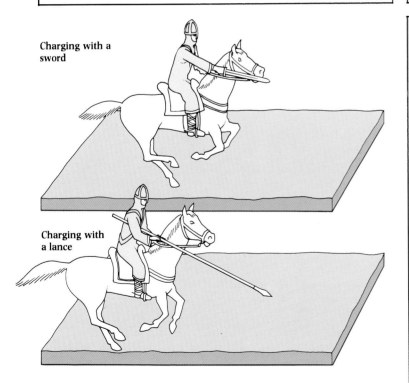

Charging with a sword

Charging with a lance

During the middle ages knights carried a lance, a sword and often a shield as well. The lance was about 3 m (10 ft) in

length, with a pointed blade, carried tucked under the arm and directed forward. The lance usually

broke on first impact; thereafter the knight relied on his sword, which sometimes replaced the lance in a charge.

The victory at Arsuf—the only major battle of the Third Crusade—followed close on the fall of Acre and enhanced Christian morale, for Richard I had broken the spell of Saladin's invincibility. But it was Richard as diplomat who contributed most to the Third Crusade. Although Jerusalem and the True Cross eluded him, his treaty with Saladin re-established the Frankish principalities along the coast and guaranteed Christian pilgrims free access to the shrines of the Holy Land. Few Crusaders could claim to have achieved so much.

The long-term effects of the Third and other Crusades, notably the Fourth, were profound. Trade between western Europe and the Levant increased from the twelfth century onward, the influence of Arab Islamic culture spreading westward along the trade routes developed in the Crusade period. A large number of crops—spices, lemons, oranges, peaches, maize, rice, dates and sugar cane, among much else—became generally known in the West for the first time. Moreover, Arabic art in the form of oriental carpets, jewellery, enamel work, glassware and ivory carvings, became much sought after. Perhaps most important, words of Arabic origin—notably in astronomy and the sciences—found their way into western languages. By the time the Crusade movement declined, the cities of the Levant had achieved such economic and political power that they could raise military support for themselves, and trade between east and west continued to flourish without interference.

Crécy/*26 August, 1346*

In 1337, the first blows were struck in what developed into 116 years of intermittent fighting between England and France. Hostilities reached a peak in 1346, with sieges and counter-sieges in disputed Aquitaine. Edward III resolved to invade northern France and raised an army of 10,000 experienced troops for the purpose: more than half of them were yeomen archers.

On 11 July 1346, he and his men embarked at Portsmouth and landed in Normandy the next day. He was cut off in hostile territory when his fleet, mistaking their orders, prematurely sailed for home. Edward then had no option but to march north toward Flanders, an area friendly to him. By the time the English reached the River Somme near Abbeville, Philip VI of France had mustered an intercepting force which far outnumbered the invaders.

Discovering that all the bridges in the area were either destroyed or too well defended to force, and that the French were closing in on him, Edward had hastily to find a means of crossing the wide waterway to avoid being cornered. Offers of a large reward had the desired effect. A certain Gobin Agache valued English gold above loyalty to France and guided Edward and his troops to a ford at Blanque Taque.

On the other side of the river, 16 km (10 mls) north of Blanque Taque, Edward happened on a position that was admirably suited to a defensive battle featuring the concentrated fire of his longbowmen. There, at Crécy-en-Ponthieu, he decided to stand and fight.

On the morning of Saturday 26 August, the English deployed themselves in battle array along a ridge, running roughly southwest to northeast for some 1,800 m (2,000 yds) between the villages of Crécy and Wadicourt. To the front, the ridge fell away gradually to open ground; behind lay the thick woods of Bois de Crécy Grange.

Edward's front line was drawn up across the entire forward slope. It comprised two phalanxes of foot soldiers and dismounted men-at-arms—1,800 on the right and 800 on the left—each supported on both sides by formations of up to 1,000 archers, angled steeply outward. The bowmen thus formed a 'V' in the centre, linking the two wings of Edward's army. Pits had been dug and spikes driven into the ground in front of the archers to prevent their being ridden down by cavalry; these defences would also serve to funnel attacking horsemen into the infantry, exposing the horses' flanks to a flurry of arrows.

A second line, drawn up centrally a little behind the two front divisions, or battles as they were then known, contained 700 men-at-arms, either mounted or standing

Edward III's army landed at St Vaast on 12 July and the next six days were occupied unloading men and stores. He then moved south to St Lô, with his fleet at first accompanying him close to the shore. Pillaging as they went, the army moved eastward. Edward reached Acheux on the very day that the Flemish, his allies, unaware he was so close, broke camp and retired eastward. On 24 August, the English crossed to the other bank of the Somme, near Crécy.

Edward III drew up his army along a ridge, some 1,800 m (2,000 yds) long, with his right flank resting on the Maye River, and his left on Wadicourt. The ground dropped away on both sides, making this a strong defensive position. Although the French had been within striking distance since afternoon, no attack was made until after 6 pm, the hour of vespers. Bright sunshine, following a brief rain storm, shone directly into the faces of the French army.

Edward III and his second line of knights, **1**, were stationed to the rear, with a body of archers at each side.

Crécy

Numerous antagonisms between England and France led, in 1337, to the outbreak of the Hundred Years War. Successive English monarchs had been obliged to pay homage to the French kings for their possessions in present-day France, a vexation to a man of Edward III's proud nature. There were other grievances, too, that drove Edward to war. For a long time, there had been intermittent naval engagements between English and French ships in the Channel and, more important, the French consistently gave comfort and support to Scotland, with which England was at war.

Then, in 1328, Charles IV of France died without leaving an heir. Philip of Valois was crowned and demanded homage from Edward III, but the English King, who had a claim himself, albeit remote and through the female line, recognized that this issue was his most plausible excuse for going to war.

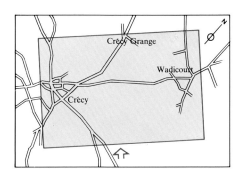

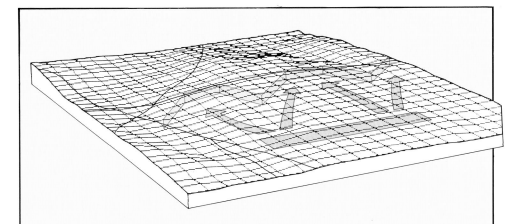

Edward's wagon park of baggage and horses, **2**, was positioned to the rear, close to a wood. From there, supplies of arrows could be brought rapidly forward, and, in an emergency, the wagoners could seek the protection of the dense wood.

The main English force comprised two battles, or divisions, of foot-soldiers and mounted knights, with about 1,000 archers jutting forward in arrowhead formation between them, **3**. To the right and left of the foot-soldiers were more archers, also in arrowhead formation.

Though the battle did not begin until shortly after 6 pm and the French army, much of it still coming up, was in disorder, no fewer than 15 charges were made by French knights before they abandoned the field. They made frontal attacks, and their horses were exposed to enfilade fire from the deadly longbows—just as the English had planned.

Once it became clear that Philip's main attack was coming from the left, English men-at-arms advanced to threaten the French right, **4**.

Those Genoese cross-bowmen, who had survived both the first onslaught by English archers and the wrath of their French masters, fled in disordered terror, **5**.

The French, **6**, would have been well advised to wait until the next day before engaging, but, fearful that their enemies might withdraw, they came on, although in disorder. Philip VI tried to form his army into coherent battles, but the soldiers pressing on from behind made this impossible.

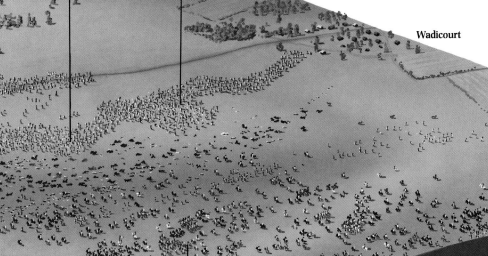

Wadicourt

The King of France persisted in his attacks until dark, finally bringing up his third battle. This merely added to the chaos and caused him to lose even more of his knights.

French horses shied away from the deluge of arrows and, bolting out of control, galloped straight at the English men-at-arms—especially on the English right, **7**, which was ostensibly commanded by the 17-year-old Prince of Wales.

At times, when the French drew back, Welshmen, who carried long knives, rushed forward and killed fallen French knights. This was against Edward's orders, for valuable ransoms were thereby lost.

Fallen and dead horses and knights littered the ground between the two armies, impeding ensuing charges by the French.

to horse, with 2,000 archers on its flanks. Here Edward stationed himself.

In the late afternoon a lookout in the windmill (the hillock on which it stood can still be seen) warned that Philip's army was approaching. Some sources place his strength at 12,000, others go as high as 40,000. The lower figure is more likely.

On the road from Abbeville, the French ranks were in confusion. Philip had intended to make camp in sight of the enemy and join battle on the morrow, but he could not control his troops, who, thirsting for a fight, pushed on in disorder to Crécy. The sanguinary ardour of the leading elements soon cooled, however, when they realized the strength of Edward's position. The front ranks halted, then fell back; the rear ranks cannoned into them.

Accepting that a battle that evening was now inevitable, the French king tried to instil some order by bringing to the front his Genoese mercenaries with their cumbersome crossbows, thinking—falsely, in the event—that these weapons were more effective than the longbow.

Battle began with a volley of bolts from the Genoese crossbowmen. In reply, Edward's yeomen took a pace forward, drew their longbows and let fly a tornado of arrows, which so convulsed the Genoese that they broke and ran. A slight alteration of aim, and mounted men-at-arms became the target of the English archers. Fleeing crossbowmen, rearing and bucking horses and growing numbers of dead and wounded clogged the French front but did not deter battle-crazed riders spurring on from behind. The French cavalry galloped through the turmoil, laying about the Genoese with their swords to clear a way to the enemy. Charging up the incline, they made straight for the English men-at-arms, as Edward had expected, and were flayed by close-range enfilade fire from thousands of longbows. Time and again, uncoordinated clutches of armour-clad knights rode into Edward's lines to engage in vicious hand-to-hand combat.

Darkness had fallen when Philip's remaining knights launched their fifteenth and final charge. This was repulsed, and they relinquished the field in defeat.

Some reports claim that more than 10,000 French dead lay before them. This may be an excessive estimate, but what is certain is that the nearly blind King of Bohemia, the Duke of Lorraine, 10 counts and more than 1,500 knights and squires perished at Crécy. Edward's losses have been placed at about 100, which seems improbably low considering the duration of the battle and the number of men believed to have been involved.

English society in the 14th century was governed by the feudal system, under which military service and homage were given by vassals in return for an allotment of land. In this way the king could, in times of need, call on the services of his subjects, however humble. Edward III's archers, however, were a well-paid force of selected men, who had undergone rigorous training in the use of the longbow, weekly practice in the butts being obligatory. Archers, justly prized, received the high pay of 6 pence a day. They wore leather jerkins, a cap of leather (often reinforced with iron) and a cloak, used both to sleep in and to protect their bowstrings from rain. During the Crécy campaign, each archer was mounted on a fast pony for transport, but he fought on foot.

The longbow, of Welsh invention, was incorporated into English armoury by Edward I. By the time of his grandson, Edward III, its power and the skill of the bowmen had been so developed that even the strongest armour was not always adequate against its fire. Longbows were 1.8-m (6-ft) staves of yew or elm, tensioned by a bowstring and capable of propelling, with great accuracy, a 92-cm (36-in) steel-tipped arrow some 256 m (280 yds). Each archer carried an iron-tipped stake, which, in battle, he plunged into the ground in front of him, and which afforded him stout protection against cavalry.

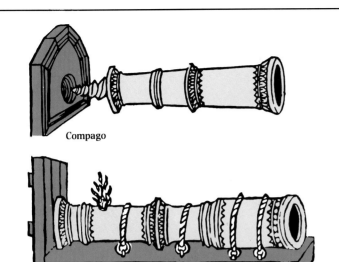

Compago

Tormentum

Woodcuts from the late 15th century give an indication of the type of cannon that Edward III possessed, although particulars are not recorded. The King is thought to have had three cannon at Crécy, which he posted with his archers. Thus at the time of the longbow's greatest triumph, the weapon that would ultimately replace it was already deployed.

During the Hundred Years War, France had a population five times that of England and greater wealth in natural resources. French defeats at English hands were inflicted largely by the longbow's astonishing speed of fire. Why, then, did not the French adopt this weapon themselves?

The answer, in part, stems from the rigid feudal structure of French society. It had seemed inconceivable to the nobility that they could be broken by mere English yeomen; even after Crécy they were slow to learn the lesson. Furthermore, they were equally contemptuous of their own peasant levies and did not deign to spend money on arming or time on training them. Equally important, they feared to put so formidable a weapon into the hands of those who might revolt and use it against them. From this stemmed all their ensuing reverses, culminating in the Battle of Agincourt in 1415, and great loss of land. Almost all of their territory was to be recaptured, however, during the reign of England's hapless King Henry VI.

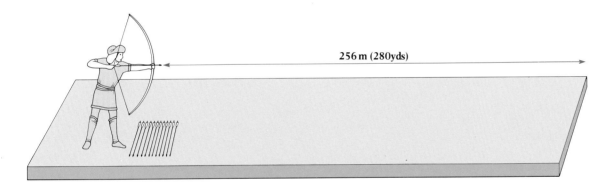

256 m (280yds)

The longbow was cut from springy sapwood for the ends and dense heartwood in the middle for strength. At the time of Crécy, it was slightly outranged by the crossbow but was more efficient. The overwhelming advantage of the longbow, however, lay in the speed with which trained bowmen could fire the weapon—up to 10 arrows a minute. Moreover, since longbowmen leant into their bows and fired facing sideways, a great many archers could be deployed within a small area.

320 m (350 yds)

The 14th-century crossbow fired either arrows or bolts. It was an extremely accurate weapon, since the top of the bolt could be used for precise sighting. The crossbow's great drawback lay in its having to be wound up before each shot, allowing the bowman to discharge only one bolt a minute.

Breitenfeld/*17 September, 1631*

In 1611, when he was only 17 years old, Gustavus Adolphus succeeded to the Swedish throne. A keen but critical student of warfare, he quickly evolved a military force that differed in almost every respect from those of other European powers.

When the struggle between Roman Catholic and Protestant nations, known as the Thirty Years War, was in its twelfth year, and the fighting had spread to Germany's Baltic shore, Gustavus feared a direct threat to Sweden. Rather than wait for the conflict which was engulfing Europe to spread to his own country, he decided to support the wavering Protestant cause.

At the head of his disciplined, well-armed, well-equipped and—by the standards of the day—exceedingly mobile army, Gustavus Adolphus established a bridgehead at Usedom in Pomerania, north Germany, on 6 July 1630. At that time, Germany comprised several principalities, ruled by Electors, and it was evident that not all of them welcomed the presence of the 36,000-strong Swedish army, with its leavening of Scottish and German mercenaries, despite the threat by Count Tilly and his 40,00 men. Tilly championed the cause of the Holy Catholic League, led by the Habsburg emperor, Ferdinand II.

The aftermath of the siege of Magdeburg changed their minds. Gustavus had been denied permission to march across the Electors' territories to the aid of the surrounded city, which fell on 20 May 1631. In the looting that followed, Magdeburg was set on fire, and contemporary reports record that more than 20,000 citizens perished in the flames.

This horrifying event marked the end of Protestant apathy, and several states allied themselves to the Swedes. The Elector of Saxony, however, still hesitated until, early in September, Tilly's marauding army crossed his frontiers and threatened to destroy Leipzig as it had Magdeburg. He then offered his forces to serve under the Swedish banner; the two columns met at Duben and set out to relieve Leipzig, 24 km (15 mls) to the south.

A mist covered the plain near Breitenfeld at dawn on 17 September, as the Swedes moved to confront Tilly. Predictably, Tilly drew up his 40,000 men in typical Spanish formation across the brow of rising ground, but Gustavus arranged his battle order in his own innovative fashion. In the centre were four infantry brigades, supported by a further two and a regiment of cavalry, with three more brigades and two regiments of horse in reserve. Strung out in squadrons on the right were six regiments of cavalry, interspersed with platoons of musketeers, with another cavalry regiment in support

The Thirty Years War, which began in Germany in 1618, was originally a struggle between Roman Catholics and Protestants, the *casus belli* being a dispute over the crown of Bohemia. Germany then was divided into principalities, all eventually to be engulfed by the war. Outside help for the Protestant princes' fight against the Habsburg Empire came first from King Christian IV of Denmark, in 1624, then from King

Gustavus Adolphus of Sweden in 1630, when he perceived a Catholic threat to his own country. His intervention pleased Cardinal Richelieu, Chief Minister of France, which, although Catholic, wanted to break Habsburg power.

On 20 May 1631, the Imperialists sacked Magdeburg. The city was razed to the ground and 20,000 citizens are alleged to have perished in the fires that followed. For civilians, it was the most terrible massacre in the annals of the Thirty Years War. It shook the Protestant world and inflamed the Protestant cause. Shocked out of their intransigence, the Electors welcomed Gustavus as their champion and at last gave him freedom to cross their lands. John George, Elector of Saxony, joined his

army to the Swedes' and together they marched on Leipzig, which was under threat from Tilly of a repeat of the Magdeburg horror. The destruction of Magdeburg so outraged Europe that, as a result, the concept of 'limited' warfare was born.

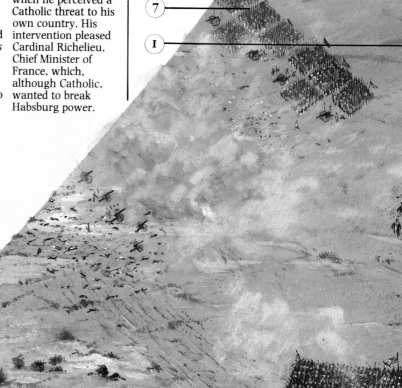

As Tilly's infantry bore slowly down on the Swedes, their ranks were thinned by Gustavus's light regimental guns, **4**. These canister-firing 4-pounders were easy to re-site rapidly.

The Saxons quit the field without a fight when Tilly's cavalry approached. They stopped only long enough to loot the baggage train of their Swedish allies.

To strengthen the extremity of his improvised left flank, Gustavus moved across infantry, **5**, from his central reserve force.

After Tilly's cavalry, 6, had driven off the Saxons, they were sent to attack the Swedish rear.

3

The Battle of Breitenfeld was fought on a front 3.2 km (2 mls) long, on 17 September 1631. By early afternoon, the situation on the Swedish left seemed critical after the collapse of their Saxon allies, but Gustavus was quick to react.

When Tilly saw the Saxons flee, uncovering the Swedish left, 1, he ordered his huge infantry formations, 2, to manoeuvre and deliver a blow against the enemy's exposed flank. Such a move would have beaten a conventional foe—but not Gustavus.

As soon as Gustavus noted Tilly's flanking move, he had the forces on his left, mainly cavalry, 3, swiftly change front and meet the astonished enemy with a hail of fire. Later, the Swedish King led the rest of his horse from the right into the fray.

King Gustavus Adolphus, the Lion of the North, is portrayed here by Jean Walther at Breitenfeld in 1631. An inspired leader, he was the finest militarist of his age.

The left-centre of the Swedish line, 7, stood firm while the enemy manoeuvred to change front. They became involved only when the battle had developed.

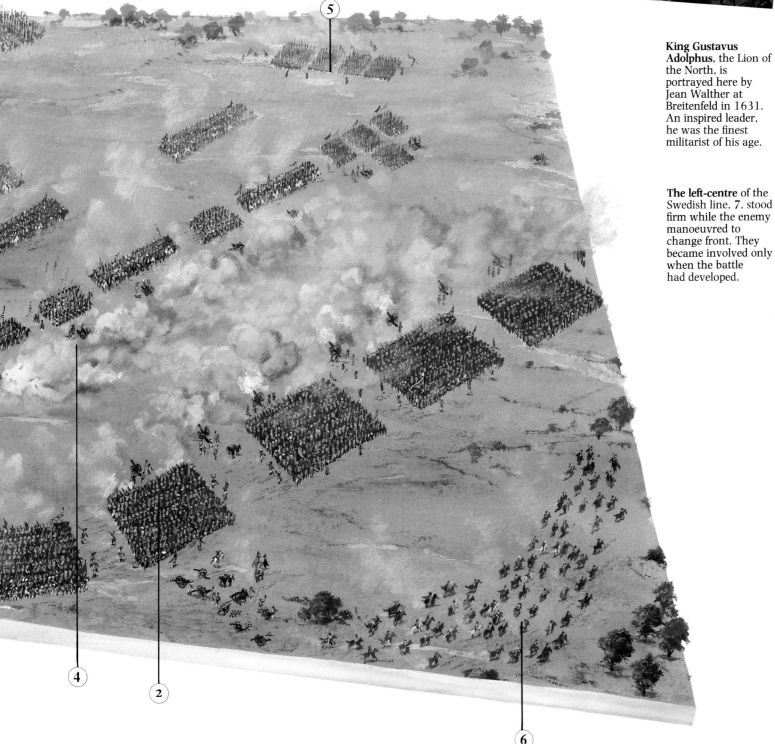

and four squadrons in reserve. On the left were three cavalry regiments, with two platoons of musketeers and a reserve of two regiments. Beyond the Swedish left, the Saxon contingent drew up in a formation that was unrecorded. Each Swedish infantry regiment had its light guns, and the King ordered the heavy artillery to be positioned slightly forward of his centre.

Battle commenced with a cannonade lasting two and a half hours, in which the Swedish gunners gave a convincing demonstration of their superior firepower. The effect of their bombardment on the enemy left was so shattering that Count Pappenheim, its commander, broke ranks without Tilly's authority and charged at the head of 5,000 horse. Seven times they performed the *caracole* in the face of deadly fire from Gustavus's cunningly positioned musketeers. All their attacks failed, and Pappenheim's cavalry was driven off in disorder by a massive, galloping countercharge by the Swedish horse.

On Tilly's right flank, the cavalry took a lead from Pappenheim and also charged without orders. They trotted up to the Saxons who, to the astonishment of all, turned and fled, leaving the Swedes' left flank dangerously exposed.

Tilly, who belatedly took control of his wayward army, seized the opportunity and began slowly to turn his unwieldy masses of infantry to envelop the Swedes' left, while his cavalry was dispatched to circle around and fall on their rear.

In ordinary circumstances, this move would have decided the outcome. But Gustavus Adolphus was able to change his front quickly and to present a united firing line to the surprised enemy forces bearing down on him. As Tilly's troops recoiled, Gustavus Adolphus led the cavalry, which he had brought over from his secure right, in a charge at his opponent's left. The Swedes then poured in close-range artillery fire, even turning captured guns on their former owners. For a time, Tilly's infantry bravely grappled with their assailants, but their lines ultimately broke, and they streamed from the field. They were pursued by the Swedish cavalry, led by Gustavus Adolphus himself.

The forces of the Holy Catholic League lost 13,000 men; Swedish losses numbered fewer than 3,000 casualties, most of whom fell during the early cannonade.

The engagement at Breitenfeld was a triumph for King Gustavus Adolphus and laid the foundations for a complete change in European battle tactics. A year later the King led his troops to another victory at the Battle of Lützen, but he was killed during the action.

Gustavus had long realized what Tilly was probably too old to learn—that Spanish military methods were outmoded. His method of conducting a cavalry charge—a terrifying dash made at full gallop with drawn swords—was in marked contrast to the manoeuvre known as the *caracole*, employed by Tilly's horsemen. This Spanish type of cavalry attack, made at a trot in ranks ten deep, relied more upon the pistol than the sword. The men discharged their pistols and then wheeled to the rear to reload before advancing again.

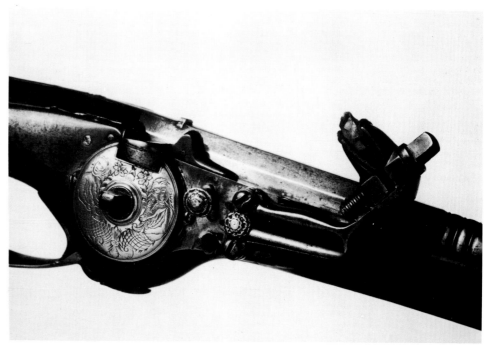

The wheel-lock, *above*, had a mechanism similar to that of a modern cigarette lighter.

The wheel was wound up on a spring, with a wrench rather like a piano tuner's key. Pulling the trigger set the wheel spinning and brought down a piece of iron pyrites, held in the doghead. The sparks produced by the flint striking the serrated edge of the wheel ignited the priming powder in the pan.

Being armed with wheel-locks enabled the Swedish army to fire off three rounds to their enemies' one so that, as one writer put it, they were able to 'quail, daunt, and astonish them three times more'.

The almost continuous fire of his musketeers was Gustavus's chief weapon, but he also retained large numbers of pikes in his army, not merely as an adjunct to the musket but as an integral part of his war machine. By exploiting the characteristics of each weapon, Gustavus produced a combination of shot and pike, which was improved upon by the introduction of the fixed bayonet later in the 17th century.

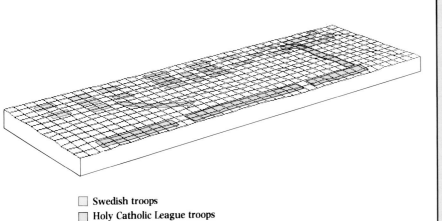

☐ Swedish troops
☐ Holy Catholic League troops

The Swedish victory at Breitenfeld turned the tide of the Thirty Years War. Gustavus was applauded as the Protestant champion and his success laid the foundations for the considerable increase in Swedish power and prestige that was to make her one of the leading powers in Europe over the next half century. Cardinal Richelieu was not pleased. He had hoped that Gustavus would counterbalance Imperial power, not destroy it. Within three months, Gustavus controlled all northwestern Germany; he then moved southward. Forced to withdraw into Saxony, he gave battle at Lützen, near Leipzig. The Imperial forces were driven from the field, but the Protestant cause suffered an irreparable loss in the death of Gustavus. Had he lived, it was probable that he would have attempted to build a Protestant confederation under Swedish leadership. This project was stillborn, and within two years Swedish forces had been defeated at Nordlingen. France was forced to enter the war, a bloody struggle that was to last for another 14 years.

At the climax of the battle at Breitenfeld, it was the Swedes' ability to form, without delay or confusion, a new front on the flank exposed by the flight of the Saxons that proved decisive, despite the weight of numbers ranged against them. Such mobility was due to the regular training and discipline of Gustavus's troops—perhaps really possible only in a conscript army—and to the small, mobile troop deployments he had evolved. This could hardly have been in greater contrast to Tilly's heavily accoutred phalanxes. Since the early 16th century, Spanish methods of deployment had dominated European warfare. Typical of the Spanish troop disposition was the *tercio, right,* a massive formation consisting of a central group of pikemen surrounded by a 'sleeve' of musketeers, who were also ranged in dense squares at the corners. Each *tercio* could consist of between 1,500 and 3,000 men; though formidable in action, it was unwieldly for rapid changes of tactic in mid-battle.

It was Gustavus Adolphus's genius that revolutionized almost all aspects of the warfare of his time. Eager to exploit new technological developments, he streamlined armaments, making muskets and field guns lighter and more manageable. The lightened musket could be operated without a rest or tripod to support it, and the lengthy and complex loading procedure was simplified by introducing paper cartridges, *above,* which contained both powder and shot. Ten of them were issued to each musketeer, who bit off the end with his teeth before loading. Paper cartridges had already been proposed by Leonardo da Vinci in the 15th century.

Gustavus Adolphus II (1594–1632) was King of Sweden for 21 years. His army was the forerunner of all modern European armies, and his inspired leadership was admired by Napoleon, who compared him with Alexander the Great. Perhaps the only real strategist of the Thirty Years War, he remains to the Swedes the epitome of the hero-king.

Count Johannes Tilly (1559–1632). In the service of Duke Maximilian I of Bavaria, Tilly commanded the army of the Catholic League. Small in stature, but fierce in appearance, Tilly was a stern disciplinarian. He was defeated again by Gustavus Adolphus in 1632 at the crossing of the Lech, where he was fatally wounded.

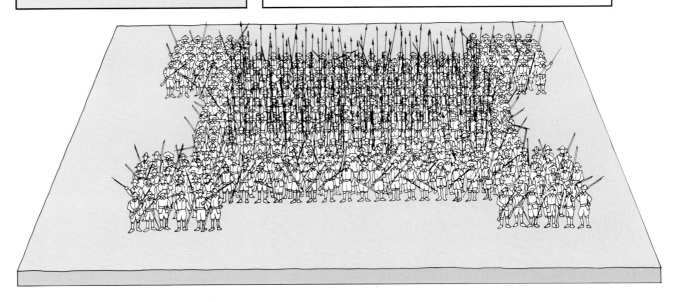

Naseby/*14 June, 1645*

In February 1645, the English Parliament consented to a plan to reconstitute various bodies of Roundhead troops into one professional force called the New Model Army. Sir Thomas Fairfax was appointed its first commander.

The New Model Army marched west to raise the siege of Taunton on 30 April 1645, but at Blandford they received new orders to turn north and invest Oxford, the King's wartime capital. But Charles I and his army were not at Oxford. Having rejected Parliament's peace terms early in May, the Royalists were marching to the assistance of their besieged stronghold at Chester, when news came that the siege had been lifted. The King then determined to assault the prosperous but ill-fortified Parliamentary town of Leicester.

After Leicester had fallen, Charles decided to march south to relieve Oxford, and, on 5 June, the Royalist army reached Market Harborough. That same day Fairfax lifted the siege on Oxford and moved north to bring the King's men to battle.

At Daventry, 40 km (25 mls) from Leicester, Charles learned that the New Model Army was advancing upon him and he resolved to retreat farther north. On 13 June, Fairfax, knowing that the Royalists were near by, decided to bring them to battle—a decision that met with the strong approval of his Lieutenant-General of Horse, Oliver Cromwell, who had brought an additional 700 cavalry into the Parliamentary camp at Kislingbury. Learning that the Parliamentarians were now only a short distance behind him and moving more quickly than expected, Charles made up his mind to stand and fight. Although his army was small, probably no more than 9,000 in all to the Roundheads' 13,000, it was well trained and confident after its recent victory at Leicester.

Saturday 14 June found the Royalists, with their considerable train of artillery, occupying a strong position on a ridge 6 km (4 mls) north of Naseby. The Roundhead camp was 4.8 km (3 mls) to the south, but when Cromwell and Fairfax inspected the ground at dawn, they decided it was too marshy for the cavalry and Cromwell obtained permission to move the Parliamentary army to Red Hill, a ridge 1.6 km (1 ml) to the rear, on the outskirts of Naseby.

Seeing this rearward movement and thinking that Parliament's new army was retiring, Prince Rupert of the Rhine, the Commander-in-Chief of the Royalist army, was encouraged to take precipitate action. Without waiting for the cannon, he hurried his forces forward.

Large numbers of men can be concealed in the rolling countryside around Naseby. It

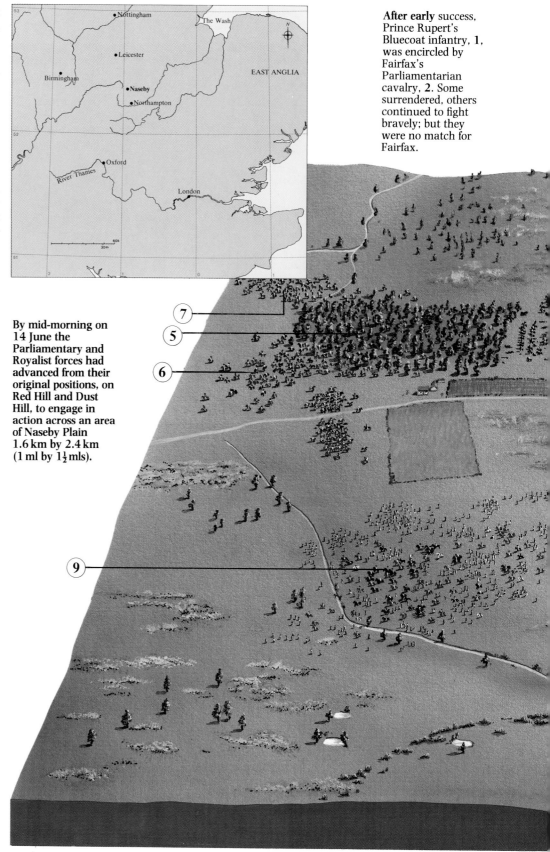

By mid-morning on 14 June the Parliamentary and Royalist forces had advanced from their original positions, on Red Hill and Dust Hill, to engage in action across an area of Naseby Plain 1.6 km by 2.4 km (1 ml by 1½ mls).

After early success, Prince Rupert's Bluecoat infantry, **1**, was encircled by Fairfax's Parliamentarian cavalry, **2**. Some surrendered, others continued to fight bravely; but they were no match for Fairfax.

The volleys and charges of Fairfax's troops, **2**, gave way to close combat with musket-butts and swords.

Cromwell and his cavalry, **3**, relieved their hard-pressed infantry by attacking the Royalist flank and rear in three waves.

The encirclement of the Royalist infantry was completed by Okey's dragoons, **4**, in a sweeping cavalry-style movement.

Langdale's Royalist cavalry, **5**, was routed early on and driven back into Long Hold Spinney. Some rallied around the

On 22 August 1642, King Charles I raised his standard at Nottingham and signalled the start of the English Civil War. The event came as no great surprise: the clash of interests between King and Parliament had been coming to a head for a considerable time. Fragmentary struggles broke out around the country as the supporters of each side sought control over local militias, the only substantial armed force in England.

After an early victory at Edgehill, in 1643, Charles lost the initiative and squandered a chance to seize London. Increasingly, the greater financial resources and manpower of Parliament began to tell. But having failed to capitalize on their triumph at Marston Moor, in 1644, the Parliamentarians entered the Battle of Naseby with their morale at a low ebb.

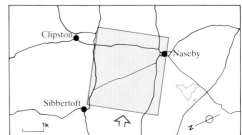

Prince Rupert was absent during the crucial action: after wreaking havoc on Ireton's left, **10**, his cavaliers pursued the survivors off the field.

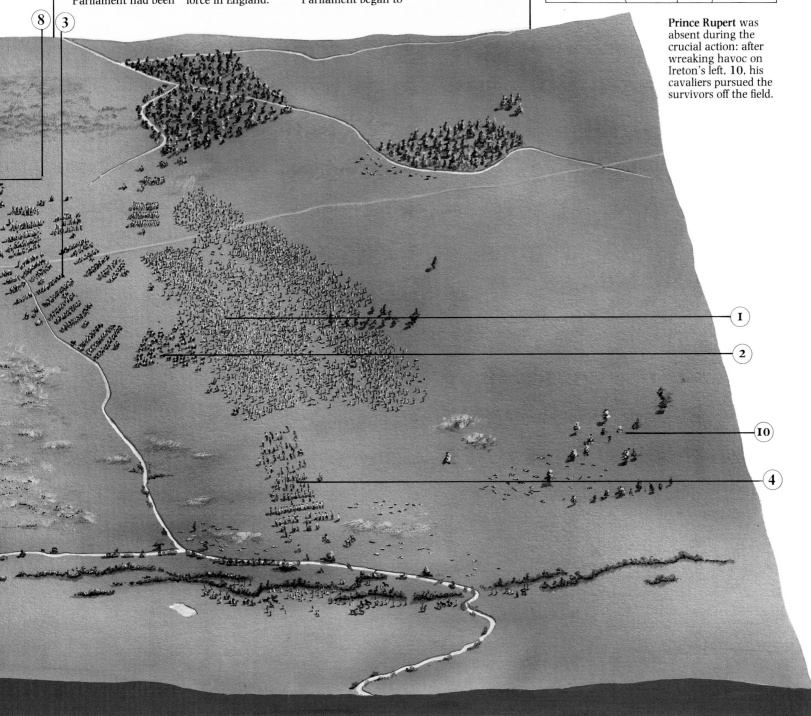

King, **6**, while others, **7**, who had been denied leave, seized the chance to flee back to their homes in Yorkshire.

Two Parliamentary cavalry regiments, **8**, remaining in line on pain of death, prevented Langdale's return to the field.

In the confusion, many of the King's reserves, **9**, thought the battle lost and eagerly followed a cry to retreat.

The King was forcibly prevented by the Earl of Carnwath from rallying his Lifeguard of Horse to rescue his endangered infantry.

The pikemen and musketeers of the New Model Army were resplendent in scarlet, a colour which became synonymous with the British army over the next 250 years and is still worn by many regiments on ceremonial occasions.

must have been with great astonishment, therefore, that Prince Rupert breasted the crest of Dust Hill and discovered the assembled might of the New Model Army drawn up in battle array, less than 1.6 km (1 ml) distant.

It was too late for the Prince to call a halt. Langdale and a body of Northern and Newark Horse advanced on the left, only to be repulsed by Cromwell's charging troopers. In the centre, Sir Jacob Astley had insufficient infantry to extend along the whole front line of the Parliamentarian musketeers and pikemen, but his veterans drove into as many of their opponents as they could and broke several regiments.

On the right, Prince Rupert led his considerably outnumbered cavalry against Commissar-General Henry Ireton's squadrons. Rupert's attack quickly gathered momentum and a fierce mêlée developed. As the Cavaliers charged, they came under flanking fire from Colonel Okey's dismounted dragoons, who had been skilfully positioned behind Sulby Hedges, at right angles to the Roundhead left. Although the Royalists were getting the better of Ireton's men, the Parliamentary commander suddenly diverted part of his force to assist the reeling infantry in the centre.

Prince Rupert meanwhile had broken the remaining Parliamentary cavalry and, instead of turning to help Astley's infantry, now heavily engaged in close combat with the Roundhead second line, embarked on a dashing pursuit. It was only when the Royalist cavalry encountered Fairfax's baggage train some 3.2 km (2 mls) on, that they drew rein and, without pressing an attack, rode back to the battlefield. In the hour that he had been absent, the Royalist position had deteriorated and it was now too late for him to influence the outcome of the battle.

Having driven off Langdale's force, Cromwell had turned his disciplined cavalry inward to set upon the flank and rear of the Royalist foot, and Fairfax had ordered uncommitted infantry regiments into the fray. On the other side of the field, Colonel Okey and his remounted dragoons rode out from behind Sulby Hedges into the Royalist right flank. Virtually surrounded, the King's soldiers began to lay down their arms. Fairfax ordered a general advance, and the King and his remaining troops left the field pursued by Roundhead cavalry.

The Battle of Naseby was not particularly bloody—the Royalists are calculated to have lost about 1,500 men, killed and wounded, and 4,500 taken prisoner; the Roundheads lost fewer than 1,000. Nevertheless, the final destruction of Charles I's army was complete.

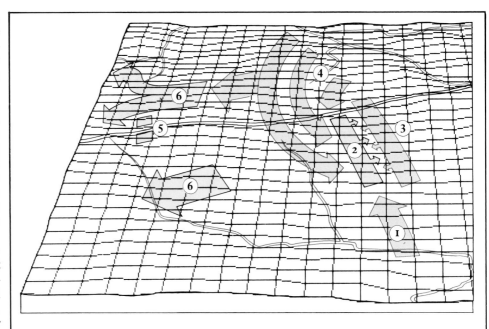

The armies originally faced each other across Broad Moor from Dust Hill and Red Hill. Battle was joined when Prince Rupert's cavalry charged through the Parliamentary left flank and, under fire from dragoons, 1, at Sulby Hedges, went on to attack a baggage train some 3.2 km (2 mls) distant. But Rupert met unexpected resistance and did not return until all was lost.

Meanwhile, the outnumbered Royalist infantry, 2, engaged the centre of the Parliamentary line, 3, while Cromwell's cavalry, 4, counter-charged the Royalist left flank. Three waves of cavalry, flung against flank and rear, set up an envelopment which the dragoons, 1, advancing from Sulby Hedges, completed. The King, 5, tried to rally his troops, but many had already fled, 6.

The matchlock musket provided the infantry's main firepower during the English Civil War. Cheaper to produce than the more efficient flintlocks, which were just being introduced into the New Model Army, matchlocks were rather ungainly.

A musketeer needed the cover of pikemen to perform the lengthy reloading process: a musket ball and wadding was rammed down the muzzle; a primed flash pan was filled with one of 12 measured charges, known as the 'Twelve Apostles'. A piece of slow-burning match, kept permanently alight, was then placed in a serpentine catch. The cover was swivelled off the pan, and the trigger was pulled, pivoting the serpentine backward into the pan and igniting the charge.

In wet weather, the matchlock was often liable to a 'hang fire' delay, which made it specially unreliable. Many accidents occurred when a burning match was left too close to an open powder-barrel.

1. Marching with a match constantly alight at both ends.

2. Priming the musket in the 'cast-about' position.

3. Ramming ball and wadding down the muzzle.

4. Priming the flash pan with fine powder.

5. Blowing on the coals to improve the burn of the match.

6. Aiming the musket with the help of a fork-tipped rest.

Sir Thomas Fairfax (1612–1671) was knighted by the King in 1640, following his Scottish campaign. But, by 1645, he was the natural choice as Lord General of all Parliament's forces, having experienced their changing fortunes in the Civil War. Normally quiet, he became in battle an inspirational figure, whose 'countenance', a witness reported, 'discovered an Embleme of True Valour.'

Prince Rupert of the Rhine (1619–1682) was only 23 years old when his uncle, King Charles I, appointed him General of Horse. His headstrong cavalry charges at Edgehill and Naseby have overshadowed his considerable ability (acquired in campaigns in the Thirty Years War) as a shrewd strategist, who wished to avoid confrontation at Naseby.

At Naseby, Charles I lost his last chance of countering the Parliamentary forces and the English Revolution moved toward its climax. The last Royalist forces in the west of England were forced to surrender and, by May 1646, Charles gave himself up to the Scots at Newark. A month later, the last Royalist stronghold, at Oxford, surrendered.

The power of the Army became so great that Parliament moved to disband it, unpaid. Mutiny followed, and Cromwell, though at first hesitant, supported the radicals. A manifesto was issued declaring that the Army would not disband until its legitimate grievances had been met. It then occupied London. Negotiations between the King and the Generals produced the Heads of the Proposals, a moderate document which envisaged a limited role for the monarchy.

But while Cromwell was forced to deal with radical elements within the Army—the Levellers—the King continued to negotiate with possible allies and a second phase of the Civil War ensued. The Royalist revolts in the southeast and South Wales were easily crushed and Charles's last hope, the Scottish Royalists, were defeated at Preston in 1648.

The King, inflexible to the end, refused to compromise; on 30 January 1649, he was sent to the block. The monarchy and House of Lords were abolished, and England was declared a republic.

Pikemen, six ranks deep, locked together and advanced 'at push of pike'. The weapons, between 3.6 m (12 ft) and 5.5 m (18 ft) long, were held in the left hand and braced by the right foot, leaving the right hand free to wield a sword.

The Boyne/*1 July, 1690*

When James II and his French troops landed in Ireland, they were given generous support. Soon that wild and desolate country was under his control, with the exception of Derry and Enniskillen in the north. From September 1689, William's forces, led by the aged Duke of Schomberg, a veteran of the Thirty Years War, campaigned against the Irish Jacobites, but without much success. In the following summer, William himself arrived, together with reinforcements from several European countries which had combined to resist Louis XIV's plan to dominate Europe.

After reviewing his 36,000-strong army, which was better trained and better equipped than James's force, William marched toward the Irish capital. The Jacobites fell back before him until they reached the south bank of the River Boyne, a tidal waterway some 48 km (30 mls) north of Dublin, where James decided to make a stand. He placed the bulk of his 25,000 men—a large proportion of whom were inexperienced recruits—on high ground at Oldbridge, a town dominating the ford at the apex of a big northward loop of the river. Here he expected the enemy would try to cross. There was only one bridge in the area: at Drogheda, 4.8 km (3 mls) east, which was held by a strong Jacobite detachment.

The opposing forces first sighted each other on 30 June and at once engaged in a cross-river artillery duel, which lasted into the evening. Meanwhile, William's cavalry had been reconnoitring along the banks of the Boyne and had discovered more fords both above and below the village. These were taken into account at the King's council of war that night, when it was decided to make a feint to the west to draw off Jacobites from the centre and then to launch the main force against Oldbridge.

In dawn mist, on 1 July, Count Meinhard Schomberg, aged 49, the son of William's Captain-General, moved west toward the ford at Rosnaree at the head of 10,000 men. When William learned that Schomberg was over the Boyne, he sent another brigade under Lieutenant-General James Douglas in support and succeeded in convincing the Jacobites that he was shifting his main body to fall on their exposed left flank. In a move which presaged defeat, James divided his army and sent two-thirds of it, including his best French infantry regiments, away from Oldbridge to take up a position 6.4 km (4 mls) southwest across the Rosnaree to Duleek road. In the event, the only service these troops performed was to secure a line of retreat because there was an impassable bog between them and William's diversionary force.

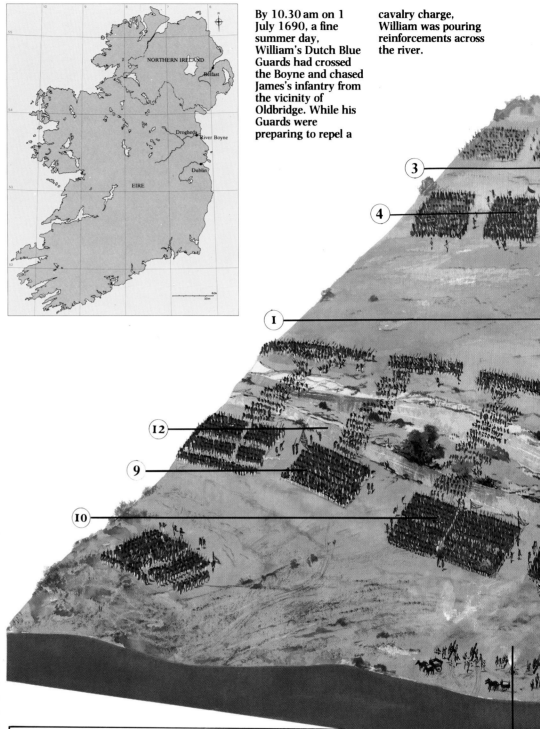

By 10.30 am on 1 July 1690, a fine summer day, William's Dutch Blue Guards had crossed the Boyne and chased James's infantry from the vicinity of Oldbridge. While his Guards were preparing to repel a cavalry charge, William was pouring reinforcements across the river.

Major religious differences lay at the root of the dispute which brought the armies of James II and William III face to face on the banks of the Irish River Boyne. James II's Roman Catholicism had rankled with his largely Protestant subjects, but they were content to wait for the accession of his ardently anti-Catholic daughter Mary and her husband William, the Prince of Orange.

Then James II had a son, a new heir to the throne, who was brought up in the Catholic faith. The tolerant mood of the country abruptly changed. In 1688, William and Mary were invited to share the crown of Great Britain and Ireland.

James, lacking adequate support, was obliged to flee abroad, where he sought the help of the Catholic monarch, Louis XIV of France in regaining his crown. Jacobite sympathies were strongest in Ireland, to which James, backed by troops and arms supplied by King Louis, travelled in March 1689.

Three battalions of Dutch Blue Guards, **1**, William's élite troops, drove the Jacobites out of their breastworks and the shelter of Oldbridge, **2**, then re-formed in fields beyond the village to await reinforcements. There they came under attack from enemy cavalry, which they stood off by calmly forming squares.

Three wild charges were launched against the Dutch Blue Guards by 1,000 Jacobite cavalrymen, **3**, led by the Duke of Berwick. All were repulsed.

Although heavily outnumbered, the Jacobite infantry, **4**, fought well but could not hold Oldbridge, **2**. They regrouped to meet new enemy crossings to the east.

Oldbridge was deserted by its inhabitants on the approach of the two armies. The Jacobites fortified the town to guard the ford, and these positions were heavily bombarded by William's guns. The church, **5**, was badly damaged, as were several houses.

Once his guards had secured Oldbridge, King William ordered up reinforcements. Two Huguenot regiments, **9**, and two English regiments, **10**, supported by a Dutch regiment, **11**, began to cross the river at Grove Island, **12**, downstream from the town. They were attacked as soon as they had crossed.

Irish Protestant regiments, **8**, started to ford the Boyne in support of the Dutch Blue Guards, who had cleared the town of Oldbridge without other support.

William's battery of 6-pounder cannon, **7**, on high ground overlooking Oldbridge, caused much damage.

The Jacobites built a line of breastworks, **6**, along the south bank of the Boyne, to command the river crossing.

At Oldbridge, shortly after 10 am, when the tide was at its lowest, William ordered forward his Dutch Blue Guards, later followed by Huguenot, English and loyal Irish regiments. The Dutchmen, armed with the latest infantry weapons—flintlock muskets with bayonets—waded waist-deep across the Boyne, while the enemy poured fire at them. Once on the far bank, they became involved immediately in a furious mêlée, principally with James's crack Irish Guards, who suffered severe losses.

Sheer weight of numbers began to tell in the fierce house-to-house fighting, and the defenders were eventually pushed out of the village. The Earl of Tyrconnell, James's Captain-General, decided that now was the time to intervene with his cavalry. His squadrons charged down on the élite Blue Guard, which quickly formed squares and presented a *chevaux de frise* of bayonets. This, backed by volleys of musketry fire and the arrival of reinforcements, halted the waves of attacking horsemen.

An hour after his opening attack, William sent 12,000 men, mainly Danes, to cross the Boyne below Oldbridge, where he knew the enemy thought it was unfordable. This new threat, which was met by cavalry, then infantry drawn from the main fight upriver, spelled the beginning of the end of Jacobite resistance. When the remainder of William's cavalry forded the Boyne at Drybridge, 3.2 km (2 mls) west of Drogheda, in the early afternoon, the three-hour fight was nearly over.

The Jacobite infantry retreated up the hill of Donore behind the village, made a brief stand on its summit, then withdrew toward Duleek, the only escape route open to them. Meanwhile, Tyrconnell and his cavalry had achieved considerable success by charging time and again to protect the retreat of the Jacobite foot. This time they were up against mostly matchlock-armed troops, who were virtually defenceless when the horsemen crashed into their ranks. By their desperate courage, the Jacobite cavalry bought a delay of half an hour in William's advance. This allowed the rest of the Jacobite army to slip away, but casualties had been heavy.

On the Jacobite left, where most of the army had been unemployed for several hours, James learned of the collapse at Oldbridge. He ordered an immediate attack on Count Meinhard Schomberg's forces but there was no way around the marshy ground that lay between them. Then William's troops began to move as if to cut off the road to Duleek behind the Jacobites: retreat was inevitable. James rode on ahead to Dublin and within three weeks had taken ship back to France.

King James II going into exile after the Battle of the Boyne.

By 1690, the pike, following the invention of the musket bayonet, was falling into disuse as a weapon, and the number of pikemen in a regiment was, at most, one to every five musketeers.

Unless they were required in the front to help repel a cavalry attack, the pikemen were drawn up behind the musketeers, who were deployed in six ranks, as shown above.

The first three ranks fired as a unit, the front rank generally lying flat, the second kneeling and the third standing. These ranks then removed to the rear of their unit to reload, while the three ranks behind stepped forward, one rank behind the other, to fire their muskets in the same manner. The process could be continuous, enabling the unit to keep up almost constant fire.

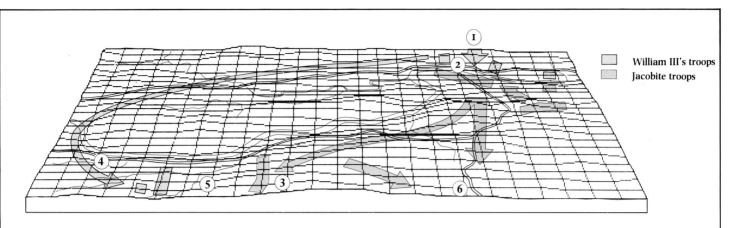

The River Boyne formed a barrier to William's advance, **1**, although it was fordable in places. Unfortunately for the Jacobites, the area around Oldbridge, **2**, although the best position that could be found by them on the river in that area, entailed their disadvantageously occupying a loop in the river. Moreover, the Jacobite forces were depleted when a large section, **3**, was hastily detached to meet William's troops, which were sweeping in a wide movement toward Rosnaree, **4**, as if to attack the Jacobite rear. The movement—a ploy to split the Jacobite force—was successful; but in fact no fighting took place at Rosnaree

because the two sides were separated by a marsh, **5**. The Jacobites were later to join their defeated comrades from Oldbridge in the retreat to Duleek, **6**. Many writers on military tactics have pointed out the danger of entering into such a loop, since the position gives the enemy the opportunity to attack with enfilade fire before forcing a crossing. Nearly 200 years later, General Sir Francis Clery recorded in a book on tactics how desirable it was to find an enemy in this situation. Despite this, he himself forgot the lesson at the Battle of Colenso in 1899, when a large body of men was sent into a loop of the Tugela River.

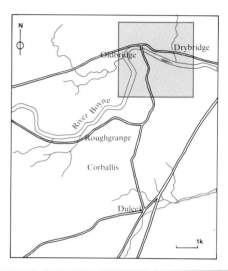

William III (1650–1702), a grandson of Charles I, was married to James II's daughter, Mary, and was thus closely related to the Stuart royal family. After his father-in-law, James, came to the throne, he ceaselessly plotted against him and eventually brought about his downfall. An experienced and able soldier, but a cold and calculating politician, William was the strongest opponent of Louis XIV of France in the struggle for European domination.

James II (1633–1701) became a Roman Catholic in about 1668, but, although unpopular for this reason, he succeeded his brother, Charles II, in 1685, without opposition. His unpopularity increased when he filled offices of authority with Catholics and issued two Declarations of Indulgence, suspending the laws against Catholics and dissenters. In the end, opposition to his rule became overwhelming; in 1688 he fled to France.

The 'Glorious Revolution', so called because it was brought about without bloodshed, was a landmark in English constitutional history. It ensured, through the Bill of Rights in 1689, that no Roman Catholic could ever again be the sovereign, that Englishmen possessed inviolate civic and political rights, and—most important of all—its provisions gave political supremacy to Parliament. William III and his queen, Mary II, accepted these conditions on ascending the throne. The King remained the most important and influential man in the land, but a major advance toward democratic government, in which voters rather than the monarch would appoint government ministers, had been taken. During the 50 years following the Battle of the Boyne, the Jacobites strove to regain the throne for the Roman Catholic Stuarts, but their cause was finally destroyed at the Battle of Culloden.

Blenheim/*13 August, 1704*

Marlborough, Captain-General of the forces of the Second Grand Alliance—England, Austria and the United Provinces of the Netherlands—was a far-sighted, original military thinker whose skills were at their height in the early years of the War of the Spanish Succession.

Anticipating that the critical area of operations, in the summer of 1704, would be on the Upper Danube, Marlborough resolved to march to the aid of the Austrians with a large army of mixed English, Dutch and German troops. In May, 'Corporal John', as he was nicknamed, began to transfer 40,000 men from one theatre of war, the Low Countries, to another, 402 km (250 mls) away. On 21 June, the Allied army reached the Upper Danube and joined forces with the commands of two Imperial Austrian generals, Prince Eugene, and Prince Louis of Baden. As a result of his rapid and superbly organized march, Marlborough held the initiative and could plan to relieve Leopold I of Austria in Vienna, where he faced a French attack.

In the path of the Allies, on the north bank of the Danube, lay the fortress town of Donauwörth, which, garrisoned by 14,000 men, guarded a main crossing into Bavaria. Marlborough devised a two-pronged, uphill assault against this position and, after furious fighting, the vital fortress fell.

Though dismayed by the loss, the Elector of Bavaria stubbornly refused to negotiate terms. He and Marshal Marsin, the French commander, decided to avoid battle until another French army under Marshal Tallard joined them. Prince Eugene, who had been standing off another large French force at Strasbourg, broke off and followed Tallard north. Meanwhile, Marlborough had moved south of the Danube and was laying waste Bavaria in an attempt to incite the Elector to battle. Tallard reached the Elector and Marsin at Augsburg on 5 August, and a Franco-Bavarian army 60,000 strong was now in the field preparing to sever Marlborough's lines of communication.

Marlborough realized that he and Prince Eugene would have to bring on a general engagement if the initiative were to be regained. Prince Louis, who disagreed with Marlborough's strategy, was quickly sent to besiege Ingolstadt.

On 11 August, Prince Eugene confirmed that Tallard, Marsin, the Elector and all

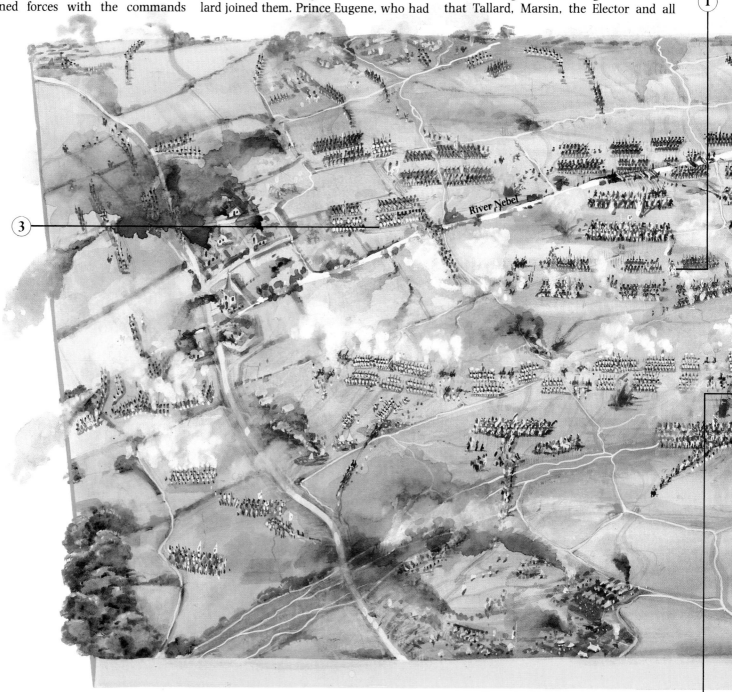

When Prince Eugene, on his right, was finally in position, facing the Bavarian forces, Marlborough opened hostilities at 12.45 pm along a 6.4-km (4-ml) front.

Marlborough was strong in cavalry but relatively weak in infantry. He sought to concentrate his cavalry in the centre, 1, and to weaken the French centre by drawing away French infantry to the flanks. Using his cavalry, Tallard hoped to crush Marlborough after he crossed the Nebel, a river flowing across the French front line.

The long struggle of the Protestant states against the ambitions of Louis XIV had continued unceasingly since 1685. In 1700, the danger the anti-Louis coalition faced was the partition of the vast Spanish Empire on the death of Charles II. The absorption of Spain and her territories into France would give Louis overwhelming strength and bring all Europe under his sway. To avoid this, a series of treaties was signed with France, dividing the spoils between all the interested parties. These efforts reckoned without Charles II's will, which left his dominions to Louis's grandson, later Philip V.

Blenheim village

Lord Cutts on the left, 2, feinted toward Blenheim, where the French became so crowded that, as a Frenchman wrote, 'they could not even fire, let alone receive or carry out any orders.'

Prince Holstein-Beck commanded the infantry on the right-centre of the Allied army, 3. He aimed to draw French infantry away from their centre by feinting toward the village of Oberglau. Only Marlborough's personal intervention here averted defeat.

The French army between Oberglau and Blenheim was situated on a gradual, undulating slope, 4, beyond the Nebel. Tallard hoped to catch Marlborough off-balance as his troops re-formed after the river crossing.

their troops had come over the river at Hochstadt 32 km (20 mls) from the Austrian camp at Munster. While preparing to retire to Donauwörth, Eugene wrote to Marlborough: 'Everything, milord, consists in speed and that you put yourself forward in movement to join me tomorrow, without which I fear it will be too late.' Marlborough acted at once, and, by 12 August, the whole army was encamped around Munster.

While Marlborough and Prince Eugene were working in close cooperation, the opposite happened in the Franco-Bavarian lines. The Elector wanted to attack what he thought was a tired and divided force, but Tallard was more cautious. They compromised by advancing a few miles nearer the enemy, to a strong position near Blenheim. Tallard felt sure that the Allied army, outnumbered without Prince Louis, would not make a frontal assault and would retreat north to Nordlingen. But the French Marshal underestimated his opponent, who made war according to his own rules. Far from retiring, Marlborough ordered a reconnaissance of the Franco-Bavarian position. Scouts reported 60,000 men and 90 guns, occupying a front 6.4 km (4 mls) wide that connected the villages of Blenheim, Oberglau and Lutzingen. The French right flank was anchored on the Danube, their left on rising, thickly wooded ground beyond Lutzingen. In front of them lay a further obstacle: the River Nebel, a tributary of the Danube.

Marlborough's staff officers thought it foolhardy to attack such a formidable position with the 56,000 troops and 60 cannon at their disposal, but Marlborough was resolved. As darkness fell on 12 August, Tallard and the Franco-Bavarian army retired to their tents, confident that by all known precepts of war an attack against them was unthinkable.

In the middle of the night, the Allied army began a 14.5-km (9-ml) march on Blenheim. At dawn, thick mist hid their approach from the unsuspecting enemy. Even when the alarm was sounded in the Franco-Bavarian camp, it was not taken seriously: at 7 am, Tallard was writing to King Louis XIV of France that he still expected Marlborough to retreat north to Nordlingen.

An hour later, when Marlborough's assembled force began to spread out into battle formation, the astonished Tallard at last realized that he was being brought to battle. Hurriedly, he deployed his command to defend the area from the Danube to Oberglau, while Marsin and the Elector were to hold the line from Oberglau to Lutzingen. The three villages were heavily fortified and linked by lines of infantry and

John Churchill, Duke of Marlborough (1650–1722) served his military apprenticeship in Flanders during the 1670s. He deserted his patron, James II, after the 'Glorious Revolution' and won the favour of the new King, William III. Marlborough continued to correspond with James, however, and, a victim of his own duplicity, was for a time imprisoned. He was later reinstated in William's favour and, during the War of the Spanish Succession, became the most powerful man in England after the King.

Prince Eugene (1663–1736) was a favourite of Louis XIV. When his mother was banished from Versailles after a scandal, Louis decided that Eugene should enter the church. Eugene refused, fled from France and, in 1683, entered the service of Emperor Leopold I of Austria. He served with distinction against the Turks and, in 1694, was appointed Commander-in-Chief of the army. After the French advance on Vienna, he joined forces with Marlborough; their friendship was so harmonious that medals were struck likening them to Castor and Pollux.

Camille, Comte de Tallard (1652–1728) was sent to London in 1698 as Minister to the Court of St James. He was popular in London and was able to warn Louis of the dangers of his policy. When, in September 1701, Louis acknowledged James Stuart as King of England, William III dismissed Tallard, who returned to France to command an army. More a temporizer than a man of action, he consoled himself after Blenheim with the thought that things might have been worse. Few others, and certainly not Louis XIV, shared his view.

Maximilian Emmanuel, Elector of Bavaria (1662–1726), like previous rulers of Bavaria, was a traditional ally of France against the Habsburgs. The ambitious Elector had extended his dominions in 1691, when he became Governor of the Spanish Netherlands. When Marlborough invaded Bavaria in 1704 and laid waste the principality, bribes were offered to induce the Elector to change sides, but he refused—word had reached him that Tallard was coming to his rescue. After the defeat at Blenheim, he was not allowed to return to Bavaria until 1714.

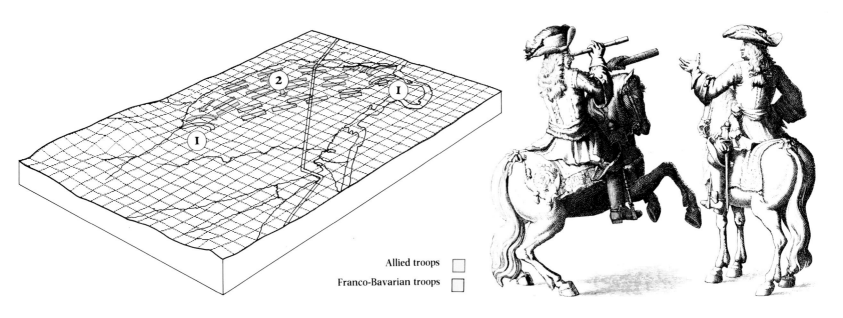

Allied troops ☐
Franco-Bavarian troops ☐

While the two armies were of similar strength (around 56,000 men), Marlborough was stronger in cavalry than in infantry. To capitalize on this strength, he feinted toward the villages on the French flanks, **1**, hoping to draw the French infantry away from the centre. His tactic was successful and he promptly mounted a massive cavalry charge on the French centre, **2**. At the same time, there was a risk that the French might launch a cavalry attack on his centre before he was ready. To avoid this, Marlborough interwove lines of cavalry with lines of infantry to ensure cooperation.

The partnership of Marlborough and Prince Eugene was one of the most successful in military history. Meeting just a few days before the battle, they immediately struck up a warm friendship and founded a smooth working relationship on the basis of mutual respect and lack of jealousy. Marlborough's charm was legendary, but Prince Eugene did not need to be won over as he already hated Louis XIV and was determined to humble the *roi soleil*. He gave Marlborough the type of whole-hearted cooperation he had rarely received from his other allies.

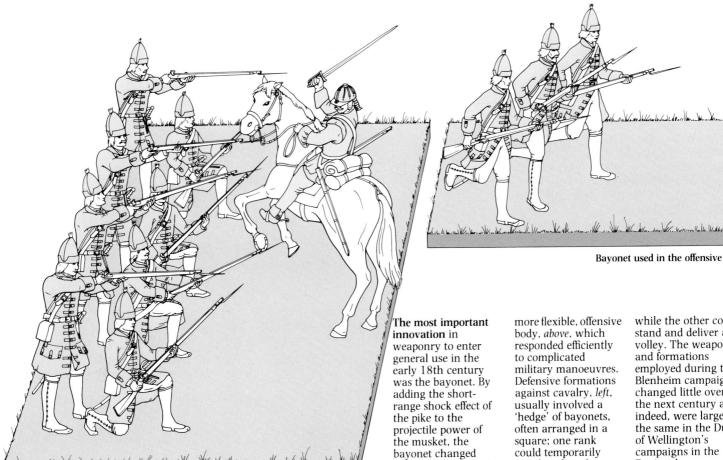

Bayonet used in the offensive

The most important innovation in weaponry to enter general use in the early 18th century was the bayonet. By adding the short-range shock effect of the pike to the projectile power of the musket, the bayonet changed infantry into a much more flexible, offensive body, *above*, which responded efficiently to complicated military manoeuvres. Defensive formations against cavalry, *left*, usually involved a 'hedge' of bayonets, often arranged in a square; one rank could temporarily rest, kneeling down, while the other could stand and deliver a volley. The weapons and formations employed during the Blenheim campaign changed little over the next century and, indeed, were largely the same in the Duke of Wellington's campaigns in the Peninsula.

cavalry, supported by artillery. Tallard's plan was that between Lutzingen and Oberglau all Allied attacks should be stopped on the Nebel, while between Oberglau and Blenheim the enemy should be allowed to cross. As they advanced, they would be disorganized by enfilade fire, then charged by cavalry and sent fleeing back across the river in disarray.

Surveying Tallard's deployment, Marlborough saw that Tallard's right wing was stronger than the rest of his line and calculated that the enemy would not expect him to launch his opening attack on their most heavily defended sector. Marlborough proposed to do precisely that, in conjunction with a diversionary attack on the Franco-Bavarian left by Prince Eugene.

Shortly after 9 am, Eugene set out on a circling march through rough country to a position facing the enemy at Lutzingen. It took longer to accomplish than expected and caused Marlborough much anguish, for many hundreds of his soldiers were killed or maimed by artillery fire while they awaited the order to advance.

It was not until 12.30 pm, when the August sun was at its highest, that news came that Prince Eugene was finally in position. Marlborough swiftly ordered his officers to take post and, at 12.45 pm, Lord Cutts, on the Allied left, sent forward an English brigade to attack nine enemy battalions in Blenheim village. Two consecutive assaults failed to penetrate the defences, but the ferocity of the fire unnerved the commander of the French, Lieutenant-General the Marquis de Clerambault, who called up seven support and eleven reserve battalions. Marlborough declined a third attempt to take the village: he had achieved what he wanted—27 crack infantry battalions isolated in Blenheim, and the French centre gravely weakened.

Meanwhile, the *Gendarmerie*, the élite of the French cavalry, tried to aid the hapless defenders of Blenheim, who were packed tight in burning buildings and being picked off by volleys of English musketry. Eight squadrons were met head-on by five Allied squadrons. Tallard saw his finest soldiers retreat before a much smaller force.

Shortly after 2 pm, when the majority of Marlborough's troops had crossed the Nebel and regrouped, the Allies suffered a reverse at Oberglau which might have proved disastrous but for Marlborough's presence of mind.

Ten assault battalions under Prince Holstein-Beck were routed by the Marquis de Blainville's nine French battalions, uncovering the right flank of Marlborough's centre. Just as Marshal Marsin was gathering a huge force of horse with which to roll

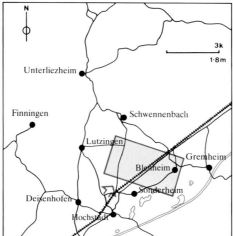

By 4 pm the climax of the battle was approaching. The sun had shone brightly all day. Since it was usual in 18th century warfare to destroy most obstacles in the field, many buildings in the vicinity were set ablaze and clouds of smoke blew across the battlefield.

The terrain around the village of Blenheim was soft and marshy and intersected by small streams, which hampered the movement of infantry.

The French army lacked an infantry reserve to support its cavalry attack because so many troops, drawn off to the villages on the flanks, could not now be extricated to help in the centre.

Marlborough's army displayed much better cooperation between infantry and cavalry than the French, whose failure was epitomized by their futile fight at the village of Blenheim.

Marlborough, **1**, had concentrated an overwhelming force against the French centre. For Tallard, it seemed the only way to stave off disaster was to launch a cavalry attack.

The French cavalry charge, led by the Marquis d'Humières, was repulsed with heavy casualties, **2**. Marlborough's relentless wearing down of the French centre was nearing completion.

The only infantry forces left to Tallard in the centre were nine battalions of new recruits. **3**. On Marlborough's command, they were flayed by artillery fire.

At 5 pm, Marlborough rode along the front and ordered the trumpets to summon his fresh cavalry through the intervals in the infantry's ranks, **4**. The French cavalry gave way under the impact of the charge.

Marlborough's tactics, which were reminiscent of Gustavus Adolphus's tactics over 70 years previously, were triumphantly successful. Once their centre had been broken, the French army dissolved. The pursuit was pressed until nightfall and thousands of panic-stricken French soldiers were drowned trying to cross the Danube.

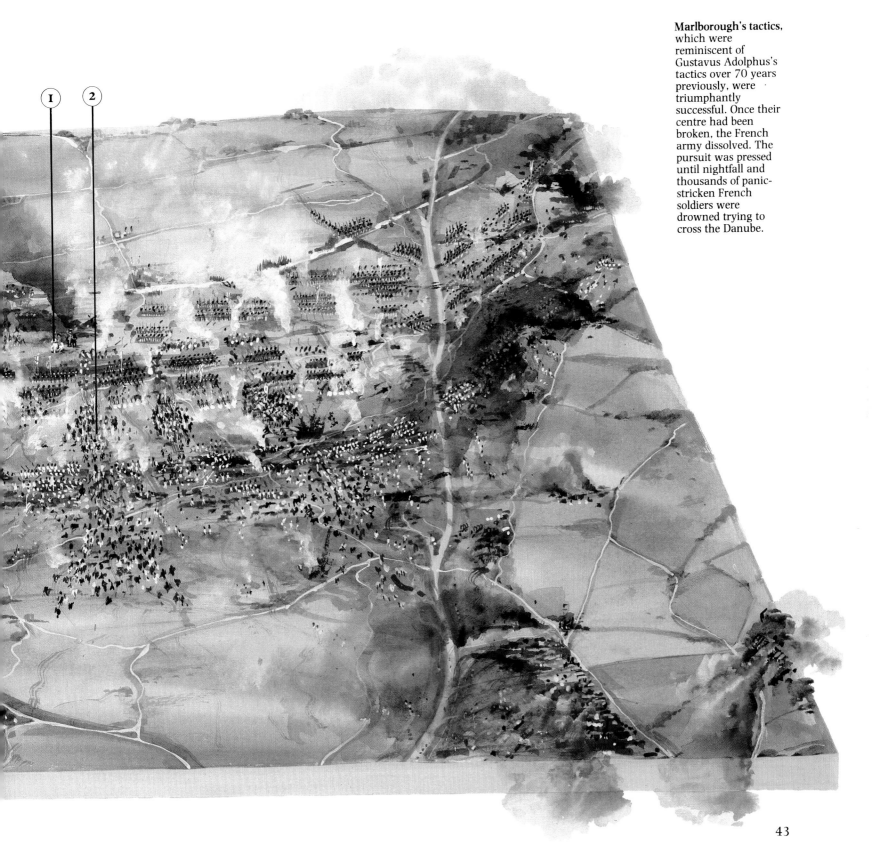

43

up the Allied line, Marlborough dispatched a message to Prince Eugene, urging him to send Fugger's cavalry brigade to the rescue. In an act of supreme generosity, for he was hard pressed himself, Eugene immediately sent Fugger—his only reserve—to assist his Captain-General. The Austrian *cuirassiers* arrived in time to repel Marsin's charge and to stabilize the Allied centre. Another infantry attack was launched against Oberglau, and this time it managed to pin down de Blainville's garrison.

With two enemy strongpoints contained and the Franco-Bavarian left fully occupied by Eugene, the way was now clear for Marlborough to throw in his 80 squadrons of cavalry and 22 battalions of infantry against the 60 squadrons of horse and nine battalions of foot, which were all the forces the French could muster between Blenheim and Oberglau.

At about 4.30 pm, when he learned that Prince Eugene was closing in on Lutzingen, Marlborough ordered forward his entire centre, led—unusually—by the cavalry. Tallard, whose tidy defensive trap had been neutralized by Marlborough's bold attack on Blenheim in the opening minutes, now mounted a desperate stand and, for a time, succeeded in checking the weight of Marlborough's advance. But the result of the contest was now beyond all doubt.

The Allies fell back slightly to regroup while a battery of guns swept the French lines with canister at close range. Shortly after 5 pm, Marlborough's troops once more surged forward—and this time they could not be stopped. French infantrymen were killed where they stood, while their cavalry galloped for safety to the rear. Many headed for a pontoon bridge over the Danube, west of Blenheim, and were drowned when it collapsed.

Tallard was taken prisoner; Marsin and the Elector retreated. The only resistance still offered was at Blenheim, where some 11,000 French infantry remained bottled up inside their cramped perimeter. Now, however, they were without Clerambault, their commander; he had deserted them earlier, only to be drowned in the panic at the Danube crossing.

A final bloody clash was avoided when the French agreed to accept terms and then marched out honourably into captivity. For the loss of 12,000 killed and wounded, the Allies had inflicted 20,000 casualties on the Franco-Bavarian army and taken 14,000 prisoners, 129 colours, 171 standards and all their artillery.

Austria and the Second Grand Alliance were secure and the might of the French army—for so long the dominant force in Europe—had been dealt a massive blow.

Generalship at the time of Blenheim was a solitary burden. Generals had to act as their own chiefs of staff, intelligence officers and quartermasters. To be successful, commanders had to make themselves masters of detail— Marlborough supervised even minor tactical movements in person, and his coolness and detachment always impressed those around him. Like Wellington, he always displayed 'British phlegm' in moments of crisis.

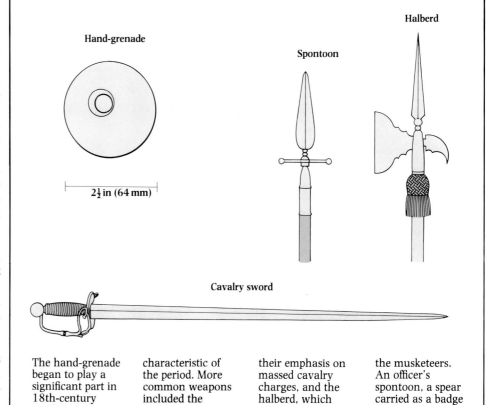

Hand-grenade

Spontoon

Halberd

2½ in (64 mm)

Cavalry sword

The hand-grenade began to play a significant part in 18th-century warfare, particularly in the protracted sieges which were characteristic of the period. More common weapons included the cavalryman's sword, so vital to Marlborough's campaigns with their emphasis on massed cavalry charges, and the halberd, which weighed as much as 7.7 kg (17 lbs) and was primarily designed to protect the musketeers. An officer's spontoon, a spear carried as a badge of office, was 2 m (7 ft) long, and was useful for aligning muskets.

Representations of the battles of this period can be misleading: the neat lines and squares of this contemporary engraving of Blenheim, *below*, give little idea of what conditions were actually like. The elaborate drills of the later 18th century were only in their infancy, and the movements of large formations were often muddled. Most armies were still composed of mercenaries. In the early 18th century, monarchs tried to make warfare pay for itself. Soldiers had to forage for themselves in enemy territories. The arrival of soldiers in a region, *above*, meant that they would have to be fed and housed. Discipline was often weak, resulting in the countryside being put to the sword. Marlborough ravaged Bavaria systematically, burning some 400 villages.

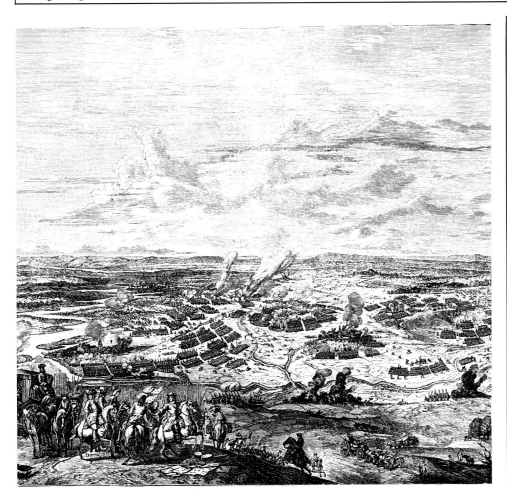

The Battle of Blenheim was the major turning point in the War of the Spanish Succession. It reversed Louis's early run of success, saved Vienna, and thus the Grand Alliance. Soon after the battle, all Bavaria fell to the Allies. Indeed, Blenheim was the first major blow to French arms for over half a century, and the victory raised Marlborough's military reputation to great heights.

He returned to the Low Countries to inflict three further defeats on French armies, at Ramillies (1706), Oudenaarde (1708), and Malplaquet (1709), before the conflicting interests of the Allies and the obstinacy of Louis could accommodate a lasting settlement.

The Treaty of Utrecht in 1713 resolved the Spanish Succession crisis by confining Philip to the Spanish throne but forcing him to renounce his rights to the French. Of more lasting importance, Blenheim made clear that Great Britain had emerged as the world's greatest power, holding the balance of power in Europe while building up an empire in India and North America.

Culloden/*16 April, 1746*

The last flickering hope of restoring a Stuart king to the British throne was brutally extinguished at Culloden Moor on Wednesday, 16 April 1746.

The brief, bloody, decisive battle on a rain-sodden hillside near Inverness marked the end of an adventure begun 10 months before, when a young man of 25 landed in Scotland with a handful of followers, a few arms and not much money, but with the resolve to regain the British throne for the Stuart dynasty.

Prince Charles Edward Stuart ('Bonnie Prince Charlie') came to seize the kingdom for his father, James Edward, whose father before him, King James II, had been forced into exile in 1688 as a result of his intolerant Roman Catholicism.

Almost 60 years had passed, and the Protestant House of Hanover, presently represented by King George II, was exercising a benign and not unpopular rule. But there were those who believed that James Edward Stuart in Rome was their lawful monarch—'the King over the water'. They were dubbed Jacobites, and most were to be found among the clans of the Scottish Highlands. It was, therefore, to them that Prince Charles Edward turned after the Roman Catholic King Louis XV of France abandoned plans to invade England and restore the Stuarts.

Even the Jacobites thought Prince Charles was ill-advised, for he faced daunting odds; but he persisted. The early, albeit grudging, support of the Camerons and Macdonalds, two large and influential clans, encouraged others to rise. Soon the Prince was marching south at the head of a wild tartan army, comprised of men who owed greater allegiance to their clan chiefs than to him.

Events then began to gather momentum, throwing England into panic. Less than two months after Prince Charles's landing, Edinburgh, the capital of Scotland, fell to him without a fight. Five days later, his Highlanders surprised a royal army at Prestonpans, a few miles east of the city, and inflicted a crushing defeat.

While Prince Charles held glittering court at the royal palace of Holyroodhouse in Edinburgh, the ranks of his force swelled. The upsurge of Jacobite sympathy following his victory brought more recruits, now from the Lowlands as well as the Highlands.

Mistakenly believing that his 5,000 ill-disciplined followers were invincible, Prince Charles enlarged his plans and resolved to march on London. Despite protests from his senior officers, who urged delay until the help, freshly promised by the French king, arrived, the headstrong Prince

The Scots had been divided in their loyalties since the 'Glorious Revolution' of 1688, when James II, a Roman Catholic and the last Stuart king to sit on the English throne, fled the kingdom and was succeeded by the Protestant monarchs, William and Mary.

Most Highlanders, but not all, hankered for the return of the Stuart dynasty, while most Lowlanders, being Presbyterians, would never again accept a Roman Catholic king. In the Highlands, however, there was a general resentment of the English, for, in 1701, the English Parliament had passed the Act of Settlement, which stipulated that the crown could pass only to a Protestant. Moreover, in 1707, the Act of Union joined England and Scotland as one country, Great Britain, with one parliament and one flag. Almost all the advantages, however, devolved on the English side.

Despite the defeat of an uprising in 1715, led by James II's heir, James Edward, many still plotted a Stuart restoration. When James Edward's son, Charles Edward ('Bonnie Prince Charlie' of ballad and legend) landed in Scotland in 1745 to claim the throne for his father, he was at first crowned with victories—but ultimately lost all on the terrible field of Culloden.

The two armies were drawn up opposite each other across flat moorland. Cultivated areas on either side of the Jacobite army were enclosed with 2-m (6-ft) high drystone walls. The extension wall was of turf and in poor repair.

The Jacobites, 1, faced east across the exposed moor—straight into blinding rain and sleet, whipped by a keen wind. The rain abated, but the wind continued to blow cannon smoke toward their lines.

The English troops, 2, well equipped and fed, had their backs to the wind and enjoyed an uninterrupted view of their enemy.

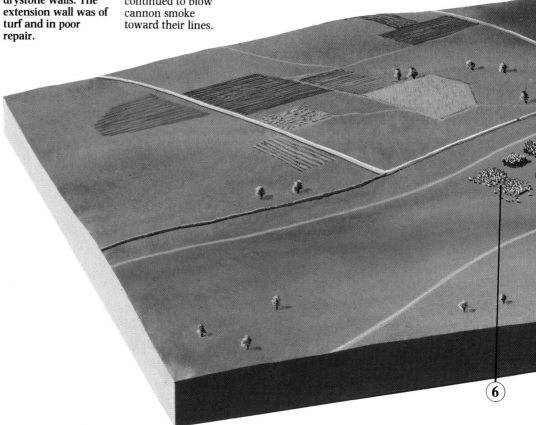

(6)

The Duke of Cumberland (centre), like Prince Charles, was a conspicuous figure on a grey mount. In this contemporary woodcut, the English forces are shown inflicting heavy casualties on the Jacobites. The building in the centre background is a representation of Culloden House, the Prince's headquarters on 16 April 1746.

Once established in Scotland, the Prince had but two options: he could raise more troops in readiness for the inevitable English attack or take the offensive and march south. The latter course was adopted, but soon there was an ominous sign: Englishmen were not rallying to the Jacobite cause. At Manchester, where their unruly columns were led into the city by a whore and a drummer boy, they attracted only 200 recruits. By the time the Jacobites reached Derby, their number had been much reduced by desertion; retreat to Scotland was the only course. But the English followed tenaciously, allowing no respite.

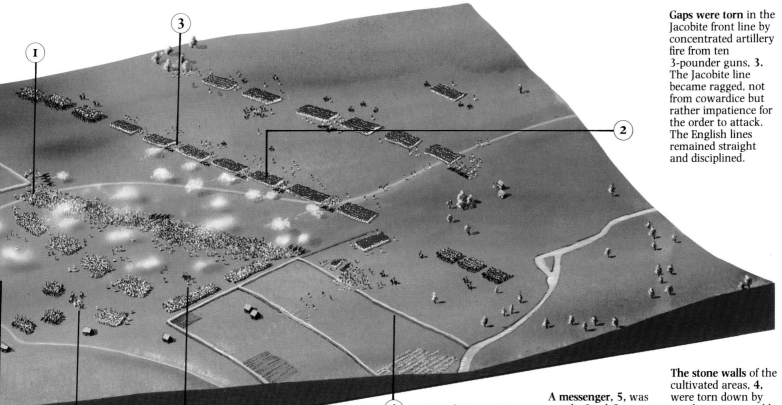

Gaps were torn in the Jacobite front line by concentrated artillery fire from ten 3-pounder guns, 3. The Jacobite line became ragged, not from cowardice but rather impatience for the order to attack. The English lines remained straight and disciplined.

The Prince's standard, 8, first raised just after his landing, was his father's royal standard of red and white silk.

Prince Charles, 7, was stationed to the rear of his army, but not in a commanding position. For much of the time he was out of sight of the action.

French troops, 6, who had been sent by King Louis XV, were held in reserve and used only to cover the disordered retreat of the Jacobites.

A messenger, 5, was sent by Lord George Murray on the Jacobite right to ask permission to attack, since he could not hold his troops in the face of cannon fire for much longer.

The stone walls of the cultivated areas, 4, were torn down by royal troops to enable them to attack the Jacobite rear. The rebel Adjutant-General had said they would not attempt to do this.

ordered an advance across the border. It was December, winter had set in, and even before his army reached England, some 1,000 clansmen had deserted to their familiar glens.

From Carlisle, the Prince's army moved south through Preston and Manchester to Derby. There, however, the rebellion began to lose momentum. English Jacobites had not flocked to his standard as expected, there was no word of a French landing, and 30,000 royal troops were marching against him. With bad grace, the Prince submitted to a retreat. Unknown to him, George II, in London, had ordered his own possessions to be packed and was preparing for flight.

Once more in Scotland, Prince Charles's fortunes briefly improved. His army was reinforced and now included a token three regiments, sent at last by Louis XV; and, on 17 January, he attacked and scattered a much stronger royal force at Falkirk in Stirlingshire. But instead of exploiting this success, the Prince procrastinated with a pointless siege of Stirling Castle. Bored by inactivity, Highlanders began to desert. So numerous did this exodus become that Lord George Murray, the Jacobites' able Lieutenant-General, considered the army unfit to stand against the large body of English regulars now advancing upon them. This force was led by George II's younger son, William, Duke of Cumberland.

Withdrawal into the Highland fastnesses, there to raise a 10,000-strong army and return to the fray in the spring, was the course agreed upon, despite Prince Charles's angry protestations. To confuse the enemy, one wing of the depleted army marched up the east coast under Lord George Murray, while the other, under the Prince, started north through the mountains. In the last week of February, they reunited at Inverness, where the scene was set for the final act in the drama known as 'the Forty-Five Rebellion'.

While Jacobite raiding parties were marauding the Highlands, attacking forts and other government outposts, the Prince was enjoying himself, hunting and dancing, his ardour for military activity temporarily abated.

Barely 160 km (100 mls) distant in Aberdeen, the Duke of Cumberland was training his infantry in a new drill, devised to repel the Highlanders' much-feared broadsword charge. Instead of engaging the man to the front with his 41-cm (16-in) fixed bayonet, the redcoat was taught to go for the clansman on his right, stabbing the side exposed by his upraised sword arm.

By the middle of March, Cumberland was ready to resume his pursuit of the rebels. On

Prince Charles Edward Stuart (1720–1788). Although slight of build, the Prince was a strong, active man, capable of enduring long marches under harsh conditions. His light-hearted manner and handsome presence were forceful assets to the Jacobite cause. No one ever doubted his personal courage, but he lacked one crucial attribute, which his opponent, Cumberland, possessed in high degree: military experience. After the battle, the Prince escaped to France and then to Rome. All hope of restoration gone, he degenerated into a drunken, physically unattractive old man.

William, Duke of Cumberland (1721–1765). The third son of George II, Cumberland had, from an early age, been devoted to soldiering: when aged only five, he was found drilling a company of boys outside his nursery. He gained wide experience of warfare in Europe, where his large frame, mounted on a 17-hand horse, was a familiar, reassuring sight to his soldiers. He was both admired and feared by them: admired for his ability, but feared for his undeviating severity to any who disobeyed or opposed him, as the defeated Highlanders were to learn to their cost after the Battle of Culloden.

Lord George Murray (1694–1760). A tall, strong, fearless man, Murray was not only a brilliant strategist but was always diligently attentive to military detail. Unquestionably the most able commander on the Jacobite side, he was nevertheless regarded with suspicion by his comrades, for he had been in the pay of the Hanoverians and joined the Prince only at the last moment; this was to have farreaching and ultimately disastrous results, since it caused his advice to be often ignored. After the Battle of Culloden, he resigned his commission and fled to Europe, where he remained in exile for the rest of his life. On a number of occasions over the next few years, he asked to see the Prince, also in exile, but Charles Edward, believing that Murray had betrayed him, always refused.

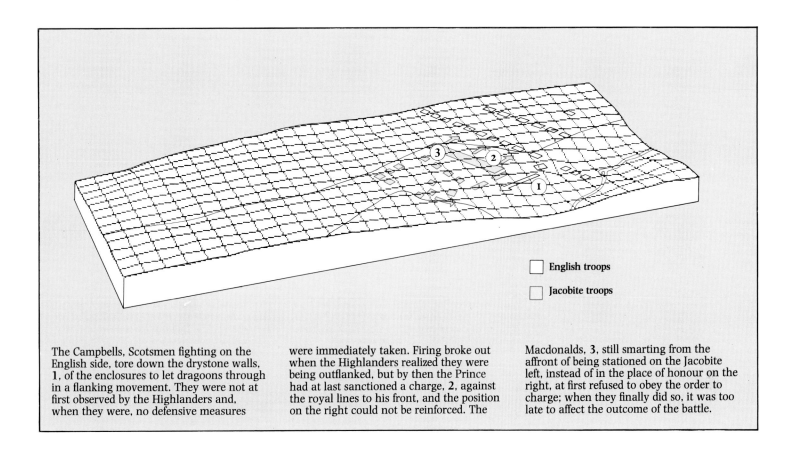

The Campbells, Scotsmen fighting on the English side, tore down the drystone walls, **1**, of the enclosures to let dragoons through in a flanking movement. They were not at first observed by the Highlanders and, when they were, no defensive measures were immediately taken. Firing broke out when the Highlanders realized they were being outflanked, but by then the Prince had at last sanctioned a charge, **2**, against the royal lines to his front, and the position on the right could not be reinforced. The Macdonalds, **3**, still smarting from the affront of being stationed on the Jacobite left, instead of in the place of honour on the right, at first refused to obey the order to charge; when they finally did so, it was too late to affect the outcome of the battle.

English troops

Jacobite troops

Much of the credit for the English victory at Culloden must go to Cumberland, marred though it was by his barbaric conduct after the battle. He had taken command of an army much demoralized by repeated defeats at Jacobite hands, despite their having greater numbers and better weapons. Moreover, the English feared the Highland Charge and were liable to panic. In the months preceding the battle, he had subjected his troops to strict training, turning them into an efficient, confident force. Contemporary illustrations, *above*, show English foot-soldiers of the time fixing bayonets, one of the disciplines that was constantly practised by Cumberland's troops.

14 April, the royal army reached Nairn, just 26 km (16 mls) from Inverness. Prince Charles, shaken out of his temporary lethargy, ordered his troops to concentrate on Culloden Moor, a bleak tract of heather and peat 9.5 km (6 mls) east of the town.

Lord George Murray was dismayed, for the ground chosen by the Adjutant-General, John William O'Sullivan, an incompetent Irishman with a high opinion of himself and a favourite of the Prince, was the very worst for Highlanders to fight upon. It was open, flat and generally firm—excellent for the enemy artillery and cavalry but ill-suited to the Highlanders. Murray later remarked that not one common clan soldier would have fought there had he been given a choice.

While the Jacobites began to muster on Culloden Moor, the royal army remained at Nairn on the 15th, celebrating their commander's twenty-fifth birthday with extra rations and a plentiful supply of liquor.

Learning of this, Prince Charles proposed to take the 4,000 men he had available and surprise the royal army, which was erroneously estimated to be 18,000 strong, twice their actual number. At first, none of the senior officers would countenance such a gamble. The men on the moor were starving (the commissariat had forgotten to bring up supplies) and expected reinforcements had not arrived.

When a further clan regiment came in and the cavalry reported no movement in Cumberland's camp, Murray softened his opposition to the scheme, which, in any event, the Prince was adamant should proceed. Possibly thinking that it was better to try a desperate attack than offer battle on such unsuitable ground, Murray devised a two-pronged attack on Cumberland's sleeping regiments. Surprise was essential, so a night march was organized to put them in position for the assault at daybreak.

What followed should have served notice of impending disaster. Murray, with 2,000 men, set off at a good pace, but soon became separated from Lord John Drummond's column, behind which came the Prince and the French troops. Drummond fell farther and farther behind in the darkness, while matters were exacerbated by a confusion of orders and counter-orders. When the first streaks of dawn lit the sky, Murray found himself still 3.2 km (2 mls) from the enemy's camp and with too few men at his back to press an attack. There was no alternative but to return to Culloden, for already the drums were beating reveille in the royal lines.

Prince Charles, ever the military optimist, argued against retreat and swore that he had been betrayed. When the dispirited

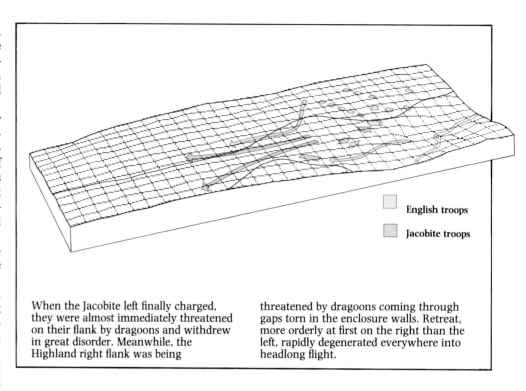

English troops

Jacobite troops

When the Jacobite left finally charged, they were almost immediately threatened on their flank by dragoons and withdrew in great disorder. Meanwhile, the Highland right flank was being threatened by dragoons coming through gaps torn in the enclosure walls. Retreat, more orderly at first on the right than the left, rapidly degenerated everywhere into headlong flight.

The beginning of the Jacobite rout. Their attacks, first on the right and then on the left, were repulsed by a combination of cannon fire and deft bayonet action by Royalist infantry. The Jacobite army, enveloped in cannon smoke, began to disintegrate, and streamed from the field, with cavalry and Campbells in pursuit. Many, including wounded, were cut down, both then and after the battle. Corpses littered the field.

The Irish Piquets, 1, regulars loaned to the Prince by Louis XV of France, tried to delay the Royalist cavalry with volleys of fire from the cover of an enclosure wall.

The Jacobite left, having at first refused to advance, found their flank exposed when they did so; they retreated, **2,** pursued by dragoons.

50

The conventional method of attack was for musketeers, with pikemen in support, to advance against their foe, discharging volleys as they did so. Muskets, however, were time-consuming to reload—a failing that the Highlanders were quick to exploit. Highland troops would advance to within range of the enemy and then discharge a volley, to which there would be an immediate reply. At once, while the enemy was struggling to reload, the Highlanders would throw aside their muskets, draw their swords and, screaming their terrifying war-cries, hurl themselves ferociously against their adversaries.

Muskets were without bayonets until the late 17th century, and those attacked had only musket butts or pikes with which to defend themselves. The former were no match for Highland swords, while the latter were rendered harmless by the simple expedient of each man's receiving a pike thrust on his wood and leather shield and then severing the embedded pike head from its shaft with a slash of his broadsword. Small wonder, then, that defenceless and terrified lines usually broke within five minutes of a Highland Charge being launched.

By the year of Culloden, however, refinements in equipment had rendered the Highland Charge ineffectual; fire-lock muskets, which took less time to reload, and bayonets were potent weapons. The period of Highland triumph was over.

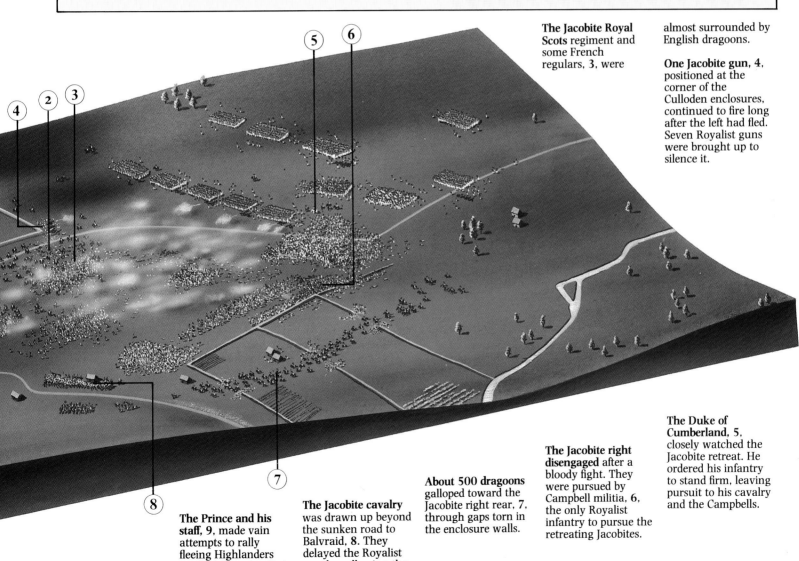

The Jacobite Royal Scots regiment and some French regulars, **3**, were almost surrounded by English dragoons.

One Jacobite gun, 4, positioned at the corner of the Culloden enclosures, continued to fire long after the left had fled. Seven Royalist guns were brought up to silence it.

The Prince and his staff, 9, made vain attempts to rally fleeing Highlanders on the left centre. But by then the battle was already lost.

The Jacobite cavalry was drawn up beyond the sunken road to Balvraid, **8**. They delayed the Royalist cavalry, allowing the Jacobite right to retreat in good order.

About 500 dragoons galloped toward the Jacobite right rear, **7**, through gaps torn in the enclosure walls.

The Jacobite right disengaged after a bloody fight. They were pursued by Campbell militia, **6**, the only Royalist infantry to pursue the retreating Jacobites.

The Duke of Cumberland, 5, closely watched the Jacobite retreat. He ordered his infantry to stand firm, leaving pursuit to his cavalry and the Campbells.

Jacobites straggled back to Culloden Moor at about 6 am, it was estimated that more than 2,000 men had slipped away to forage for something to supplement the one biscuit apiece issued the day before. Many of those remaining, faint from hunger and the exertions of the night, fell asleep in the heather—but not for long.

When Cumberland heard of the abortive night march, he resolved to give no respite to the exhausted rebels. Shortly after 5 am no fewer than a dozen battalions of infantry, three regiments of horse and a train of artillery were marching rapidly along the road to Culloden.

Cumberland's advance guard of cavalry was spotted by Jacobite pickets when it was about 6 km (4 mls) from the moor. Uproar erupted in the Prince's camp, as frantic efforts were made to rouse the sleeping and round up the foragers. There was no time to revise the order of battle: that of the previous day had to suffice. This placed on the left the Macdonalds, who by tradition held the right of the line, an affront to their honour which continued to rankle, even in the face of the enemy.

To the rattle of drums from the Lowland and French regiments and the wild skirling of the clan pipers, the weary Jacobites stood to arms. They faced east across the exposed moor—straight into blinding rain and sleet, whipped by a biting wind. Their muster-roll showed a strength of 8,000 but no more than 5,000 were present. They were drawn up, two lines deep, on a 640-m (700-yd) front, each flank resting on the walls of cultivated enclosures.

Wet, hungry and bedraggled, the Scots watched as the approaching scarlet and white column of some 9,000 royal soldiers smartly formed a three-deep line of battle and then advanced to within 460 m (500 yds) of their position. At about one o'clock, Lord Boyd, a Coldstream Guards' officer on a mounted reconnaissance of the Jacobite front line, attracted a cannon shot—and immediately battle began.

The rebels had 12 assorted guns, but they had no professional gunners to work them and the effect of their fire was minimal. Not so the effect of royalist artillery. Five batteries, each of two three-pounders, posted at intervals between the front-line battalions, opened a regular and devastating fire, lasting almost half an hour. Casualties, dreadful in their number, were sustained in the Jacobite ranks before the Prince, who was stationed in the rear out of sight of the havoc being wrought, finally consented to an attack.

The rain had ceased, but the wind blew the choking gunsmoke into the faces of the rebel centre and right, which broke into an uncontrolled charge. Many men forgot to discharge their firearms in the mad race to meet the enemy hand to hand.

Volleys of musketry discharged by disciplined soldiers, coupled with barrages of grapeshot, erupted from the English ranks, mowing down Mackintoshes, Stewarts and Camerons in hundreds. The two regiments bearing the burden of the vicious onslaught split, allowing about 500 clansmen to penetrate. But the regiments in the second line brought many down, and most of the rest were taken in the flank by the quickly recovered royalists.

Murray's Atholl Brigade, which had lost direction in the fog of battle, was trying to attack, but, bunched up along a turf dyke on the Jacobite right, it ran into heavy enfilade fire from Wolfe's regiment. Regular soldiers, who had been at the Battle of Fontenoy and other battles in Flanders, said they had never seen a field strewn with so many dead and wounded.

Devastating fire and deft bayonet work at close quarters forced the Jacobite centre and right to retire. Jacobite forces on the left had made no sustained attack, and, when the clan regiments moved forward, making feints to draw the royalist troops' fire, they found their flank exposed and threatened by dragoons—so they also withdrew, but not in such good order as the mangled right flank managed.

While Murray, one of the few front-line officers to escape unscathed, brought up some French troops from the second line to cover the retreat, the retiring rebels were taken on the right flank by cavalry. The royal troops had done the very thing that the unimaginative O'Sullivan had sworn

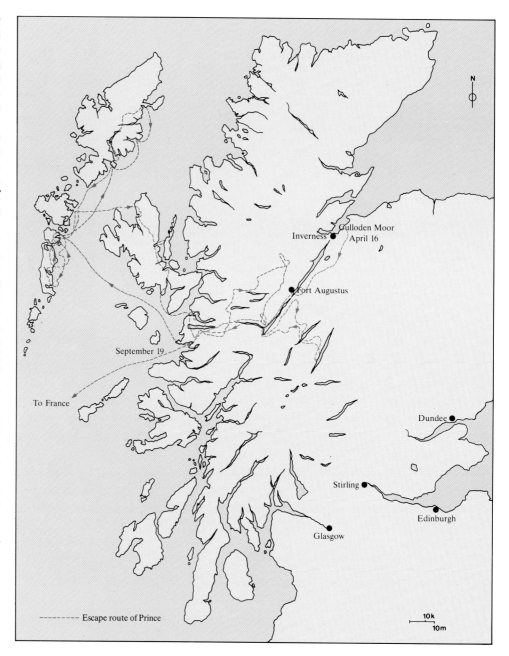

Inverness ● | Culloden Moor
April 16

● Fort Augustus

September 19

To France

Dundee ●

Stirling ●

Edinburgh ●

Glasgow ●

-------- Escape route of Prince

10 k
10 m

After the rout of his forces at Culloden, Prince Charles Edward became a fugitive. He wandered by night from place to place, *left*, often reduced to living in caves or huts. Disguised as a woman, he was rowed to the island of Skye and there housed by the valiant heroine Flora Macdonald—for which selfless act she was for some time imprisoned in the Tower of London.

During his wanderings in Scotland, a price of £30,000—an enormous sum in the 18th century—was placed on his head. Yet not one single Scotsman or woman vouchsafed information as to his whereabouts. The Prince was rescued after six months and taken into exile by a French ship.

they would not do when he picked that ill-fated ground: they tore down the high stone walls of the Culloden Park enclosures and then came swinging through behind the Jacobite lines.

Bar a few pockets of resistance, the battle was over. The Prince, who had watched incredulously as his army disintegrated, was led from the field. He was to spend the next six months as a fugitive before being taken into exile by a French ship.

Although 14,000 troops were on Culloden Moor, it is unlikely that more than 3,000 took an active part in the fighting. Many regiments on both sides never fired a shot. For the cost of a mere 50 killed and 259 wounded, the Duke of Cumberland's army is estimated to have despatched the best part of 2,000 Jacobites, about half their total number.

Much of the killing occurred after the rebels broke off the action. The cavalry gave chase and began an orgy of death and mutilation. Not only were fleeing Jacobites, both wounded and unscathed, mercilessly cut down, but so too were Highland women and children and bystanders, who had unwisely come to view the battle, albeit from a distance.

Parties of infantry later moved about the field and the surrounding area, executing all the wounded rebels they could find. A false rumour that the Jacobites had been ordered to give no quarter in the battle fired their thirst for revenge. So it was that their violent excesses earned for their royal commander the odious soubriquet 'The Bloody Butcher'. It was the last battle to be fought on British soil and frustrated forever all hopes of a Stuart restoration.

The Hanoverian victory at Culloden was shamefully marred by Cumberland's merciless retribution exacted upon the Highlanders, for no quarter was given. The wounded were shot, as were many of the prisoners; others were taken into England, then swiftly tried and executed. Some 1,000 prisoners were sold to American cotton plantations as slaves.

The Highlanders' cattle were seized and their homesteads destroyed. Clan chiefs were stripped of their authority, thereby permanently undermining Highland social structure. No Highlander was permitted to speak Gaelic, play Highland bagpipes, own weapons or wear the tartan, offenders being either imprisoned or executed.

More roads and bridges were built to facilitate the movement of Hanoverian troops about the region, thereby making further revolt impossible. In this way Cumberland eliminated support for the Jacobite cause, but, in doing so, he left for many years a heritage of hatred. One good was to emerge, however: Highland military prowess was soon channelled into new Highland regiments, which in future years were to stand among the élite of the British army.

Saratoga/*19 September - 7 October, 1777*

Great Britain's colonies in North America declared their independence on 4 July 1776, but the fledgling nation did not gain recognition from the European powers until 15 months later, after its decisive victory over the British at Saratoga.

Lieutenant-General John Burgoyne's strategy, conceived in 1776, was designed to restore the rule of King George III in his rebellious American colonies. General George Washington's Continental Army had defeated Lieutenant-General Sir William Howe's British troops at Trenton and then at Princeton, and a waterborne offensive by way of Lake Champlain, led by the Governor-General of Canada, Sir Guy Carleton, had to be abandoned after sustaining heavy losses in a naval action.

Carleton's second-in-command, Burgoyne, saw an opportunity to win himself an important field command. The British government, at Burgoyne's instigation, issued orders for him to mount a summer offensive from Canada into America by way of Lake Champlain and the Hudson River. A small force under Lieutenant-Colonel Barry St Leger was at the same time to come along the Mohawk valley from Lake Ontario, and a large contingent from Howe's main British army, based on New York City, was to strike north up the Hudson. The three columns were to converge on the town of Albany and then to cut off New England, the centre of the revolution, from the other colonies.

The plan was doomed from the moment that Howe, without reference to Burgoyne, was simultaneously authorized to conduct a separate campaign of his own against Washington in Pennsylvania. This entailed leaving only a small force in New York under Major-General Sir Henry Clinton, severely limiting operations on the Hudson.

An enthusiastic and confident Burgoyne launched his expedition on 21 June 1777. His army comprised six brigades of British regulars and German mercenaries, supplemented by 400 Indian scouts and some 250 mixed Canadian and American Loyalist irregulars. Nearly 8,000 men and 138 guns were crowded on to 200 flat-bottomed boats which then sailed down Lake Champlain.

At first the expedition accorded with all Burgoyne's hopes. Fort Ticonderoga, which dominated the American end of Lake Champlain, fell almost without a shot being fired. The 3,000-strong garrison, finding themselves exposed to British cannon on heights they had believed impassable to guns, evacuated the fort. One column marched to join Major-General Philip Schuyler's army 64 km (40 mls) to the south, while another escaped in boats.

Territories of vast expanse, notably in North America, fell to the British after their victories over the French in the Seven Years War. 'To quiet the minds of the Indians', as George Washington wrote, the British government forbade the purchase or settlement of the frontier lands—a justifiable order but a source of grievance to colonists seeking to make their fortunes.

The British were also determined that the North American colonies should pay their proportion of the expenses of garrisoning the New World—a not unreasonable demand, since England had supplied the bulk of men and money in the fight for their protection against the French in the recent wars. But taxes produced little

revenue and much antagonism; 'No taxation without representation!' became the colonists' cry. Colonial revolutionary leaders then emerged, who disputed the legality of direct taxation levied from London. Those seeking a

break with England fostered resentment, and in 1775 there were skirmishes at Lexington and Concord; these were followed by that at Bunker Hill and, two years later, came the decisive battle at Saratoga.

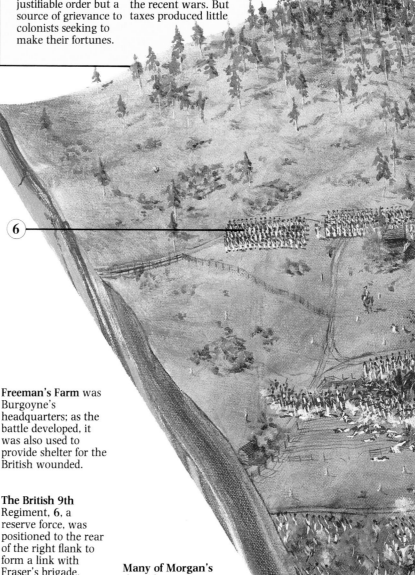

Freeman's Farm

Freeman's Farm was Burgoyne's headquarters; as the battle developed, it was also used to provide shelter for the British wounded.

The British 9th Regiment, **6**, a reserve force, was positioned to the rear of the right flank to form a link with Fraser's brigade, which was 0.8 km ($\frac{1}{2}$ ml) to the west.

Many of Morgan's sharpshooters were sited high up in the trees, **5**, from which vantage points they used their powerful Pennsylvania rifles to deadly effect. British officers, in their distinctive gold-laced uniforms, were especially vulnerable.

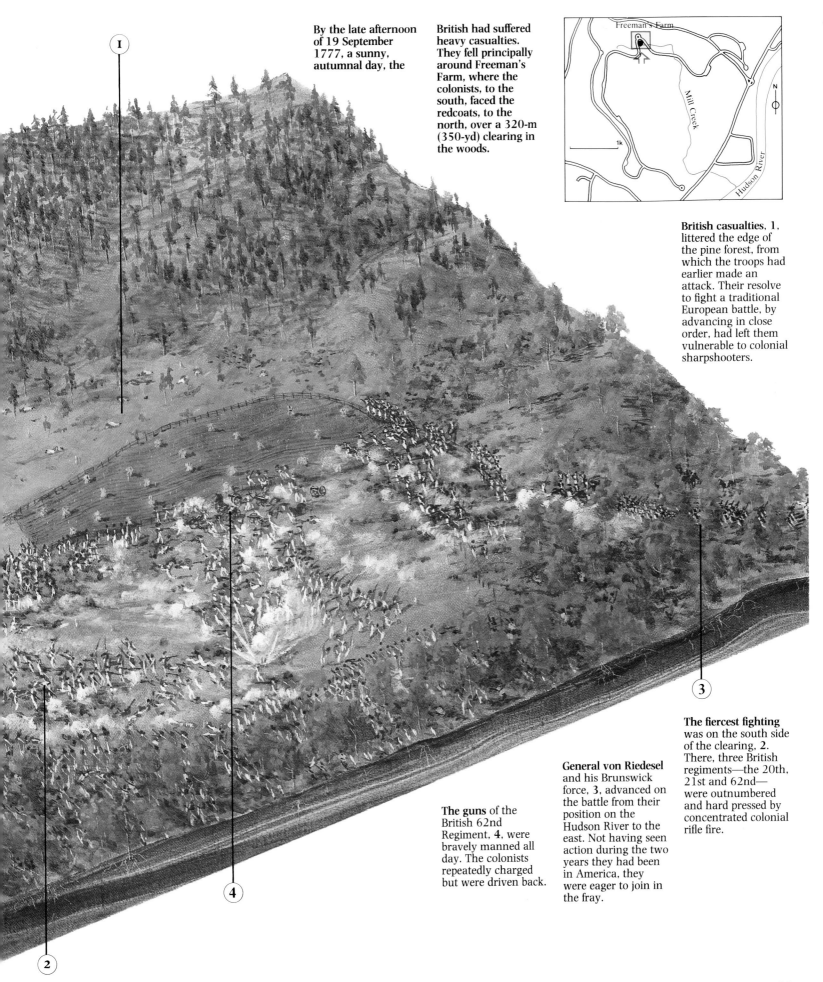

By the late afternoon of 19 September 1777, a sunny, autumnal day, the British had suffered heavy casualties. They fell principally around Freeman's Farm, where the colonists, to the south, faced the redcoats, to the north, over a 320-m (350-yd) clearing in the woods.

British casualties, **1**, littered the edge of the pine forest, from which the troops had earlier made an attack. Their resolve to fight a traditional European battle, by advancing in close order, had left them vulnerable to colonial sharpshooters.

The fiercest fighting was on the south side of the clearing, **2**. There, three British regiments—the 20th, 21st and 62nd— were outnumbered and hard pressed by concentrated colonial rifle fire.

General von Riedesel and his Brunswick force, **3**, advanced on the battle from their position on the Hudson River to the east. Not having seen action during the two years they had been in America, they were eager to join in the fray.

The guns of the British 62nd Regiment, **4**, were bravely manned all day. The colonists repeatedly charged but were driven back.

Brigadier-General Simon Fraser, commanding the élite British Grenadiers and light infantry, pursued them overland, met their rearguard at Hubbardton, on 7 July, and won decisively in a sharp fight.

Burgoyne meanwhile, having been obliged to detach two regiments to garrison Ticonderoga, overtook the retreating rebel flotilla at Skenesborough, capturing their boats, guns and stores. He then opted to march his unwieldy army, with 220 wagons and 42 guns, 96 km (60 mls) to Albany through rough country. Short of supplies, Burgoyne sent 800 men to raid an American supply depot at Bennington, Vermont; they were overwhelmed, and a relief column was badly mauled.

In the interim, in the Mohawk valley, Colonel St Leger's 1,500-strong column had been halted before Fort Stanwix (now Fort Schuyler), 193 km (120 mls) west of Albany, and was soon in retreat. Howe, confident of Burgoyne's ability to take care of himself after his early successes, was fighting his own battles in Pennsylvania and would not be able to send a sizeable supporting force north before winter set in.

Burgoyne was now deep in enemy territory, with 15 per cent of his army lost, daily reports of ever-increasing numbers of Americans ranged against him and with no hope of significant help from other British forces. On 13 September, resupplied and reinforced by some German companies, he gambled on reaching Albany, even though he had to sever his lines of communication with Canada to do so. When his depleted force crossed a pontoon bridge near Saratoga, now Schuylerville, on the west bank of the Hudson, he knew that they were without supporting allies. Now under the command of General Horatio Gates, who had replaced Schuyler, the Colonial army had the day before taken up positions on Bemis Heights, about 40 km (25 mls) north of Albany, to block the British advance. Behind strong earthworks, Gates had 7,000 men and 22 guns. As well as numerical superiority, he possessed a formidable advantage in 500 sharpshooters, led by Colonel Daniel Morgan and sent to him by General Washington.

Thick mist lay in the Hudson valley as the King's men marched from their camp at 10 am on 19 September. They advanced in three columns—Brigadier-General Fraser with 2,500 men on the right and Burgoyne with 1,400 in the centre, while the more heavily equipped Germans and the artillery, under Baron von Riedesel, moved down the river road on the left. Many of Gates's senior officers, notably Major-General Benedict Arnold, pleaded to take the initiative against Burgoyne's divided,

Lieutenant-General John Burgoyne (1722–1792) was a capable military commander, who had become a hero in England after his capture of a Portuguese citadel during the Seven Years War. In his North American campaign, however, he revealed two shortcomings: though admiring the colonists' courage, he consistently underestimated their military capabilities, and he never mastered the techniques necessary for fighting local troops in a wild terrain.

General Benedict Arnold (1741–1801) was a commander of great personal courage, but he had taken deep offence when five junior brigadiers had been promoted over him. However, in 1780, he was appointed commander of West Point. In financial difficulties, and now married to a woman with Loyalist sympathies, he conspired with Clinton to betray West Point in return for a large sum of money. The plot was discovered, and, although Arnold escaped, his name became synonymous with infamy.

General Horatio Gates (c. 1727–1806) was born in England and, after enlisting at an early age, served in North America. Later, having resigned his commission, he settled in present-day Virginia. He espoused the Colonial cause, and his triumph at Saratoga, although the outcome was little due to his leadership, made him a hero. However, in 1780, he was routed at the Battle of Camden and was permanently disgraced by fleeing from the field, outdistancing his men in his haste to escape.

Colonel Daniel Morgan (1736–1802) led some 500 sharpshooters at Saratoga. Morgan became, in the colonists' eyes, the hero of the battle, for it was his buckskin-clad frontiersmen, firing from the cover of trees, who had wrought such havoc on the British troops. Immediately after the war, he retired into private life.

British infantry in the War of Independence were mostly equipped with the 'Brown Bess', a smooth-bore musket which saw service from about 1720 until the 1840s. The model of this period had a 107-cm (42-in) long barrel.

The colonial sharpshooters were armed with the Pennsylvania rifle (sometimes incorrectly called the Kentucky rifle), a .44 calibre weapon with a longer than usual barrel. It was a more accurate and powerful weapon than the 'Brown Bess' and took less time to load.

Muskets before the 19th century were inaccurate and time-consuming to load. To compensate for this, one rank of infantry fired while another reloaded, or both ranks fired at once and immediately made a bayonet charge.

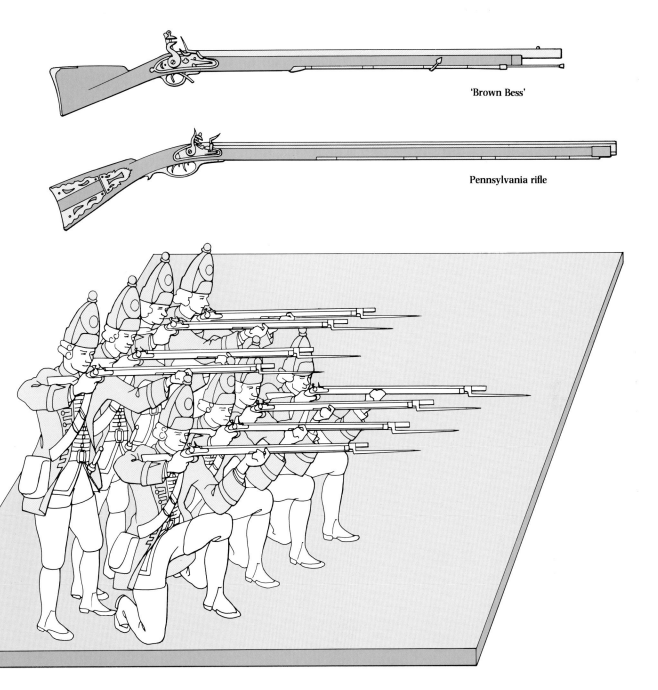

'Brown Bess'

Pennsylvania rifle

In the 18th century, a trained soldier could fire three rounds a minute. A good marksman could hit an enemy up to a distance of 80 m (87 yds); beyond that range, he might or might not strike his target. Shot became spent at about 183 m (200 yds). Despite the lack of accuracy at a range greater than 80 m (87 yds), compact fire was still effective against large numbers.

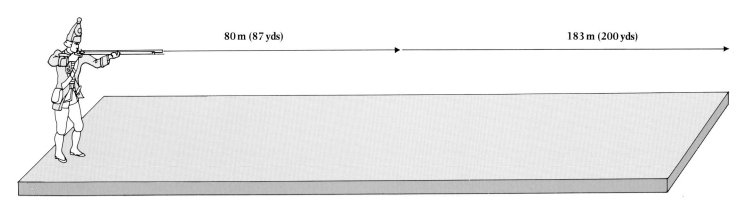

80 m (87 yds)

183 m (200 yds)

slow-moving army, but Gates would submit only to a reconnaissance in force by Morgan's sharpshooters.

At 1 pm, near a clearing by Freeman's Farm, the British advance guard of the centre column came up against the colonial riflemen, who saturated them with fire. As the survivors fell back in disorder, Morgan's men rushed after them—straight into the concentrated musketry of the main column, which was hurriedly deploying on the open ground. It was the rebels' turn to break and run.

Morgan then tried to turn Burgoyne's right flank, but was repulsed by Fraser, holding a strong position on rising ground to the west of the farm. Later, reinforced by New Hampshire militia sent up by General Arnold, Morgan again turned to the clearing, where Burgoyne had stationed 900 men of the British 20th, 21st and 62nd Regiments and four six-pounder cannon in a line of battle 277 m (300 yds) long.

All afternoon, the rattle of musketry and the boom of guns echoed through the forest. Six major assaults were made by the colonists; six fierce counter-attacks were launched by the redcoats. Just as Burgoyne's situation was becoming critical, Baron von Riedesel brought up his Brunswick force from the left on his own initiative and executed a well-timed bayonet charge against the Colonials' exposed right flank, driving them off. The rebels hid in the cover of the woods and fired individually until night fell.

With less than a month's rations left, Burgoyne's only hope was a message from Sir Henry Clinton saying that he was preparing to mount a diversionary attack on the Hudson forts south of Albany. Shelving all thoughts of moving forward until he had more news of Clinton, Burgoyne had three earthwork lines thrown up to protect his army from attack: the Balcarres, Breymann and Great Redoubts. By October, still with no news from Clinton, Burgoyne's situation had become desperate. He decided to carry out a reconnaissance in force with a view to mounting a major assault later. On 7 October, 1,500 of his best remaining men marched out at 11 am, taking 10 pieces of artillery with them.

An hour later, the column reached a wheatfield 0.8 km ($\frac{1}{2}$ ml) southwest of the Balcarres Redoubt, where Burgoyne deployed his troops. Meanwhile Gates was receiving a detailed account of the British foray. For once, this ultra-cautious general acted decisively. Colonel Morgan and his riflemen, some light infantry and two militia brigades were ordered to work their way around a heavily wooded hill on the British right and attack Burgoyne in the

The afternoon of 7 October 1777, when the second Battle of Saratoga was fought, was another fine, clear day, ideal for marksmen. By now, however, the British had constructed a fortified line from the Hudson River to the

Breymann Redoubt. Its strongest point lay on Freeman's Farm, where eight cannon were mounted.

Breymann Redoubt, 1, was occupied by German troops. They would not be attacked until the end of the battle, after the British line had broken. It was here that Benedict Arnold was wounded.

Some redcoats, 2, from the British left flank, their positions overrun, retreated to the shelter of the Breymann Redoubt.

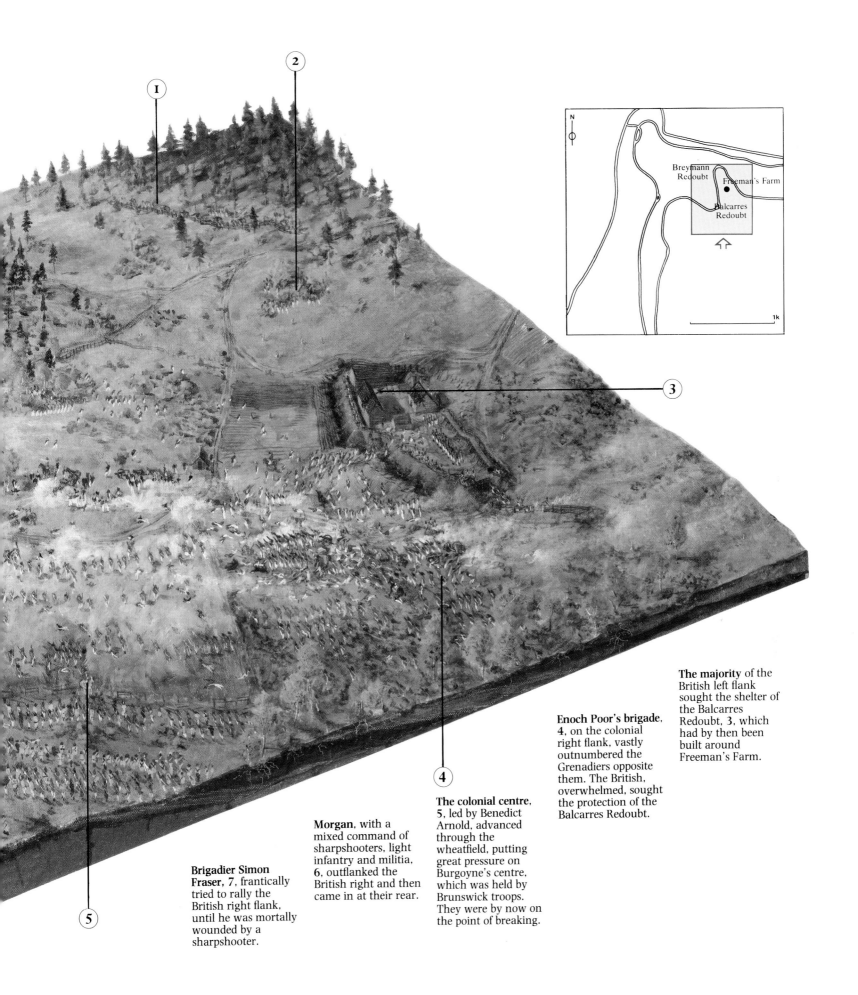

Brigadier Simon Fraser, 7, frantically tried to rally the British right flank, until he was mortally wounded by a sharpshooter.

Morgan, with a mixed command of sharpshooters, light infantry and militia, **6**, outflanked the British right and then came in at their rear.

The colonial centre, 5, led by Benedict Arnold, advanced through the wheatfield, putting great pressure on Burgoyne's centre, which was held by Brunswick troops. They were by now on the point of breaking.

Enoch Poor's brigade, 4, on the colonial right flank, vastly outnumbered the Grenadiers opposite them. The British, overwhelmed, sought the protection of the Balcarres Redoubt.

The majority of the British left flank sought the shelter of the Balcarres Redoubt, **3**, which had by then been built around Freeman's Farm.

59

flank and rear; at the same time, General Enoch Poor's brigade was to assail his left. As soon as the King's troops pivoted to fend off these assaults, General Ebenezer Learned's brigade was ordered to rush the weakened centre.

Although he had been relieved of his command, following a disagreement with Gates after the fight at Freeman's Farm, the impetuous General Arnold could not resist riding toward the sound of the guns. General Arnold, ignoring Gates's order to return to camp, took charge of the fighting at the front, backed by no greater authority than that conferred by his domineering and flamboyant personality.

The British put up a spirited resistance but could not fend off the overwhelming rebel attacks for long. Before an hour had passed, they were reduced to fighting back to back, while the colonists surged around them. The left was the first to crack; then the right was shaken by a wild assault coming from three directions at once. Displaying brilliant leadership, Brigadier Fraser rallied the remnant of his troops and regrouped farther back.

The Colonial battle plan was running perfectly, for Learned's brigade then streamed out of the woods to storm Burgoyne's centre. Outnumbering the British and Germans by more than five to one, they forced them to retreat. Brigadier Fraser, resplendent in scarlet regimentals, bravely galloped over to attempt to halt the rout, but was spotted and shot down by one of Morgan's marksmen. Nothing now could stop the stampede to escape.

Firing died away only as the light began to fade and, under cover of darkness, Burgoyne withdrew his battered troops to the Great Redoubt. He had lost another 600 men in the second Battle of Saratoga. The colonists lost 200.

The following night, Burgoyne ordered a retreat on Saratoga town, intending to recross the pontoon bridge there and fall back to Fort Ticonderoga. After a two-day struggle through dense rain and impeding mud, the long-suffering British and German force finally completed the 13 km (8 mls) to Saratoga—only to find the colonists already there, with guns trained on the vital bridge over the Hudson.

On 17 October, Burgoyne accepted defeat and secured terms of surrender that generously allowed the British troops to return to England, on a promise that they would never again serve in North America. The Continental Congress subsequently reneged on this agreement. They were prepared to accord brave soldiers due honour, but they insisted that for the rest of the war the British troops should be imprisoned.

General Burgoyne, among other British commanders, made much use of Indians, both as scouts and warriors. They were willing allies, since the colonists had seized their land without paying compensation. But after the débâcle at Bennington, most of Burgoyne's Indians abandoned his cause. There were about 100 serving with the British at Saratoga.

Infantrymen were strictly trained in loading drill for flintlock muskets so that they could maintain their rate of fire in battle. The procedure, shown left to right, *below*, was 1, to bite the paper cartridge to release the powder; 2, to pour the powder down the barrel, priming the pan in the process; 3, to place the shot and paper wad in the muzzle; 4, to ram the charge home, and, 5, to cock the lock. The soldier was then ready, on command, to fire his weapon, 6.

The consequences, both immediate and long term, of the British surrender at Saratoga were momentous. The colonists were seen to be capable of winning the war and immediately gained European allies, notably France, which was anxious to avenge her defeats at the hands of the British during the Seven Years War. The French fleet for a time broke the British blockade of the east coast of North America and allowed supplies of ammunition to be sent to the insurgents, without which they must have failed. Moreover, war between England and France pinned down many British troops in Europe and elsewhere, troops that might otherwise have been sent to fight the colonists. Before the Battle of Saratoga, colonial hopes of independence were forlorn; after it, they would inevitably be fulfilled.

Great Britain, in direct consequence of the battle, lost her North American colonies, and a new nation, soon to be more prosperous and powerful than any in Europe, was born. This new nation, one dedicated to the twin principles of liberty and democracy, produced an immediate effect on world affairs. The colonists' successful uprising inspired French revolutionaries, which in turn led to the horrors of the Napoleonic Wars. Nearer home, the revolution was shortly to be emulated by those in South America who sought to overthrow their Spanish and Portuguese masters and establish independent nations.

Many colonial troops, such as Morgan's marksmen, dressed as they pleased, although most wore buckskin jackets. The majority were equipped with the Pennsylvania rifle, which was longer than contemporary rifles, was more accurate and had a greater range. As a matter of national pride, however, the majority of colonial riflemen, **1**, and, **3**, were issued with a uniform, designating their regiment. The British Grenadier, **2**, was armed with a smooth-bore musket, as were the Germans and most colonials. Grenadiers wore mitre-shaped caps. When throwing grenades, they slung their muskets on their backs, a movement easier to accomplish in a cap than in a tricorn hat.

Brigadier Simon Fraser, who had been mortally wounded during the second Battle of Saratoga, asked to be buried in the Great Redoubt. Burgoyne ordered this to be done, despite its causing a dangerous delay in the British retreat. The gathering of mourners was seen by the colonists who, suspecting it presaged military action, opened fire with their artillery. Although shots landing close by covered the mourners with dust, the chaplain delivered a lengthy sermon. Von Riedesel, who, with Burgoyne, attended the service, called it a 'real military funeral'.

Austerlitz/*2 December, 1805*

Napoleon, the greatest soldier in Europe, had to resort to subterfuge to extricate his cold, hungry and outnumbered army from an exposed position in Moravia (now Czechoslovakia) in the winter of 1805. His long march into central Europe from France, which culminated in the Battle of Austerlitz, began in September of that year. The combined might of Austria and Russia—the Third Coalition, as their pact with Great Britain was called—had obliged the recently self-crowned Emperor of the French to give up ambitious plans for an invasion of England and march east to confront them. On transferring his troops from the Channel coast, Napoleon changed their title from the *Armée d'Angleterre* to the *Grande Armée*, a name that was to become famous throughout Europe.

To take the Austrians and Russians by surprise before they could mass their considerable strength, Napoleon marched 200,000 soldiers in a lightning offensive across the River Rhine. Sweeping through southern Germany, his army encircled a 60,000-strong Austrian force at Ulm, forcing it to capitulate almost without a shot being fired.

In the Inn valley of Austria, 160 km (100 mls) to the southeast, lay a Russian army under the Allies' Commander-in-Chief, Marshal Mikhail Kutuzov, which had advanced to relieve the hapless thousands captured by the French at Ulm. Napoleon resolved to bring the Russians to battle. Kutuzov was a cautious, 60-year-old veteran, who chose to delay action until his army was stronger. With considerable skill, he withdrew in good order eastward, as far as Vienna, then turned north into Moravia, where he joined forces with Lieutenant-General F. W. Buxhowden's outposts, on 19 November 1805.

With the French in close pursuit, Kutuzov continued to retire. From Brünn (Brno) he marched to Olmütz (Olomouc), where reinforcements increased his army to some 89,000 men and 278 guns. There Kutuzov was relegated to being the Commander-in-Chief in name only, for both Tsar Alexander I and Francis I, Emperor of Austria, were in the camp. The Tsar, a soldier of extremely limited experience, was opinionated as to how the campaign should be directed; Francis deferred to him. Alexander's dearest wish was to win glory by defeating Napoleon; there was, therefore, no question of further retreat.

The *Grande Armée* was at that time in a vulnerable situation. Its strength had been reduced on the march, as more and more men were shed to guard the ever-lengthening lines of communication; and, as the commissariat became over-burdened

At about 1 pm on the cold wintery day of 2 December 1805, French infantry, occupying the hard-won Pratzen Heights, the central position on the battlefield of Austerlitz, came under strong attack from the Russian Imperial Guard. The Guards' initial success posed a momentary threat to Napoleon's plans for the destruction of the Austro-Russian army, but the French soon repulsed them.

Riding at the head of the cavalry of the Russian Imperial Guard, **1**, Tsar Alexander's brother, the Grand Duke Constantine, ordered his squadrons to attack the French left flank, **2**, causing havoc and putting some units to flight.

The 10,000-strong Russian Imperial Guard, **3**, the Allies' sole reserve, broke the French first line with a bayonet charge.

When Napoleon, 4, rode on to the Pratzen Heights to get a closer view of the action, he was met by fleeing French infantry, **5**, comprising two battalions. One had lost its Eagle standard, the only one captured by the Allies at Austerlitz.

The French second line was spared the Russian onslaught, thanks to its artillery, **6**, which flayed the enemy with canister.

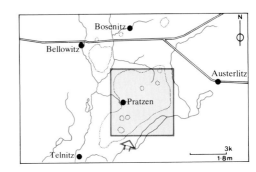

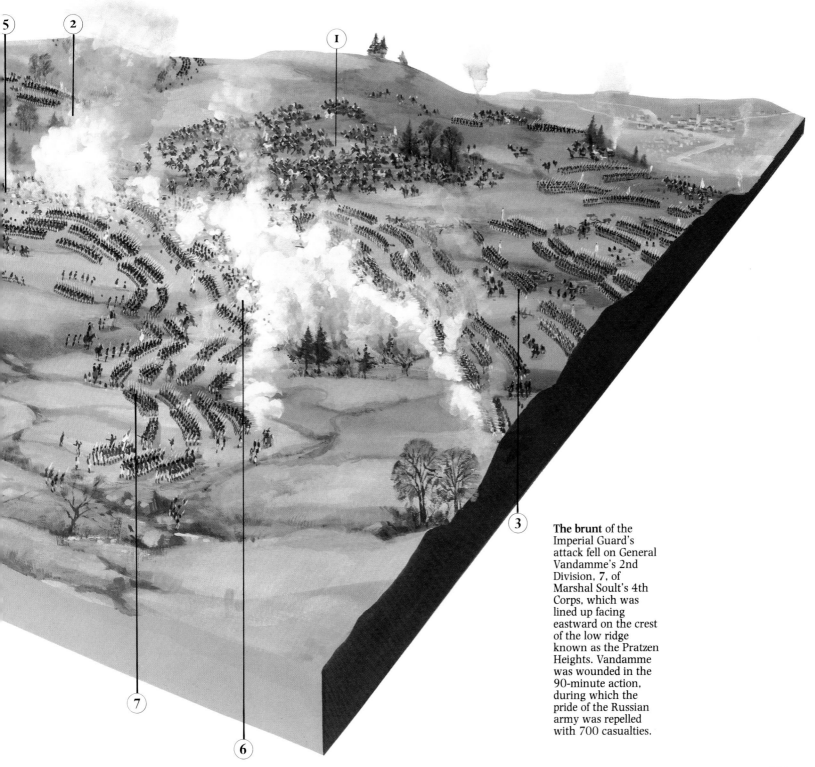

The brunt of the Imperial Guard's attack fell on General Vandamme's 2nd Division, **7**, of Marshal Soult's 4th Corps, which was lined up facing eastward on the crest of the low ridge known as the Pratzen Heights. Vandamme was wounded in the 90-minute action, during which the pride of the Russian army was repelled with 700 casualties.

and bitter weather set in, the number of stragglers grew to alarming proportions. At his camp south of Olmütz, Napoleon had only 55,000 poorly supplied men, who huddled around their fires in hostile country 965 km (600 mls) from the French border. Then the ominous news arrived that Prussia was poised to join the Third Coalition against France.

The Emperor's options were few: retreat was discarded as unthinkable, and a head-on advance against a much stronger force would be foolhardy. He decided to lure the Allies to him quickly and to fight a battle on his terms and on ground of his choosing, to give himself the best chance of regaining the initiative.

A well-laid scheme was set in motion to deceive the Allies into thinking that the French army was on the point of collapse. Napoleon let it be thought that morale was low, while his forward patrols were ordered to flee on sight of the enemy. He fell back several kilometres to Austerlitz (Slavkov), where he purposely failed to occupy the strategically important Pratzen Heights to the south of the village. Then, as a final subterfuge, he sued for peace.

Completely deceived, the Tsar ordered the Allied army to march on Austerlitz, where he was certain he would defeat the demoralized French. Kutuzov was not so sure; he said so—but was ignored.

Tsar Alexander should have heeded his Marshal. As the Austrian and Russian divisions filed on to the Pratzen Heights on 1 December, the situation in the French camp to the west, on the other side of the River Goldbach, was very different from what the Tsar supposed.

Napoleon had, unknown to the Allies, brought up Marshal Bernadotte's 1st Corps from Iglau, and by that evening the leading units of Marshal Davout's 3rd Corps would be arriving after a forced march from Vienna. The French lines faced east on an 8-km (5-ml) front, secured on the left by the fortified Santon Hill and resting on the Telnitz lakes on the right. The deployment was a carefully designed trap in which to catch the Austrian and Russian armies.

In a display of supreme tactical skill, Napoleon concentrated the bulk of his troops on his centre and left, making use of dead ground to conceal the size of his force, while leaving his right flank along the River Goldbach and on toward Telnitz undermanned. He was tempting the Allies to weaken their centre on Pratzen Heights in favour of an all-out attack on his lightly held right, to cut off a French withdrawal down the main road to Vienna. Napoleon would then take the high ground and swing around behind the enemy left.

Field Marshal Mikhail Ilarionovich Kutuzov (1745–1813). A soldier of wide experience, Kutuzov strongly advised against engaging Napoleon at Austerlitz; his advice was ignored and disaster ensued. Kutuzov again met Napoleon in battle in 1812, when he commanded the Russian forces against the invading French. At Borodino, a village 110 km (70 mls) west of Moscow, he tried to delay the enemy advance in a head-on fight, which caused terrible carnage. The Russians withstood three major attacks before a heavy bombardment, followed by a cavalry charge, broke their lines and cleared the way to Moscow. When Napoleon was obliged to retreat from the Russian capital, Kutuzov pursued him with a tenacious fury, inflicting heavy casualties on the *Grande Armée*.

Alexander I (1777–1825), Tsar of Russia. In the early years of his reign, Alexander pursued liberal policies for the betterment of the serfs. However, after Russia's defeat of Napoleon (1812–13), when Alexander was one of the most powerful figures in Europe, he was preoccupied with suppressing revolutionary movements. His increasing conservatism was in part due to his devout Christianity, which led him to uphold Christian morality and the *status quo*. After his death, rumours spread that he had in reality become a hermit in Siberia. In 1926, the Soviet government ordered his tomb to be opened. It was found to be empty and the mystery remains.

Francis I (1768–1835), Emperor of Austria, was also the last Holy Roman Emperor (as Francis II), that confederation being dissolved by Napoleon in 1806. At the Battle of Austerlitz, Francis, prematurely old and discredited by earlier defeats, deferred to the young and impetuous Tsar Alexander. Despite his defeat at Austerlitz and later humiliations, Francis agreed, during a period of peace with France, to Napoleon's marrying his daughter Marie Louise. This, together with his fear that Russia and Prussia might grow too strong, led him to propose lenient terms on Napoleon's defeat in 1814, as opposed to the Prussians, who argued for the total overthrow of 'the Corsican ogre'.

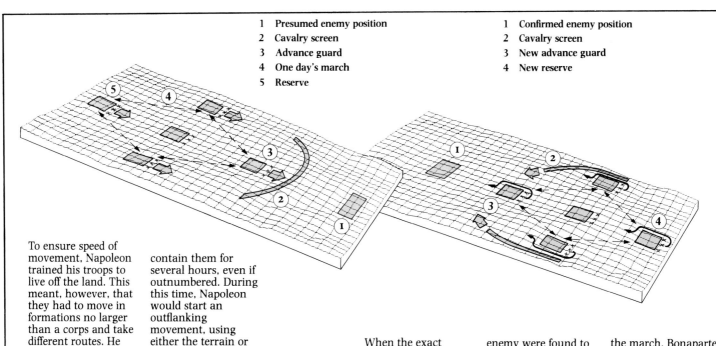

To ensure speed of movement, Napoleon trained his troops to live off the land. This meant, however, that they had to move in formations no larger than a corps and take different routes. He overcame the problem of a divided army by moving his corps with no greater distance between them than a day's march. Since all corps were of equal strength, whichever first made contact with the enemy was able to make a feint against them or to contain them for several hours, even if outnumbered. During this time, Napoleon would start an outflanking movement, using either the terrain or cavalry as a screen. The feint at the enemy's front usually lured them forward into the trap while the outflanking manoeuvre was completed and the reserve came forward to support the engaged corps. The result was usually devastating.

When the exact location of the enemy was unknown, there was an additional advantage in this formation. If the enemy proved to be in a position other than to the French front, any of the other three corps would take over the role of advance guard. Thus, if the enemy were found to be on the French right flank, that corps became the advance guard, and the left flank the reserve. The old advance guard then became the left flank and the reserve the right flank. This great rapidity of manoeuvre vastly increased Napoleon's military options. On the march, Bonaparte stayed in the rear, but when action commenced he moved up. 'A general who has to see things through other people's eyes will never be able to command an army as it should be commanded,' he said.

Napoleon, conscious of the importance of a soldier's loyalty to his unit as well as to himself as emperor, issued flags to his regiments and mottoes with which to embellish them. Great attention was also given to uniforms. Each infantryman, **2**, wore white breeches and waistcoat and a blue coat with scarlet piping. The bearskin, or helmet, had by now replaced the traditional three-cornered hat. Soldiers on parade were gorgeously attired, even dandified. Moustaches were obligatory, and each man was required to grow a queue, or pigtail, to the precise length of 15 cm (6 in). This was tied with a meticuously arranged bow of black ribbon. Each night, soldiers of the élite Imperial Guard put their hair in curling papers and, in the morning, a barber arranged it.

Soldiers were promoted to Napoleon's Imperial Guard solely on merit. In Russia, they were given that honour more for their stature and strength, and with padded shoulders and tall helmets or bearskins, they looked like supermen, **1, 4**.

Drastic cuts in Austria's military budget in the years preceding Austerlitz had seriously run down the efficiency of the national army. Most of the infantry, **3**, who wore tall shakos and green tunics, carried the old 1754 Maria Theresa musket, for which ammunition was often in short supply.

Major-General Weyrother, an Austrian favourite of the Tsar, had produced a plan that called for a mass attack across the Goldbach by some 50,000 men under General Buxhowden, to cut the Olmütz to Vienna road and roll up the French army. While this manoeuvre was in progress, a mixed force of 17,000 infantry and cavalry, commanded by Lieutenant-General P. I. Bagration and Prince John of Lichtenstein respectively, was to threaten the Santon fortifications. The Russian Imperial Guard would form the reserve on the Allies' right.

Few commanders, however, knew the operational details. Marshal Kutuzov slept throughout Weyrother's lengthy briefing, and by the time the verbose Austrian's orders had been translated into Russian for the benefit of more than 60 per cent of the force, it was almost dawn on the day that battle would be joined. Officers did not have time to read their orders properly, let alone understand them. The result was chaotic.

A thick mist blanketed the armies as they stood to their arms in the early hours of 2 December. For the Allies, already confused by events, poor visibility made forming-up even more difficult. Units became intermingled, and hopeless congestion occurred as they struggled from the heights down into the Goldbach valley.

Buxhowden's milling men suddenly came under unexpectedly brisk fire from the French right but quickly made gains against limited defence. Davout's 3rd Corps shortly arrived on the scene, however, and, though weary, made its presence felt to such an extent that Buxhowden called for reinforcements from the centre—just as Napoleon had planned that he should.

From his command post on Zurlan Hill on his left flank, Napoleon watched as the fog began to clear from the high ground, at about 8.30 am, revealing many Allied regiments leaving Pratzen and moving south. When most of them had disappeared toward the fighting on his right, he ordered two divisions of Marshal Soult's 4th Corps, which were hidden from the enemy by mist in the valley bottom, to move out and storm the heights. Surprise was complete. The French soon controlled Pratzen and brought up cannon with which to bombard the crowded Austro-Russian left flank.

Meanwhile, Bagration and Lichtenstein on the Allied right had precipitately launched a full-scale attack on Santon Hill, only to be repulsed by the combined weight of Marshal Lannes's 5th Corps, Bernadotte's 1st Corps and Marshal Murat's cavalry. Until then, hardly a shot had been fired in this sector. Now, however, Napoleon ordered Marshal Bernadotte to move on Blasowitz village in support of

After securing the Pratzen Heights in the centre of the battlefield around 2.30 pm on 2 December 1805, Napoleon then concentrated on destroying the left wing of the Allied army, commanded by General Buxhowden. The French fell on the unfortunate Austrians and Russians from the front, right flank and rear, driving them in disorder toward the Telnitz lakes.

Snow was beginning to fall around 4 pm, when the last act of the Austerlitz tragedy was played out for the defeated Allies. As some units surrendered and others retreated, the order was given to break ranks and scatter, so that individuals might have a chance to make good their escape. Many chose to flee across the frozen Satschan Pond, 1, one of the Telnitz lakes.

French troops, 2, converged on the retreating Allies, 3. General Buxhowden escaped, leaving most of his men behind.

The day after the Battle of Austerlitz, the Austrian Emperor, Francis I, sent an officer to Napoleon asking for terms. The two Emperors met on 4 December, at Spaleny Mill, near Austerlitz (the scene depicted in the painting) and an armistice was agreed, to take effect on the next day.

Napoleon is reputed to have ordered his artillery to smash the ice on the pond, **4**, causing the fleeing Allied soldiers to fall in and drown.

A combination of snow and gathering darkness brought the battle to a close at 4.30 pm, leaving the French undisputed masters of the field.

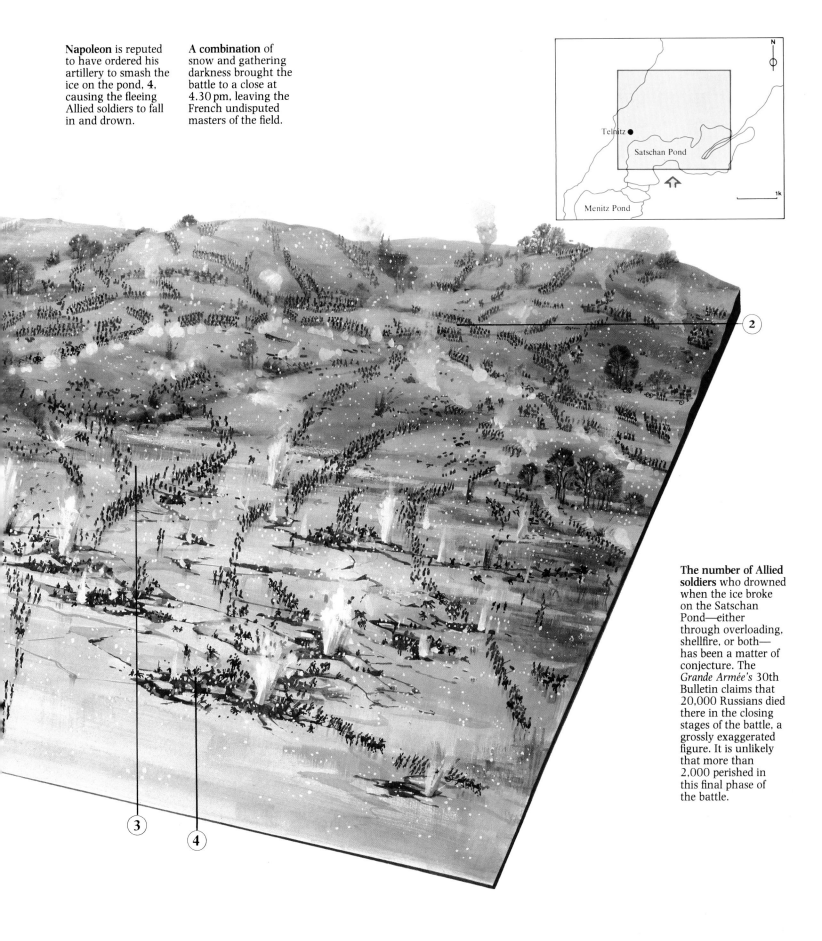

The number of Allied soldiers who drowned when the ice broke on the Satschan Pond—either through overloading, shellfire, or both—has been a matter of conjecture. The *Grande Armée's* 30th Bulletin claims that 20,000 Russians died there in the closing stages of the battle, a grossly exaggerated figure. It is unlikely that more than 2,000 perished in this final phase of the battle.

the attack of Marshal Soult's to the south.

The advance at first made good progress, but, at about 9.30 am, the village was recaptured by Russian light infantry. Within the space of half an hour, violent fighting had erupted around Blasowitz when Murat's cavalry, together with infantry under Lannes, advanced to halt the Allied infantry and cavalry, commanded by Bagration and Lichtenstein. French troopers, despite being outnumbered by about ten to one, dismounted and let loose concentrated carbine fire into the Allied ranks. Then they remounted and charged, bringing Lichtenstein's attack to a halt. Bagration, however, quickly replied with another attack on Santon Hill, but the French line held.

Shortly afterwards, Lannes retook Blasowitz, and Murat, seeing his opportunity, charged forward to drive a wedge between Bagration and Kutuzov to the south. The outcome briefly hung in the balance, but then the Allied cavalry broke. Bagration's force was in full retreat by noon, and Bernadotte was able to come to the support of the attacking French centre.

Throughout the morning, the Allies had made several attempts, all abortive, to regain the Pratzen Heights. In the early afternoon, they committed their reserve, the élite Russian Imperial Guard, in yet another effort to regain the lost ground, and in so doing gave Napoleon momentary anxiety. Their furious onslaught smashed through his first line and caused some units to flee in disorder before the cavalry of his Imperial Guard could restore the position.

By 2.30 pm, the heights were in the undisputed possession of the French, and Napoleon was free to begin the systematic destruction of Buxhowden's huge force, which was now hemmed in on its front, right flank and rear. Many were killed and thousands surrendered. Of those who managed to evade the deadly encirclement, many were drowned when the ice broke as they fled across the frozen Telnitz lakes. Some say the French smashed the ice by artillery fire; it is more likely that it cracked under the weight of the fleeing soldiers.

Toward late afternoon, a driving snowstorm put a stop to the fighting and gave some respite to the Allied forces, now so lacking in cohesion that they could hardly be described as an army. Their losses totalled 27,000, Napoleon's only 8,000.

The Battle of the Three Emperors, as Austerlitz is sometimes called, was a memorable victory for France against daunting odds, destroying the Third Coalition in the process. Austria immediately sought peace terms, while the humiliated Russians withdrew to their own country.

The Battle of Austerlitz

The 4-pounder cannon was the lightest piece in the powerful French artillery corps, of which Napoleon, a former gunnery officer, was particularly proud. This weapon, of 85 mm calibre, was manned by six gunners.

In serving their pieces, artillerymen followed a precise procedure for loading, aiming and firing. There was no recoil system, so once a gun had been fired, it had to be pulled back with drag ropes to its firing position. The spongeman then plunged a wet sponge into the bore to extinguish any smouldering particles from the shot just fired. The loader put a new cartridge and shot in the bore and rammed them home with a wooden rod. The ventsman then pierced the cartridge with a pricker, inserted a firing tube, and checked the gun's elevation. Finally the firer placed his portfire to the firing tube and the gun discharged its projectile.

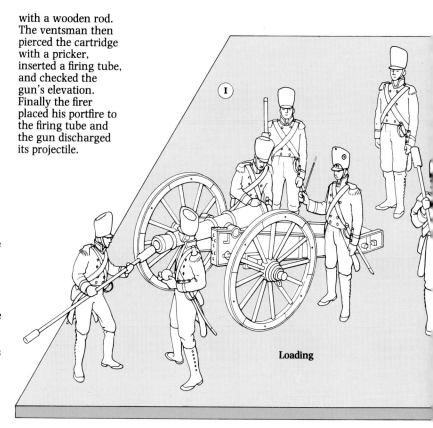

Loading

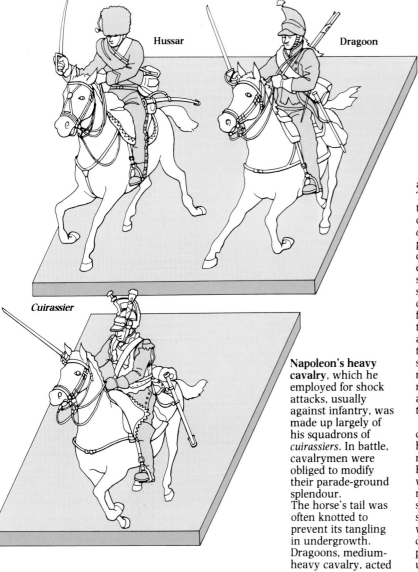

Hussar

Dragoon

Cuirassier

Napoleon's heavy cavalry, which he employed for shock attacks, usually against infantry, was made up largely of his squadrons of *cuirassiers*. In battle, cavalrymen were obliged to modify their parade-ground splendour.
The horse's tail was often knotted to prevent its tangling in undergrowth. Dragoons, medium-heavy cavalry, acted as mounted infantry. They and sometimes the hussars carried carbines, whereas *cuirassiers* had only pistols in holsters. All cavalrymen were equipped with swords, usually sabres—swords with curved blades, used for slashing. Usually the more lightly armed the cavalry, the more curved their sabres, but the design might vary from regiment to regiment and often from year to year.
Napoleon used light cavalry, especially his hussars, mostly for reconnaissance. Bearskins (*kolbaks*) were worn by all ranks in élite squadrons. In other squadrons, the men wore a shako: a cylindrical hat with a peak and a short upright plume.

Austerlitz, the most tactically perfect of Napoleon's battles, had important political results, both immediate and long term. A day after the battle, the Austrians sued for an armistice, which was agreed to. Meanwhile, the Russian army marched homeward. Tsar Alexander had been chastened by his defeat and, until Napoleon invaded his country in 1812, adopted a pro-French policy. All of Great Britain's plans had been brought to ruin, and her only remaining ally, Prussia, was annihilated in the following year at the Battle of Jena.

Despite his great victories, however, Napoleon and his empire were doomed, for victories stimulated resentment, which led to more battles, leaving the vanquished further scores to settle. Great Britain's only hope lay in the expectation that Napoleon would overreach himself. This he did, in 1808, by invading Spain and Portugal, thereby giving Great Britain the chance to field a major land army, supported from the sea. The army was led by a British commander of military genius comparable to that of the Emperor Napoleon—Wellington, the 'Iron Duke'.

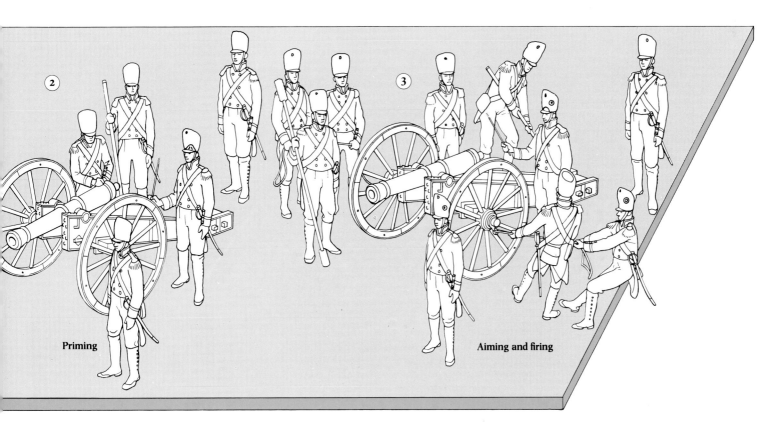

2

3

Priming

Aiming and firing

Waterloo/*18 June, 1815*

The battle that Napoleon Bonaparte confidently predicted would be 'a picnic' turned into a wake for his dynastic ambitions, as well as for the cream of the French army.

Less than four months had passed since the man who was once Emperor of France and master of western Europe had caused trepidation in the capitals of Europe by escaping from exile on the Mediterranean island of Elba. When the Allies, meeting at the Congress of Vienna to redraw the map of Europe torn up by the Napoleonic Wars, learned of his return, they branded him an outlaw and mobilized to crush him.

In the spring of 1815, two large armies gathered in Belgium to threaten France's northern frontier. From his headquarters in Brussels, the Duke of Wellington commanded a mixed force of British, Dutch, Belgian, Hanoverian and Brunswick troops: some 83,000 men. He called it 'an infamous army'. At Liège, Prussia's 72-year-old Marshal Gebhard von Blücher mustered some 113,000 men, but many were recruits.

After detaching forces to guard his other frontiers, Napoleon swiftly concentrated 124,000 soldiers in the north. They were outnumbered by almost two to one, but this was not so disadvantageous as it sounds, for most were battle-hardened veterans of his old *Grande Armée*.

Exhibiting undiminished audacity, Napoleon resolved to strike first, drive a wedge between Wellington and Blücher and then defeat each in turn. Before the Allies realized what was happening, the French invaded Belgium on 15 June, crossed the River Sambre at Charleroi and began to march on the capital, Brussels, 64 km (40 mls) away.

Blücher rushed three corps to Ligny, 16 km (10 mls) northeast of Charleroi, but was slow to inform Wellington of his movements. Wellington, meanwhile, concentrated his forces in the area of Mont St Jean and Nivelles, about half way down the main road between Brussels and Charleroi.

As soon as the French patrols reported Prussians in strength at Ligny, Napoleon decided to divide his army, a tactic against which he had always warned his marshals. He himself took 63,000 men to deal with Blücher, while Marshal Ney marched on Brussels.

The crash of battle echoed and re-echoed around Ligny on 16 June. Next morning, the Emperor made the first of what were to prove several mistakes in the campaign. Wrongly assuming that the Prussians were retreating east toward the River Rhine, he ordered Marshal Grouchy, an unimaginative man, to take 30,000 men and give chase, thereby reducing his army yet further. It was the last he would see of

The scene at about 11.30 am on 18 June, viewed from French positions: the Anglo-Dutch army under Wellington occupied the ridge of Mont St Jean, across the Charleroi to Brussels road. The battlefield was small for the number of men engaged: 3.6 km (2¼ mls) north to south and 6 km (4 mls) from east to west.

Wellington, unaware that Napoleon thought the Prussians were in retreat, calculated that the Emperor was most likely to attack the British right or to manoeuvre to the west and advance on Brussels. To counter the former possibility, he placed a force of 15,000 men at Halle, **1**.

Wellington fortified a number of buildings in advance of his front, notably the château at Hougoumont, **2**, on his right and the farm at La Haye Sainte, **3**, to his centre front. His purpose was to blunt enemy attacks by pouring enfilade fire into the flanks as the French advanced toward his main position.

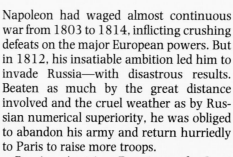

Napoleon had waged almost continuous war from 1803 to 1814, inflicting crushing defeats on the major European powers. But in 1812, his insatiable ambition led him to invade Russia—with disastrous results. Beaten as much by the great distance involved and the cruel weather as by Russian numerical superiority, he was obliged to abandon his army and return hurriedly to Paris to raise more troops.

Russia, Austria, Prussia and Great Britain united and advanced on France. Unable to repel invasion, Napoleon was forced to abdicate in 1814 and was then exiled to the island of Elba.

In 1815, he escaped and landed with fewer than a dozen supporters near Nice, on 1 March. He marched on Paris, gathering support on the way. Eighteen days later he entered the capital and by June had raised a force of 124,000 men. Napoleon then struck northeast to seize Brussels: but between his army and the Belgian capital lay Wellington and Blücher—and Waterloo.

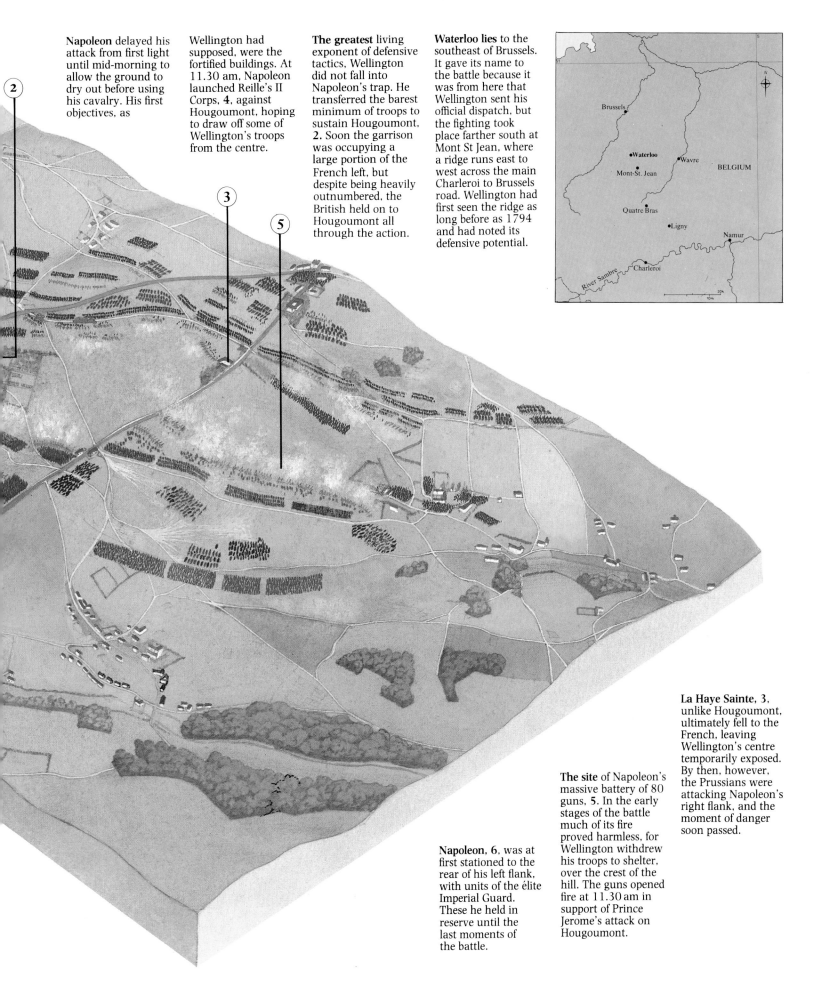

Napoleon delayed his attack from first light until mid-morning to allow the ground to dry out before using his cavalry. His first objectives, as Wellington had supposed, were the fortified buildings. At 11.30 am, Napoleon launched Reille's II Corps, 4, against Hougoumont, hoping to draw off some of Wellington's troops from the centre.

The greatest living exponent of defensive tactics, Wellington did not fall into Napoleon's trap. He transferred the barest minimum of troops to sustain Hougoumont, 2. Soon the garrison was occupying a large portion of the French left, but despite being heavily outnumbered, the British held on to Hougoumont all through the action.

Waterloo lies to the southeast of Brussels. It gave its name to the battle because it was from here that Wellington sent his official dispatch, but the fighting took place farther south at Mont St Jean, where a ridge runs east to west across the main Charleroi to Brussels road. Wellington had first seen the ridge as long before as 1794 and had noted its defensive potential.

La Haye Sainte, 3, unlike Hougoumont, ultimately fell to the French, leaving Wellington's centre temporarily exposed. By then, however, the Prussians were attacking Napoleon's right flank, and the moment of danger soon passed.

The site of Napoleon's massive battery of 80 guns, 5. In the early stages of the battle much of its fire proved harmless, for Wellington withdrew his troops to shelter, over the crest of the hill. The guns opened fire at 11.30 am in support of Prince Jerome's attack on Hougoumont.

Napoleon, 6, was at first stationed to the rear of his left flank, with units of the élite Imperial Guard. These he held in reserve until the last moments of the battle.

nearly a quarter of his force. The next day, while eating strawberries outside an inn 24 km (15 mls) from the battle, Grouchy was to hear the cannon pounding at Waterloo; but, mistaking this for thunder, he remained inactive.

The Emperor and the remainder of his victorious force rejoined Ney, who had been involved in a bloody encounter at Quatre Bras on 16 June. Ney thought that the entire Anglo-Dutch army was defending the strategically important crossroads, but, in fact, only an advance guard of 30,000 was blocking his path.

Across the lines, Wellington, who assumed that Blücher had won at Ligny, received an unpleasant surprise when a second belated Prussian message informed him that the old Marshal had retreated to Wavre, a few miles south of Brussels. Now that the Prussians were northeast, in his rear, Wellington ordered an immediate withdrawal to a previously reconnoitred defensive position at Mont St Jean near Waterloo, only 19 km (12 mls) from Wavre. There he awaited the arrival of Blücher's two corps, promised for the morrow.

Expertly screened by a rearguard of cavalry and horse artillery and assisted by torrential rain, Wellington's regiments broke contact with Ney and retired in good order. That stormy night his miserable troops lay deployed along a 4-km (2½-ml) front, stretching east to west across the Brussels to Charleroi road. They were on a slight ridge, covered with standing corn, which backed on to the vast forest of Soignes. To protect a vulnerable section of the lines on his right, Wellington took the unorthodox step of placing a garrison in the château of Hougoumont, almost 0.4 km (¼ ml) in front of his main position. Farm buildings at La Haye Sainte, in the centre, and at Papelotte, on his left, were also turned into strongpoints.

Reasoning that Napoleon would not expose his army to a flank attack by Prussians advancing from Wavre, Wellington judged that he would assault his right or, possibly, manoeuvre to the west and push on to take Brussels. As a counter to the latter possibility, Wellington sent a 15,000-strong detachment to block the Mons to Brussels road at Halle. His assumptions, however, were wrong.

Bonaparte and his equally wet and bedraggled soldiers, lying a mile or so to the south around La Belle Alliance, did not know that the Prussians were just a short distance to their right. As the rain cleared and the sun rose on the morning of Sunday, 18 June, the Emperor was planning two diversionary attacks on the wings of Wellington's army, to be followed by a

The Duke of Wellington (1769–1852), commander of the Anglo-Dutch force, was renowned throughout the British army for his calm under stress, a quality that was to stand him in good stead during the battle. On the evening he learned that Napoleon had crossed the Belgian border, he was attending the Duchess of Richmond's ball in Brussels, and, though surprised, was seen to take the news calmly. During the battle itself, many men remarked on his indifference to shot and shell. His staff officers also repeatedly expressed concern for his safety, for he was irreplaceable, and none doubted that he was truly fearless and totally preoccupied with his and his enemy's movements.

Gebhard von Blücher (1742–1819), the Prussian commander, was an amiable, friendly man who referred to his troops as 'my children', while Napoleon assiduously maintained his dignity, and Wellington feigned detachment. Blücher was 72 years old at the time of the battle, but despite his age and being rolled on by his horse at Ligny (and while prostrate having two cavalry charges pass over him), he continued in the saddle until victory was assured. He was a man of his word, and it was his keeping of his promise, although he was painfully bruised, to join Wellington if he were attacked, that sealed Napoleon's fate.

Napoleon Bonaparte (1769–1821) and Wellington were both in their mid-forties at the time of Waterloo but, whereas Wellington was fit and active, Napoleon had recently grown fat and suffered from bouts of lethargy. Throughout much of the battle he was unwell. Only three people knew of the malady: his doctor, his valet and Prince Jerome, his brother, who later revealed the truth. Napoleon was certainly suffering from a severe attack of haemorrhoids and probably cystitis. Moreover, his period in exile and, more especially, his enormous mental and physical exertions since his return to France had left him exhausted. These ailments probably account for the many mistakes he made during the campaign, mistakes he might not have made a few years earlier.

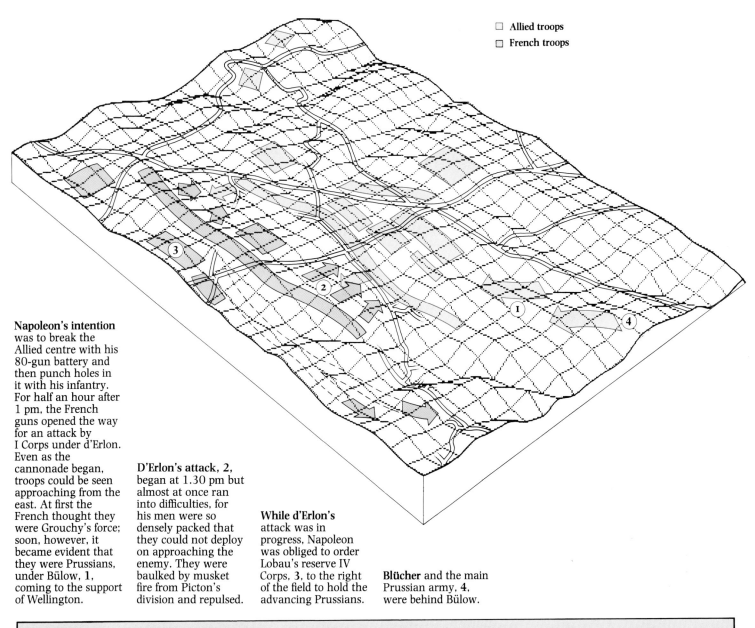

Allied troops
French troops

Napoleon's intention was to break the Allied centre with his 80-gun battery and then punch holes in it with his infantry. For half an hour after 1 pm, the French guns opened the way for an attack by I Corps under d'Erlon. Even as the cannonade began, troops could be seen approaching from the east. At first the French thought they were Grouchy's force; soon, however, it became evident that they were Prussians, under Bülow, **1**, coming to the support of Wellington.

D'Erlon's attack, 2, began at 1.30 pm but almost at once ran into difficulties, for his men were so densely packed that they could not deploy on approaching the enemy. They were baulked by musket fire from Picton's division and repulsed.

While d'Erlon's attack was in progress, Napoleon was obliged to order Lobau's reserve IV Corps, **3**, to the right of the field to hold the advancing Prussians.

Blücher and the main Prussian army, **4**, were behind Bülow.

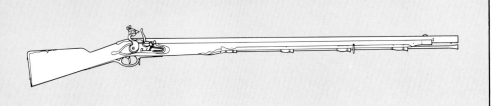

The Baker rifle was one of the first to come into service in the British army and was widely used between 1800 and 1840. It was equipped with a detachable sword bayonet, which fitted on the side of the muzzle.

The Charleville musket was the standard French weapon; it fired an iron ball 19 mm ($\frac{3}{4}$ in) in diameter. While it was deadly on impact, by modern standards it was inaccurate even at close range. The musket took its name from the town of Charleville, which, from the 17th century, had been an important centre of arms manufacture.

powerful thrust at the centre. The presence of Wellington and a large contingent of British regulars at their immediate front worried some senior French officers, who had suffered at their hands in the Peninsula campaign. Irritated by this, Napoleon told his Chief of Staff, Marshal Soult, 'I tell you that Wellington is a bad general, that the English are bad troops and that this will be a picnic.'

The French army received its battle orders at 11 am, and half an hour later the first cannon shots thundered out in support of Prince Jerome's division, feinting against the château of Hougoumont. Dutch infantry in woods and orchards around the buildings were driven back, but the attack foundered at the stone perimeter walls, lined at first by just four Light Companies of the Brigade of Guards. Met by an impenetrable storm of musket fire, the enraged French then brought up more and more reinforcements. Eventually most of Reille's corps became heavily engaged there.

At first Wellington thought it was the expected assault on his right wing, but, when he observed a mass of uncommitted French troops opposite his centre, he resisted the temptation to throw in a large force to support Hougoumont's gallant defenders. His caution paid dividends. Although the château was to be the scene of bitter fighting throughout the day, it never fell—and Wellington made good use of his precious reserves elsewhere.

Napoleon next planned a 'softening up' bombardment before the main assault and ordered an 80-gun battery to be brought up to shock the opponents he held in such contempt. But before the barrage opened, the Emperor himself received a shock. From the summit of a little rise near Rossomme, he had been peering northeast through his telescope at an ant-like column about 10 km (6 mls) long. Could it be Grouchy's force rejoining him? No—it was the Prussians!

Four divisions were dispatched at the double to counter this unexpected threat.

The massed cannon—24 of which were 12-pounders, the biggest field pieces then available—began to pound the Mont St Jean ridge in a fury of shot and shell, but without doing significant damage. Wellington had drawn up his army on the reverse slope, out of reach of the cannon balls, many of which plunged harmlessly into the ground on the front slope.

At 1.30 pm, the French drums beat the insistent rattle of the *pas de charge*, and four divisions of infantry marched forward, the sun glinting on 16,000 bayonets. Up the ridge they marched, rank upon closely packed rank, straight into the waiting field artillery's scything, point-blank fire. Oblivious of the slaughter, the French uttered a great cheer for their Emperor and plunged on. Papelotte fell, while La Haye Sainte was

There was a pause after d'Erlon's charge and Uxbridge's counter-attack. At about 3 pm, French guns opened fire in preparation for heavier cavalry charges. The 460-m (500-yd) long front is shown from the Allied side.

Marshal Ney, seeing his enemies draw back over the crest of the hill and mistakenly thinking them in retreat, personally led a cavalry charge of 5,000 men, **1**, without the support of either artillery or infantry. The horses, sighting the infantry squares, swerved to either side of the formations. Ensuing charges suffered the same fate.

Wellington formed 20 hollow infantry squares, **2**, with sides three ranks deep. The front rank knelt with rifles held outward at 45°, presenting a hedge of bayonets, while the standing rear ranks discharged volleys of fire. Two further merits were that gaps torn in the ranks could be quickly compressed, and cavalry attacks, since horses would never charge at solid blocks, were diverted.

At various times during the battle, Wellington, for protection, moved some of his men behind the crest of Mont St Jean, where, for additional safety, they were ordered to lie down. The French cavalry, mistaking this for retreat, prepared to charge. Wellington, seeing Ney's regiments massing below, could not at first believe that they would attack unsupported by infantry or field artillery. When he realized that they meant to come on, he ordered the squares to be formed. Thus, when the French came over the crest they were confronted by 20 squares of infantry, three ranks deep and with bayonets at the ready. Some cavalrymen paused, only to be pushed forward by those behind; others galloped on but could not control their horses, who swerved to right or left between the squares. As they milled about in disorder, they became easy targets for the disciplined British infantry.

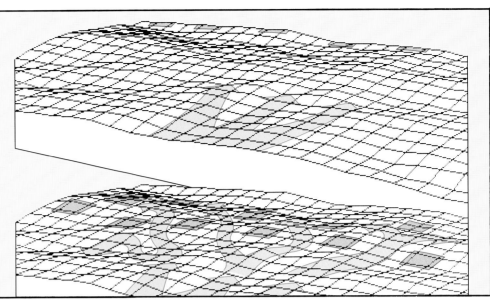

Wellington, 3, mounted on his chestnut horse, Copenhagen, shelters inside a square.

Mercer's battery, 4, remained in action throughout repeated attacks, giving heart to raw troops.

Hougoumont, 5, was under fierce attack by the French. La Haye Sainte garrison, **6,** and the remnants of cavalry had suffered in earlier actions.

Gunners and their horses took refuge inside squares, while cavalry attacked. They left their guns in

position—some as much as 90 m (100 yds) in front of the squares—and

brought them into action again as soon as the waves of cavalry fell back.

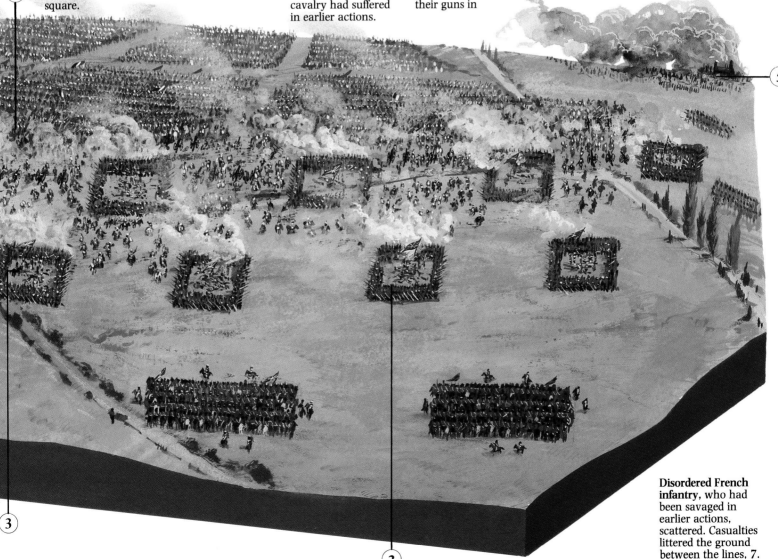

Disordered French infantry, who had been savaged in earlier actions, scattered. Casualties littered the ground between the lines, **7.**

surrounded, the French *cuirassiers* smashing the Luneburg Landwehr battalion, which had hurried to assist the garrison. In the centre, a demoralized Belgian unit broke and ran, but, before the French could pour through the gap, General Sir Thomas Picton confronted them with a British brigade of Peninsula diehards. He lost his life, but the defence held.

As Napoleon and his staff were congratulating themselves on what looked to them like a hold being won on the centre of the ridge, Wellington was watching how disordered the French ranks were becoming as they bravely pressed their attack. Judging the time nicely, he launched his two heavy cavalry brigades in a counter-attack, creating havoc among the French.

First to charge was the Household Cavalry, led by the dashing Lord Uxbridge. They crashed through the *cuirassiers*, trying to re-form after their sortie at La Haye Sainte, then on into the infantry, slashing with their sabres as they rode.

Hard after them came Ponsonby's Union Brigade, so called because it comprised the Scots Greys, the Inniskillings and the Royal Dragoons. As the Greys rode through Picton's ranks, the 92nd—the Gordon Highlanders—yelled, 'Scotland for ever!' and ran forward in the charge, too, until outdistanced by the cavalry.

A kind of battle madness gripped the horsemen as they galloped headlong at the French in one of the most terrifyingly spectacular charges ever made by British cavalry. The beautifully formed infantry divisions of Marcognet and Donzelot were shattered, but still the cavalry pressed on. Deaf to all calls to rally, they ploughed through the gun batteries and into the very midst of Napoleon's position. Out of breath, out of formation, their horses blown, Wellington's heavy cavalry was surrounded and cut to pieces.

It was now mid-afternoon and, apart from the continuing inferno around Hougoumont, hand-to-hand action slackened. Almost at once, however, came the crash of the French bombardment reopening with even greater intensity. Casualties were mounting alarmingly, so Wellington ordered his troops back behind the protection of the reverse slope.

Thinking that the Anglo-Dutch army was withdrawing, Marshal Ney—to whom Napoleon had unwisely entrusted field command of the battle—made a bold move for a quick victory. Instead of waiting for his scattered infantry to regroup, he led 5,000 heavy cavalry to sweep the ridge. Wellington, astonished that such an attack should be countenanced without the support of foot-soldiers and horse artillery, had

Wellington fortified the château of Hougoumont, *above*, during the night before the battle. The complex comprised a farmhouse, granaries, cowsheds and barns. All the gates to the yard formed by the buildings were closed except the main gate on the north side, which was left open to admit supplies. The complex was flanked by an orchard on one side and a wood on another. Hand-to-hand fighting was so ferocious that the British were taken wholly by surprise when French troops came undetected through the orchard and rushed the still-open main gate. About 100 of the enemy got in, but Colonel Macdonnel, commanding the Scots and Coldstream Guards, and four others forced the gate back against the French and secured the door. All the French trapped inside were killed. Had Hougoumont fallen, the outcome of the battle might have been different.

Napoleon had twenty-four 12-pounders in his 80-gun battery. They were far less manoeuvrable than the lighter Allied artillery, and the French had difficulty in positioning them on the rain-sodden ground. Each gun was accompanied by three caissons, sturdy ammunition carts. The caissons were positioned some 27 m (30 yds) behind the gun site. Each one contained 48 rounds of solid shot (the most commonly used artillery projectile at that time), 12 rounds of large canister and 8 rounds of small canister. In addition, the gun's limber box contained 9 rounds of solid shot. Thus each gun went into the field with a stock of 213 rounds of ammunition.

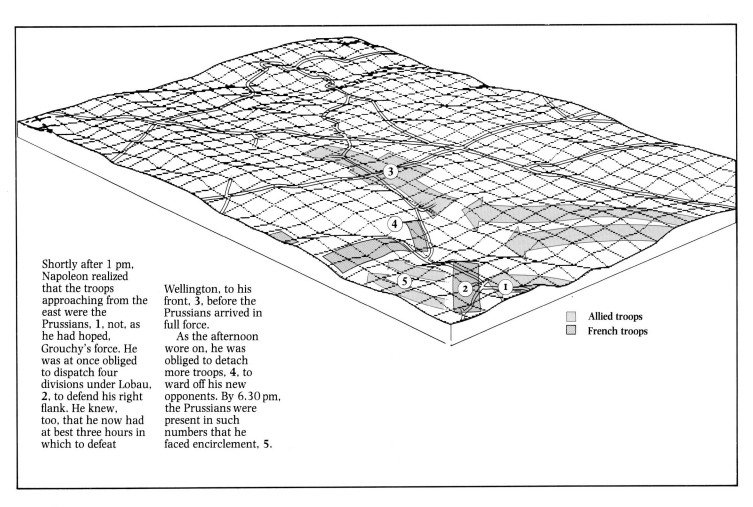

Shortly after 1 pm, Napoleon realized that the troops approaching from the east were the Prussians, **1**, not, as he had hoped, Grouchy's force. He was at once obliged to dispatch four divisions under Lobau, **2**, to defend his right flank. He knew, too, that he now had at best three hours in which to defeat

Wellington, to his front, **3**, before the Prussians arrived in full force.

As the afternoon wore on, he was obliged to detach more troops, **4**, to ward off his new opponents. By 6.30 pm, the Prussians were present in such numbers that he faced encirclement, **5**.

☐ Allied troops
☐ French troops

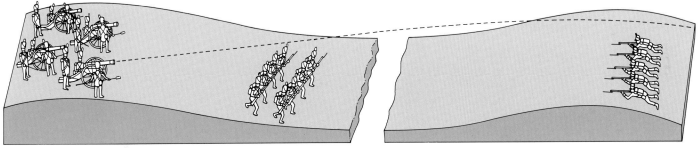

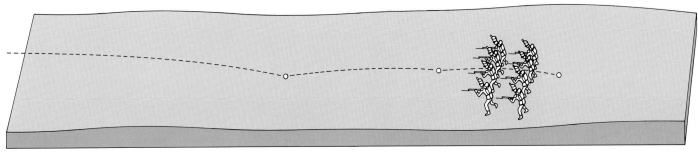

There were three main types of projectile: canister shot, cannonball or roundshot, and shells. The last could be fired only by howitzers.

Roundshot, a solid iron ball, depended on velocity for its effect. It was thus generally fired from long-barrelled guns, which give the greatest muzzle velocity.

Canister shot, consisting of a cylinder of thin tin crammed with metal balls, was used only at short range. The cylinder disintegrated as it was discharged, scattering the balls.

The correct positioning of forward troops was crucial, since a gun's elevation had to be such that its projectile passed over their heads, yet reached the enemy.

Roundshot was fired almost parallel to the ground to devastate enemy ranks. The iron ball lost speed after bouncing two or three times along the ground, but though it

was ultimately slow enough to be seen, it could still easily decapitate a man.

his troops form battalion squares in echelon across the hillside. Then the ominous order rang out, 'Prepare to receive cavalry.'

As the resplendent French squadrons came over the crest, they saw before them a chilling spectacle: 20 infantry squares, each presenting a barrier of long, glittering bayonets held firmly by a kneeling rank, backed by two standing ranks of levelled muskets. In the path of the rapidly approaching horsemen were Royal Artillery field batteries, which took a deadly toll before the gunners retreated to the safety of the infantry squares.

Time and again the cavalry came charging out of the swirling smoke to hurl themselves against the squares, each time to be repulsed by deadly volleys of close-range musketry. Throughout the bloody fighting, Wellington, a grey-coated figure with a black cocked hat, rode from square

to square, giving words of encouragement: he had an unerring instinct for appearing wherever the action was fiercest.

While Wellington's men were bearing the brunt of the main attack, the Prussians were at last coming up, obliging Napoleon to send reinforcements to the four divisions already sent to delay their advance.

The hot afternoon was drawing into evening, and his exhausted, now depleted, cavalry was beginning to drift away from the unbroken squares, when Napoleon decided to renew the assault with his reserve horse, in a bid to break Wellington before Blücher arrived in force. Once more, valiant French troops spurred over the battle-churned ridge, only to be turned aside by fierce, defensive fire. Realizing at last that he badly needed infantry support, Ney galloped back and rounded up as many of the milling foot-soldiers as he could,

together with such guns as were available.

Some of the battered Allied squares were beginning to waver, La Haye Sainte was on the point of falling, and Ompteda's brigade of the King's German Legion, which moved forward to support the defenders, was practically wiped out. There was now a dangerous gap in Wellington's line.

While Wellington calmly drew spare units from his right and left and placed them in his weakened centre, Marshal Ney was appealing to Napoleon for more infantry to exploit his considerable gains. The Emperor, who was absorbed in a grim holding action to prevent the ever-increasing Prussian army from encircling him, would not spare Ney any, even though he had reserves.

A little later, Napoleon changed his mind, but by then Ney's very real chance of victory had passed. The sun was beginning

Early evening: the final stages of the battle, seen from the Allied positions. At 6 pm Ney led his reserve infantry in an all-out attack on La Haye Sainte, which fell soon afterward. French guns could now be pulled forward to bombard Wellington's centre. The moment was hazardous for Wellington, but Ney's request to Napoleon for infantry reserves to exploit the new situation was refused. This gave Wellington time to pull in troops from his left, now supported by the Prussians, so as to strengthen his centre.

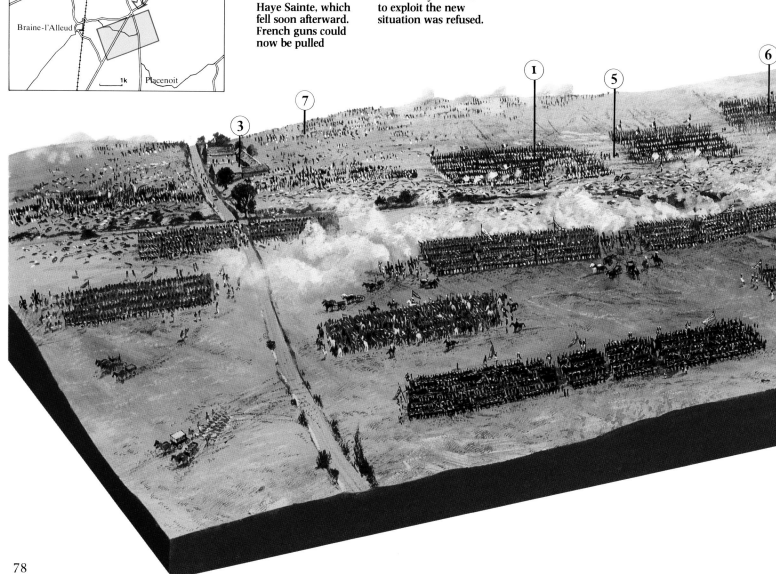

Uniforms at the time of the Battle of Waterloo had two purposes apart from clothing the men. They enabled troops to distinguish friend from enemy and deceived the enemy into thinking that the troops were bigger, and therefore stronger, than they actually were. All helmets and bearskins were tall, giving the impression of greater height, and epaulettes gave breadth to the shoulders. These embellishments appeared gallant on the parade ground, but, during the battle, the reality was otherwise. Troops had slept in their uniforms for at least three days during intermittent rain; they were sodden, muddy and, as the battle progressed, saturated with the blood of their comrades.

At about 7 pm, Napoleon made his last bid: he advanced the Imperial Guard, **1**, and attacked diagonally, between Hougoumont, **2**, and La Haye Sainte, **3**, at Wellington's right centre.

The leading 2,000-strong Imperial Guard topped the ridge—to be confronted by Maitland's brigade, **4**. They were repulsed, and Napoleon's final attempt to breach the Allied lines failed.

One of the two 6-gun field batteries, **5**, that accompanied the Imperial Guard on its attack. Their close-range fire inflicted heavy casualties on the Allied forces.

The second column of the Imperial Guard, **6**, also 2,000-strong, was beaten off by Adam's brigade.

The day-long fight for Hougoumont, **2**, continued unabated. This position, never taken by the French, protected the Allied right flank during the battle.

The French infantry were forced off the ridge, **7**. When the Imperial Guard's attack failed, they, like the cavalry, started to flee from the field.

to set over the smoke-cloaked carnage when Napoleon, his threatened right rear momentarily secured, once more turned his attention north, for a last, desperate attempt to smash the Anglo-Dutch forces. It was to be yet another frontal attack, made this time by the famous Imperial Guard, which had never yet failed to carry an assault. In reserve, Napoleon kept a few battalions of the Old Guard.

Wellington, supported now by Ziethen's Prussian corps on his left, carefully made his dispositions to receive the expected onslaught, the main weight of which he knew would fall between Hougoumont and La Haye Sainte. Amid a punishing cannon-ade, his battle line, four ranks deep, took what cover it could—and waited. Welling-ton himself took station with Maitland's Guards brigade, who were lying camou-flaged in a cornfield.

In the gathering dusk, the proud Imper-ial Guard, immaculate in blue coats with red epaulettes and white crossbelts, was led forward for part of the way by Napoleon himself. They advanced as on parade and, in a mighty clash of arms, achieved some gains before Allied reinforcements were poured into the danger spots to cut them down. Only two French regiments suc-ceeded in winning the crest of the ridge. When their tall, red-plumed bearskin hel-mets appeared over the top of the hill, Wellington called out, 'Now, Maitland! Now is your time.' With that, the British Guards scrambled up and delivered de-vastating volleys into the very faces of the astonished Frenchmen, who thought they had broken the Allied line. For the first time in their history, they fled.

At the foot of the hill, they regrouped and attacked again, together with some cavalry, but once more were driven off. Incredibly, the Imperial Guard began re-treating in disorder, harried mercilessly by the Allied cavalry. Panic seized what was left of Napoleon's forces. Only the Old Guard maintained its stern discipline, as Wellington ordered his cheering troops to commence a general advance. Formed in two squares to cover the retreat of their Emperor and his vanquished men, the élite of the French army refused several calls to surrender and were shot down.

Wellington, who later described his de-cisive victory as 'a damned near-run thing', and Blücher, whose belated arrival was the guarantee of success, finally met at La Belle Alliance at 9 pm—a more aptly named venue for their historic meeting would be difficult to find. All around lay the victims of the frightful battle, which had cost the Allies 22,000 men and the French as many as 30,000.

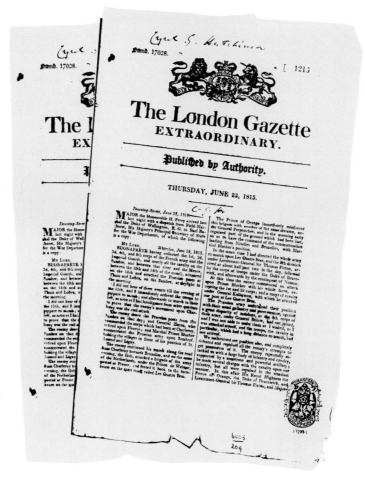

These army pensioners, *above,* reading the Waterloo Despatch, *left,* outside an inn in London were depicted by Sir David Wilkie R.A. in 1822. Newspaper correspondents vied with one another to get their reports to London before those of their rivals. *The Times,* making use of pigeons, was adept at this. Pensioners such as these might have served under Wellington in the Peninsular War; many would have known men who fought at Waterloo.

Napoleon's defeat at Waterloo was absolute, and in his haste to escape he was obliged to abandon his carriage, *above opposite,* and mount his charger.

Looting the dead and wounded was, from time immemorial, the privilege of victorious soldiers. After Waterloo, there was much to be had, especially from officers: purses, watches, pistols and swords. False teeth, usually of ivory, were also worth taking for later sale to dentists. Many of those wounded who resisted the looters were promptly killed, while others parted with all they had for a drink of water. When dawn came, Belgian peasants moved in, like vultures, to purloin the final pickings. Some were so heavily laden with clothing and valuables that they could only stagger. It was four days after the battle before the last of the wounded of both sides were discovered and taken by jolting carts to hospitals, there to endure primitive surgery.

After Waterloo, the Allied powers convened to draw up a peace treaty with exhausted France. The Prussians, following their defeat at Jena in 1806, had suffered grievously at French hands and were clamorous for revenge; Wellington, however, sensed that the best hope of securing enduring peace lay through clemency—and Wellington, after Waterloo, was the most influential man in Europe. Clemency was indeed shown, but no consideration was given to the aspirations of European nationalities.

Men of the French Revolutionary period and the Napoleonic Empire, though ruthless and careless of life, had spread the ideals of liberty and nationalism throughout Europe, but at the peace treaty the autocratic powers of Prussia, Russia and Austria restored their old rule. Although these boundaries remained unchanged for over a hundred years, until the Treaty of Versailles (1919–20), they were deeply resented and led to widespread uprisings in 1832 and 1848.

Nevertheless, Europe was spared further major conflict, save for the Crimean War, for the greater part of a century. By the outbreak of the First World War, the technological advances of the nineteenth century had given armies a new arsenal of weapons, which radically altered military practice. Machine-guns had been introduced, grenades were more deadly and rifles more accurate; most important of all, artillery could inflict greater damage than ever before. Never again would battles be fought in the time-honoured style of Waterloo.

Balaclava/*25 October, 1854*

At Balaclava in the Crimea, on 25 October 1854, Queen Victoria's poorly provisioned soldiers distinguished themselves in a three-phase action against much stronger Russian forces. This battle, on a plateau above an Allied supply base, was the second confrontation since Great Britain, France, Turkey and Sardinia had carried the conflict on to Russian soil less than six weeks earlier by invading the Crimean Peninsula.

Tsar Nicholas I's Black Sea naval base at Sebastopol was the target of the ill-starred, but ultimately successful, campaign. Despite having defeated the Russian Army on the River Alma, on 20 September, the Allied force of 57,000 men could not break into the fortress from the north. The invaders then invested Sebastopol from Balaclava, on its south side.

The hard labour necessary to fortify camps in readiness for an expected Russian attempt to relieve the Sebastopol garrison took a particularly heavy toll on the undernourished, badly-clad British troops. Even so, the Allies were caught slow-footed, when a Russian attack came out of the early morning mist on 25 October. While defeated Turks were abandoning a string of redoubts guarding the approaches to Balaclava, the alarm was sounding in the British and French cantonments as far as 4.8 km (3 mls) away.

First to respond to the threat was the Earl of Lucan's British Cavalry Division, comprising the Heavy Brigade and the Light Brigade. Horses went unwatered and troopers unfed as the order to mount was sounded and squadrons moved out to cover the retreating Turks.

There was at first a lack of infantry on the field. While the British 1st and 4th Divisions and two brigades of French infantry were being moved up from their lines before Sebastopol, the route to Balaclava harbour was barred by only 550 men of the 93rd Highland Regiment, supplemented by a few men from other units, all under the command of General Sir Colin Campbell.

From a viewpoint on the Sapoune ridge, high above the battleground, the British Commander-in-Chief, Lord Raglan, his staff and some civilian spectators, looked on with mounting apprehension as a strong force of Russian cavalry bore down on the Highlanders. Less brave soldiers might have faltered when faced with a force of yelling, charging horsemen. The feather-bonneted Highlanders merely laughed, stood firm and coolly delivered two crashing volleys, destroying the attack.

Soon after the gallant stand of the 93rd, those watching from the ridge had more to applaud.

At 11.20 am, on 25 October 1854, a sunny, autumnal day, the order was given for the Light Brigade to charge down the North Valley, a distance of about 2.4 km (1½ mls). The valley, formed by a bow-shaped cluster of hills to the north and a low ridge to the south, is about 1.6 km (1 ml) wide, but the cavalry were deployed over less than a fifth of its width. At first they advanced at a brisk trot, breaking into a gallop when they were a mere 92 m (100 yds) from the Russian guns. During the charge, they were also subjected to artillery and musket fire from the flanks.

Cardigan, 1, a vain but brave commander, insisted on being at the head of the Brigade throughout the charge; men who drew level were ordered to fall back behind him.

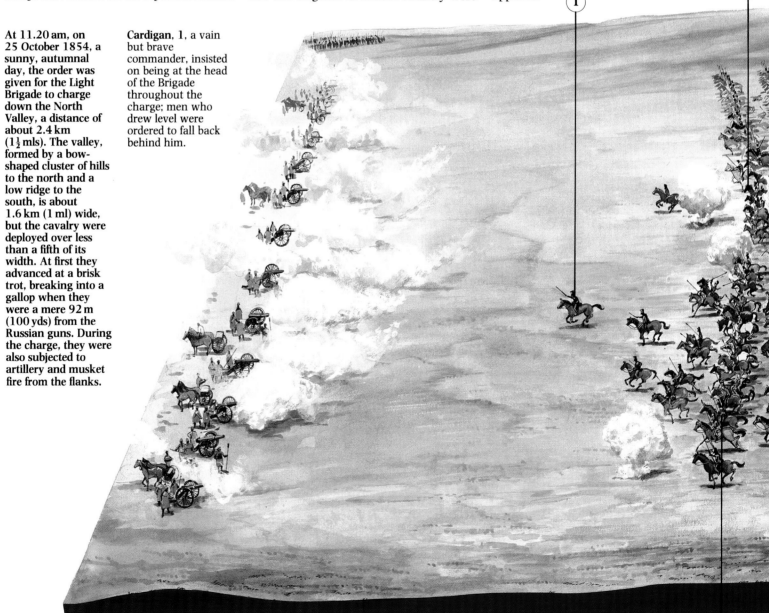

The Crimean War (1853–1856) was the outcome of the disintegration of Turkish influence in the Balkans and the threatened collapse of the Turkish Empire itself, exacerbated by Russian imperialism. The immediate cause of the outbreak of hostilities was a dispute between France and Russia over guardianship of the holy places in Palestine. While Russia, an Orthodox country, claimed the rights of guardianship, France had secured from the Sultan certain privileges for the Roman Catholic Church. On 4 October 1853, after Russia had already begun to mobilize, Turkey declared war. In March 1854, Great Britain and France declared themselves the allies of Turkey and, in September, landed a force in the Crimea with the object of capturing the great Russian naval base of Sebastopol.

Those men of the 17th Lancers, **2**, and 13th Light Dragoons, **3**, in the front rank, who reached the guns, hacked mercilessly at the Russians in revenge for the fearful havoc they had caused.

The 11th Hussars, **4**, and 4th Light Dragoons, **5**, rode 366 m (400 yds) behind the first rank. Their advance was impeded by corpses and wounded and by terrified riderless horses.

The 8th Hussars, **6**, in the rear, was the only formation to reach the guns in good order. But by then the smoke was so thick that they could see little of what lay ahead.

The entire action was over within 20 minutes. Of the 673 men who charged, only 195 answered the first muster. Many of those who ultimately reached safety had sustained dreadful wounds.

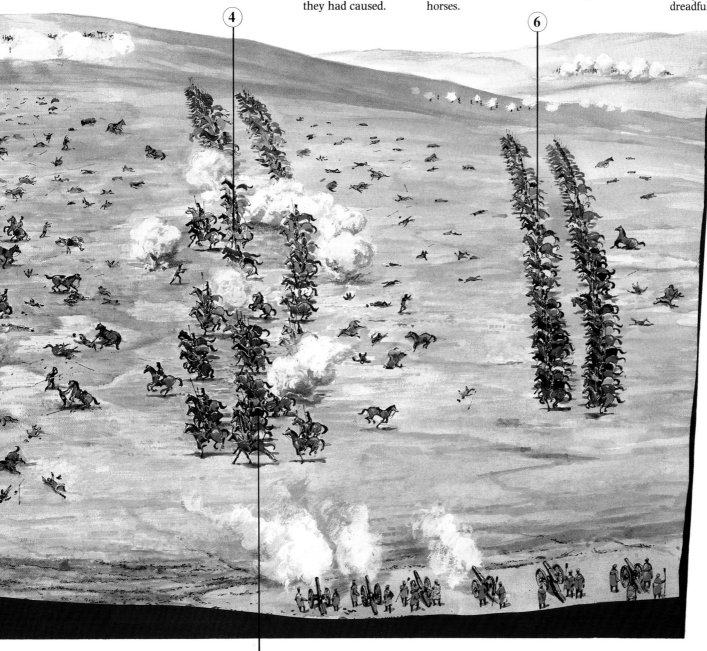

General Sir James Scarlett's Heavy Brigade, reduced by sickness to about 600 cavalrymen, was positioned in a dip in the ground; this concealed from it the dangerous fact that it was about to be attacked by a force of Russian cavalry, which outnumbered it by six to one.

As 3,500 Russian troopers galloped toward them and drew up 365 m (400 yds) away, the Scots Greys and Inniskillings calmly dressed ranks before their trumpets called the 'Charge'. The broken ground would not permit a trot, far less a gallop, so they advanced upon the Russians at no more than a smart walk. The fury of British swordplay had a devastating effect on the Tsar's cavalry, and it was only a few minutes before the centre squadrons of Greys and Inniskillings had cut a path clean through their dense formation. From the flanks, the 4th and 5th Dragoon Guards pitched into the milling Russians, causing further disruption among their troopers.

The Heavy Brigade's triumph prevented further activity in the area, known as South Valley, immediately above Balaclava. After another of the lulls that punctuated the fighting, action switched to North Valley on the other side of Causeway Heights. This was a low ridge running along the Woronzow Road, which was the Allies' main supply route, linking Balaclava with their camps before Sebastopol. The road was guarded by the redoubts which the Russians had seized from the Turks at the start of the battle.

By moving the Cavalry Division into North Valley, far ahead of the infantry, Raglan prepared the way for one of the most daring, but futile, feats of British arms—the Charge of the Light Brigade. Seeing what he thought was an attempt by the enemy to drag away guns from the lost redoubts on Causeway Heights, the British commander decided to stop them.

Because his order to Lord Lucan was urgent, it was given not to the duty aide-de-camp but to Captain Louis Nolan of the 15th Hussars, a brilliant horseman. He took a dangerous shortcut to deliver it. Lucan read the written order: 'Lord Raglan wishes the cavalry to advance rapidly to the front, and try to prevent the enemy carrying away the guns . . .' Lucan then asked for clarification because, from his position, he could not see any Russians moving guns.

Laying quite the wrong interpretation on Raglan's instruction, Nolan deliberately pointed to the Russian artillery lined up 2.4 km (1½ mls) away at the far end of North Valley and told Lord Lucan 'There is the enemy, there are the guns, sir.'

Apart from some cannon in front, there was a battery on each flank; behind the guns lay a Russian army. It was a suicidal mission, but Lucan had been given a direct order, which could not be disobeyed. He detailed the Light Brigade under Lord Cardigan, his brother-in-law, but with whom he was not on speaking terms, to mount the attack. The Heavy Brigade, which was still re-forming after its earlier engagement, was held in reserve.

Cardigan was astonished by the order, for unsupported cavalry had never before charged lines of guns. Nevertheless, he formed his small command for its desperate task. Illness had reduced his five regiments to a mere 673 men, whose mounts were in poor condition.

When Raglan and his staff realized what was happening, there was consternation on the Sapoune heights. Messengers were swiftly despatched to the valley below, but it was too late. 'The gallant six hundred', as they were later immortalized by Lord Tennyson, were already on their way to destruction.

The Light Brigade closed up as gaps were torn in their ranks by cannon balls. Through clouds of smoke, spiked with flashes of gunfire, Cardigan led the remnants of his first wave into the Russian batteries, lancing or cutting down any artilleryman who could not reach shelter beneath his field piece.

The Light Brigade reached the guns against all odds, but had no means of disabling them. Those brave troopers who remained in the saddle rallied as best they could and rode back to the Allied lines.

As small groups of British cavalrymen, some hideously wounded, began to make their way back, they were harried by Cossacks, attacking from the Russian right, as well as by enfilading musketry and gunfire.

Four survivors of the 17th Lancers, wearing their medals.

Two Coldstream Guardsmen, in the dress uniform of the period.

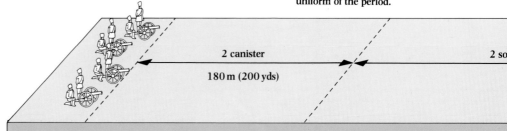

2 canister

2 solid sh

180 m (200 yds)

366

In the 19th century, cavalry crossed the ground from their starting position to the enemy in a set sequence of walk, trot, gallop and finally all-out charge. The time taken to cover a distance of 915 m (1,000 yds) was about 7 minutes. While they were still 915–550 m (1,000–600 yds) away, each enemy gun had time to fire nine rounds of solid shot or shrapnel. As the distance closed to

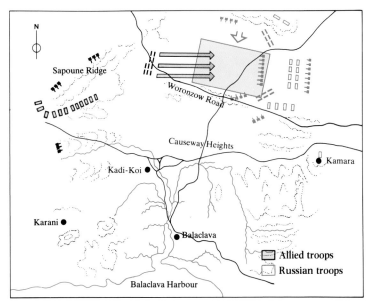

In 1855, the accession of Tsar Alexander II, who was anxious to restore peace, together with the capture of Sebastopol by the Allies, led to negotiations toward a peaceful settlement. The result was the Treaty of Paris, signed in 1856, in which Russia acknowledged Turkish independence and renounced her claim to Turkish territories. Russia also agreed to the declaration of the Black Sea as a neutral zone open to all shipping. The Sultan was obliged to improve the status of his Christian subjects.

The Treaty did not prove to be a lasting solution. Turkey's promises of reform went unfulfilled while Russia took advantage of the Franco-Prussian War to denounce the clause of neutralization of the Black Sea. The 'Eastern Question' remained a European problem until the map was redrawn after the First World War.

In Britain, the incompetence and discomfort experienced by the military led to army reforms and improvements in the conditions of service.

Early on the morning of 25 October, the Russians attacked the Allied defensive perimeter around Balaclava and quickly overran a string of redoubts overlooking the Allies' supply route. Later, after two Russian cavalry attacks had been successfully repulsed by his forces, Lord Raglan observed the Russians dragging guns away from the redoubts. In order to prevent this, he moved his Light Brigade over Causeway Heights and positioned them for what was to be one of the bravest, if most futile, cavalry charges in history.

Captain Louis Nolan of the 15th Hussars held obsessive views on the superiority of his arm of the service. Whether he misunderstood the message Raglan ordered him to take to Lord Lucan or deliberately misinterpreted it to prove his theory of the unstoppable power of light cavalry is still a matter of conjecture. Ironically, Nolan was among the first to be killed.

Field Marshal Lord Raglan, who had lost an arm at Waterloo, first gained military recognition in the Peninsular War. Brave but unimaginative, his limitations were exacerbated during the Crimean War by his joint command with the French leader, Marshal Saint-Arnaud, and by the inefficiency of British government departments. He died before the war ended, the object of much criticism.

'All that was left of them, left of six hundred.' A painting by R. Caton Woodville.

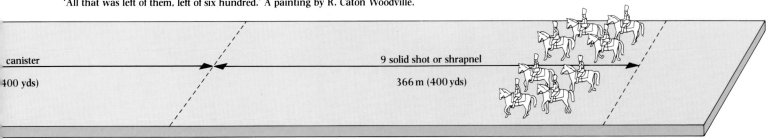

canister ... 9 solid shot or shrapnel

400 yds) ... 366 m (400 yds)

550–180 m (600–200 yds), guns could fire either two rounds of solid shot or three of canister; during the last 180 m (200 yds), which was covered at a gallop, two rounds of canister shot could be discharged before the impact.

Roundshot, the most effective and reliable projectile, accounted for some 70 per cent of the ammunition fired. A single shot could shatter a wagon; moreover, when fired into a column, roundshot could tear through several ranks of cavalry. In view of these facts the Light Brigade's advance straight at Russian artillery was knowingly suicidal.

Solferino/*24 June, 1859*

No one could have foreseen the impact an eyewitness account of the horrors of the Battle of Solferino would have on civilized nations. The carnage around Solferino, on 24 June 1859, was at first viewed as just another defeat for the Austrians, but from it was born the International Red Cross.

The war was instigated by Piedmont's wily Prime Minister, Count Camillo di Cavour, as a preliminary toward achieving his ambition of creating a united Italy, free from foreign intervention. Piedmont-Sardinia, a monarchy ruled by King Victor Emmanuel II, had tried to achieve this on its own in 1848, but had been frustrated by the Austrian Marshal Radetzky. Subsequently, Cavour formed an alliance with France, with the intention of securing her military assistance in the next confrontation, which was inevitable, over the sovereignty of Lombardy and Venetia.

Cavour found a willing partner in Napoleon III, who sought to emulate the martial prowess of his uncle, Napoleon Bonaparte. But Napoleon expected recompense: Piedmont would have to cede to France the region of Savoy and also Nice.

By the second half of April 1859, the Austrians had lost patience with the warmongering Piedmontese. On 22 April, the day before Emperor Franz Joseph's ultimatum demanding Piedmontese demobilization expired, Napoleon was hurrying to establish his troops in Piedmont in time to check the Austrian onslaught. Some of the French regiments went by sea to Genoa, but for the first time in history a major movement of forces to a war zone was carried out principally by train. Without any disruption to civilian timetables, France's efficient rail network speedily transported more than 8,000 men and 500 horses a day.

On 17 May, 100,000 Frenchmen and 50,000 Piedmontese, supported by 400 guns, occupied an 80-km (50-ml) front north of Alessandria; they faced 120,000 invading Austrians, with 480 guns. Three days later, the Franco-Piedmontese force advanced and made contact with the enemy at Montebello. During the ensuing month, through a number of small actions and one pitched battle at Magenta, they advanced deep into Lombardy.

On 23 June, Napoleon and the French, with Victor Emmanuel and the Piedmontese on their left, lay along the River Chiese, preparing to move off early next morning to continue their pursuit of the Austrians, who were thought to be defending a line behind the River Mincio that stretched from Peschiera on Lake Garda in the north, southward to the fortress town of Mantua. But the reinforced Austrians, now

Although battle had been joined at 6 am on 24 June, the outcome was not decided until early afternoon when, in intense heat, French infantry successfully stormed the key village of Solferino in the centre of the Austrian line. The steep slopes leading to this hilltop hamlet were bitterly contested by the Austrians.

The tower and castle of Solferino, 1, dominated the village, which was crammed with Austrian infantry, 2, and artillery, 3.

A neat row of shellbursts over the Austrian positions, 4, demonstrates the superiority of the French artillery. Their rifled guns could bring fire to bear with great accuracy.

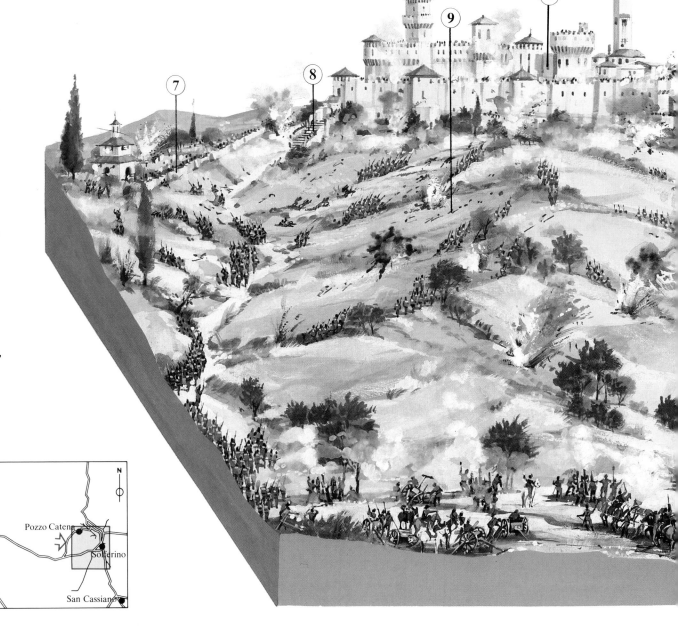

Napoleon III had to seek glory abroad in order to underpin his fragile legitimacy in France. To this end, he determined to remove Austrian influence from northern Italy by supporting Piedmontese aspirations.

In a secret treaty, Napoleon promised his support to Piedmont, which mobilized its forces in March 1859. The Austrians demanded their immediate disbandment, and, by April, had invaded Piedmont. Napoleon seized the chance to intervene. The invaders were checked at Montebello, but Napoleon was a mediocre commander, so confusion prevailed.

In a series of indecisive battles, the Austrians were pushed back. They retired into the formidable defensive box formed by the fortified cities of Mantua, Peschiera, Verona and Legnano, regrouped, then blundered into a confrontation with Napoleon before they were ready for it.

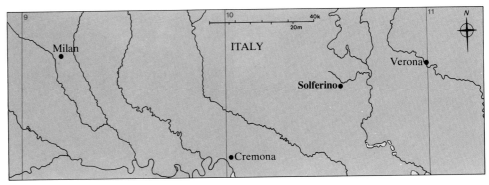

The major battle of the short war between Austria and the Franco-Piedmontese alliance was fought on a 24-km (15-ml) front centred on Solferino, in northern Italy.

Column after column of French troops toiled up the hot, dusty hill before Solferino and threw themselves against the defenders. Between 1 pm and 2 pm, the élite Imperial Guard, **5**, charged and took a little knoll covered with cypress trees, **6**, to the right of the village. The entire Austrian position then began to disintegrate.

Just after the Guards took the cypress hill, line infantry on the left succeeded in breaking the Austrians' defence of the walled cemetery, **7**. They carried the fighting into the village streets and took many prisoners.

Steep, narrow paths up to Solferino from behind the Austrian lines, **8**, were often under fire, making it almost impossible to reinforce the garrison in the village.

Despite excellent artillery support, the French paid dearly for their mass assaults on Solferino village. The rows of dead and wounded, **9**, on the face of the hill show all too clearly that the closeness of their ranks presented the Austrians with an easy target.

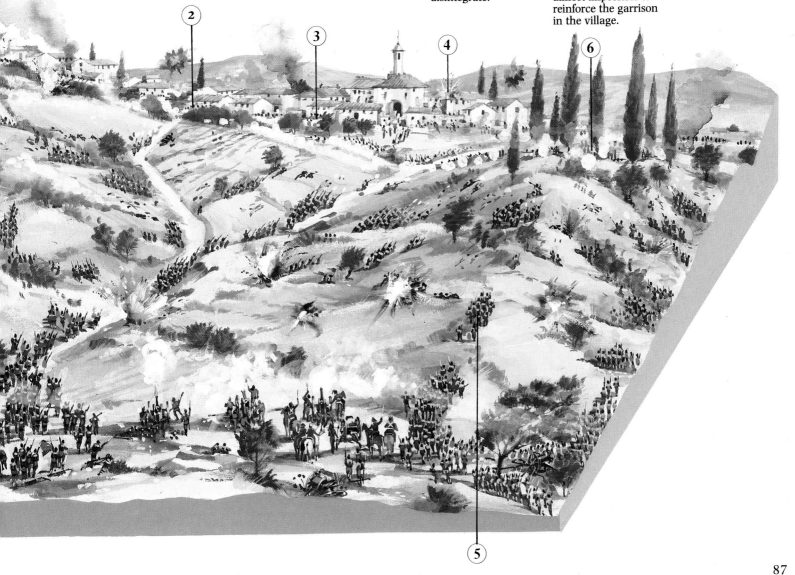

commanded by their Emperor, had re-crossed the river and occupied a ridge of high ground, centred on the village of Solferino, in readiness to launch an offensive.

Reconnaissance in both armies was poor, and both were ignorant of the other's exact position. Observers in a balloon above the French lines detected dust on the west bank of the Mincio late on the 23rd, but Napoleon dismissed it as a scouting column. In the early hours of the 24th, the French advance guards ran into Austrian pickets, who fell back on their main line, running from Medole in the south, through the hill villages of Cavriana, Solferino, Madonna del Scoperta and San Martino, up toward the south shore of Lake Garda.

The French attack on the Austrian left flank opened shortly after 6 am. By the time Napoleon reached the front an hour and a half later, battle had been joined, each side feeding in about 150,000 troops. At 10.30 am, Medole fell on the Austrian left, but no further French progress had been made. The centre stood firm and, on Franz Joseph's right, General Benedek's corps was stubbornly resisting repeated assaults by the entire Piedmontese army.

Fearing the approach of strong Austrian reinforcements from the south, which could turn his vulnerable right flank, Napoleon resolved to make an all-out attack to break the enemy centre at Solferino. His batteries of rifled artillery poured shells on the heavily-defended village. Shortly afterwards, the infantry stormed up, led by the élite Imperial Guard. After heavy fighting in stifling heat, Solferino was finally captured at 2 pm, and the French began to drive a wedge between the Austrian lines.

As the afternoon wore on, dark clouds gathered above the battlefield. On the Austrian right, Benedek still held his ground, but at the other end of the line there were scenes of fearful carnage as the French gradually forced the Austrians back. In the centre, the Austrians withdrew to Cabriana, after being driven out of Solferino. Then, just as the French were carrying that village also, a cloudburst all but brought the fighting to a halt.

When the rain ceased, Napoleon's regiments cheered at seeing the whole Austrian army in full retreat across the Mincio. Combined casualties totalled more than 40,000 men after nine hours of combat. The French had lost almost 17,000, the Piedmontese 5,000 and the Austrians more than 22,500. A jubilant Napoleon telegraphed his Empress in Paris: 'Great Battle. Great Victory.' But the wounded lay in agony in their thousands and were scattered over a wide area.

Emperor Napoleon III (1808–1873), the nephew of the great Napoleon, seized power as Prince President in a *coup* in 1851. The following year he proclaimed the Second Empire. His regime was unstable and he sought to reinforce it with successes in foreign policy. This effort led him into an alliance with Great Britain and involvement in the Crimean War. In 1859, he declared war on Austria. In reality, Napoleon III was vacillating, irresolute and dominated by his wife, the Empress Eugénie. His prestige relied upon his skilful exploitation of the Bonaparte legend. The campaign of 1859 revealed that that was all he had in common with his uncle.

Emperor Franz Joseph (1830–1916). The tragic reign of Franz Joseph was one of the longest in history and corresponded with the decline and fall of the Habsburg monarchy in central Europe. Franz Joseph was of a pessimistic disposition and had had no experience of field command before 1859. He was deeply shocked by the carnage of Solferino and never commanded in the field again. It was said that after Solferino Franz Joseph always expected the worst from his army—that it would always be defeated. His fears were confirmed and after 1859 Austrian power went into eclipse.

Victor Emmanuel II (1820-1878). The King of Piedmont had served a military apprenticeship by commanding a brigade against Austria in 1848. One of his first acts as King was to appoint the wily and ruthless Count Cavour as Prime Minister. The result of the Solferino campaign was the liberation of Lombardy from Austrian rule and, the following year, Tuscany, Modena and Parma revolted. Since Garibaldi had already liberated Sicily and Naples, the scene was set for the unification of Italy, with Victor Emmanuel as her first King. He was a skilful diplomat and conscientious ruler.

The biggest single advantage which the French had over the Austrians lay in their ordnance. A keen artilleryman, Napoleon III had recently re-equipped his army with bronze 4-pounder muzzle-loading rifled cannon. They fired a fused conical shell with great accuracy up to 3,200 m (3,500 yds)—twice the range of the smoothbore Austrian field pieces, which still relied on old-fashioned bouncing roundshot.

Napoleon had been experimenting with rifled cannon ever since the British army first introduced them in the Crimean War. The success of his bombardments at Magenta and then Solferino pointed the way to all the armies of the Western world adopting rifled ordnance.

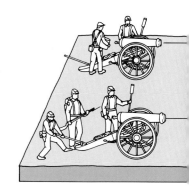

After Solferino, France and Austria were ready to seek a settlement. Emperor Franz Joseph had lost two major battles and was threatened by discontent in Hungary. Napoleon, mindful of the growing anti-war lobby in France, realized that to lose a battle might cost him his throne; moreover, the Prussian attitude to his involvement in northern Italy was increasingly warlike.

The two monarchs met privately at Villafranca on 8 July, excluding King Victor Emmanuel, and agreed to armistice terms, later ratified by the Treaty of Zurich. Lombardy was ceded to Piedmont, except for the fortresses of Peschiera and Mantua; Austria retained Venetia. This enraged the majority of Italians, and, with the country in turmoil, the stage was set for its unification under King Victor Emmanuel.

Henri Dunant was an impressionable young Swiss banker who visited the field of Solferino while on holiday; and, like most tourists, he looked forward to a great spectacle. The reality of war—the carnage and the suffering—deeply shocked him, and in his subsequent writings, including the famous tract *Un Souvenir de Solferino*, he called for the creation of a neutral body to care for the wounded. The result was the foundation, in 1864, of the International Red Cross.

The first skirmishing at Solferino was scarcely an hour old before Napoleon III was riding to the sound of the guns, moving up from his headquarters in the rear. Throughout the action, he rode about the field directing troops hither and thither, as in the contemporary engraving, *top*, but there was little scope for textbook generalship. The battle quickly degenerated into a grim hand-to-hand struggle between uncoordinated masses of infantry, as depicted in this artist's impression, *above*, showing the French Colonel Maleville being struck down at the head of the 55th Regiment.

2,377 m (2,600 yds) max.
Austrian artillery

3,200 m (3,500 yds)
French artillery

Gettysburg/*1-3 July, 1863*

'War with all its desolating evils is upon our Good Old Commonwealth! The Rebel Invaders are upon our Soil, with Fire and Sword desolating the once happy homes of our people. Come to the Rescue!'

Bombastic recruiting posters such as this appeared in towns and villages throughout Pennsylvania in the early summer of 1863. The American Civil War was now in its third year, and, for the second time within the space of nine months, Confederate forces were invading the North. The fears of the people of Pennsylvania, so far untouched by conflict, were well founded, for General Robert E. Lee was advancing into the state with his seemingly invincible Army of Northern Virginia—75,000 veterans who had trounced the Union Army of the Potomac time and again.

On 3 June, the Confederate army had slipped away from Fredericksburg, Virginia, where it had been barring the path of Major-General Joseph ('Fighting Joe') Hooker's dispirited men. Lee marched west, then north up the Shenandoah Valley into the enemy's well-stocked hinterland.

For almost a month, confusion was constant in both armies. It took Hooker nine days to discover that the Confederate main body had left his front. Contrary to Lee's expectation, Hooker then wanted to thrust at Richmond; he was, however, forbidden to do so by President Lincoln and his government, who reminded him that his priorities were the defence of Washington and the destruction of the invaders. But Hooker did not know exactly where the Army of Northern Virginia was. Reports from his cavalry ranged from inaccurate to absurd. Though badly hampered by this lack of reliable information, he moved off, keeping his army between the capital and where he thought the Rebels might be.

Across the Blue Ridge mountains, Lee was equally ill-informed. He normally relied on reconnaissance digests collected by Major-General J.E.B. ('Jeb') Stuart, his brilliant cavalry leader, but Stuart and his hard-riding troopers were absent on a raid and had been out of touch for days.

Until 28 June, Lee believed that the Army of the Potomac was still somewhere in Virginia. It was with considerable disquiet that he learned from a spy that the Union forces were at Frederick, Maryland, just 40 km (25 mls) away. He heard, too, that the boastful but incompetent Hooker had been replaced by a more skilful opponent, Major-General George Meade. 'General Meade will commit no blunder on my front,' Lee prophesied, 'and if I make one he will make haste to take advantage of it.'

Lee immediately revised his plans, ordering his three corps, at present strung out, to

The scene in and around Gettysburg shortly after 4 pm on the first day of the great battle shows elements of two corps from General Robert E. Lee's Army of Northern Virginia, pressing in from the west and north against two corps from General George G. Meade's Army of the Potomac. The Union right flank has started to collapse and will retreat nearly 3.2 km (2 mls) back through the town before rallying and taking up new positions on Cemetery Hill.

Gettysburg, the principal town of Adams County, Pennsylvania, was a quiet rural community of no particular note until advance guards of the Union and Confederate armies encountered each other on its northwestern outskirts on the morning of 1 July 1863. Twelve good roads converged on the town from all points of the compass, making it easy to concentrate large bodies of troops there. As a result, Gettysburg became the site of the biggest battle ever to be fought on the soil of North America.

Toward the end of 1860, the Republican candidate, Abraham Lincoln, was elected President of the United States. The Presidential campaign had centred on the questions of slavery and States' rights. Lincoln by no means wished to lead a crusade against slavery; rather, he sought to prevent the extension of the 'peculiar institution' of slavery to the Territories, vast areas in the west that had yet to be granted statehood. The southern States, however, made the right of States to secede from the Union the main issue. On Lincoln's election, they formed their own independent confederacy of slave-owning states and, from that moment, civil war could not be avoided.

At the outset, many Southerners were serving in the north in the United States army. Most, notably Colonel Robert E. Lee, returned to the south to serve the Confederacy. Lee, possibly the most able soldier of his generation, was soon to command the principal Confederate army. But what should he attempt? The North had twice the manpower of the South and all the factories; a long war would be to their advantage.

Lee resolved on attack. 'An invasion of the enemy's country,' he argued, 'breaks up all his preconceived plans, relieves our country of his presence, and we subsist while there on his resources.'

Lee had once already briefly penetrated the North, but, in 1863, in the Gettysburg campaign, he made his most determined attempt at invasion.

Troops from General Ambrose P. Hill's Confederate 3rd Corps, **1**, were involved in the opening skirmishes and became heavily engaged as the battle developed. Advancing from the northwest, they pushed the enemy off Seminary Ridge by the end of the first day's fighting.

The cupola of the Lutheran Seminary, **2**, afforded a dramatic view over the whole Gettysburg area. It was to be used by both sides— but mostly the Confederates—as an observation post.

Seminary Ridge was unsuccessfully defended by the Union 1st Corps, commanded by General Abner Doubleday, the man credited with introducing baseball to America. He fell back in good order toward Cemetery Hill.

The Rebel 2nd Corps, **3**, led by General Richard Ewell, approached Gettysburg from the north and broke the Federal 11th Corps, taking many prisoners.

When General O.O. Howard's 11th Corps, **4**, started retreating, Doubleday's right flank was dangerously exposed, making his position on Seminary Ridge untenable.

In the van of the 11th Corps' retreat, **5**, was General Schimmelfennig's 3rd Division. This former Prussian officer spent the rest of the battle hiding in a cellar in the town.

Culp's Hill, **6**, a thickly wooded knoll, was occupied by Union troops on the evening of 1 July and became the anchor of General Meade's right wing for the rest of the battle. It was never taken by the Rebels.

Formerly a Federal reserve area, Cemetery Hill, **7**, became a rallying point for Howard's retreating corps. This high ground was ideal for defence and was soon consolidated into a stronghold.

Doubleday's left flank was protected by troopers of General John Buford's 1st Cavalry Division, **8**, who had played a large part in the fighting since dawn, when one of their patrols had first been fired on.

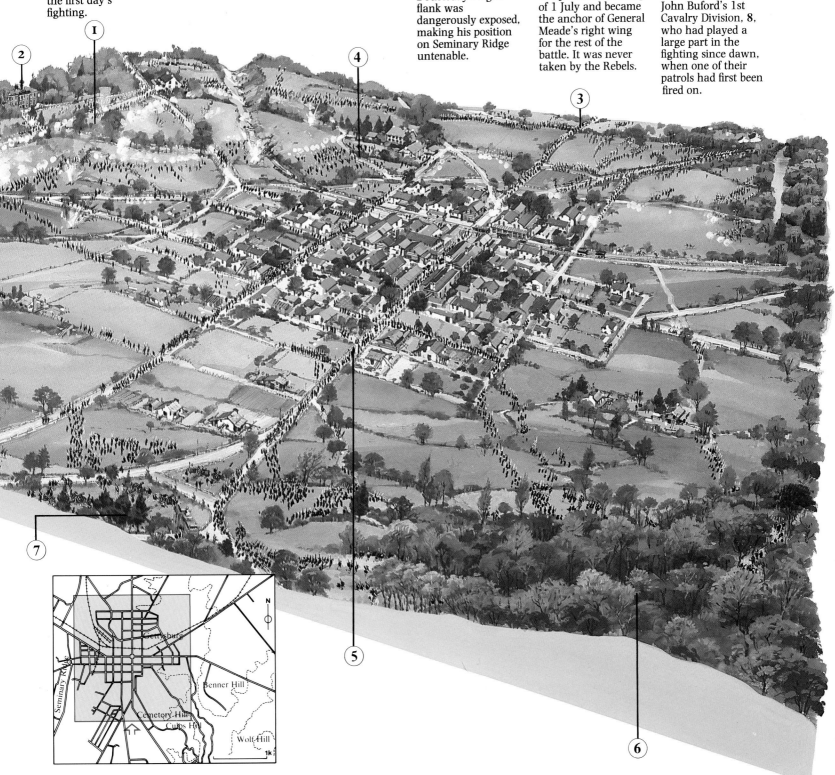

Gettysburg/2

concentrate on the village of Cashtown. Meade, meanwhile, had moved forward to a position on Big Pipe Creek. The gap between the armies was narrowing, and both sides had strong patrols out.

On the afternoon of 30 June, forward elements first sighted each other west of Gettysburg. The Confederate infantry withdrew on seeing Union cavalry, but returned in strength the following morning.

Just after 5 am, a Corporal Hodges of the 9th New York Cavalry spotted figures coming along the Chambersburg turnpike toward his outpost on McPherson's Ridge. He moved forward to get a better view—and a volley of shots rang out. The Battle of Gettysburg had begun.

Fortune was, for once, on the Union side, for Brigadier-General John Buford, commander of the 1st Cavalry Division, was the right man in the right place. A professional soldier, years ahead of his time as far as cavalry tactics were concerned, Buford believed in using horses for mobility, then dismounting troopers and deploying them as infantry. To make his men more effective in this novel role, he armed them with seven-shot Spencer repeating carbines. These 'horizontal shot towers' in the hands of four squadrons delayed two Rebel brigades while reinforcements came up.

Neither Meade nor Lee, who were both some distance away when fighting broke out, wanted to fight a major battle at Gettysburg, but the decision had been made for them. The town was at the junction of 12 roads, leading to all points of the compass and thus making concentration and supply easy for both sides. There was now no holding back, for fighting was rapidly increasing as more and more troops arrived and flung themselves into the fray.

By the time Lee reached Gettysburg in the early afternoon, his infantry had gained the upper hand in fierce fighting for the ridges to the west and north of the town, during which Major-General John Reynolds, the Union's senior field commander, had been killed.

Then fortune was with the North again. Meade had sent forward Major-General Winfield Scott Hancock to assume field command. An able tactician, he at once set about forming a defensive line on rising ground south of Gettysburg. He garrisoned Culp's Hill, a high, wooded knoll, then fortified nearby Cemetery Hill and Cemetery Ridge, anchoring his left flank on two small hills, Little Round Top and Big Round Top. The position, 4 km (2½ mls) long and shaped like an inverted fish-hook, was strong with good interior lines of communication.

As soon as Lee saw Union soldiers milling

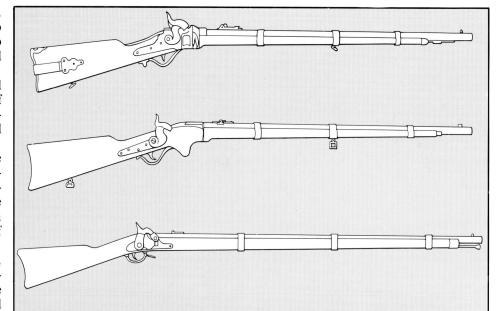

The .58 calibre Springfield rifle musket, *bottom*, the standard rifle of the Union Army, was very accurate to about 550 m (600 yds). The Confederates used many Enfield rifles, imported from England. This .577 calibre weapon had the bonus of taking Springfield cartridges, enabling Confederates to use captured Union ammunition.

The Sharps carbine, *top*, a .52 calibre, single-shot, breech-loader, was tough and reliable. A few units of the Union Army had the seven-shot repeating Spencer carbine, *centre*, a rugged .56 calibre weapon, which was loaded by thrusting a tubular magazine into the breech through a hole drilled in the butt.

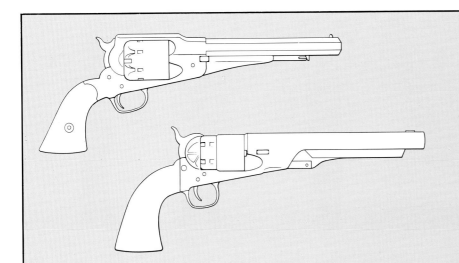

Probably the most popular handgun of the Civil War was the 1860 New Model Army Colt, *above*, a large .44 calibre, six-shot, cap and ball revolver with a 203-mm (8-in) barrel. Many came with an attachable rifle stock, which was said to improve accuracy. The Confederates produced copies of this weapon. Almost as widely used was the Union's 1861 Remington .44 calibre percussion revolver, *top*. Unlike the Colt, a solid frame enclosed its six-shot revolving cylinder, making it more rigid and thus more accurate.

Many Confederate officers carried one of the most formidable handguns ever made—the LeMat pistol. It was designed by a Confederate colonel, Jean LeMat, and had a nine-shot, .40 calibre cap and ball cylinder, swivelling around a large central bore that contained a 16-gauge charge of buckshot. It was used as a single-action pistol, but, at close quarters, an officer could flick its hammer to a second position and discharge buckshot from the lower barrel. It was commonly called the 'grapeshot revolver' by the Confederate troops.

The stages in loading and firing a rifle of the Civil War period are depicted in this painting by Gilbert Gaul. The soldier on the right is ramming home a cartridge, while the one on the left is fitting a percussion cap over the nipple of his Springfield rifle; others are aiming, from either a kneeling or standing position. After the battle, rifles were found on both sides with as many as a dozen charges down the barrel: soldiers, in the heat and horror of battle, had forgotten to squeeze the triggers.

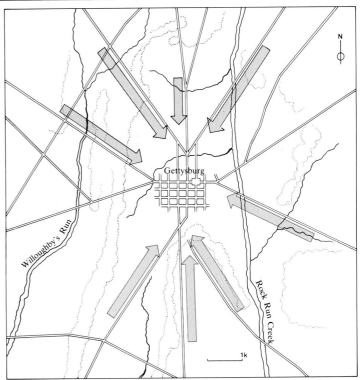

Battles are often won or lost by a general's choice of time and terrain. At Gettysburg it was otherwise. Advance patrols met there on 30 June, while the rival commanders— Lee and Meade— were far distant. Gettysburg's location, at a point where a railway and 12 roads converged, meant that reinforcements poured rapidly to the scene. The biggest battle of the Civil War unfolded with neither commander seeking it.

about on the slopes beyond the town, he realized that they must be driven off before they had a chance to re-form and dig in. The man he turned to was Lieutenant-General Richard Ewell, now commanding the troops once led by the redoubtable 'Stonewall' Jackson, who had been mortally wounded by his own men at the Battle of Chancellorsville two months earlier. Ewell, who had lost a leg at Second Manassas, lacked Jackson's offensive spirit and flair—as Lee was to discover more than once at Gettysburg.

Not wishing to inhibit the commander on the spot with direct instructions, Lee, as usual, issued a discretionary order asking for Cemetery Hill to be attacked 'if practicable'. Jackson would have plunged in immediately; Ewell, used to specific orders, took his chief literally. It had been a hard day, the infected stump of his amputated leg was paining him, casualties had been heavy, and he considered that his remaining·men were too tired to launch a major assault. True, he went through the motions of reconnoitring and probing around Cemetery Hill and Culp's Hill well into the night, but he did not attack. He did not think it practicable.

At midnight, when the Army of the Potomac's new Commander-in-Chief arrived at the front, he found his mauled regiments recovering from their close brush with disaster and desperately fortifying and filling out the line drawn by General Hancock. Meade approved of what he saw: it was a good position and he resolved to defend it.

At his headquarters near the Lutheran Seminary that gave its name to the low ridge now occupied by much of the Confederate army, Lee was pondering his next move while struggling against dysentery. The Rebel leader was also suffering from a heart complaint that would ultimately cause his death.

Much to the dismay of Lieutenant-General James Longstreet, the Confederates' senior corps commander, his plan to manoeuvre around Meade's left flank, threaten Washington and fight a decisive battle on ground of their choice, was vetoed by Lee. Still without Stuart's cavalry, Lee refused to move 'blind' in the face of the enemy. He, too, would fight at Gettysburg.

Next morning, on 2 July, Longstreet's 1st Corps was scheduled to make an early assault from the southern end of Seminary Ridge, northeast across the Emmitsburg Road, to where it was thought the Union left flank rested. Lee expected the onslaught to roll up the Union's defences all along Cemetery Ridge. Ewell was to demonstrate against the right flank, which he had so

Fancy uniforms had vanished from Civil War battlefields by the time of Gettysburg. Of those illustrated here, only the Union army infantry fatigue marching order was in general use on active service. In fact, all arms of the Federal forces were never short of their familiar blue uniforms because most of the clothes manufacturers were based in the North and fulfilled army contracts throughout the war. Full dress in the Union Army was reserved for the likes of the Headquarters guard and for formal parades.

The Confederate Army started out with natty uniforms, but hard campaigning soon took its toll on their finery, which was almost impossible to replace, given the South's limited manufacturing resources. Homespun cloth, dyed Confederate grey or a brown shade called 'butternut', was fashioned into garments by soldiers' families, giving the Rebel troops a rough-and-ready appearance.

Sergeant, Cavalry, C.S.A.

Corporal, Artillery, C.S.A.

Private, Infantry, C.S.A.

Infantryman with overcoat, C.S.A.

Sergeant Major, Artillery, U.S.A.

Private, Infantry, U.S.A.

Corporal, Cavalry, U.S.A.

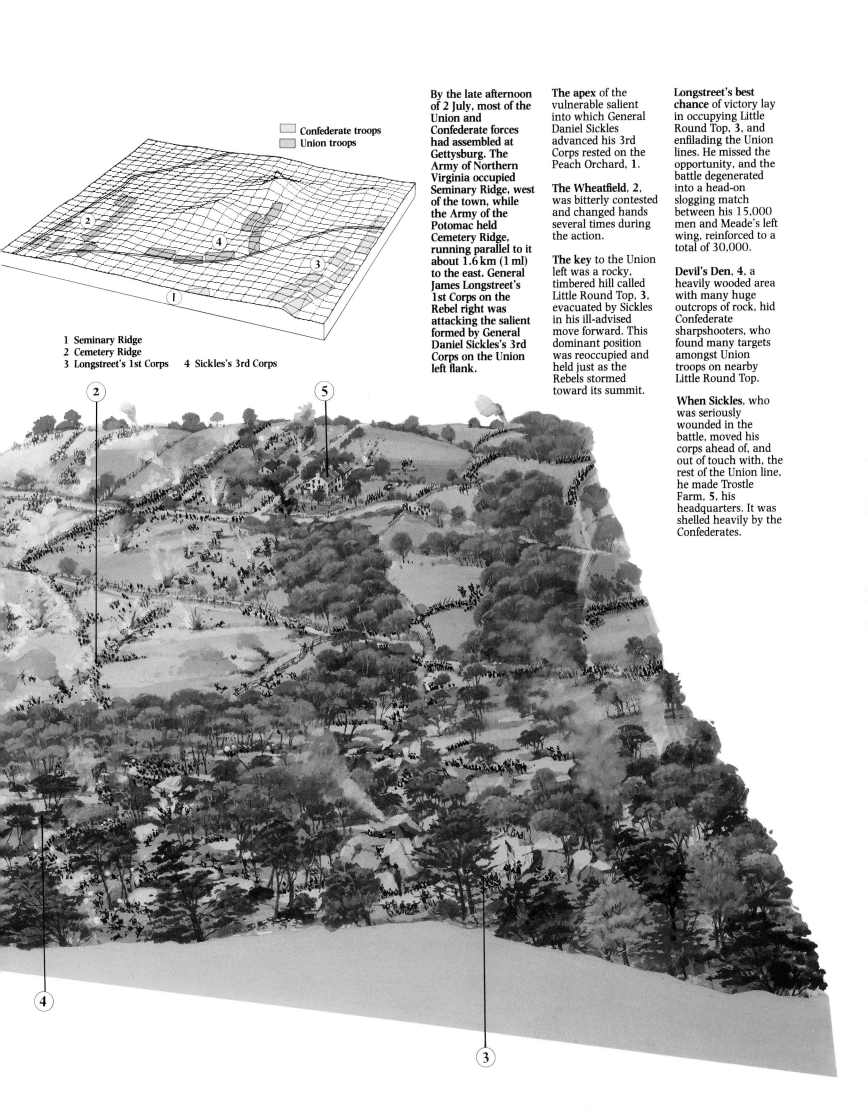

Confederate troops
Union troops

1 Seminary Ridge
2 Cemetery Ridge
3 Longstreet's 1st Corps 4 Sickles's 3rd Corps

By the late afternoon of 2 July, most of the Union and Confederate forces had assembled at Gettysburg. The Army of Northern Virginia occupied Seminary Ridge, west of the town, while the Army of the Potomac held Cemetery Ridge, running parallel to it about 1.6 km (1 ml) to the east. General James Longstreet's 1st Corps on the Rebel right was attacking the salient formed by General Daniel Sickles's 3rd Corps on the Union left flank.

The apex of the vulnerable salient into which General Daniel Sickles advanced his 3rd Corps rested on the Peach Orchard, 1.

The Wheatfield, 2, was bitterly contested and changed hands several times during the action.

The key to the Union left was a rocky, timbered hill called Little Round Top, 3, evacuated by Sickles in his ill-advised move forward. This dominant position was reoccupied and held just as the Rebels stormed toward its summit.

Longstreet's best chance of victory lay in occupying Little Round Top, 3, and enfilading the Union lines. He missed the opportunity, and the battle degenerated into a head-on slogging match between his 15,000 men and Meade's left wing, reinforced to a total of 30,000.

Devil's Den, 4, a heavily wooded area with many huge outcrops of rock, hid Confederate sharpshooters, who found many targets amongst Union troops on nearby Little Round Top.

When Sickles, who was seriously wounded in the battle, moved his corps ahead of, and out of touch with, the rest of the Union line, he made Trostle Farm, 5, his headquarters. It was shelled heavily by the Confederates.

conspicuously failed to penetrate the night before, and make an all-out attack if the opportunity presented itself. Lieutenant-General Ambrose Powell Hill's 3rd Corps was to carry out a diversionary operation in the centre to keep Meade uncertain where the real blow would fall. What Lee's plan most called for was coordination: he did not get it.

Longstreet, who was often heard to mutter, 'I never like to go into battle with one boot off,' excelled his previous records for lethargy. It was 4.30 pm before he was finally in position to attack.

By that time, to Meade's justifiable anger, the Union line had been altered for the worse just at the point where it was about to be assailed. Major-General Dan Sickles, whose corps had been placed at the bottom end of Cemetery Ridge and around Little Round Top and Big Round Top to secure the left flank, suddenly moved forward to what he thought was a better line—an order he gave without consulting his Commander-in-Chief. The salient he thus formed in front of, and out of touch with, the main Union position almost brought about defeat.

An alert signaller on the summit of the now undefended Little Round Top reported enemy troop movements to the front, which was confirmed by Brigadier-General Gouverneur Warren, whom Meade had sent to investigate. Realizing that if the Rebels took the hill, they could enfilade the whole of Cemetery Ridge, Warren managed to rush some more troops to the top of the hill just as the Southerners hurled themselves up the rocky slopes. For this swift initiative, Warren was later hailed, not without justification, as 'the saviour of the Union army'.

All across the woods and fields to the west of Little Round Top, Longstreet was pressing his attack. For four hours some of the fiercest fighting of the war raged around Devil's Den, the Peach Orchard and the Wheatfield, names which have become synonymous with violent death to generations of Americans. Vigorous though his attacks were, Longstreet could not break through because Meade showed remarkable skill in moving troops around in the thick of battle to plug every weak spot.

Not until the firing had all but died away in the south did Ewell begin to tackle the northern flank. His efforts came too late in the day and were repulsed by Union reinforcements, rushed to the scene from farther down the ridge. Talking of Gettysburg afterward, Ewell admitted, 'It took a great many mistakes to lose the battle. And I myself made most of them.'

Fighting on its own territory put steel into the oft-derided Army of the Potomac.

General Robert E. Lee (1807–1870) had served with distinction in the United States army for almost 20 years by the time of the Civil War. A kindly, considerate man of deep religious conviction, he was opposed to slavery on moral grounds and to secession for practical reasons. However, his primary allegiance was to his home state of Virginia. By Lincoln's order, he was offered the command of the Union army. He refused; and when, a few days later, Virginia seceded, he resigned his commission and returned to his home state. There, four days later, he was offered, and accepted, the command of all Virginian military and naval forces. Though undoubtedly the outstanding strategist and tactician of the Civil War period, even Lee could not ultimately withstand the North's greater resources in men, money and materials.

Major-General George G. Meade (1815–1872) learned with astonishment three days before the Battle of Gettysburg that President Lincoln had appointed him to lead the Army of the Potomac. A quick-tempered, irascible man, he was nevertheless cautious in battle. He never made either a foolish or a brilliant decision, but his skill in moving troops rapidly from one danger point to another at Gettysburg frustrated all Confederate attacks and ensured Union victory.

The North, backed by a massive arms industry, used six-gun batteries equipped, in almost all cases, with the same calibre of weapon to simplify ammunition supply. The South, without thriving ordnance factories, favoured four-gun batteries of whatever cannon could be found.

Popular with both sides was the bronze, smoothbore 12-pounder 'Napoleon', *top*, which had a range of 1,554 m (1,700 yds). Designed by Napoleon III of France in 1853, these sturdy muzzle-loading guns could fire solid shot, exploding shell or canister with equal facility.

Many Union army batteries of horse artillery were equipped with the Parrot 10-pounder, *bottom*, a rifled muzzle-loader which was more accurate and had a slightly longer range than the 'Napoleon'. This gun, made of cast iron, with a wrought-iron strengthening 'collar' encircling the touch-hole, was cheap to manufacture but was prone to burst because of imperfect casting.

In the war's biggest cannonade, the Union Army of the Potomac fired 32,000 rounds of ammunition while the Confederate Army of Northern Virginia discharged 20,000 rounds.

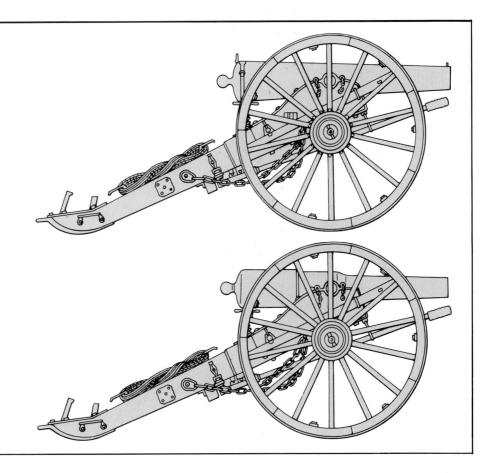

Almost a year had passed since the Battle of Gettysburg when these four senior U.S. Army officers posed for this photograph. They were serving together again after recovering from wounds received in the huge three-day battle of the previous summer, when Lee's invasion of the North was effectively blocked.

They are Major-General Winfield Scott Hancock (seated), commander of the 2nd Corps, and (left to right) Brigadier-General Francis Barlow, 1st Division, 11th Corps; Major-General David Birney, 1st Division, 3rd Corps and Brigadier-General John Gibbon, 2nd Division, 2nd Corps.

Gettysburg claimed an unusually high proportion of general officer casualties on both sides. Four died for the Union and six for the Confederacy (including one in the retreat to Virginia). Twelve senior officers in each army were wounded.

This was not the same demoralized force that Lee had trounced on the battlefields of the South. At the close of the second day's fighting, it was clear that the Army of Northern Virginia had encountered very determined opposition. No one could predict the outcome if combat were to be resumed on 3 July.

That night, at a meeting held in his headquarters in a farmhouse behind Cemetery Ridge, Meade forecast that Brigadier-General John Gibbon, commanding the Union centre, would bear the brunt of the Rebel assault should Lee attack again.

As the third day dawned over the battle-scarred countryside, the Confederates' idolized commander resolved to continue the assault where he had left off—but the Federals forestalled him. At 4.30 am they launched a surprise offensive to drive Ewell's troops out of the tiny foothold they had gained on Culp's Hill, thus ruining Lee's plan for a concerted pincer attack on the Union flanks. With Ewell's corps heavily engaged, and Longstreet, on the right, still reluctant to take the offensive, Lee turned his attention to the Federal centre, which had shown signs of weakness the day before. It was as Meade had earlier predicted.

Lee proposed to take Major-General George Pickett's division of Longstreet's corps, which had recently arrived on the field, add to it troops from Hill's 3rd Corps—a total of 15,000 men—and launch them directly at the middle of the Union lines.

Longstreet was horrified. Bluntly he told his superior, 'It is my opinion that no fifteen thousand men ever arrayed for battle can take that position.' Lee was unconvinced.

Once again, however, his subordinates displayed agonizing slowness. Preparations dragged on for the rest of the morning, and it was not until 1 pm that Longstreet ordered 150 guns to pound Cemetery Ridge to 'soften' the way for the infantry. The Federals at once replied with 80 field pieces. For the next two hours, the air was rent with the biggest cannonade ever heard on the North American continent. It was thunderous and impressive—but not especially effective.

As the Rebel barrage died away for want of long-range ammunition, General Pickett led his 15,000 shock troops out of the cover of the trees at the bottom end of Seminary Ridge. As many eyewitnesses testified, they formed in line and began to cross the 1.6 km (1 ml) of open, gently sloping farmland in review order, their red flags waving bravely in the warm sunshine.

It must have been a stirring spectacle, Napoleonic in its grandeur. But on Cemetery Ridge, around the little clump of trees

John Burns, a 72-year-old veteran of the War of 1812 and the Mexican War, also saw action at Gettysburg. When the fighting started on 1 July, he grabbed his old musket and stood in the U.S. line with the 7th Wisconsin Volunteers. He was wounded three times and left for dead but nevertheless survived to earn President Abraham Lincoln's personal congratulations.

The only civilian killed in the three-day bloodbath at Gettysburg was a young woman named Jennie Wade. When the armies clashed, she was at her married sister's home on Baltimore Street, near Cemetery Hill, helping to look after a new baby. A stray bullet smashed through two doors of the little brick house and struck 20-year-old Jennie in the back, fatally wounding her.

Remnants, 7, of the shattered first wave of Pickett's attack begin to make their way back to the Confederate lines on Seminary Ridge.

As Pickett's charging troops bunched, Union infantry, **6,** wheeled to send enfilading volleys crashing into the Confederates' right flank.

In a slight fold in the ground behind Codori Farm, **5,** about 460 m (500 yds) from the nearest enemy positions, Pickett's units paused to dress ranks before continuing their assault.

This little house, 4, behind Cemetery Ridge was General Meade's headquarters until it was badly damaged by Rebel artillery fire.

Against Longstreet's advice, Lee insisted on trying to break the centre of the Army of the Potomac on Cemetery Ridge 1.6 km (1 ml) east of the Confederate positions, across open countryside. He chose his freshest 15,000 men, placed them under the command of Major-General George Pickett, and sent them forward in the wake of a huge—but ineffective—bombardment. By 3.30 pm less than half an hour after starting out, Pickett's charge had been repulsed with dreadful casualties.

While 15,000 Confederates under General George Pickett were attempting to pierce the centre of the Union line along Cemetery Ridge, another action was taking place 3.2 km (2 mls) to the east—behind Meade's position. The dashing Rebel cavalry leader, General 'Jeb' Stuart, got into a sharp fight with U.S. cavalry, who successfully prevented him from breaking into the Army of the Potomac's rear and possibly altering the outcome of the battle.

General Lee chose this clump of trees, 1, as the axis of advance for the Confederate attack on the Union centre on Cemetery Ridge. It stood out clearly on the skyline.

Only Brigadier-General Lewis Armistead, followed by about 150 Rebel infantrymen, 3, managed to penetrate the Union defences, 2. Armistead was mortally wounded.

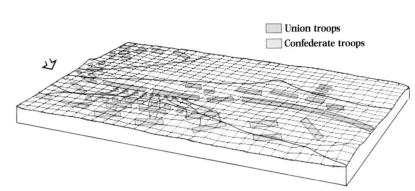

Union troops
Confederate troops

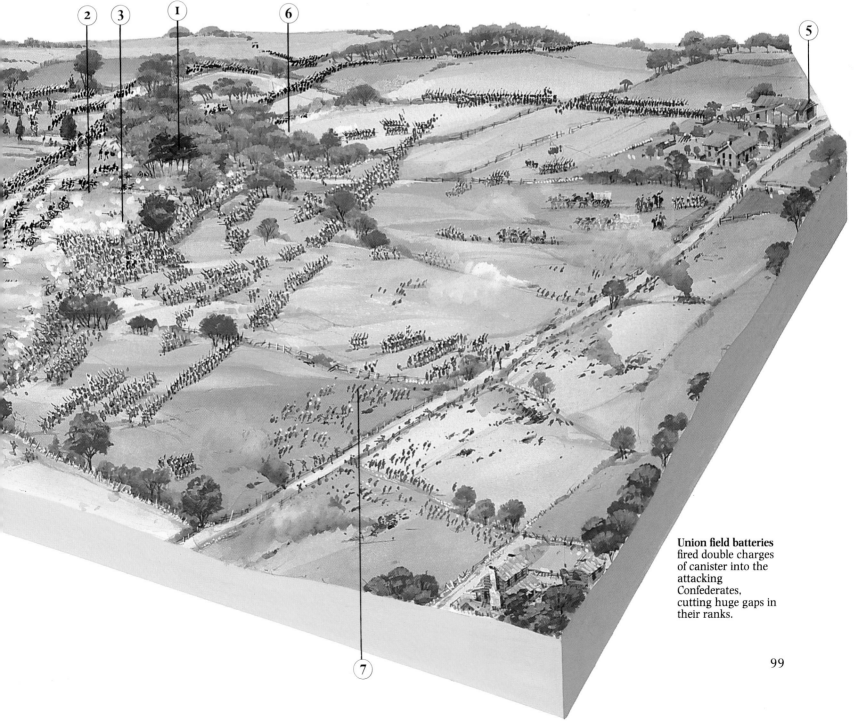

Union field batteries fired double charges of canister into the attacking Confederates, cutting huge gaps in their ranks.

which marked the axis of the Confederates' steady advance, the weapons trained on them were more accurate and powerful than anything Napoleon had known.

When the long grey lines drew closer, they were raked by devastating volleys of rifle fire and bombarded with canister shot from waiting batteries. Closing up the great swaths cut in their ranks, the Southerners pressed on relentlessly, their famous Rebel yell rising above the din of battle. Perhaps 150 men actually penetrated the Union's heavily defended lines. They were led by Brigadier-General Lewis Armistead, waving his hat on his sword point. He paid for his gallantry with his life.

Unsupported by Longstreet, who would not commit any more troops, Pickett's glorious charge soon lost its momentum. The survivors found their position untenable and began to fall back under fire, leaving behind about 7,000 casualties.

'All this has been my fault,' General Lee told the returning soldiers, whom he ordered to form a line in case the Federals counter-attacked. He disguised his disappointment at their reverse and they acknowledged him with cheers.

While Pickett's magnificent, but doomed, assault was in progress, Stuart and his cavalry, at last returned from raiding, were 4 km (2½ mls) to the east, behind the enemy lines. They posed an empty threat, however, for they were effectively blocked by a strong force of Union cavalry, among whom was an ambitious Brigadier-General named George Armstrong Custer.

So ended the biggest and bloodiest battle ever fought on American soil. The North lost some 23,000 killed, wounded, captured or missing out of some 97,000 men; the South about 27,000. All the next day, Independence Day, the exhausted armies faced each other without seeking combat.

That afternoon, the fine weather of the previous few days broke, just as a Confederate wagon train, 27 km (17 mls) long, set out to carry the many wounded on a long, jolting, painful journey back to Virginia. After nightfall, when he was sure the Union army would not attack, Lee ceded victory by withdrawing from the field.

Meade was not certain that the Rebels had gone until the middle of Sunday, 5 July. His pursuit was not vigorous, and his failure to force a decisive battle before Lee crossed the Potomac River to safety has been the subject of controversy ever since.

Battered, but still proud, the Army of Northern Virginia fought on valiantly for two more years before Lee finally surrendered at Appomattox. The South had lost the war of attrition, which it had not the *matériel* to sustain.

A few of the 21,000 wounded left behind at Gettysburg when the war moved on. For weeks after the battle, the whole area was a vast hospital. Army medical services were hard put to it to cope with such huge numbers, but they received considerable help from the civilian Sanitary Commission, a forerunner of the Red Cross.

After the battle, the bodies of 3,155 Federals and 3,903 Confederates lay in the fields and woods surrounding Gettysburg. Some were recovered and sent home for burial, either embalmed or sealed in the special metallic coffins advertised *right*. Most were hastily buried in mass graves where they had fallen. Later on, the remains of 3,564 Federal soldiers were exhumed and reburied in a National Military Cemetery, created in a corner of the battlefield near the town.

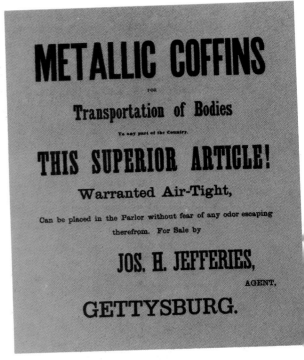

The day after the Battle of Gettysburg, the Confederacy sustained another grievous reverse: their garrison at Vicksburg was finally starved into surrender, leaving the entire length of the Mississippi River in Federal hands. This day, 4 July 1863, marked the turning point of the war, although the full consequences were not immediately perceived. It was at once clear, however, that Lee had lost—and could never replace—27,000 men out of his 75,000; and without them his reputation as an invincible force was also lost.

Lee led his troops down the Shenandoah valley to their earlier positions behind the Rappahannock and Rapidan Rivers, knowing that, although they remained a formidable fighting force, he would never again have sufficient men and materials to invade the North. The Confederacy did not lose the war because of Gettysburg alone, but after it, Federal victory was inevitable.

'Home of a Rebel Sharpshooter' is a famous photograph taken by Alexander Gardner at Gettysburg in July 1863. It purports to show a dead Rebel marksman among the rocks of Devil's Den on the right flank of the Confederate position. Examination of his other negatives reveals that this same soldier was struck down near by, then carried to the rocks by Gardner.

'**Four score and seven years ago**, our fathers brought forth upon this continent a new nation, conceived in liberty and dedicated to the proposition that all men are created equal ...' So began President Abraham Lincoln, *circled right*, when he rose to speak at Gettysburg on 19 November 1863. It took him just 2 minutes and 15 seconds to utter ten sentences to a crowd of some 15,000 people, who had come that day to the site of the previous July's great battle to see a corner of the field dedicated as a National Military Cemetery for fallen men of the Union army.

President Lincoln's brief remarks—271 words in all—contrasted sharply with the 1 hour and 57 minute eulogy delivered by Edward Everett, the elderly scholar recognized as the country's leading orator.

Very few listeners rated the President's speech. In fact, Lincoln himself turned to another member of the platform party after he sat down and said, 'It is a flat failure.' Yet when his fellow-countrymen read and re-read his simple, direct words, they realized that he had been misjudged. In those few lines, immortalized as The Gettysburg Address, Lincoln had managed to encapsulate all that nascent America stood for—and was prepared to die for.

Sedan/*1 September, 1870*

Gallic anger instigated the outbreak of hostilities on 19 July 1870. The France of Emperor Napoleon III, though boastful of its military prowess, was, as events were to prove, ill-equipped to fight a major war, but across the Rhine, more than 380,000 well-supplied Prussian troops were massed on the border, facing Alsace and Lorraine.

On 1 August, Napoleon found himself at the head of 250,000 men, who were not yet ready for combat. Putting his faith in the legendary *élan* of the French soldier, he ordered an advance into enemy territory. It was the first error in a series of ill-considered manoeuvres that culminated in the débâcle of Sedan.

Recoiling before the Prussians, two large French forces fought and lost four battles, at Worth, Spicheren, Mars la Tour and Gravelotte. After the defeat at Gravelotte on 18 August, Marshal Bazaine's army was forced to retire behind the fortifications of Metz, where it was besieged by 150,000 Prussians. Marshal MacMahon's forces, defeated at Worth, fell back nearly 240 km (150 mls) to Chalons on the River Marne, where they were joined by Napoleon III. By 20 August, the Army of Chalons had been formed and the French government insisted that it should join Bazaine, who was planning to break out of Metz and move north. Napoleon, lacking the military foresight of his namesake, agreed to advance. MacMahon, therefore, led the Army of Chalons on a left-flanking march northeast toward the Belgian frontier, in an attempt to avoid the Prussians, before striking south again to link up with Bazaine.

The Prussians at once took advantage of this incompetent manoeuvre by wheeling the Third Army and the Army of the Meuse north to catch the French in a pincer grip. At Beaufort, on 30 August, the Prussians, commanded by Helmuth von Moltke, caught up with the French. After losing 5,000 men and more than 40 guns in a sharp fight, MacMahon retired to Sedan.

On 31 August, the Army of Chalons occupied Sedan and its environs, a triangular 'island' formed by three rivers—the Meuse, the Floing and the Givonne. The French positions were surrounded by commanding hills, which made ideal platforms for the Prussian guns which had been brought up to bombard the town.

At dawn on 1 September, the attack opened. The Prussians, who outnumbered the French by some 90,000 men, were equipped with an obsolete rifle, the 1841 Dreyse needle-gun, but possessed many batteries of modern, Krupps breech-loading

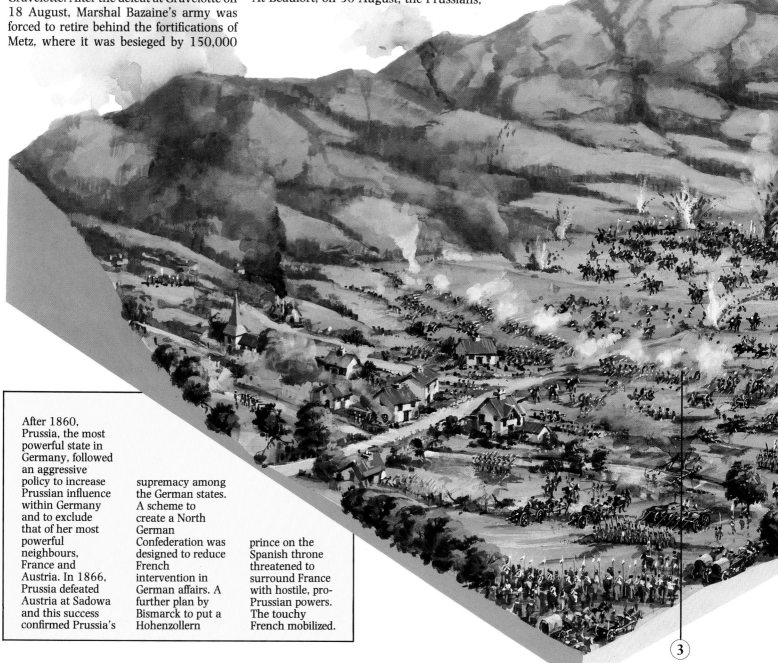

After 1860, Prussia, the most powerful state in Germany, followed an aggressive policy to increase Prussian influence within Germany and to exclude that of her most powerful neighbours, France and Austria. In 1866, Prussia defeated Austria at Sadowa and this success confirmed Prussia's supremacy among the German states. A scheme to create a North German Confederation was designed to reduce French intervention in German affairs. A further plan by Bismarck to put a Hohenzollern prince on the Spanish throne threatened to surround France with hostile, pro-Prussian powers. The touchy French mobilized.

③

At 2.30 pm on
1 September 1870,
after two charges
had failed to break
out, the French tried
to restore order in
their shattered lines
to prepare for yet
another charge. It
was a beautiful
summer's day, clear
and sunny, with
superb visibility.

The town of Sedan
lies in a fertile valley.
To the north, the
ground rises sharply
toward the Ardennes.
The Prussians held
the village of Floing,
2.4 km (1½ mls) to the
northwest. To break
out from Sedan, the
French had to seize
the village.

The French cavalry
had to charge down a
steep, uneven slope,
1, toward Floing. The
ground was so
broken and rough
that it was difficult to
maintain the
momentum of the
charge without the
horses stumbling and
falling.

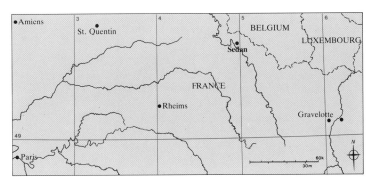

Sedan's strategic
importance was due
to its position on the
River Meuse—the
only major natural
obstacle between the
German border and
the city of Paris.

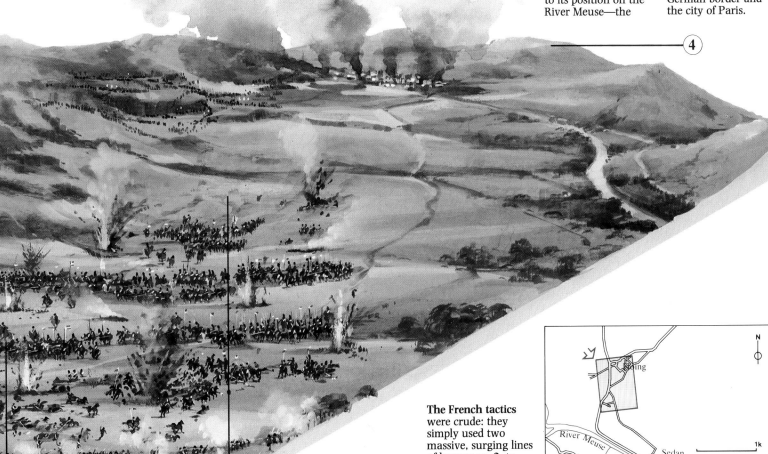

One of the Prussian
artillery officers later
wrote of the height of
the battle: 'The
spectacle of the
carnage was horrible;
the fearful cries of the
victims of our shells
reached as far as
where we stood.'

With the front
crumbling and the
horse twice repulsed,
General Ducrot
ordered yet a third
cavalry charge. The
crowded ranks met a
hail of fire and, as
Gallifet and the
remains of his gallant
command withdrew,
the Prussians stopped
firing and allowed the
survivors to pass
unharmed. Their
officers saluted.

The King of Prussia,
soon to be Kaiser
Wilhelm I, took a
keen interest in
military matters and
watched the battle
from a ridge, 4, near
Sedan. When the
French horse moved
out for the third
charge, he exclaimed
with admiration, 'Ah!
the brave men!' The
astonishing bravery
of the French cavalry
before Floing
epitomises that
transitional phase of
warfare in which raw
courage was pitted
against bullets.

The French tactics
were crude: they
simply used two
massive, surging lines
of horsemen, 2, to
break through the
encircling Prussian
lines, 3. When asked
by General Ducrot
whether the charge
could be successfully
repeated, General
Gallifet replied, 'As
often as you like, *mon
général*, so long as
there's one of us left.'

Prussian soldiers, *right*,
were well-disciplined
conscripts with a
serious attitude to
war. Within 18 days,
380,000 men had
been transported to
the frontier with
France—a formidable
achievement.

rifled artillery. Napoleon's troops had the superior Chassepot rifle, with twice the range of the Dreyse, some old-fashioned muzzle-loading cannon, and the *mitrailleuse*, a machine-gun capable of firing 125 rounds a minute. Unfortunately, development of the *mitrailleuse* had been kept so secret that officers did not know how best to deploy it in action. In the event, Prussian artillery dominated the battle and decided its outcome.

In the early hours of the struggle, Marshal MacMahon was wounded and handed over command to General Ducrot. Appreciating the hopelessness of the French position, Ducrot decided to withdraw and secure a line of retreat before the converging Prussian armies succeeded in encircling Sedan. When General de Wimpffen, who had arrived the day before, heard this, he produced written orders from the Minister of War authorizing him to assume command should anything happen to MacMahon. Thus the Army of Chalons received its third commanding general in the space of little more than four hours.

De Wimpffen countermanded the withdrawal and rashly boasted that he would drive the enemy into the river within two hours. The plan was without hope, for more and more Prussian artillery was being brought to bear, and the storm of shells was exacting a terrible toll.

At about 11 am, the Prussian armies joined forces to the north of the town. Encirclement was complete, and the tempo of gunfire increased further. While the Emperor began to face the prospect of capitulation, an attempt was made to force a way out of the Prussian vice, northward through the village of Floing.

General Marguerite's cavalry division was to form the point of the battering ram, supported by General Ducrot's infantry corps. Marguerite, however, was killed before he had completed a reconnaissance of the enemy lines. General Gallifet, a dashing cavalryman, took his place and gallantly led no fewer than three desperate charges against Floing. As he and the remnants of his squadrons retired after the third attempt, he was saluted by admiring Prussian officers, who held their troops' fire to allow the survivors to return.

There could now be no escape. The Emperor had a white flag raised over the town. At first, de Wimpffen refused to give in; but having failed to persuade his troops to mount a counter-attack, he finally accepted defeat. It was an overwhelming victory for the Prussians. For fewer than 9,000 casualties, they had inflicted 17,000 on the French, taken 104,000 prisoners and captured all their guns and baggage.

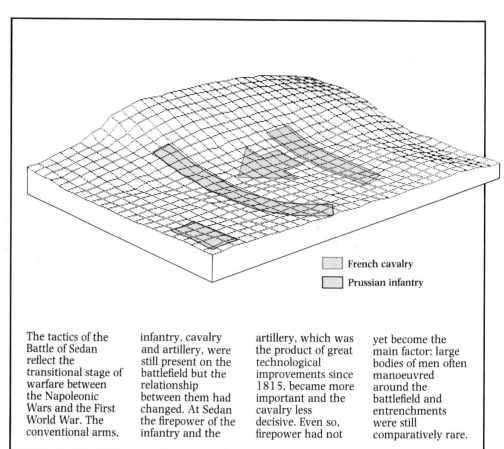

French cavalry

Prussian infantry

The tactics of the Battle of Sedan reflect the transitional stage of warfare between the Napoleonic Wars and the First World War. The conventional arms, infantry, cavalry and artillery, were still present on the battlefield but the relationship between them had changed. At Sedan the firepower of the infantry and the artillery, which was the product of great technological improvements since 1815, became more important and the cavalry less decisive. Even so, firepower had not yet become the main factor: large bodies of men often manoeuvred around the battlefield and entrenchments were still comparatively rare.

Marshal MacMahon, Duc de Magenta (1808–1893), *above*. Though dashing and recklessly brave, his military experience in Africa and the Crimea had not prepared him for the Prussians, but his reputation survived the defeat at Sedan. **General Emmanuel Felix de Wimpffen (1811–1884)**, *above left*. At Sedan, his ambition blinded him to the desperateness of his situation. In defeat, it was his unenviable task to negotiate a peace against a history of 22 years of animosity between France and Prussia. **Helmuth von Moltke (1800–1891)**, *left*, a soldier of exceptional ability, with an unequalled grasp of technical military matters, was appointed Chief of the Prussian General Staff in 1857.

The *mitrailleuse*, a primitive form of machine-gun, was the product of Napoleon III's interest in weaponry. The French had been experimenting with it since 1860, and it had been produced in strict secrecy since 1866. Its strange appearance, however, contributed to the suspicions of the French generals, who saw no role for it in their army. The *mitrailleuse* had 25 barrels, each of which could be fired in sequence by turning a handle. It had a range of almost 1,830 m (2,000 yds), a rate of fire of 125 rounds a minute and was a reliable weapon. The French generals did not realize its potential; they sited it in the open and used it ineffectually as an ordinary piece of artillery.

The Prussian Dreyse needle-gun, *below*, was an early form of breech-loading rifle. When the trigger was pulled, a needle-like firing pin pierced the base of the cartridge, passed through the powder and ignited a cap at the base of the bullet. This gun greatly improved the accuracy and rate of fire of the infantry, but it was unreliable and sometimes exploded in the face of its firer. The basic design was adapted and improved by the French, who sealed the breech with a rubber ring. The range was also greatly enhanced from 550 m (600 yds) to 1,463 m (1,600 yds). It was most effective against cavalry charges.

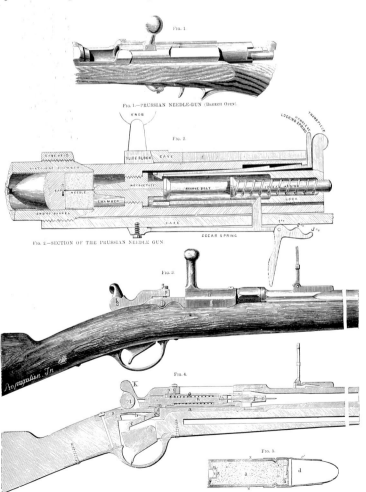

The humiliation of French arms at Sedan decided the outcome of the war. The surrender of Napoleon III was a catastrophic blow to the Second Empire, and the Bonaparte dynasty, unstable and increasingly unpopular, could not survive. On 4 September, the Empire was overthrown by a popular uprising in Paris. Napoleon followed his Empress into exile in England, and the Third Republic was proclaimed by Léon Gambetta.

Within a fortnight, the Prussians had advanced on Paris and begun a long and harrowing siege of the city. Gambetta escaped to the south by balloon to raise new armies. Three successive sorties by the Paris garrison failed. Trochu, the military governor, sought an armistice and on 29 January 1871, at the Convention of Versailles, all French regular troops surrendered. Paris was occupied by the Prussians and at Versailles Wilhelm I, King of Prussia, was proclaimed German Emperor.

In May 1871, under the terms of the Treaty of Frankfurt, France was forced to cede Alsace and two-thirds of Lorraine. Germany had replaced France as the greatest European land power.

Little Big Horn/*25 June, 1876*

George Armstrong Custer pursued glory all his life, but only in death did he attain international fame, when he and his entire command were slaughtered in the incident immortalized as 'Custer's Last Stand'.

Custer graduated from the United States Military Academy in 1861, the year the American Civil War broke out, and two years later, aged 23, gloried in being hailed as a 'boy general'. Ever boisterous and flamboyant, Custer led numerous daring actions. His sheer raw courage was never in doubt, but his brigade paid for their leader's dash with heavy casualties.

General Phil Sheridan, who had moulded the U.S. cavalry into a cohesive fighting force, took a liking to Custer and, by the end of 1864, Custer was a major-general in charge of a division, the darling of the northern Press and lionized by society. In July 1866, a year after the war's end, Sheridan had Custer, by then reduced in rank from his wartime, brevet major-generalship of U.S. Volunteers to a lieutenant-colonel in the regular U.S. army, lead a punitive expedition against the Cheyenne and Arapaho tribes. Custer and 700 troopers of the 7th Cavalry found an Indian camp on the Washita River. Without making a proper reconnaissance, Custer split his command into four columns and attacked, killing men, women and children, and ponies in one of those frenzies of slaughter that so disgraced the U.S. army in the latter half of the nineteenth century. Seeing some Indians escape, Major Joel Elliott and 19 men spurred after them. A scout reported continuous firing from farther down the valley but, again without investigating, Custer retired with his regiment almost intact.

Another column found the luckless Elliott and his troopers lying mutilated less than 3.2 km (2 mls) from the village that Custer had devastated. It was a grim fore-shadowing of the fate awaiting the man who had now shaken the confidence both of his troopers and of his superior, Sheridan. Eight years later, in 1874, Custer led an expedition to explore the Black Hills of Dakota. Reports of gold sparked a rush to the area, which had been ceded to the Sioux, and roused the Indians of the northwest—the Sioux and the Cheyenne— to combine to form the largest warrior army ever assembled.

Sheridan's three-pronged campaign against the Indians was for General Crook to come north from Fort Fetterman, Colonel Gibbon to approach eastward from Fort Ellis and General Terry to march west from Fort Lincoln. Terry's force included the 7th Cavalry, whose colonel, Custer, was suspended from duty for having displeased the

The Battle of the Little Big Horn took place in the afternoon of 25 June 1876, across an area of 1.6 km (1 ml). Confident of his men, reckless in his tactics, Custer belonged to the 'see the enemy and charge' school.

The massacre exacted a heavy toll on the Custer family. Lying close to George, **1**, were the bodies of his brothers, Tom, a cavalry captain, and Boston, a civilian, as well as his teenage nephew, Autie Reed. Farther across the hillside was the body of his brother-in-law, Lieutenant Calhoun, **2**.

The Black Hills and Yellowstone River regions in Montana were granted to the Sioux in perpetuity by a treaty of 1868. But by 1873, the Americans were pressing the Government to open the hills for gold prospecting. This, combined with the encroachment of the railroad and the depletion of the buffalo, roused the Indians at last to anger and a fierce determination to fight for their lands, their freedom and their independence.

During the decade before 1876, the transcontinental railroad cut across Indian territory, and the buffalo herds so vital to the Indian economy were slaughtered. The excessive killing of buffalo was both for commercial gain and a deliberate policy of starving the Indians into submission. Despite this aggressive policy, the United States army was thinly spread over the Central Plains and it was, therefore, possible for the Indians to concentrate in large numbers to annihilate an isolated force of American troops. Opposition to American policy grew as a result of the influence of two Sioux chiefs, Crazy Horse and Sitting Bull, who undermined the older, more accommodating chiefs. Both were determined to maintain control of the Sioux hunting grounds south of the Platte River, the cession of which in 1873 posed a threat to the Sioux 'holy land' in the Black Hills. Negotiations continued, and the Sioux chiefs demanded $600 million for the Black Hills. U.S. Commissioners offered $6 million, but the offer was refused, and eventually, in the spring of 1876, the Department of the Interior handed over the problem of 'pacifying' the area to the army.

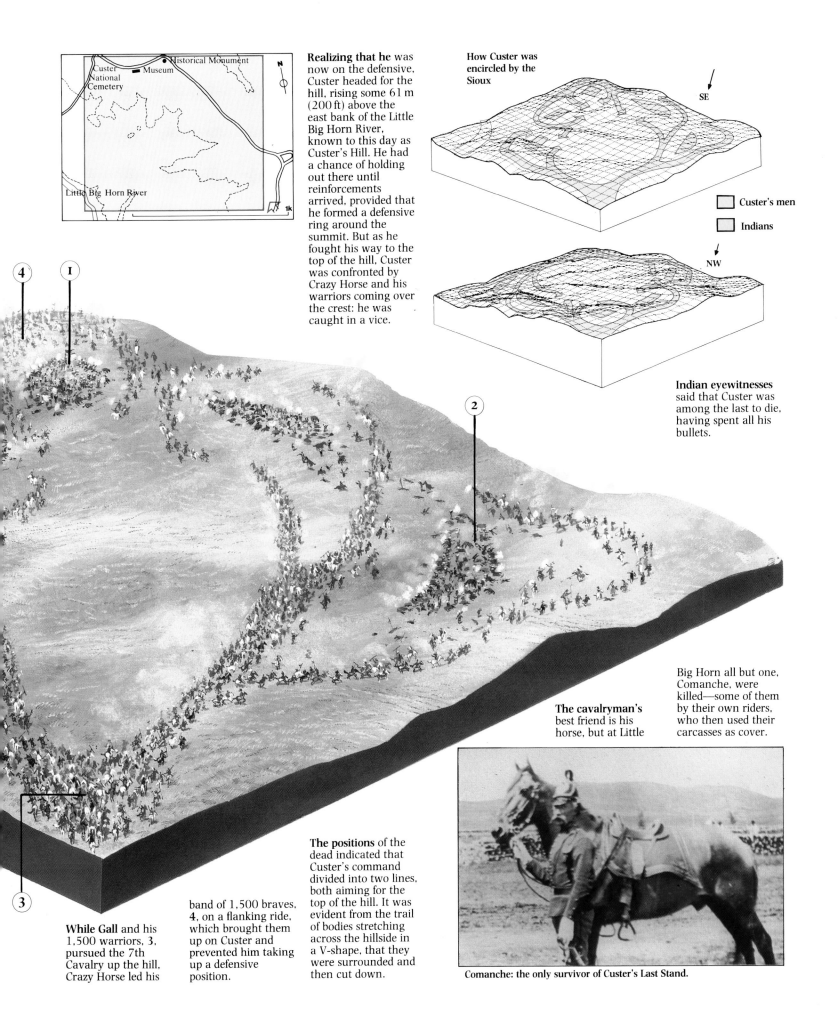

Realizing that he was now on the defensive, Custer headed for the hill, rising some 61 m (200 ft) above the east bank of the Little Big Horn River, known to this day as Custer's Hill. He had a chance of holding out there until reinforcements arrived, provided that he formed a defensive ring around the summit. But as he fought his way to the top of the hill, Custer was confronted by Crazy Horse and his warriors coming over the crest: he was caught in a vice.

How Custer was encircled by the Sioux

SE

☐ Custer's men

☐ Indians

NW

Indian eyewitnesses said that Custer was among the last to die, having spent all his bullets.

Big Horn all but one, Comanche, were killed—some of them by their own riders, who then used their carcasses as cover.

The cavalryman's best friend is his horse, but at Little

While Gall and his 1,500 warriors, **3**, pursued the 7th Cavalry up the hill, Crazy Horse led his band of 1,500 braves, **4**, on a flanking ride, which brought them up on Custer and prevented him taking up a defensive position.

The positions of the dead indicated that Custer's command divided into two lines, both aiming for the top of the hill. It was evident from the trail of bodies stretching across the hillside in a V-shape, that they were surrounded and then cut down.

Comanche: the only survivor of Custer's Last Stand.

President, Ulysses S. Grant. But General Terry wanted Custer with him because he knew the plains, and Grant relented.

On 21 June, at the confluence of the Rosebud and Yellowstone Rivers. Terry acceded to Custer's dearest wish—a detached command. He was to march 160 km (100 mls) up the Rosebud, then turn west into the valley of the Little Big Horn River. In his belief that the 7th Cavalry could defeat all the warriors of the northwest plains, Custer rashly refused Terry's generous offer of four extra troops from the 2nd Cavalry and two Gatling guns. At noon on 22 June, he and his men rode off to their fate.

Custer insisted on a demanding pace and managed to cover more than 112 km (70 mls) before nightfall on 24 June. Tired as his men and mounts were after two and a half gruelling days, Custer would not halt. He set off on a night march toward the Little Big Horn, which exhausted the 7th Cavalry still further. When they finally bivouacked in the early hours of 25 June, Custer gave orders that the troops were to rest in preparation for an assault on 26 June—by which time Gibbon should have arrived.

By breakfast, however, Custer learned that the biggest encampment his scouts had ever seen was only 24 km (15 mls) to the northwest. Another report followed saying that the Indians seemed to be getting ready to move. It was too tempting for Custer to resist, and he began to issue orders for an attack before the Indians could get away.

His scouts warned that there were more Sioux and Cheyenne ahead than the 7th Cavalry had cartridges, but Custer reportedly just smiled, confident that his seasoned troopers could disperse a pack of savages, which he thought to be no more than 1,500 strong. He underestimated the Indians' true number by some 2,000, as he would have discovered had he undertaken a proper reconnaissance.

Custer adopted much the same plan as he had used previously on the Washita, dividing his command to attack from different angles. Three cavalry troops went with Major Marcus Reno, another three with Captain Frederick Benteen, while one, under Captain Thomas McDougall, stayed with the ammunition pack-train in the rear. Custer himself took five troops. Benteen was to move southwest toward the Little Big Horn River to 'pitch into anything he might find' and to cut off any escaping Indians; Reno was to attack the southern end of the encampment, and Custer would move north behind the cover of bluffs and come in on the camp from the opposite side.

Custer believed he would catch the Indians off balance as they rushed south to

Colonel Custer with his Indian scouts in front of a Northern Pacific railroad tent during the Yellowstone River Expedition of 1873. On his right is his favourite scout, Bloody Knife, of the Crow tribe. He was with Reno on the 25th and was one of the first to be killed.

Custer delighted in eccentric dress. As a major-general of U.S. Volunteers during the Civil War, he wore a black velvet uniform designed by himself. Later, as shown in the photograph, his habitual dress was a fringed buckskin jacket, blue trousers, red scarf and a dark, broad-brimmed hat. It was in this garb that he appeared at Little Big Horn. The Indians knew him as 'Long Hair' for his other affectation—his shoulder-length flaxen hair.

meet Reno's attack. The reverse happened. Crazy Horse knew that Custer was behind the bluffs, but his scouts had not reported Reno's movements.

From the top of a bluff, Custer looked down on a huge sea of tepees, where life was going on as normal; the Indians were not on the run at all. Realizing that he had detached Benteen unnecessarily, he turned to his bugler and told him to fetch the captain as fast as he could, together with the ammunition supplies.

As the trooper, an Italian immigrant with a poor grasp of English, was leaving, the adjutant scribbled a note and gave it to him. It read, 'Benteen: Come on. Big village. Be quick. Bring packs. W.W. Cooke. P.S. Bring pacs.' That hastily written note, with the mis-spelt postscript underlining its urgency, was the last that was heard of George Armstrong Custer and his 225 men.

At that moment, Major Reno was in sight of the Sioux lodges. His exhausted men and horses were in no condition to charge, so his troopers dismounted and began to pour carbine fire into the camp. The warriors reacted swiftly by sending out a strong party. The Major ordered a retreat to the shelter of trees along the west bank of the river and then made a dash for the protection of the bluffs across the Little Big Horn. It was a withdrawal in panic, and losses

began to mount when his command was caught in the open.

Not long afterwards, Captain Benteen and the remainder of the 7th Cavalry joined Reno. To their credit, they attempted to obey their commanding officer's last order, but they were confronted with an overwhelming force of Indians and had to fall back on their own defensive perimeter.

Riding down from the bluffs, it is likely that Custer and his troops found their way blocked by at least 1,500 war-painted Indians. As the exhausted troopers came under sustained and violent attack in the open, they turned to their right and tried to reach a hill at the north end of the bluffs, there to form a defensive ring and await reinforcements.

But Crazy Horse had planned otherwise. While the soldiers were desperately fighting their way up the hill, he led another 1,500 warriors on a fast, flanking ride up the west bank of the Little Big Horn, crossed it and swept down behind Custer, catching him in a lethal vice before he and his men could reach the summit.

It was probably all over in less than half an hour. The Indians lost about 40 men in the day's fighting; the only survivor in the U.S. cavalry was an officer's horse. After the battle, the Press and public hailed Custer as a hero; posterity has judged otherwise.

Crazy Horse was notoriously camera-shy, but this photograph (taken by S.J. Morrow) is generally thought to be a portrait of him. Renowned for his bravery and skill, Crazy Horse was revered by all the Oglala Sioux as their greatest leader. Certainly at Little Big Horn he showed an understanding of generalship unusual among the Indians.

Sitting Bull, perhaps the most famous of all the Indian chiefs, admitted that he did not take part in the fighting. He remained in his tepee 'making big medicine.'

To the Sioux, and later to the white man, Crazy Horse and Sitting Bull were names synonymous with Indian freedom and the determined resistance to white encroachment.

The significance of the Battle of the Little Big Horn is that it numbers among the handful of victories gained by indigenous warriors over the invading forces of Western states. But though the Indians triumphed in the battle, they had little hope of winning the war. The United States was roused to fury by the death of Custer. The forces ranged against Sitting Bull and Crazy Horse were strengthened and immediate and massive retribution was promised. In the ensuing Battles of Crazy Woman Fork and Wolf Mountain, the Sioux were no match for artillery and were scattered and isolated. Sitting Bull escaped with a few braves to Canada. Crazy Horse eventually surrendered and was confined at Fort Robertson, where, some weeks later, he was bayonetted 'trying to escape'. The greatest triumph of the Indians turned to tragedy, and the man whose foolish vanity had so contributed to their victory, George Armstrong Custer, became revered as a folk hero.

With their traditional weapons—tomahawks, clubs, scalping knives, bows and lances—the Indians were, surprisingly, better armed for hand-to-hand fighting than Custer's men, who, in order to move stealthily, had left their sabres behind. In their magazine-loading 1866 Winchesters, too, the Indians had a weapon far superior to the .45/70 1873 Springfield 'trapdoor' breech-loading carbines. These guns, one of which is being fired here by a U.S. Army trooper, were standard issue to the regular army until the 1890s.

The Springfield, named after the town in Connecticut where the State Armoury was operational from 1794 to 1966, had to be cleared and reloaded after every shot. It was much slower than the .44 Winchester repeating rifle, which could fire 13 rounds at a time.

Designed to be fired from the back of a horse, the Winchester was a very reliable weapon. Adopted by frontiersmen, it presaged the gun that 'won the West', although, ironically, it was also popular with the Indians, who secured it from traders. It is thought that as many as one in five braves may have had a Winchester at Little Big Horn.

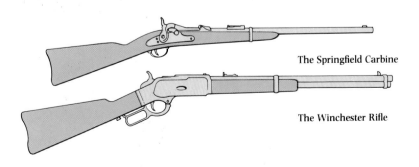

The Springfield Carbine

The Winchester Rifle

Omdurman/2 September, 1898

General Gordon, a devout Christian who had done much to suppress the slave trade in the Sudan, reached Khartoum in February 1884 to supervise British withdrawal. He quickly formed the opinion, however, that it would be infamous to abandon the Sudanese people to the Mahdi's ferocious Dervishes. Gordon called for reinforcements from London. Gladstone, reluctant to become involved in a colonial war, delayed. When he finally succumbed to mounting public indignation and sent a relief force, he was too late: it reached Khartoum two days after the town had been taken by the Mahdi and Gordon speared to death on the steps of the governor's palace. Gladstone was regarded by many of his countrymen as a murderer.

The Mahdi died soon after, but his successor, the Khalifa, was equally bloodthirsty and repeatedly sought conflict with the Anglo-Egyptian forces on the border between Egypt and the Sudan. In 1896, Lord Salisbury's Conservative government sanctioned the reconquest of the Sudan to avenge Gordon's death, to extinguish the slave traffic and to restore orderly government to the area.

General Sir Herbert Kitchener was given the task of quelling the Sudan, an inhospitable region of northeast Africa. A stern disciplinarian, Kitchener was Sirdar (Commander-in-Chief) of the British-trained and led Egyptian army, which contained several superb battalions recruited from the tall, black-skinned natives of southern Sudan—men who detested the Dervishes. Kitchener had little experience of commanding troops on active service, but he was a Royal Engineer with a flair for organization and administration, qualifications that were to stand him in good stead during the campaign.

To defeat the enemy would be straightforward; the problem was how best to reach them since they were concentrated deep in the desert. There were, in addition, the questions of how to keep the army adequately supplied in so distant a place, how to keep open extended lines of communication and how to evacuate casualties.

The River Nile provided some of the answers. Troops and *matériel* could be transported easily by steamer as far as the First Cataract at Wadi Halfa, some 800 km (500 mls) south of Cairo. From there, however, the river looped far to the west, away from the direct line of march to Khartoum in the heart of the Sudan.

Kitchener decided to build a railway. The proposal was at first dismissed as being impracticable, but his critics reckoned without the Sirdar's determination, and he had time on his side to undertake such a

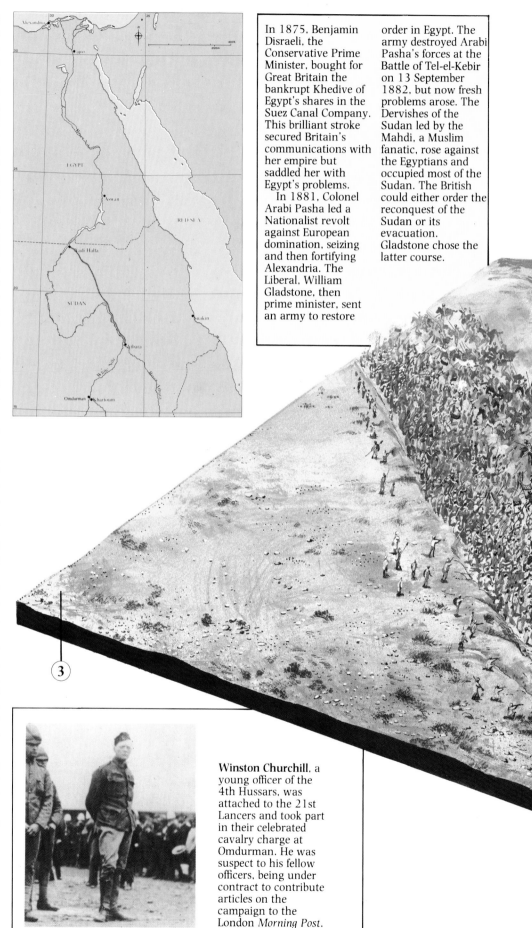

In 1875, Benjamin Disraeli, the Conservative Prime Minister, bought for Great Britain the bankrupt Khedive of Egypt's shares in the Suez Canal Company. This brilliant stroke secured Britain's communications with her empire but saddled her with Egypt's problems.

In 1881, Colonel Arabi Pasha led a Nationalist revolt against European domination, seizing and then fortifying Alexandria. The Liberal, William Gladstone, then prime minister, sent an army to restore order in Egypt. The army destroyed Arabi Pasha's forces at the Battle of Tel-el-Kebir on 13 September 1882, but now fresh problems arose. The Dervishes of the Sudan led by the Mahdi, a Muslim fanatic, rose against the Egyptians and occupied most of the Sudan. The British could either order the reconquest of Sudan or its evacuation. Gladstone chose the latter course.

Winston Churchill, a young officer of the 4th Hussars, was attached to the 21st Lancers and took part in their celebrated cavalry charge at Omdurman. He was suspect to his fellow officers, being under contract to contribute articles on the campaign to the London *Morning Post*.

Shortly before 9 am, on 2 September 1898, the 21st Lancers launched what was to prove the last charge by British cavalry. They attempted to cut off what was mistakenly thought to be a force of fewer than 1,000 retreating Dervishes. In fact, some 2,700 Dervishes lay hidden in a *khor* (a dry watercourse) about 410 m (450 yds) long, lying between Surgham Hill and the River Nile.

This composite Victorian painting depicts all the actions during the Battle of Omdurman as happening simultaneously. British troops are shown in ceremonial scarlet, while in reality they wore khaki uniforms, which had been introduced into the British army in India, in 1848.

The Dervishes, 12 ranks deep, 1, rose as one man when the lancers, 2, were a mere 91 m (100 yds) away.

The British cavalry, 2, although momentarily astonished, at once increased their pace and a fearful impact and mêlée ensued. Every man fought for himself, the Dervishes stabbing at horses and riders, even pressing their rifle muzzles into the lancers' bodies before firing; the British hacked at them without pity.

The impact of the British charge was such that it carried their squadrons through the Dervish lines, 3. They re-formed and, with many of those unhorsed quickly remounted, charged back again. This time the Dervish lines broke and fell into headlong flight.

vast and complex engineering project.

Built by teams of native labourers under French-Canadian railway expert, Edouard Girouard, the railway was pushed forward at the astonishing rate of 2 km ($1\frac{1}{4}$ mls) a day. By the end of 1897, the railhead terminated at the confluence of the Nile and Atbara rivers, and an assortment of locomotives and rolling stock was taking merely 36 hours to carry down men, horses and equipment from Wadi Halfa.

While the bulk of the Egyptian army, together with a British brigade, was pouring into Atbara, the Khalifa dispatched Emir Mahmoud and 16,000 warriors to harass the invaders. The Dervish leader remained with a huge army 322 km (200 mls) farther south at Omdurman, his headquarters across the Nile from Khartoum. He was acting on a dream, in which he had won a great victory at Omdurman.

At Atbara, Mahmoud pitched camp a few miles from the Anglo-Egyptian base, instead of making a frontal assault. The two forces watched each other for a time; then, on 8 April, Kitchener opened a brisk bombardment on the Dervishes, followed by an infantry attack. The Dervishes fled before the lowered bayonets, leaving thousands of dead and wounded as well as 4,000 prisoners—including Mahmoud himself.

His railhead secure, the Sirdar then built up three months' supplies, reinforced his command with more British troops and assembled gunboats to dominate the Nile between Atbara and Khartoum.

Only when he was thoroughly prepared did Kitchener permit his army to march on Omdurman. By 1 September, he had almost 25,000 men, a battery of Maxim machine-guns, 46 artillery pieces and 10 heavily-armed gunboats within sight of his goal.

That night his troops slept under arms between the river and a 3-km (2-ml) long barrier of thorn bushes, a *zereba*, which was strongly patrolled, for the cavalry had reported 50,000 Dervishes merely 8 km (5 mls) away behind a ridge.

Reveille sounded at 4.30 am, while it was still dark. First to move were squadrons of British and Egyptian horse, sent to probe the enemy position. Then, an hour later, in the grey half-light of dawn, the whole army stood to behind its thorny redoubt, facing west across the wide Kerreri plain in a semi-circle, its flanks resting on the Nile and protected by gunboats.

In another 20 minutes it was daylight, and word came back from the cavalry that the Dervishes were moving rapidly forward, strung out on an 8-km (5-ml) front.

As soon as the first howling phalanx came into view, Kitchener's artillery opened fire from 1,829 m (2,000 yds); then

British officers watching the preliminary movements of the Dervishes through field-glasses.

Lieutenant-Colonel Hector Macdonald (1853–1903), a crofter's son, was remarkable in Victorian England in that, through courage, ability and tenacity, he had risen from the ranks. Later, he was to be promoted major-general, knighted and appointed an aide-de-camp to Edward VII. Churchill attributed British success at Omdurman in high measure 'to the great military qualities of Macdonald.' The Press dubbed him 'Fighting Mac' after Omdurman, and he became renowned throughout the Empire.

General Sir Herbert Kitchener (1850–1916), at the time the youngest general in the British Army, was overbearing with his subordinates and sycophantic with his superiors, but he was loyal and reliable. He drove his men hard and himself harder. Although no military expert, he was an ideal choice to oversee the reconquest of the Sudan, since he was an engineer of great skill and a master of logistic detail—two attributes that were to prove crucial in this particular campaign.

A line of Maxim guns was stationed between British and Egyptian brigades prior to the Battle of Omdurman. These early machine-guns were fully automatic, unlike the earlier hand-cranked guns of the 1870s. The Dervishes, though unequalled in courage, had no defence against the Maxim's rapid fire.

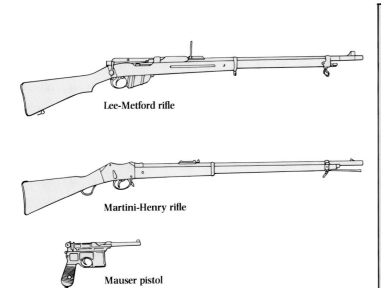

Lee-Metford rifle

Martini-Henry rifle

Mauser pistol

The Lee-Metford was the British army's first repeating rifle. Introduced in 1888, it was the most up-to-date infantry weapon of the time. It combined an American Lee bolt action and eight-slot box magazine with British Metford rifling in the barrel. A .303 calibre weapon, it was superseded by the Lee-Enfield rifle.

The Martini-Henry rifle, which had been used earlier in the Sudan, was a tough 0.45 calibre weapon still on general issue to some units in the British army. It weighed 3.9 kg (8.68 lbs) and was a single-shot, underlever breech-loader. The Dervishes had some 15,000 rifles, 2,000 being Martini-Henrys.

The Mauser pistol, the first model of which appeared in 1896, was quickly adopted by many European nations; it was modified and improved during the next two decades. A 0.33 calibre, self-loading weapon, it weighed 1.13 kg (40 oz) and carried 10 rounds.

In the inhospitable terrain around Omdurman, there were few natural features to be adapted for a defence position. The British were obliged to protect their camp with a *zereba*, a stout hedge formed by embedding the severed trunks of thorn bushes in the sand and packing them tightly together. Thorn bushes were plentiful in the desert and made a formidable, waist-high barrier. Within this compound, tents and a field hospital were established; sentries continually patrolled the perimeter.

the Maxims added their deadly fire, and finally the infantry's magazine-loading Lee-Metford rifles discharged a hail of dumdum bullets. These fragmented on impact, causing massive internal injuries. In 1901–2 they were banned at the orders of the Geneva Convention.

Although the Dervishes, armed with spears and a limited number of single-shot Remingtons and Martini-Henrys, displayed fanatical courage in pressing their attack, they could not withstand Kitchener's devastating fire. About 450 m (500 yds) in front of the *zereba*, their dead and wounded mounted steadily. By 8.30 am, they were defeated—or so it seemed to the Sirdar.

Anxious to occupy Omdurman, Kitchener sent the 21st Lancers to harry the enemy's disarrayed right flank and to cut them off from the town; then he marched on the Khalifa's headquarters. By taking this action, he almost turned victory into disaster.

The Lancers—among them a 23-year-old subaltern named Winston Spencer Churchill—trotted southwest to intercept large parties of Dervishes falling back on Omdurman. What happened next was described by Churchill in a dispatch to the London *Morning Post*.

'In the foreground about two hundred Dervishes were crouching in what appeared to be a small *khor* or crease in the plain. The duty of the cavalry to brush these away and proceed at once to the more numerous bodies in rear was plain. With a view to outflanking them the squadrons wheeled to the left into columns of troops, and, breaking into a trot, began to defile across their front. We thought them spearmen, for we were within three hundred yards and they had fired no shot. Suddenly, as the regiment began to trot, they opened a heavy, severe, and dangerous fire. Only one course was now possible. The trumpets sounded "right-wheel into line," and on the instant the regiment began to gallop in excellent order towards the riflemen. The distance was short, but before it was half covered it was evident that the riflemen were but a trifle compared to what lay behind. In a deep fold of the ground—completely concealed by its peculiar formation—a long, dense, white mass of men became visible. In length they were nearly equal to our front. They were about twelve deep. It was undoubtedly a complete surprise for us. What followed probably astonished them as much. I do not myself believe that they ever expected the cavalry to come on. The Lancers acknowledged the unexpected sight only by an increase of pace. A desire to have the necessary momentum to drive through so solid a line

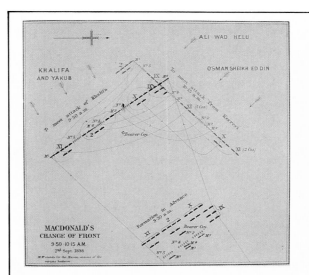

After the 2nd Sudanese Brigade had defeated the first Dervish attack, Macdonald turned his force to face the new Dervish threat, now coming from the Kerreri Hills. The Sudanese troops were so well disciplined that, despite being under fire, they executed this complicated manoeuvre to create an inverted L-shaped formation with parade-ground precision.

MACDONALD'S CHANGE OF FRONT 9·50–10·15 A.M. 2nd Sept. 1898

By 10.15 am, the second phase of the battle was being fought across about 5 sq km (2 sq mls) of the Kerreri plain. The Dervishes launched a two-pronged attack on the rearguard of Egyptian and Sudanese troops. But Dervish mistiming meant that their first force was defeated before the second advanced from the Kerreri Hills.

The first Dervish attack, **1**, led by the Khalifa, was cut down by deadly fire from Macdonald's 2nd Sudanese Brigade, **2**, some 3,450 Dervishes being killed. The fighting was at its fiercest around their Black Standard, **3**, which

they tried to keep flying, but with the loss of scores of men.

Two Dervish generals under a green standard, **10**, led some 20,000 men from behind the Kerreri Hills. When the Dervishes were about 450 m (500 yds) from the

British, their advance guard was 275 m (300 yds) ahead of them and already running out of ammunition. Many attacked the British with nothing more than their swords and spears.

The few mud-walled houses that constituted the village of El Egeiga provided a base around which the British camp was formed. Here, protected by a *zereba*, **9**, a field hospital was established.

Collinson's 4th Egyptian Brigade, **4**, was marching along the river bank when the Dervishes attacked Macdonald's rearguard formation. Collinson quickly moved across to shield Macdonald's right flank.

Broadwood's cavalry, **5**, had earlier drawn some of the Dervishes from the field, depleting their numbers and ammunition and delaying their second attack. This accomplished, the cavalry returned to their station between Collinson, **4**, and the Kerreri Hills. Macdonald, **2**, defeated Dervish attacks by changing the dispositions of his 2nd Sudanese Brigade, which was supported by the Camel Corps, **6**, at the end of the long leg of his newly formed L-shaped formation. The Sudanese, now facing the Kerreri Hills, fired frantically at the Dervishes, often without aiming. Scarcely any ammunition remained when they were ultimately relieved by the Lincoln Regiment.

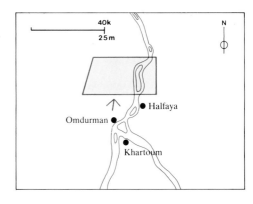

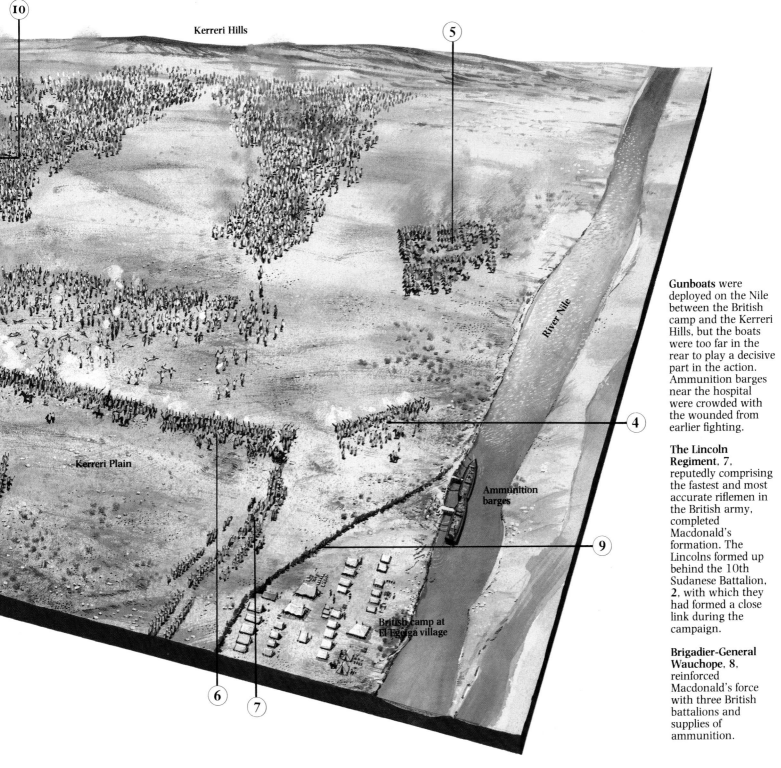

Kerreri Hills

River Nile

Kerreri Plain

Ammunition barges

British camp at El Egeiga village

Gunboats were deployed on the Nile between the British camp and the Kerreri Hills, but the boats were too far in the rear to play a decisive part in the action. Ammunition barges near the hospital were crowded with the wounded from earlier fighting.

The Lincoln Regiment, **7**, reputedly comprising the fastest and most accurate riflemen in the British army, completed Macdonald's formation. The Lincolns formed up behind the 10th Sudanese Battalion, **2**, with which they had formed a close link during the campaign.

Brigadier-General Wauchope, **8**, reinforced Macdonald's force with three British battalions and supplies of ammunition.

animated each man. But the whole affair was a matter of seconds.

'At full gallop and in the closest order the squadron struck the Dervish mass. The riflemen, who fired bravely to the last, were brushed head over heel in the *khor*. And with them the Lancers jumped actually on to the spears of the enemy, whose heads were scarcely level with the horses' knees.'

Churchill had just taken part in the last classic cavalry charge in the history of warfare. In exchange for 60 Dervishes killed and many wounded, the 21st Lancers lost 5 officers, 66 men and 119 horses in the two-minute action.

The Sirdar had meanwhile moved his army toward Omdurman without first ensuring that the Dervishes were indeed defeated. They were not, and he was now exposing his entire right flank and right rear to the enemy. His situation was vulnerable in the extreme.

It was fortunate for Kitchener that the first onslaught of fresh Dervish forces fell on his rearguard and on the 2nd Sudanese Brigade, stationed well behind the main body and commanded by Lieutenant-Colonel Hector Macdonald. 'Fighting Mac', as he was dubbed by the Press, had been commissioned from the ranks (a rare occurrence in the nineteenth century) and was renowned as a skilled, determined field officer. He quickly appraised the new danger and met it head-on with volleys of fire, which he personally directed. The Dervishes fell back in disarray.

While the Sirdar was trying to return his army to fighting formation, another force of 20,000 Dervishes bore down on Macdonald's battalions. Always a stickler for drill, he calmly manoeuvred his native infantry through a series of intricate movements to meet and repel attacks delivered from the north, west and south. When the Lincolnshire Regiment finally relieved 'Fighting Mac', it was found that many of his soldiers were out of ammunition and others had only two rounds apiece.

There is no doubt that Macdonald's skill and bravery saved Kitchener's unprepared army from an orgy of close-quarter combat, in which casualties would have been heavy and defeat not impossible.

Now the Dervishes were thoroughly beaten. Having survived a close brush with disaster, Kitchener turned to his staff before resuming the march on Omdurman and Khartoum and remarked, 'I think we have given them a good dusting, gentlemen.'

Indeed they had. The London *Daily Mail* called it 'more an execution than a battle.' The Anglo-Egyptian army sustained fewer than 500 casualties; the Dervishes lost 11,000 dead and many more wounded.

THE *SULTAN*

The Mahdi, who had died in mysterious circumstances shortly after the murder of General Gordon, was buried in a great tomb in Omdurman, *top*. This was severely damaged by British artillery.

Kitchener's river fleet, *centre*, consisted of ten steamers of recent construction, armed with artillery and machine-guns, and five lightly armed transport steamers. Each steamer was commanded by a

Royal Navy officer and carried a platoon of infantry.
After the occupation of Omdurman, Sudanese civilians looted all the buildings outside the great perimeter wall, carrying away their

spoil on their backs, in carts or on camels, *below*, Churchill wrote: 'The whole place was picked clean, and nothing escaped the vigilant eye of the Sudanese plunderer.'

After the battle, Sudanese troops made haste to loot the bodies of the dead. Many of those still living were first killed to facilitate the process. To their discredit, some British soldiers joined them in their dreadful work. In all, 11,000 Dervish corpses littered the field, with the wounded estimated at between 10,000 and 16,000.

Four Victoria Crosses were awarded for conspicuous bravery. Captain P.A. Kenna of the 21st Lancers, though under intense fire, tried to rescue a comrade, Lieutenant Grenfell, who had been unhorsed and surrounded by Dervishes. Kenna hacked his way to Grenfell's side, only to find him dead, but he brought his body back to regimental lines.

British victory at Omdurman restored her honour in the Sudan, tamed the bloodthirsty Dervishes and quickly led to the return of orderly government. Less than a week after the battle, however, news reached Khartoum that a small force of French and West African soldiers, under the command of a Major Marchand, were at Fashoda, a fort on the Upper Nile.

Their intention was to secure for France a strategic centre astride the Nile, between the Congo and Abyssinia. In this they were frustrated, for Kitchener, who went himself to Fashoda, had at his command an immeasurably stronger force. The French withdrew on 11 December 1898, but for a few weeks the so-called Fashoda Crisis, led, in both London and Paris, to alarmed speculation of impending hostilities.

This incident was the last of many clashes of interest between the two countries in Africa. Thereafter, under the growing threat of German industrial and military might, differences between them were amicably resolved. In 1904, the *Entente Cordiale* was signed, which included an agreement whereby France recognized Great Britain's interests in Egypt, in return for Great Britain's recognizing France's dominance in Morocco.

Trooper Byrne, a lancer, saw a wounded officer surrounded by Dervishes and heard him call for help. Although himself wounded by a bullet in the right arm, Byrne galloped without hesitation to the officer's aid and, despite being further wounded by a spear in his chest, rescued him. Then, his daring and heroic mission accomplished, Byrne returned to his station of duty, where he remained until, weak from loss of blood, he fainted.

Colenso/15 December, 1899

In December 1899, Great Britain was dismayed by the news from South Africa, where war with the Boers had broken out in the previous October. Was it possible that lightly armed civilians had defeated British regulars, not once, but three times, in the space of six days?

The triple disaster that befell the corps sent to relieve garrisons besieged in Kimberley, Mafeking and Ladysmith, was dubbed by the English Press 'Black Week'. Had the relief columns succeeded, Queen Victoria's suzerainty would have been imposed on the Boers in the Transvaal and the Orange Free State and peace probably quickly restored. As it was, a prolonged struggle was now inevitable.

Command of the British expeditionary force was entrusted to General Sir Redvers Buller V.C., a hero of the Zulu War, who arrived in Cape Town on 31 October. He opened a disastrous campaign by dividing his corps into three unequal columns and sending them in different directions across the empty wastes of the veld. Humiliation lay in wait for his smart, khaki-clad ranks at the hands of Boer Commandos—bands of stern, Bible-reading descendants of Dutch settlers, whose only common equipment was a Mauser rifle.

General Sir William Gatacre, who had taken 3,000 men to beat off enemy raids into the British Cape Colony, was the first to suffer defeat. In an encounter at Stormberg, on 10 December, he lost 600 soldiers and two guns; 15,000 soldiers, charged with raising the sieges of Kimberley and Mafeking, were trounced at Magersfontein. Their casualties numbered 948.

But the nadir of Black Week was reached by Sir Redvers himself, leading five brigades and 44 guns to relieve Ladysmith. The events that unfolded before the little town of Colenso in Natal were caused by indecision and ineptitude, relieved only by displays of high courage.

Buller's inconsistency was first revealed on 8 December, when he made it clear that he had no intention of forcing a crossing of the deep, fast-flowing Tugela River at Colenso, 24 km (15 mls) south of beleaguered Ladysmith. Believing that the heights beyond the river were too heavily guarded, he told the British government: 'I feel I cannot force the Boer defences between here and Ladysmith and must turn them. To do this I have to march 50 miles.'

This flanking movement was under way on 12 December, when the Commander-in-Chief inexplicably changed his mind and ordered the column to cross the Tugela at Colenso. Apparently, none of the officers commented on such an extraordinary *volte face*, but many must have wondered why

The Boer states of the Transvaal and the Orange Free State, recognized as independent states by the Treaty of Pretoria (1881), were badly governed but resisted British interference in their internal affairs. Matters were complicated by the discovery of gold in the Witwatersrand in 1886, when non-Boers streamed into the area around Johannesburg and were bitterly resented by the original settlers. By 1899, the Boers had become suspicious that a British force was being prepared to attack them. The Orange Free State then aligned itself with the Transvaal and Boer forces invaded Cape Colony and Natal, besieging the three important frontier towns of Mafeking, Kimberley and Ladysmith.

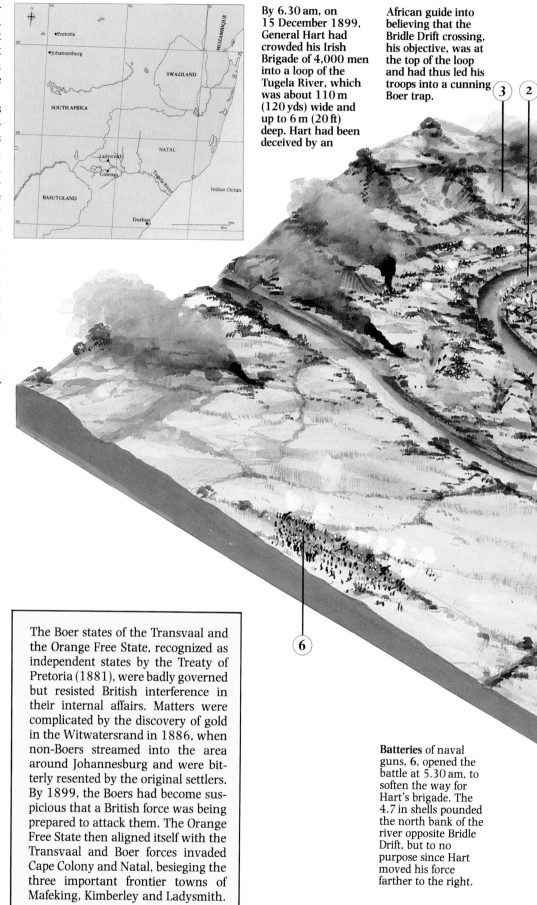

By 6.30 am, on 15 December 1899, General Hart had crowded his Irish Brigade of 4,000 men into a loop of the Tugela River, which was about 110 m (120 yds) wide and up to 6 m (20 ft) deep. Hart had been deceived by an African guide into believing that the Bridle Drift crossing, his objective, was at the top of the loop and had thus led his troops into a cunning Boer trap.

Batteries of naval guns, 6, opened the battle at 5.30 am, to soften the way for Hart's brigade. The 4.7 in shells pounded the north bank of the river opposite Bridle Drift, but to no purpose since Hart moved his force farther to the right.

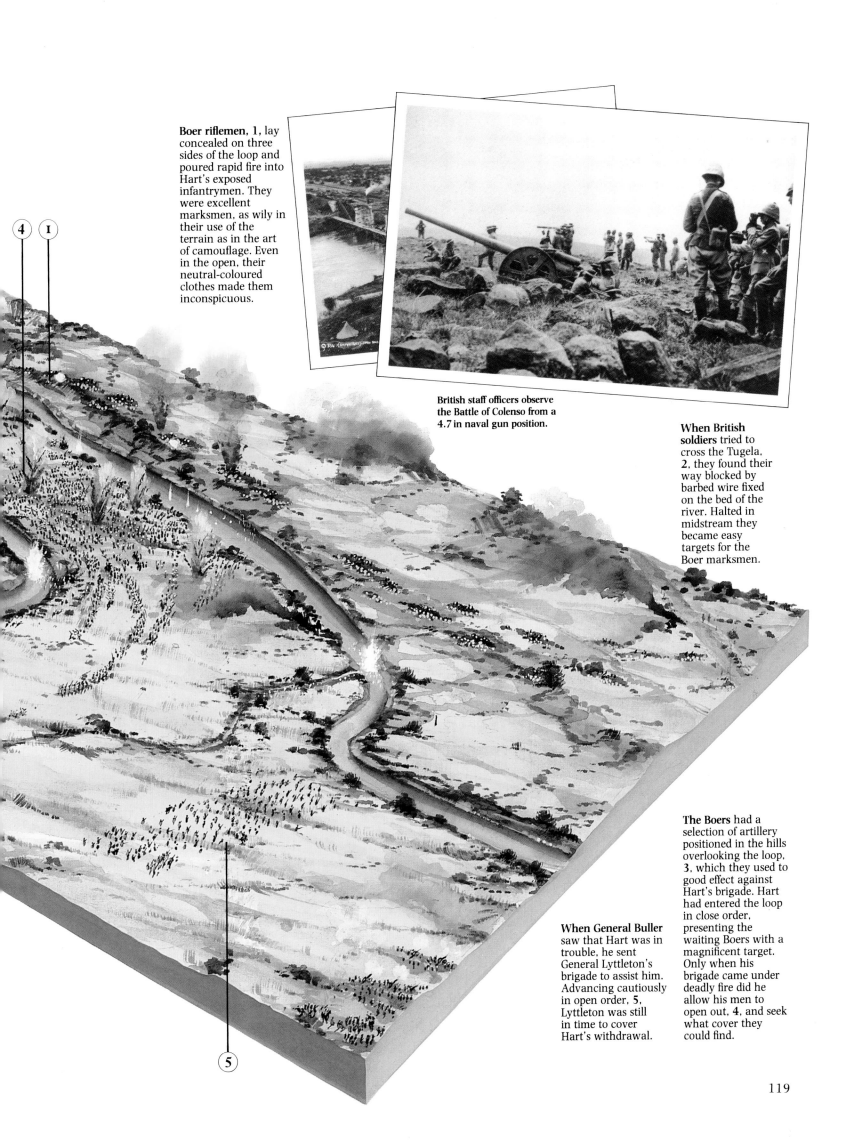

Boer riflemen, **1**, lay concealed on three sides of the loop and poured rapid fire into Hart's exposed infantrymen. They were excellent marksmen, as wily in their use of the terrain as in the art of camouflage. Even in the open, their neutral-coloured clothes made them inconspicuous.

British staff officers observe the Battle of Colenso from a 4.7 in naval gun position.

When British soldiers tried to cross the Tugela, **2**, they found their way blocked by barbed wire fixed on the bed of the river. Halted in midstream they became easy targets for the Boer marksmen.

The Boers had a selection of artillery positioned in the hills overlooking the loop, **3**, which they used to good effect against Hart's brigade. Hart had entered the loop in close order, presenting the waiting Boers with a magnificent target. Only when his brigade came under deadly fire did he allow his men to open out, **4**, and seek what cover they could find.

When General Buller saw that Hart was in trouble, he sent General Lyttleton's brigade to assist him. Advancing cautiously in open order, **5**, Lyttleton was still in time to cover Hart's withdrawal.

their general had made this contradictory and potentially dangerous decision.

Buller sent a signal to General Sir George White, commanding the garrison besieged in Ladysmith, indicating that he was advancing on Colenso and would probably attack on 17 December. White was to cooperate by mounting a simultaneous assault on his besiegers. On 14 December, however, the mercurial Buller issued orders for a dawn operation against Colenso next day. He omitted to tell White that he had advanced his plans by 48 hours.

It was Buller's intention that General Henry Hildyard's 2nd Brigade should push across the railway bridge over the river north of Colenso; General Fitzroy Hart and his 5th Brigade were to ford the Tugela at Bridle Drift, 4 km (2½ mls) west of the town, while Colonel the Earl of Dundonald was to take his Cavalry Brigade and demonstrate in the direction of Hlangwane hill, which rose steeply on the right flank—the only enemy position south of the river, which should have told Buller how important the Boer general, Louis Botha, considered it to be. General Neville Lyttleton's 4th Brigade lay in reserve behind and between the 5th and 2nd Brigades, while General Geoffrey Barton's 6th Brigade played a similar role to the rear of the 2nd and Cavalry Brigades.

As British batteries of heavy naval guns, manned by bluejackets, began to shell the north bank of the Tugela, Hart ordered forward his brigade, which was made up almost exclusively of Irish regiments. Although his map showed the best ford, Bridle Drift, farther west, the General took the word of an African guide that it was at the apex of a huge northward loop in the river. Disregarding an urgent warning from a cavalry patrol that it could see the Boers lying in wait, Hart urged on his battalions, which advanced in close order—the very worst formation under the prevailing conditions. At about 6.30 am, when the dense mass of khaki was inside the salient, the guide vanished—and the enemy opened fire from three sides with some 2,000 Mausers, a Maxim and assorted field guns.

Notwithstanding the devastating fire, five attempts were made to cross to the far bank. Each time, however, the Irishmen penetrated only as far as barbed wire entanglements anchored to the river bed by the Boers, where, immobilized, they were shot to pieces.

Buller, who had been watching the débâcle on his left to the exclusion of all else, told General Lyttleton, 'Hart has got himself into a devil of a mess down there; get him out of it as best you can.' But by the time 4th Brigade—sensibly advancing in extended line—came within range of the

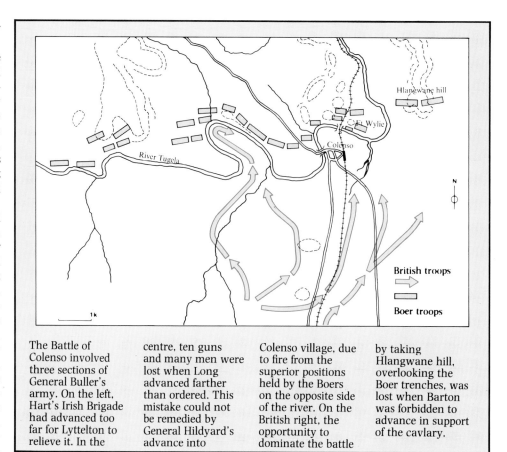

The Battle of Colenso involved three sections of General Buller's army. On the left, Hart's Irish Brigade had advanced too far for Lyttelton to relieve it. In the centre, ten guns and many men were lost when Long advanced farther than ordered. This mistake could not be remedied by General Hildyard's advance into Colenso village, due to fire from the superior positions held by the Boers on the opposite side of the river. On the British right, the opportunity to dominate the battle by taking Hlangwane hill, overlooking the Boer trenches, was lost when Barton was forbidden to advance in support of the cavalry.

General Sir Redvers Buller V.C. (1839–1908), who was given command of the British forces in South Africa when the Boer War broke out on 11 October 1899, was 60 years old and had much battlefield experience—but not as a planner. Commissioned in the King's Royal Rifle Corps in 1857, he had seen active service in Canada, South Africa, Egypt and the Sudan. Always popular with his troops, Buller looked after their welfare and, during the Boer War, established Field Force canteens to relieve the hardness and monotony of prolonged campaigning on the veld.

General Louis Botha (1862–1919) led the Boer Commandos who blocked Buller's path at Colenso. Aged 37, this was the first battle in which he was in command. Botha, a successful farmer, was a natural leader, though sensitive and unable to take criticism. He made a good soldier but had been reluctant to fight and, as a member of the Boer parliament, had abstained when the vote was taken on going to war with Great Britain.

Mauser rifle

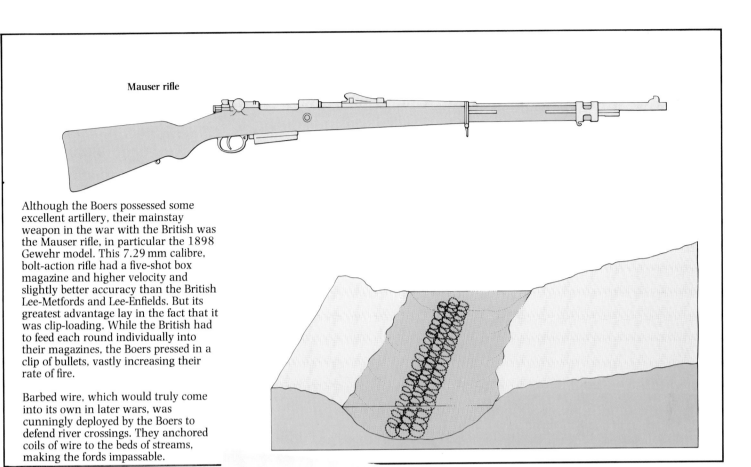

Although the Boers possessed some excellent artillery, their mainstay weapon in the war with the British was the Mauser rifle, in particular the 1898 Gewehr model. This 7.29 mm calibre, bolt-action rifle had a five-shot box magazine and higher velocity and slightly better accuracy than the British Lee-Metfords and Lee-Enfields. But its greatest advantage lay in the fact that it was clip-loading. While the British had to feed each round individually into their magazines, the Boers pressed in a clip of bullets, vastly increasing their rate of fire.

Barbed wire, which would truly come into its own in later wars, was cunningly deployed by the Boers to defend river crossings. They anchored coils of wire to the beds of streams, making the fords impassable.

A contemporary view of Colenso village, showing the open veld across which General Hildyard's brigade advanced, on the morning of 15 December 1899.

A Boer 75 mm Creusot gun position in the hills which dominated Colenso and the Tugela River. To the right of the photograph is the start of the loop in the river, in which General Hart's Irish Brigade was trapped by the Boers.

Boers, they were met by Hart's battalions retiring from the trap in which 553 men had been caught.

Meanwhile, without the knowledge of the Commander-in-Chief, another calamity was taking place on the right centre. Hildyard's attack on the Colenso railway bridge was to have been supported by artillery, commanded by Colonel C. J. Long. Although Long was supposed to advance to within only some 2,290 m (2,500 yds) of the Boers, under the protection of an infantry escort from Barton's reserve brigade, he led two horse-drawn batteries of Royal Field Artillery—the 14th and 66th—at a smart trot toward the enemy. Unmindful of Barton's repeated requests to halt, the Colonel pressed on, drawing farther away from his infantry cover and another battery of naval guns, pulled by slow-moving oxen.

Everything was quiet when, just before 6.30 am, Long sited his guns with parade-ground precision in the open, a mere 550 m (600 yds) from the Tugela. But before the batteries could come into action, a Boer gunner loosed off a single round, upon which the whole of Botha's left and centre immediately erupted. Long later claimed that he had misjudged the distance and was closer to the enemy than intended.

In this vulnerable position 1.6 km (1 ml) in front of their lines, the Royal Artillerymen calmly served their guns, while bullets and shrapnel sprayed all around them. Men and horses fell, but the survivors kept firing until about 7 am, when their ammunition was almost exhausted. The wounded, including Long, who was grievously hurt, were taken into the shelter of a donga (a dried-up watercourse) about 365 m (400 yds) in the rear of the gun positions, and it was there that the remaining able-bodied men were ordered to take cover while more shells were sent for. Unfortunately, the ammunition train was more than 4.8 km (3 mls) back across the veld and moving slowly. To the front, 12 guns, surrounded by dead gunners, stood idle but intact. When a wounded officer suggested leaving them and getting back to safety, Long roused himself to utter vehemently 'Abandon be damned! We never abandon guns.'

That was Buller's reaction also, when a shocked captain galloped up to break the news of the Colonel's self-induced disaster. In an unwise move for a commanding general, Sir Redvers took himself and his staff into the thick of the firing to direct operations from the donga. He called for volunteers to retrieve the guns: three officers and seven men at once dashed out into the teeth of intense Boer musketry. Among them was Lieutenant Frederick Roberts, a

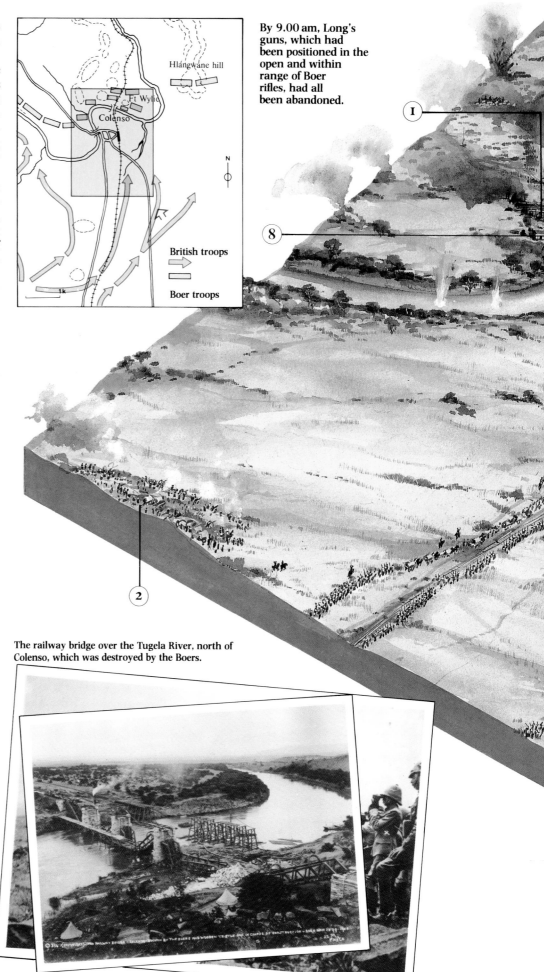

Hlángwane hill

Ft Wylie

Colenso

British troops →

Boer troops

By 9.00 am, Long's guns, which had been positioned in the open and within range of Boer rifles, had all been abandoned.

The railway bridge over the Tugela River, north of Colenso, which was destroyed by the Boers.

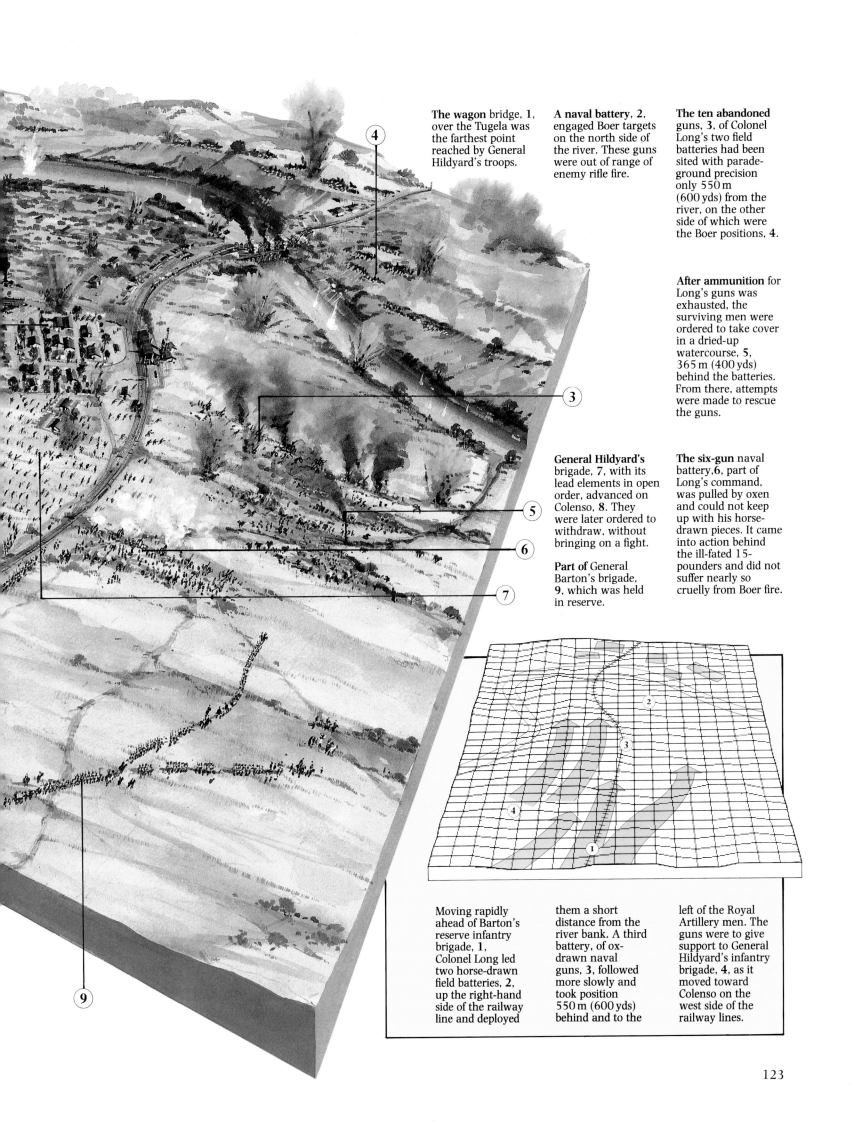

The wagon bridge, **1**, over the Tugela was the farthest point reached by General Hildyard's troops.

A naval battery, **2**, engaged Boer targets on the north side of the river. These guns were out of range of enemy rifle fire.

The ten abandoned guns, **3**, of Colonel Long's two field batteries had been sited with parade-ground precision only 550 m (600 yds) from the river, on the other side of which were the Boer positions, **4**.

After ammunition for Long's guns was exhausted, the surviving men were ordered to take cover in a dried-up watercourse, **5**, 365 m (400 yds) behind the batteries. From there, attempts were made to rescue the guns.

General Hildyard's brigade, **7**, with its lead elements in open order, advanced on Colenso, **8**. They were later ordered to withdraw, without bringing on a fight.

Part of General Barton's brigade, **9**, which was held in reserve.

The six-gun naval battery, **6**, part of Long's command, was pulled by oxen and could not keep up with his horse-drawn pieces. It came into action behind the ill-fated 15-pounders and did not suffer nearly so cruelly from Boer fire.

Moving rapidly ahead of Barton's reserve infantry brigade, **1**, Colonel Long led two horse-drawn field batteries, **2**, up the right-hand side of the railway line and deployed them a short distance from the river bank. A third battery, of ox-drawn naval guns, **3**, followed more slowly and took position 550 m (600 yds) behind and to the left of the Royal Artillery men. The guns were to give support to General Hildyard's infantry brigade, **4**, as it moved toward Colenso on the west side of the railway lines.

staff officer and only son of Great Britain's most famous living soldier at that time, Field Marshal Lord Roberts of Khandahar.

Miraculously, two guns were brought back, though not without sacrifice. A later attempt by another party failed in the face of withering fire. In all, four Victoria Crosses were earned in that rash but gallant incident, one posthumously by Lieutenant Roberts, who died of his wounds on 16 December. Eighteen Distinguished Conduct Medals were also awarded.

Buller, who was slightly wounded by shrapnel, appeared to be unnerved by the episode of Long's batteries, coming on top of Hart's disaster. By mid-morning he had changed his mind and decided to leave the guns and call off the action, even though half of his force had not yet fired a shot.

Barton, in reserve, was forbidden to reinforce Lord Dundonald at Hlangwane hill which, if taken, would have allowed the British to dominate the Boer trenches on the north bank of the Tugela. Buller apparently failed to appreciate the significance of these heights. Even Hildyard's brigade, which had made good progress in the centre and was actually in Colenso, was ordered to retire.

Buller, the Commander-in-Chief in South Africa, had lost 1,127 out of his 20,000-strong column, including 143 men killed and 240 missing, presumed captured; the remainder had been wounded, many seriously so. He also lost 10 of his 44 guns. General Botha reported only 40 casualties among his 8,000 defenders and claimed 'a brilliant victory'.

To add to his catalogue of misjudgements, Sir Redvers signalled Sir George White in Ladysmith, telling him of the defeat and suggesting that he fire off his ammunition and seek the best terms he could; Sir George ignored him.

Buller's repulsed army marched back to Frere, 11 km (7 mls) distant and the nearest place with a reliable water supply. Unaccountably, the Boers made no attempt to harass their withdrawal. At Frere, military life returned to normal, with drill and regimental parades, cricket for the men and steeple-chasing for the officers. Buller, too, regained his nerve and started to plan a flanking attack to relieve Ladysmith, but the Battle of Colenso, following so close on the defeats at Stormberg and Magersfontein, left the British government and people aghast. Buller, named 'Sir Reverse' by the Press, was not only held in high regard but was also looked upon with great affection by his troops, but he could not be retained in his command. He was replaced by Lord Roberts, whose son had died as a result of trying to save Long's guns.

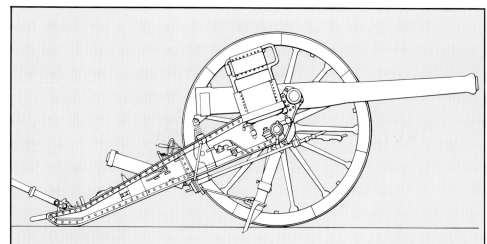

During the Boer War British field artillery batteries were equipped with the 15-pounder, breech-loading gun, which fired a 6.4 kg (14 lb) shell a maximum of 5.6 km (3½ mls). A quick-firing piece, of German design and manufacture, the 15-pounder was the first gun used by the British Army to have a full-recoil carriage. This meant that after each discharge, the gun crew did not have to manhandle it back into its firing position. Ten of these weapons were lost when Colonel Long's batteries got into difficulties at the Battle of Colenso.

Each gun in a British 15-pounder field battery, together with its limber carrying 44 rounds of ammunition, was provided with a crew of nine men and a complement of ten horses, six to pull the equipment and four to be ridden. When the Boers captured Colonel Long's ten 15-pounders, they loaded them on to railway wagons and shipped them to Pretoria, where they were put on display as war trophies.

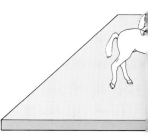

By the end of 'Black Week', Buller, an indecisive general, had been roundly beaten. The Boer War proved, as the Battle of Saratoga had before and that of Dien Bien Phu would later, that European armies using traditional tactics in a foreign terrain were at a great disadvantage when confronted by guerrillas. The British needed to adapt, but Buller was an unimaginative commander and was to suffer other defeats in Natal after being superseded as Commander-in-Chief by Field Marshal Lord Roberts, whose Chief of Staff was Lord Kitchener. Roberts at once instituted a thorough reorganization of the British forces. He knew that the Boers were more mobile than the British and that, to compensate for this, columns of mounted infantry must be formed. Ultimately, it required the whole might of the British Empire to defeat the Boers, whose military strength at no time exceeded 83,000 men and who never fielded an army of more than 40,000. British troops, on the other hand, while numbering merely 25,000 men in 1899, were increased by Imperial reinforcements over the next two years to a total strength of 500,000. The British were magnanimous in victory, and reconciliation quickly followed, so that within a few years eager South African volunteers were fighting alongside their late enemies in the two World Wars.

British troops watching the battle around Colenso from a naval 12-pounder gun position. A large portion of Buller's force was never called upon to fire a shot that day.

A Boer Commando in action. These men went to war in their everyday clothes. Their only uniform items were Mauser rifles and leather bandoliers containing their ammunition.

Port Arthur/*19 August, 1904-2 January, 1905*

In 1904, Imperial Japan embarked on the reconquest of Manchuria. Ten years previously she had taken this vast area of mainland China as part of her spoils in the Sino-Japanese War, but the combined might of France, Germany and Russia had obliged her to abandon the area.

It was thus for prestige as much as power that the Japanese wanted to reconquer Manchuria, especially Port Arthur, a deep-water harbour at the southern tip of the Liaotung Peninsula. In a lightning attack on the Russian fleet there, on 8 February 1904, the Japanese precipitated, without warning, what became known as the Russo-Japanese War. Both sides hurried huge concentrations of well-armed troops to the contested region.

The recapture of Port Arthur was assigned to General Maresuke Nogi, who landed 43 km (27 mls) north of his target, on 1 June, to take command of the Third Army, comprising about 90,000 men. His advance south, however, was slow. General Stoessel, with some 30,000 Russian troops, delayed Nogi for two months to give the engineers and the 20,000-strong garrison time to improve the town's defences. When Stoessel was finally compelled to withdraw into the town, on 30 July, he found that his sappers had done a commendable job in such a short period. The whole area bristled with gun emplacements, earthworks and trenches.

Between 19 August and 26 November, Nogi treated his disciplined infantry as cannon fodder in three separate and prolonged major frontal assaults on the Russian defences. All of them were beaten back with heavy losses. Even night attacks resulted in dreadful casualties, for the Russians made skilful use of powerful searchlight batteries to illuminate storming parties for the waiting gunners.

As the fighting progressed, all the machinery of modern war was pressed into action around Port Arthur. There were massive 11-in howitzers, capable of hurling 227-kg (500-lb) shells over 8 km (5 mls); quick-firing field artillery; Maxim machine-guns; magazine rifles; barbed wire entanglements and, above all, there were hand-grenades.

When the third big attack failed, on 26 November, leaving 10,000 Japanese dead and wounded in 15 hours of fighting on the last day alone, Nogi reluctantly accepted that Port Arthur would not fall to massed frontal assaults, no matter how bravely and recklessly they were pressed.

Under mounting pressure from Tokyo to destroy the remaining Russian battleships in the harbour before they could be joined by the enemy's Baltic Fleet, now steaming

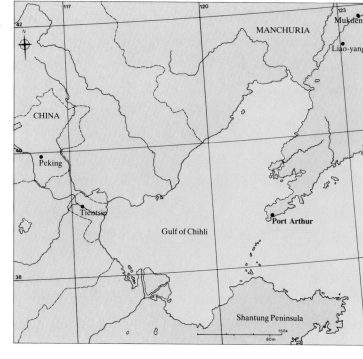

The scene at first light, on 6 December 1904, when Japanese infantry finally cleared the exhausted Russian troops, now reduced to a skeleton force, from the summit of 203 Metre Hill. Once taken, the Japanese had an observation post, from which artillerymen could direct accurate fire into Port Arthur and the fleet anchored in the harbour.

Japan developed into an industrialized nation in the late 19th century and swiftly sought to extend her political influence over mainland Asia, especially Korea and Manchuria. This inevitably brought her into conflict with Russia, which had incorporated these areas into her sphere of influence during the recent disintegration of the Chinese Empire. By 1904, Japan felt sufficiently strong to risk war with Russia to secure these areas. Victory on land depended, however, on command of the seas, which in turn required control of Port Arthur. This was Russia's sole year-round ice-free harbour on the Pacific seaboard and it provided an anchorage for her eastern fleet.

The risks Japan was about to take were enormous but the allure of the prize was irresistible.

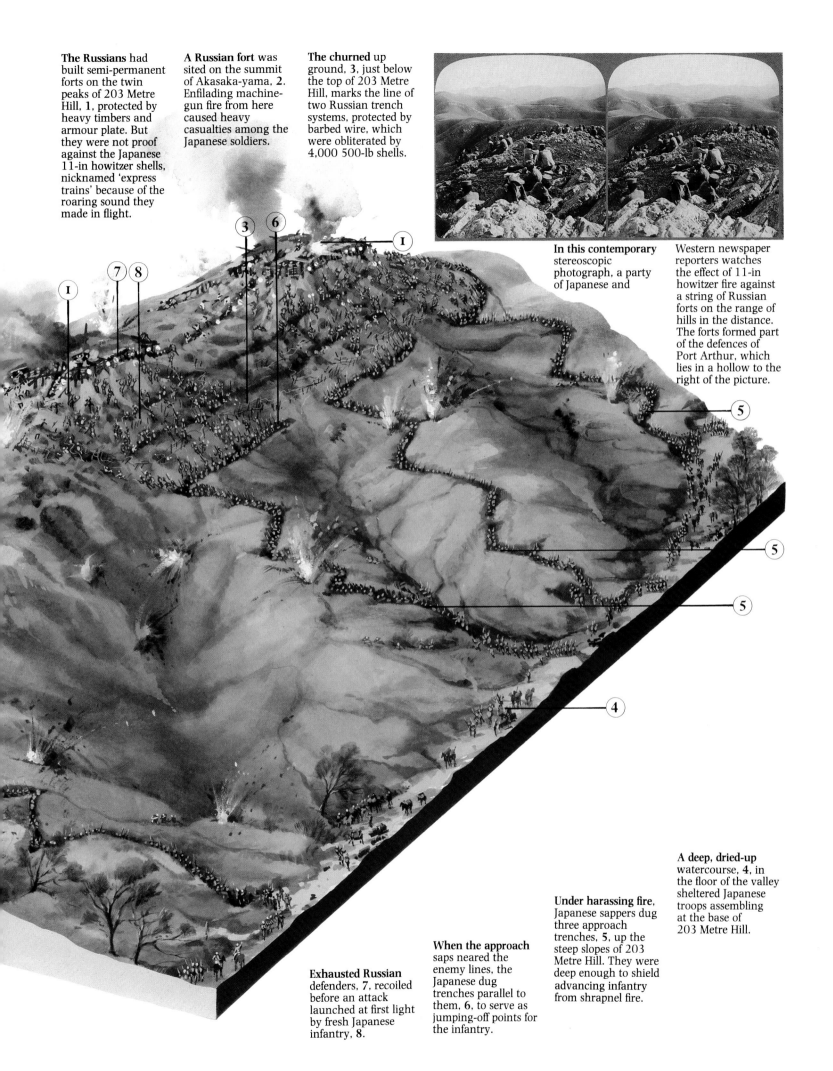

The Russians had built semi-permanent forts on the twin peaks of 203 Metre Hill, **1**, protected by heavy timbers and armour plate. But they were not proof against the Japanese 11-in howitzer shells, nicknamed 'express trains' because of the roaring sound they made in flight.

A Russian fort was sited on the summit of Akasaka-yama, **2**. Enfilading machine-gun fire from here caused heavy casualties among the Japanese soldiers.

The churned up ground, **3**, just below the top of 203 Metre Hill, marks the line of two Russian trench systems, protected by barbed wire, which were obliterated by 4,000 500-lb shells.

In this contemporary stereoscopic photograph, a party of Japanese and Western newspaper reporters watches the effect of 11-in howitzer fire against a string of Russian forts on the range of hills in the distance. The forts formed part of the defences of Port Arthur, which lies in a hollow to the right of the picture.

A deep, dried-up watercourse, **4**, in the floor of the valley sheltered Japanese troops assembling at the base of 203 Metre Hill.

Under harassing fire, Japanese sappers dug three approach trenches, **5**, up the steep slopes of 203 Metre Hill. They were deep enough to shield advancing infantry from shrapnel fire.

When the approach saps neared the enemy lines, the Japanese dug trenches parallel to them, **6**, to serve as jumping-off points for the infantry.

Exhausted Russian defenders, **7**, recoiled before an attack launched at first light by fresh Japanese infantry, **8**.

from the other side of the world to reinforce them, General Nogi turned his attention to 203 Metre Hill.

None of the Japanese positions afforded unobstructed observation of the harbour or large parts of the town, so the fire of their big guns could not accurately be directed on to the warships or other important targets. The best vantage point from which to achieve artillery domination was the summit of 203 Metre Hill, 4.8 km (3 mls) north of the port and part of the Russian outer defence system. Both it and Akasaka-yama, a lower hill branching off it to the northeast, had earth, timber and steel-plated fortifications on their crowns, while two lines of trenches, protected by barbed wire, extended across the front and around the flanks of their forward slopes. These were insubstantial defences for what the Japanese had correctly identified as the key to the enemy position.

Nogi's engineers had dug saps, or siege-trenches, up the steep hillside almost as far as the Russian front line, in order to protect their infantry's approach. But the soldiers knew that once they left the saps they would be exposed to violent resistance, mainly from high explosive. The assault on 203 Metre Hill began in the evening of 27 November and continued unabated, and with varying degrees of ferocity, until 6 December. Hand-grenades, rather than bullets and bayonets, featured in countless attacks and counter-attacks on the upper slopes. The Japanese at first poured paraffin into enemy strongpoints and set light to them; then their heavy artillery ranged in and pulverized the entire Russian trench system with some 4,000 11-in howitzer shells. Still the defenders clung to the summit and doggedly resisted the attack.

Diversionary attacks around the Port Arthur perimeter prevented the dwindling defenders of 203 Metre Hill from being relieved. They had lost 4,000 men and were on the point of exhaustion when fresh Japanese troops finally drove them off the summit in the early hours of 6 December. The operation cost Nogi more than 8,000 soldiers, but he now had the artillery observation post he so badly needed. His heavy guns immediately opened a three-day bombardment of Port Arthur, during which the Russian battle-ships were sunk and much damage was done to the town and its fortifications.

General Stoessel finally decided—more on humanitarian than military grounds—to surrender, on 2 January 1905. It had been a long and particularly bloody fight, in which the defenders suffered some 30,000 casualties; the attackers almost 60,000.

A stereoscopic photograph of a Japanese 11-in siege howitzer shelling Port Arthur

Two Russian warships, destroyed by Japanese artillery

A Japanese cookhouse, close to the front at Port Arthur

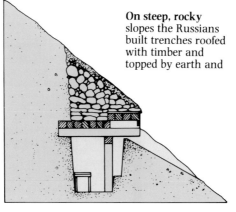

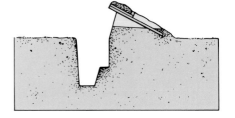

On steep, rocky slopes the Russians built trenches roofed with timber and topped by earth and boulders. They were 2 m (6½ ft) high and 1.8 m (6 ft) wide and had loopholes. More often, a trench 1.5 m (5 ft) deep, with a firing step protected by a parapet, was dug out where the soil was soft.

General Stoessel (1848–1915), the senior Russian officer at Port Arthur, suppressed signals ordering him to relinquish his command and leave by sea. After he surrendered, he was court-martialled, found guilty of unjustified capitulation and sentenced to death. The sentence was reduced to life imprisonment, but Stoessel was soon freed, although he was disgraced.

The fall of Port Arthur, together with the Japanese naval victory at Tsushima in May 1905, forced the Russian government to sue for peace. The United States mediated and, under the terms of the Treaty of Portsmouth, New Hampshire, Japan's role as the dominant power in east Asia was confirmed. Russia was compelled to surrender Port Arthur and half of the island of Sakhalin; Manchuria was to be evacuated, and Korea henceforth considered as part of Japan's sphere of influence. Russia, the sole country that could prevent Japan's encroachment on the resources of China, was thus excluded from the eastern mainland of Asia. During the next three decades, Japan attempted the outright conquest of China; then, in 1941, she tried her strength against the industrial and military might of the United States of America.

General Maresuke Nogi (1849–1912), was the commander of the Japanese forces besieging Port Arthur. It was only the Emperor's intervention that prevented Nogi from committing hara-kiri, after his last surviving son was killed while he was leading an attack on 203 Metre Hill.

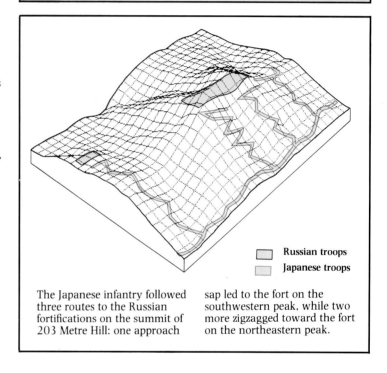

Russian troops

Japanese troops

The Japanese infantry followed three routes to the Russian fortifications on the summit of 203 Metre Hill: one approach sap led to the fort on the southwestern peak, while two more zigzagged toward the fort on the northeastern peak.

The fate of the Russian defenders of Port Arthur was sealed with the arrival, in September 1904, of batteries of Japanese 11-in Osaka siege howitzers, which fired massive 500-lb shells over ranges up to 9 km (5½ mls). The guns were set in concrete emplacements and weighed 23 tons. Eighteen of them were sent by sea from Japan to Dalny, the nearest port to the siege area. They were then manhandled over rough, muddy roads by teams of 300 soldiers because they were too heavy to be transported on the light railway. The howitzers opened fire in October; their salvoes against Port Arthur were at first indiscriminate.

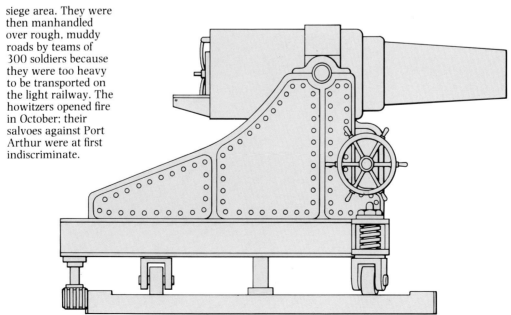

Tannenberg/26-30 August, 1914

In the early days of the First World War, Imperial German troops in East Prussia were outnumbered. While the greater part of Kaiser Wilhelm II's forces advanced through Belgium and France, his Eighth Army in the east, commanded by General Max von Prittwitz, was spread thinly across the northeastern province, which formed a vulnerable salient deep inside Russia.

Because of massive German pressure on the Western Front, the French made repeated and vociferous appeals to their ally, Tsar Nicholas II, to relieve them by opening a second front.

Though mobilization was incomplete, the Russians generously agreed to mount an offensive against East Prussia, using two armies from General Yakov Jilinsky's northwest army group, a total of about 450,000 men. Russia certainly had an abundance of manpower, but was woefully lacking in administrative ability; nor was there competent machinery to keep thousands of soldiers properly supplied in the field. A further hindrance, both to rapid troop movement and the commissariat, lay in the gauge of Russia's railway system, which was wider than that of Germany. As a defensive move to thwart invasion it was admirable, but it was equally inhibiting for offensive moves. Transport from Russian frontier railheads into East Prussia was obliged to rely on horse-drawn wagons, laboriously moving along inferior roads.

Knowing that his supply lines were in disarray, General Pavel Rennenkampf, the Russian commander in the area, nevertheless advanced on the Germans, on 17 August. His First Army was to form the right wing of a pincer movement by driving into East Prussia, through the corridor between the Baltic Sea and the north side of the huge Masurian lakes. The left arm of the pincer was formed by General Aleksandr Samsonov's Second Army, swinging around the southern end of the lakes. Unfortunately, Samsonov, who had feuded with Rennenkampf since the Russo-Japanese War of 1905, was ill prepared to invade when the First Army began its advance. It was typical of the lack of cooperation that blemished their short, disastrous campaign.

After a brush with German outposts at Stalluponen on the day Rennenkampf crossed the border, the Russians were next confronted by the left wing of Prittwitz's Eighth Army at Gumbinnen, on 20 August.

Prittwitz sought a decisive victory over the first Russian army to invade, which would then leave him free to deal with any other attack which might materialize later, doubtless aided by reinforcements transferred from the Western Front as the

When the First World War broke out, German military planning was based on the Schlieffen Plan, conceived by the Field Marshal of that name to meet the possibility of his country's having to fight on two fronts. It called for a knockout blow to France and a holding action against Russia, until such time as reinforcements could be transferred from the Western Front to deal with the threat from the east. The Russians, however, unexpectedly invaded East Prussia in large numbers, even before they were fully mobilized, thus throwing great strain on the German Eighth Army guarding the eastern frontier.

A German howitzer in action at Tannenberg.

A Russian field gun and its crew, photographed in firing position during the battle.

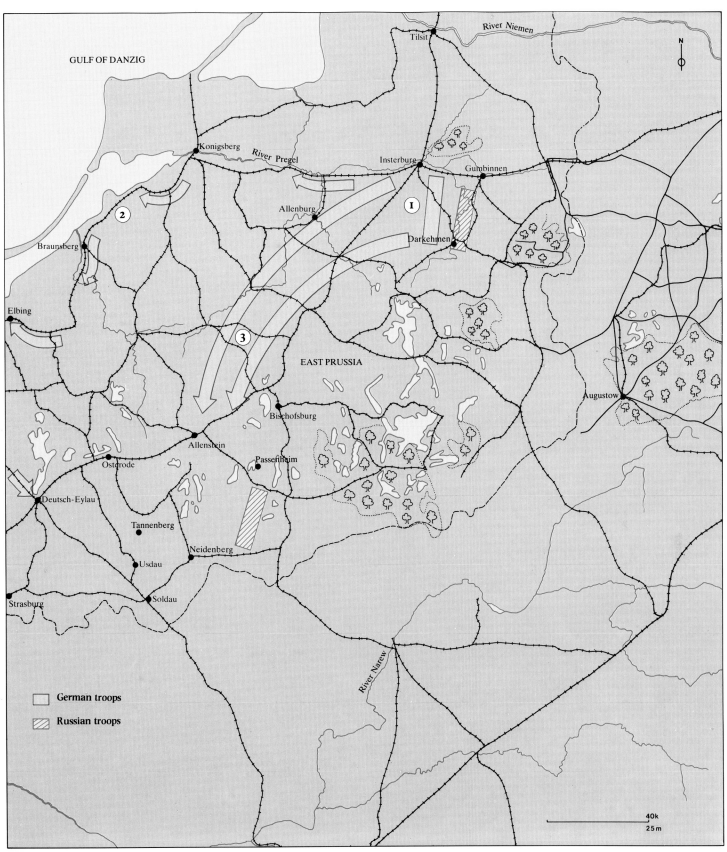

GULF OF DANZIG

River Niemen

Tilsit

Konigsberg

River Pregel

Insterburg

Gumbinnen

Allenburg

①

Darkehmen

②

Braunsberg

Elbing

③

EAST PRUSSIA

Augustow

Bischofsburg

Allenstein

Osterode

Passenheim

Deutsch-Eylau

Tannenberg

Usdau

Neidenberg

Strasburg

Soldau

River Narew

☐ German troops

▧ Russian troops

40k
25 m

After two brushes with the Russian First Army in the north of East Prussia on 17 and 20 August 1914, the German Eighth Army High Command learned with dismay that the Russian Second Army was about to invade in the south. A decision to retreat, taken in panic, was reversed when it was realized that the First Army was stationary. Leaving a thin screen of troops, **1**, to watch the enemy in the north, the Germans rapidly redeployed the bulk of their forces to join XX Corps, already in the south facing the new Russian threat. The 1st Corps and the 3rd Reserve Division were moved by rail, **2**, to form the southern flank of the new position around Tannenberg, while XVII Corps and the 1st Reserve Corps, **3**, marched to take station on the northern flank in the Bischofsburg area. By 26 August, the Germans had baited a trap for the unprepared and unsuspecting Russians.

131

Schlieffen Plan intended. The battle at Gumbinnen was inconclusive, however. The Germans broke off the engagement and withdrew westward. Inexplicably, Rennenkampf did not pursue them.

When Samsonov learnt about Gumbinnen, he assumed that German opposition in East Prussia had been broken and sought to overrun the province. Although his troops suffered greater supply problems than those of the First Army, he crossed over the frontier on 21 August.

Samsonov's advance south of the Masurian lakes astonished Prittwitz. Faced with an undefeated enemy to his front and a fresh army moving up on his right rear, he lost his nerve and ordered the Eighth Army to retire behind the River Vistula, some 320 km (200 mls) to the west. This order, greeted with dismay by his staff, had far-reaching effects, not only in East Prussia but on future operations in France.

No one was more disturbed than Lieutenant-Colonel Max Hoffman, Germany's leading authority on the Russian military machine, who was serving as a senior staff officer at Eighth Army Headquarters. He knew, from uncoded signals (corroborated by orders found on the body of a Russian officer), that Rennenkampf's forces were unable to move quickly; he knew, too, that although Samsonov had adopted an apparently threatening posture, his army was short of rations and equipment and, completely out of touch with the First Army, was, therefore, vulnerable to counter-attack.

Hoffman proposed to Count von Waldersee, the Chief of Staff, that some of the forces tied down in the north, watching the immobile Rennenkampf, should be rushed south to attack Samsonov's exposed left flank. Prittwitz saw the wisdom of the plan and cancelled his order for a general withdrawal. It was too late to save his career, however. The General had telephoned the German High Command at Coblenz to inform them of his intention to retreat behind the Vistula, but he omitted to tell them that he had changed his mind. The thought of losing East Prussia to the Russians, after token resistance only, aggrieved the Chief of the General Staff, Colonel-General Helmuth von Moltke. Suspicious of Prittwitz, he immediately ordered his dismissal and that of his blameless Chief of Staff, Waldersee. He replaced them with two soldiers who were to rise rapidly to dominate the German army throughout the rest of the First World War—General Paul von Hindenburg and General Erich Ludendorff.

Hindenburg, aged 67, a veteran of the Franco-Prussian War of 1870–1, was recalled from retirement to head the Eighth

Field Marshal Paul von Hindenburg (1847–1934) had extensive military experience, having fought in the Austro-Prussian War in 1866 and the Franco-Prussian War (1870–1). Although he ultimately led the German army to defeat, his reputation was greatly enhanced by the First World War and, in 1925, he was elected President. In 1933, when his faculties were in decline, he submitted to intense pressure and appointed Adolf Hitler as Chancellor.

General Erich Ludendorff (1865–1937), Hindenburg's Chief of Staff, was largely responsible for the German victory at Tannenberg. In 1916, when Hindenburg became supreme military commander, Ludendorff's influence greatly increased, and he intervened in civilian as well as military affairs. After the war, he advocated the new view of Aryan superiority and supported Adolf Hitler in his abortive *putsch* in 1920. He became a National Socialist member of the Reichstag in 1924, but later quarrelled with Hitler.

General Aleksandr Vasilyevich Samsonov (1859–1914) had served in the war of 1877 against Turkey and, by the age of 43, was a major-general. He commanded a cavalry division in the Russo-Japanese War and in 1909 was appointed Governor of Turkestan. Samsonov was generally liked by both his men and fellow officers, but his military talents were in decline by the time of Tannenberg, and at the close of the battle, appalled by the catastrophe, he committed suicide.

General Pavel Rennenkampf (1845–1918) was renowned in the Russian army for his dash and energy. However, he had quarrelled with Samsonov, indeed they had come to blows on the railway platform at Mukden, and they were barely on speaking terms. Thus their partnership, unlike that of Hindenburg and Ludendorff, was suspicious and uncooperative. Rennenkampf lost his nerve in 1915 and deserted his army. He was disgraced and dismissed by the service. Three years later, he was murdered by the Bolsheviks.

A group of Russian officers, photographed in 1914 with the owner of the estate on which they were billeted.

Cossacks, or light cavalry, were the élite of the Russian army and, in general, were well equipped. The great body of the army, however, was in all respects save number, inferior to the Germans, who had 10 pieces of heavy artillery to every Russian piece, a more efficient transport system and infinitely superior telephone, telegraph and wireless equipment.

Some 75 per cent of N.C.Os in the Russian army were conscripts and, among other ranks, 50 per cent, at a conservative estimate, were illiterate. Moreover, unlike the homogeneous German units, one-third of the Russian army was composed of subject races, including Balts, Letts and Poles.

Army. Ludendorff, then 49, a brilliant officer who had already distinguished himself in the advance through Belgium, was appointed his Chief of Staff.

Ludendorff learned of his appointment early on 22 August and immediately left the Western Front. He was driven to General Headquarters, where he was granted an audience with the Kaiser. Then, after a briefing meeting with Moltke, he boarded a special train to take him east. The train stopped at Hanover to pick up Hindenburg: it was the first time the two men had met.

On arrival at the Eastern Front, the new command team quickly accepted Hoffman's proposal, which was broadly in accordance with their own assessment of the situation. Satisfied that Rennenkampf would remain idle for some time, and alert to the fact that Samsonov's advance had produced a gap between his right flank and the Masurian lakes, Ludendorff saw an opportunity to encircle the Second Army. With Hindenburg's approval, he stripped the Eighth Army's left wing in order to bring sufficient numbers to bear against Samsonov, who was pressing forward in the belief that the Germans were retreating.

On 24 August, Ludendorff began the dangerous task of withdrawing two army corps in the face of Rennenkampf's forces, which were at last beginning to move. Large numbers were despatched south by train; the remainder were marched from the area down hot, dusty roads. Only two cavalry brigades remained, and for the next six crucial days they covered what Ludendorff described as 'a threatening thundercloud to the northeast.' The Germans planned to launch heavy attacks on Samsonov's flanks on the 26th, in order to force them back and so leave the three corps in his centre susceptible to double envelopment. Some of Samsonov's more perspicacious officers sensed a trap and advised against pushing too far ahead, into what seemed like a soft centre. When the General proposed to Army Group Headquarters that he should slow up the advance for that reason, Jilinsky accused him of cowardice and insisted that he press on with his 'pursuit'.

Although they were tired and ill fed, the Russian infantry fought valiantly against the German onslaught, which gathered in intensity as August drew to a close. Samsonov, whose communications had never been good, had little control over his regiments in the later stages of the battle. Despite a few local successes, which gave Ludendorff some anxious moments, Samsonov allowed his centre to drift northwest into a pocket of broken country, which the Eighth Army was poised to seal off.

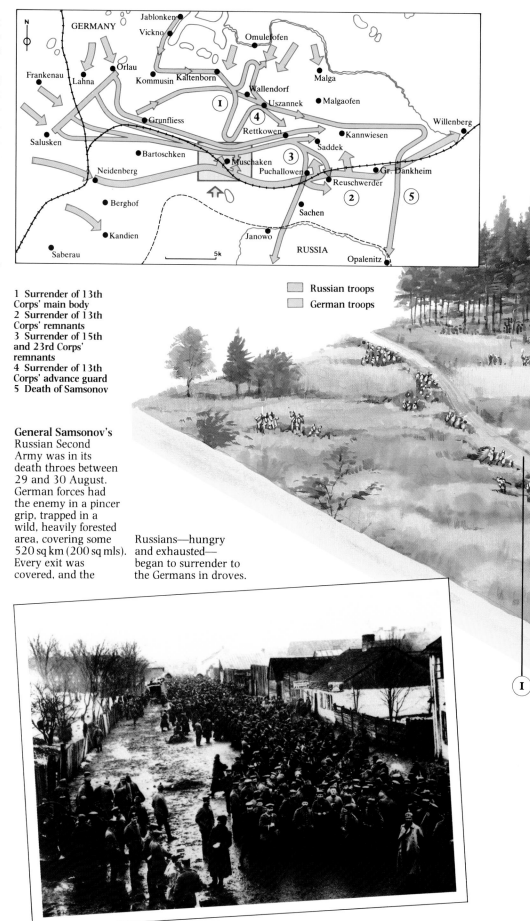

1 Surrender of 13th Corps' main body
2 Surrender of 13th Corps' remnants
3 Surrender of 15th and 23rd Corps' remnants
4 Surrender of 13th Corps' advance guard
5 Death of Samsonov

General Samsonov's Russian Second Army was in its death throes between 29 and 30 August. German forces had the enemy in a pincer grip, trapped in a wild, heavily forested area, covering some 520 sq km (200 sq mls). Every exit was covered, and the Russians—hungry and exhausted—began to surrender to the Germans in droves.

Many thousands of Russians were taken prisoner of war in the days following the battle.

Defeated Russians emerged from dark woods into bright sunlight to surrender to the waiting Germans. Scenes like this, at Muschaken, were repeated many times throughout 30 August.

On this stretch of the Neidenberg to Willenberg road near Muschaken, **1**, two battalions of German infantry, **2**, guarded every path out of the forest.

Waving anything white that they could find, column after column of battle-weary Russian soldiers, **3**, capitulated.

The Russian Army, which had been beset by supply problems, was starving when it surrendered. Most men had not eaten for several days. Their hardship was not over, however. It took the Germans until 3 September to organize rations for such a huge number of prisoners.

Sporadic rifle and machine-gun fire greeted the first Russians seen coming through the trees, but little resistance was offered to the German troops.

Members of the German staff, **4**, arrived to receive formally the Russian surrender on this sector of the battlefront.

135

On 28 August, the Germans were ready to spring their trap. The Russian flanking corps had been separated from Samsonov's main body, and, while a strong assault was launched on the centre, elements of the Eighth Army moved around toward Passenheim in the north and Neidenberg in the south to meet in the rear of the enemy.

Deserted by both Jilinsky and Rennenkampf, who failed to answer urgent appeals for help, the exhausted Second Army was in no state to break out; its only recourse was surrender. Samsonov, unable to bear the disgrace of losing his command, walked into the forest on 29 August, drew his revolver and shot himself dead.

Hindenburg called 30 August 'the day of harvesting' because thousands of Russians threw down their weapons and were rounded up into captivity. In his report to the Kaiser, he estimated that 60,000 prisoners had been taken, adding that the survivors of the flanking corps were retreating in 'hot haste'. In the event, the tally was much higher—90,000 prisoners, 30,000 casualties and 500 guns. The Eighth Army lost 10,000 to 15,000 men.

This great victory elevated Hindenburg and Ludendorff into military idols overnight. The formidable partnership dominated the war in the east for a further two years; then they were transferred to France. Never again, however, were they to repeat the great success of the Battle of Tannenberg, which was so named by Ludendorff more for historical than military reasons, for the village had not played a particularly important part in the fighting. It was at Tannenberg, however, that Teutonic knights had been defeated by Poles and Lithuanians in 1410 and Ludendorff made this gesture to level the score.

German troops on the march, *above*. Their discipline and cohesion were in stark contrast to the chaos prevailing in most Russian units, *right*.

Captured Russian infantry, with their machine-guns, being marched into captivity, *left*. After the peace treaty of Brest-Litovsk between Germany and Russia, following the Bolshevik Revolution, these and thousands more prisoners were repatriated to Russia. Because the Bolsheviks feared the presence of so many trained soldiers, however, many were summarily shot for alleged cowardice in surrendering at Tannenberg.

Russian cavalry on the move.

The stalemate on the Western Front in France, following the withdrawal of some German forces after the Battle of the Marne and the inconclusive Battles of the Aisne and First Ypres, posed a serious dilemma for Germany. The ambitious strategy of the Schlieffen Plan had failed in the area in which it had been deemed most likely to succeed. Yet at Tannenberg, in East Prussia, a striking, though not strategically decisive, victory had been won in the very theatre that Schlieffen had regarded as being of only secondary importance. The gross incompetence of the Russian commanders and the deficiencies of the Russian military machine convinced General Ludendorff that victory could be quickly achieved in the east, despite the enemy's massive resources of manpower. He planned to win in a war of manoeuvre, as opposed to the siege conditions of the Western Front. Considerable pressure was exerted on the Kaiser to support a major shift of men and *matériel* to the Eastern Front to knock Russia out of the war, while Germany stood on the defensive in the west—a complete reversal of the Schlieffen Plan. The move was resisted, however, by the Chief of the German General Staff. A compromise was eventually reached: offensives would be launched on both the Eastern and Western Fronts, but those in France would be of a limited nature. In consequence, Germany had enough strength in the east to occupy Poland and, with her Austro-Hungarian ally, advance deep into Russia, but not enough to achieve complete military victory. Hostilities on the Eastern Front drew to a close only when Russia plunged into revolution, in 1917, and the Bolshevik government then at once sued for peace.

Suvla Bay/*6 August, 1915 - 9 January, 1916*

Mounting an attack on Gallipoli was one of the few imaginative concepts of the First World War, but the officers chosen for the highest echelons of command during the campaign were either past their prime or without fighting experience, sometimes both. They allowed the operation to wither and die through ignorance, mismanagement and stubbornness. The price paid in lost opportunities, wasted lives and human suffering was appalling.

The assault was designed to break the stalemate of trench warfare in France and Flanders by destroying the power of Turkey and thereby pulling German troops to the east. The Royal Navy might have achieved this single-handed by steaming through the narrow Dardanelles straits leading to Constantinople in November 1914, when the area was still lightly defended. Instead,

British warships contented themselves with a bombardment of the shore batteries at the entrance to the straits to test the range of the enemy's guns. This succeeded only in alerting the Turks and their German commanders to the probability of further attacks in the area.

Three months later, in February 1915, the Royal Navy again appeared off the Dardanelles and found that the defences had been strengthened beyond recognition: there were now carefully laid minefields and well-sited guns, while at night the narrows were swept by searchlights.

Deciding to match might with might, Great Britain and France assembled a huge fleet, including 18 battleships, to force a passage to Constantinople. The fleet sailed perilously close to the coastal guns and sustained heavy losses: three capital ships

were sunk and three crippled. The action was broken off. Unknown to the Allies, the Turks had almost exhausted their ammunition and the fleet could have proceeded to Constantinople unmolested. Naval commanders, however, claimed that they could not force the Dardanelles unless troops were first sent to occupy the Gallipoli Peninsula in force.

Field Marshal Lord Kitchener, the British Secretary of State for War, saw such a landing as repayment to Russia for her having eased pressure on the Western Front by attacking in the east in 1914, even though she was not then fully mobilized. Now the British and French could take pressure off Russia. Kitchener assembled an army of 70,000 men, many of whom had no battle experience. The force was commanded by Lieutenant-General Sir Ian

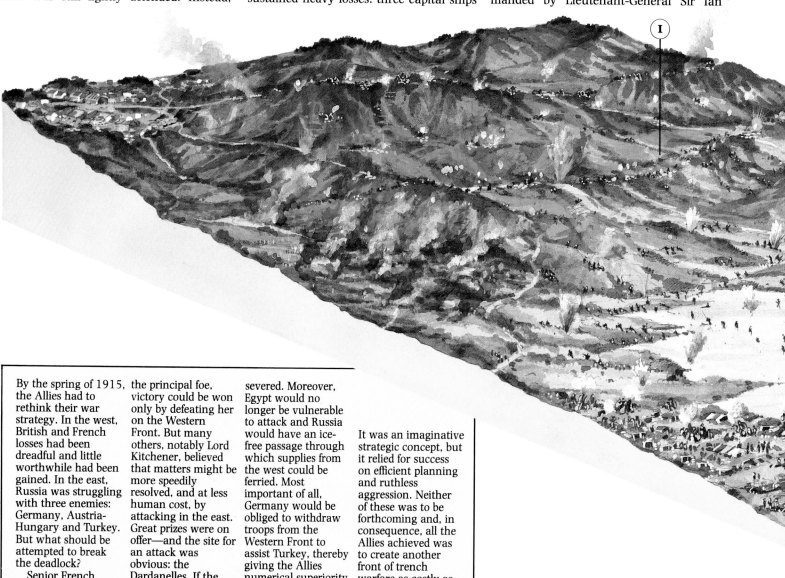

By the spring of 1915, the Allies had to rethink their war strategy. In the west, British and French losses had been dreadful and little worthwhile had been gained. In the east, Russia was struggling with three enemies: Germany, Austria-Hungary and Turkey. But what should be attempted to break the deadlock?

Senior French generals, and the French government itself, argued that, since Germany was

the principal foe, victory could be won only by defeating her on the Western Front. But many others, notably Lord Kitchener, believed that matters might be more speedily resolved, and at less human cost, by attacking in the east. Great prizes were on offer—and the site for an attack was obvious: the Dardanelles. If the attack were successful, Turkey's communications with Germany would be

severed. Moreover, Egypt would no longer be vulnerable to attack and Russia would have an ice-free passage through which supplies from the west could be ferried. Most important of all, Germany would be obliged to withdraw troops from the Western Front to assist Turkey, thereby giving the Allies numerical superiority and the opportunity to break the stalemate that was costing so many lives.

It was an imaginative strategic concept, but it relied for success on efficient planning and ruthless aggression. Neither of these was to be forthcoming and, in consequence, all the Allies achieved was to create another front of trench warfare as costly as that in the west.

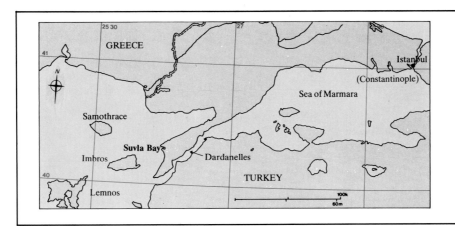

Allied troops in the southwest and south of the Gallipoli Peninsula, if deployed aggressively, could have threatened Constantinople, the Turkish capital to the northeast, with momentous consequences. After the débâcle at Suvla Bay, however, the only practical course for the Allies was evacuation.

Troop positions at about 5 pm on 21 August. Smoke blew over the battlefield from fires started by artillery shells in the brush north of Chocolate Hill. Turkish artillery was strongly positioned. Some guns were on the forward slopes, others on the reverse slope of W Hill. Fire was massed against the 2nd Yeomanry Division as it crossed Salt Lake.

Scimitar Hill, 1, was defended by Turkish infantry, who were dug in along the crest in deep, often roofed, trenches. Snipers and skirmishers were positioned to their front. The Turks were deployed in the same way on Chocolate Hill, 2, and W Hill, 3.

The 11th Division attacked Chocolate and W Hills. As with the attack on Scimitar Hill, little progress was made, but the cost in life was high.

The axis of advance of the dismounted 2nd Yeomanry Division lay across the dried-up Salt Lake area, 4. Some companies were in extended line, others in column and moving at the double. They were under continuous direct and indirect fire from Turkish batteries, which were using shrapnel.

Lala Baba, 5, the forming-up point for the British 2nd Yeomanry Division, was broken up by gullies, giving some protection from enemy fire. On Salt Lake, across which the Yeomanry had to advance, there was no cover; here they suffered their first heavy casualties.

General Stopford's army landed at Suvla Bay on the night of 6–7 August. Stores were dumped haphazardly, and the troops dug in along the shore, rather than immediately advancing to take the heights inland.

Rear echelon troops were also landed along this section, adding to the confusion.

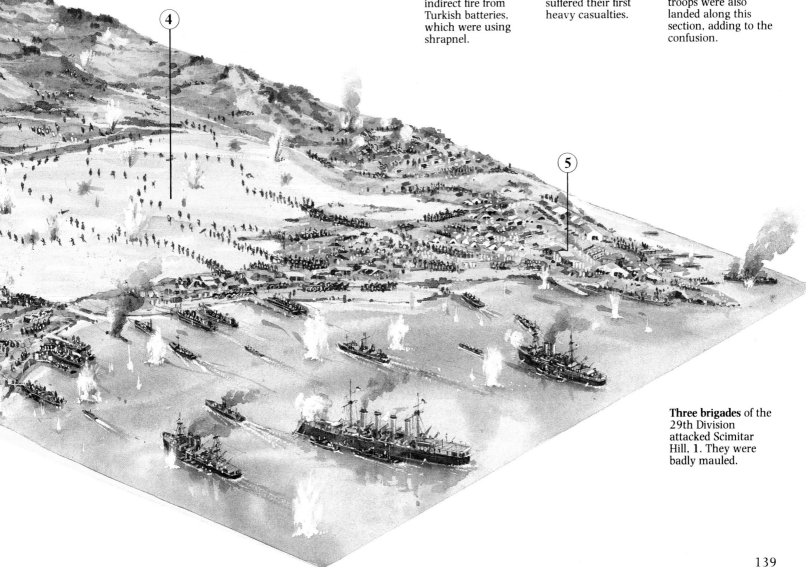

Three brigades of the 29th Division attacked Scimitar Hill, 1. They were badly mauled.

Suvla Bay/2

Hamilton, aged 62, who had more active service to his credit than any other senior officer in the army, but who was reluctant to exercise authority over his generals, a failing that was to have disastrous consequences in the ensuing campaign.

To suggest that the Mediterranean Expeditionary Force was unprepared for its Gallipoli ordeal is an understatement. Kitchener held the Turkish army in such contempt that no serious efforts were made to study its methods, command structure, strength or dispositions, even though a major offensive against it was about to be launched. To make matters worse, maps of the peninsula (some taken from tourist guide books) were out of date and often inaccurate, and no detailed reconnaissance of the landing areas had been undertaken.

Just before dawn on 25 April 1915, Hamilton's soldiers, so badly served by their commanders, started going ashore for what they thought would be 'a great adventure'. Several diversionary landings were made to confuse the Turks and to cover the two main thrusts to be made: by the Australian and New Zealand Army Corps in the southwest of the peninsula and by the 29th Division in the south.

The German commander of the Turkish forces in Gallipoli, General Liman von Sanders, had been expecting an invasion and had 84,000 men available to repel it. By luck rather than sound planning or accurate intelligence, most of Hamilton's army, which included a strong French contingent, landed in weakly held sectors. On only two beaches did his men come under heavy fire. Almost at once, however, Allied confusion and lack of cohesion, which were to typify the entire campaign, passed the advantage to the enemy. Even though the way was open for a rapid advance to occupy dominating hills, there was reluctance to achieve more than a secure bridgehead.

British officers walked unhindered to the commanding village of Krithia and up the 250-m (700-ft) heights of Achi Baba, but then returned to their lines to await orders. By the time instructions to push forward arrived, the Turks were in position. In the weeks ahead, thousands of lives were to be lost trying to take these two objectives, both of which would earlier have fallen easily, without cost.

What had been envisaged as a swift, decisive action to secure the peninsula degenerated into the horrifying conditions of trench warfare, like those on the Western Front, almost from the first day.

As casualties began to mount in the sweltering, fly-infested beachheads, the inadequacy of Allied preparations to care for

Sir Ian Hamilton, seated left, was photographed with Vice-Admiral John M. de Robeck, the British naval commander, flanked by the French naval and army leaders, *above.* Kitchener appointed Hamilton with the words, 'If you do [capture Constantinople] you will have won not only a campaign but the war.' Hamilton, however, rather than take an active part at Gallipoli, preferred his H.Q. on an offshore island.

In contrast, the German Field Marshal, Liman von Sanders, facing the camera, *top,* was a decisive commander, whose orders, often ruthless but instantly obeyed, prevented an Allied advance up the peninsula.

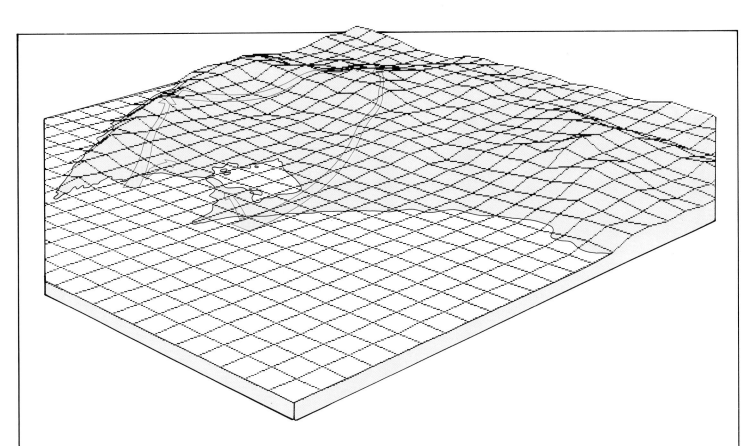

For three grim months after the landings in the Gallipoli Peninsula, Allied forces were held in check by the Turks. Hamilton, the Commander-in-Chief, determined to break the deadlock. A fresh corps was to land at Suvla Bay to the north of the Anzac Corps, and the two forces would then advance and link up on the dominating heights of the Sari Bair Hills. Once this had been achieved, Hamilton would be well placed to push forward to the Dardanelles and sever the peninsula. It was a promising concept—on paper.

Anzac troops at Anzac Bay used equipment devised in the trenches to allow soldiers to snipe at the Turks without exposing themselves to retaliatory fire. A standard .303 Lee-Enfield rifle, with a wire trigger pull, is attached to a periscope. Behind the rifleman, another soldier is using a trench periscope to scan Turkish positions.

General Sir Ian Hamilton inspecting troops at Kephalos Camp, a staging area on the Isle of Imbros. Despite heat, flies and dust, battalion parades such as this were common in the preparatory phases of the campaign. Within a few days, these smartly turned out soldiers were in the gruelling, make-shift conditions of the front line.

the wounded became painfully exposed. Too few hospital ships had accompanied the expedition, so animal transports, their stable decks uncleaned, were pressed into service to help evacuate the worst cases. On one such voyage, the only medical man on board was a veterinary officer.

For the next three murderous months, the Australians and New Zealanders grimly defended their slender foothold on Gallipoli, a mere 400 acres of steep, scrub-covered gullies and ridges. Farther south, the 29th Division, the Royal Naval Division and the French repeatedly hurled themselves against the heights that, but for their commanders' irresolution, might have been taken without loss. After failing for the third time to take Krithia and Achi Baba head-on, General Hamilton admitted in a report to Kitchener that frontal attacks in force were 'madness'. It had taken him a long time to learn the lesson.

Hamilton then planned to break out from the Anzac bridgehead. A fresh corps was to be landed at Suvla Bay to the north to protect the Australians' and New Zealanders' left as they advanced to outflank the Turks and capture the Sari Bair Hills. Once the Suvla force took the ridges to their front and linked with the Anzacs on Sari Bair, Hamilton would be poised to cut the peninsula in two, for it was only 13 km (8 mls) wide at this point and was dominated by high ground.

The plan had much to recommend it. It was doomed to failure, however, from the moment Lieutenant-General Sir Frederick Stopford was brought out of retirement to command the Suvla landings. He was elderly, in poor health, had never led troops in battle and knew nothing of Gallipoli. Solely on grounds of seniority, he was placed in command of IX Corps' twenty-two battalions, which would form the hinge on which the success or failure of the Anzac breakout would turn.

How highly Hamilton regarded his Suvla scheme may be gauged from his efforts to keep it secret. Troops in the staging areas were forbidden even to speculate on their destination. Stopford himself did not know where he was going until a fortnight before the landings. On the night of the attack, 6–7 August, there were officers in the boats heading for the beaches who had not been told their objectives and who had no maps.

All was muddle and indecision from the outset. Some units were set down on the wrong beaches, while other landing areas became chaotic because too many men had been put ashore too quickly in the darkness; supplies were dumped indiscriminately, and all the while anxious officers milled about seeking clarification of orders.

This general view of Suvla Bay shows the new motor lighters running up to the jetty to unload fodder and straw for the horses and mules.

The wheelhouses, 1, of the barges were protected by armour-plate against sniper fire. The Turks were excellent marksmen.

A field ambulance park, 2, was sited close to the jetty. Since the Allies had not expected such heavy casualties, there were insufficient hospitals and hospital ships.

Dug-outs, 3, along the shore were primitive, since they had to be made with whatever materials were available.

Fatigue parties resting at Suvla Bay, *left*. The dug-out in the foreground was more for protection from the sun than from enemy fire. Some of the resting soldiers wrapped the bolts of their rifles in rags to protect them from dust.

In the deep water of Suvla Bay, British naval and merchant ships could come in close to land, *right*. Barges ferried in supplies, while troops led pack-horses down to the shore to carry the stores inland.

Boxes of rations, 4, were dumped indiscriminately. They usually contained bully beef and biscuits, so the soldiers' diet was monotonous and badly balanced.

Stores already unloaded, **5**, lay on the quay awaiting collection. As with everything else in the campaign, supply arrangements lacked organization.

British, Empire and French troops wore regulation uniforms, which were inappropriate for the intense heat prevailing at Suvla Bay.

Beyond the ridge, 6, a couple of kilometres away, were the Turkish positions, so close that snipers had an uninterrupted view of the unloading process. But the Allied troops' proximity to the shore meant, at least, that supplies, once claimed, could be taken to the units quickly.

A stretcher party, *above*, carries a wounded comrade to the jetty to await transfer to a hospital ship. Allied medical facilities were hopelessly inadequate throughout the campaign.

Instead of immediately deploying in strength to occupy the hills around Suvla in support of the attacking Anzacs, most of IX Corps remained in the vicinity of the bay. Australians and New Zealanders, who had been fighting hard and had made some progress, could see the troops at Suvla and did not understand why they were not by now advancing.

Stopford was so intent on getting his raw soldiers ashore that he overlooked the purpose for which they had been landed. Meanwhile, on the high ground, the German commander of a hastily organized force of 1,500 Turks guarding the Suvla area must have been astonished at his good fortune. Reporting the surprise invasion to von Sanders, he remarked on the timidity of the overwhelming forces to his front. While he waited for reinforcements, his riflemen picked off British soldiers and had soon killed or wounded more than their own strength. Still there was no assault.

At Turkish general headquarters, von Sanders displayed the decisive ruthlessness so foreign to his opponents: he summarily dismissed a divisional commander who said he could not reinforce the Suvla ridges until 9 August because his men were too tired. In his place he put Colonel Mustapha Kemal, a tough, uncompromising Turk, who immediately ordered the exhausted infantry forward to plug the gap.

Despite an optimistic message from Stopford on 8 August, suggesting that worthwhile gains were being made, Hamilton dispatched an aide to see for himself and to report back. The Commander-in-Chief had his worst suspicions confirmed when his staff officer wirelessed: 'Just been ashore where I found all quiet. No rifle fire, no artillery fire, and apparently no Turks. IX Corps resting. Feel confident that golden opportunities are being lost and look upon situation as serious.'

Hamilton reached Suvla as quickly as he could and discovered that little progress had indeed been made. The majority of the troops was either relaxing or bathing; Stopford himself was asleep.

When reminded of the paramount importance of securing the encircling hills, Stopford replied that his men were hot and tired, there had been difficulties with water and other supplies and not enough guns were ashore. He would attack next morning. This was small comfort for the worndown Anzacs, who had been fighting for months in dreadful conditions.

Leaving Stopford on board the ship that served as his headquarters, Hamilton went ashore. There he found the same indolence among senior officers. In a last attempt to prevent the collapse of his plan, he uncharacteristically issued a direct order for a brigade to advance to the main ridges and dig in on the crest. It was too late: Colonel Mustapha Kemal had arrived there first.

Between 9 and 11 August, when Hamilton reported to Kitchener that most of the troops were 'strolling about as if it was a holiday', the Turks consolidated their positions. On the 15th, the feckless Stopford, who had resorted to blaming subordinates and an alleged lack of offensive spirit in his Territorial divisions for his failures, was finally relieved of his command. His nineday sojourn at Suvla had been disastrous.

In a letter to the Secretary of State for War a few days later, Herbert Asquith, the Prime Minister, wrote bitterly: 'I have read enough to satisfy me that the generals and staff engaged in the Suvla part of the business ought to be court-martialled and dismissed from the army.'

Yet even now the tragedy of Suvla Bay had not ended. Shortly after Asquith wrote

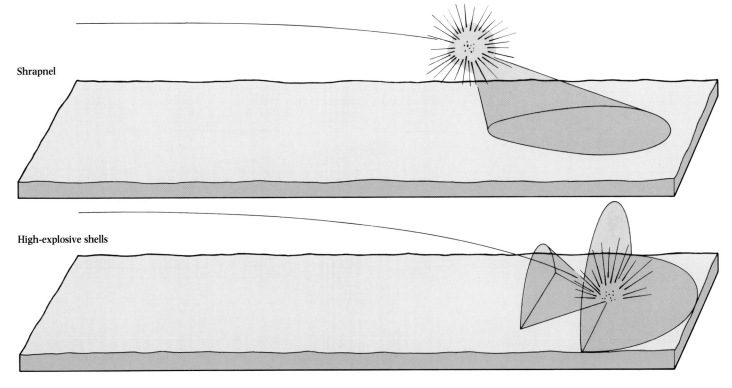

Shrapnel

High-explosive shells

Shrapnel, invented by General H. Shrapnel (1761–1842) during the Peninsular War, comprised a hollow cannister containing lead pellets, which were scattered in a shower by a bursting charge set off by a time fuse. In its earlier forms, when fuses were often imperfect, shrapnel was equipped with a device that would cause it to explode on impact.

High-explosive shells relied on impact blast, as well as fragmentation, to destroy troops in the open. Some shells at Gallipoli incorporated a fuse that delayed explosion; others could be discharged, like shrapnel, in an overhead burst, violently expelling a cone of bullets.

his letter, the new commander of IX Corps, Major-General H. de Lisle, set about attacking the ridges on 21 August.

With the blessing of his Commander-in-Chief, who had evidently forgotten about the 'madness' of frontal attacks, de Lisle launched the greater part of three divisions against strongly defended heights—in hot, but unseasonably cloudy weather. The results were bloody and predictable.

By late afternoon, when the attack was faltering, de Lisle called up his reserve, the 2nd Yeomanry Division, and ordered it to break the Turkish line. Before these dismounted cavalry regiments from the shires of England could reach the front, they had to march across the white, dried-up expanse of Salt Lake—a perfect target for Turkish artillery. In the dusk, their ranks thinned by gunfire, the troopers stormed the hills. It was a gallant attempt, but they were repulsed with heavy losses. So ended the biggest, but mercifully the last, battle fought on the Gallipoli Peninsula. Like all the others, it had gained nothing.

Sir Ian Hamilton, still groping for victory amid the stalemate of trench warfare, was recalled on 15 October. His successor, Lieutenant-General Sir Charles Monro, on assessing the dismal situation in this inhospitable corner of European Turkey, recommended evacuation. By 9 January 1916, there were no Allied soldiers on Gallipoli save the dead.

The cost to both sides had been high. Of the 480,000 British, Commonwealth and French troops who served in this incompetently conducted campaign, more than 250,000 became casualties. The Turks admitted to almost identical losses, but some estimates place their figure much higher.

In war-weary Great Britain, the successful evacuation was hailed as some kind of victory, much as that from Dunkirk would be 24 years later. The truth was that the Dardanelles remained untaken and the Turkish army, that Kitchener derided, still occupied the ridges of Gallipoli.

Stores and equipment were offloaded on the foreshore and then transported by mule cart to the waiting troops.

Territorial gunners of the 52nd Lowland Division firing a 5-in howitzer at Suvla Bay. This artillery piece, one of the most effective guns deployed during the campaign, was capable of firing about 9.5 km (6 mls). The two gunners in the foreground are setting the fuses, while the gun commander, known as No. 1, observes a shell's impact. These soldiers are in non-regulation dress, illustrating the makeshift conditions prevailing throughout the campaign.

For the Allies, failure in the Dardanelles was calamitous; the losses had been grievous. Moreover, Turkey remained active on Germany's side, and the straits to the Black Sea were still closed. Russia thus remained separated from and unsupplied by her allies, and, in 1917, following the Bolshevik Revolution, she withdrew from the war. The most immediate consequence, however, was that those senior officers who advocated a second front to save lives in France had lost the argument. Because of the fiasco at Gallipoli, Great Britain and France became committed to more years of trench warfare on the Western Front, years that would claim hundreds of thousands of lives.

The Somme/*1 July-19 November, 1916*

'It is my painful duty to inform you that a report has this day been received from the War Office notifying the death of ...' Thousands upon thousands of telegrams beginning with these chilling words arrived at homes the length and breadth of the United Kingdom in July 1916. Grim news was filtering through to cities, towns and villages, revealing the fate of husbands, fathers, sons and brothers caught in the giant mincing machine that was dignified as 'The Battle of the Somme'.

The majority of troops in action on the Somme were men who, in 1914, had answered Field Marshal Lord Kitchener's stirring appeal for volunteers. All the eager units of his so-called 'New Army' had enlisted locally and retained with pride their unofficial titles—the Accrington Pals, the Grimsby Chums, the Glasgow Boys' Brigade Battalion. Therein lay their strength—and their vulnerability. Surrounded by friends and sharing a common background, the soldiers' morale was second to none, but, should the fortunes of war go against them, whole communities would be robbed of their menfolk. This is what was presently to happen.

The British Expeditionary Force (BEF) in France had entered 1916 with a new Commander-in-Chief, General Sir Douglas Haig, who was committed to a joint offensive with the French in the vicinity of the River Somme in Picardy. The 'Big Push', as it was dubbed, was intended to coincide with major attacks by the Russians and Italians on their fronts, in a three-pronged attempt to squeeze Germany and Austria–Hungary into submission.

In February, however, the Germans forestalled Allied plans with a massive surprise assault on French positions at the fortress of Verdun. General ('Papa') Joffre's *poilus* suffered grievously in the sustained onslaught; by spring it was evident that unless an attack was mounted elsewhere to divert German pressure, the defence would inevitably crumble.

All eyes in the French High Command turned on the BEF, whose volunteers were now reaching full strength. Thus the joint offensive originally proposed turned into a largely British responsibility.

Although unhappy about the inexperience of his officers and men, Haig began to move General Sir Henry Rawlinson's newly created Fourth Army into the Somme sector, ready for action at the end of June. A straightforward infantry attack to relieve pressure on Verdun was developed by Haig into an attempt to break the stalemate of trench warfare, outmanoeuvre the Germans and end the war quickly. He planned to achieve this by pouring cavalry through

The British Somme offensive opened on 1 July 1916, a hot, sunny day. The 34th Division advanced eastward across 1.6 km (1 ml) of undulating countryside in an effort to break the German defences in the sector around La Boisselle.

(6)

In 1916, there was stalemate on the Western Front. Both sides sought a spectacular victory to put an end to the war, and, for the Germans, the target was obvious: the vast fortress of Verdun, standing on a salient in the French line. It was of no strategic importance, since it had been stripped of its guns, but for the French it was a symbol of their military might. Falkenhayn, the German Commander-in-Chief, sought to deal a blow to French pride; the French, in turn, massed reserves to defend Verdun. Thus the scene was set for one of the most futile encounters of the First World War.

Once the Germans claimed that the prize was worth fighting for, they had to persist; the French, for the same reason, had to resist. The fighting, dominated largely by artillery bombardment, raged from February to the end of June 1916. By then the French had lost 315,000 men, and the Germans 281,000.

The Allies finally brought the action to an end by drawing off German troops with an attack elsewhere. The site chosen for the attack was in Picardy, on a 29-km (18-ml) front running north of the River Somme.

The 101st and 102nd Brigades of 34th Division, **1**, moved forward at 7.30 am to assault the German trenches. Small gains were made, but many men fell before machine-gun fire.

The 2nd and 3rd Tyneside Irish Battalions, **2**, in the second wave of the attack were annihilated by machine-gun fire as they slowly advanced toward the lines of German trenches.

German Maxim machine-gun posts, **4**, sprayed No Man's Land with a waist-high curtain of interlocking fire, causing heavy casualties among the advancing British.

The German front line, **3**, was pounded by artillery—with limited effect. Deep dug-outs protected their troops, who emerged when the bombardment ceased, to mow down the British infantry.

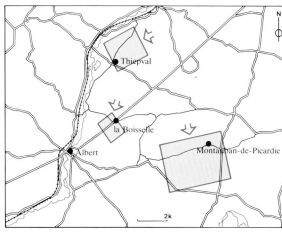

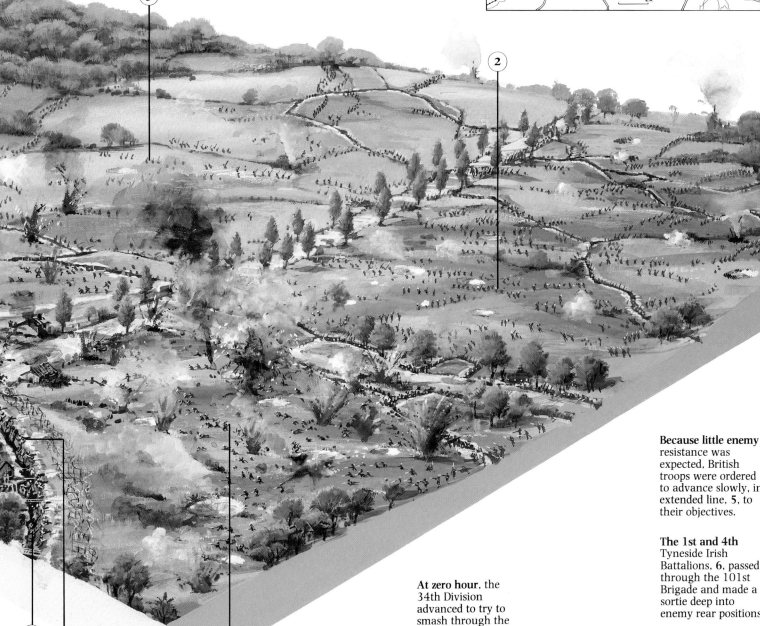

Because little enemy resistance was expected, British troops were ordered to advance slowly, in extended line, **5**, to their objectives.

The 1st and 4th Tyneside Irish Battalions, **6**, passed through the 101st Brigade and made a sortie deep into enemy rear positions.

A red flare sent up from the German lines, **7**, was the signal to bring down artillery fire on the waves of attacking British infantry.

At zero hour, the 34th Division advanced to try to smash through the German defences. Two brigades at once moved from the British front line to engage the enemy. A third brigade began a longer march over open ground to come up with them and pass through, so giving fresh momentum to their attack. The two right-flank battalions made gains but could not keep them.

gaps punched in the enemy lines by the initial assault. Three cavalry divisions were ordered up from the rear, where they had been languishing since 1914.

With their sabres and lances they were an anachronistic sight in a war dominated by artillery and automatic weapons. General Rawlinson, for one, did not place much faith in them: he preferred guns, bayonets and bombs, and therefore planned his battle around them.

From Gommecourt in the north, down through Serre, Beaumont-Hamel, Thiepval, La Boisselle, Fricourt and Mametz to Montauban, battalion after battalion of khaki-uniformed 'Tommies' occupied a zigzag of trenches 29 km (18 mls) long, cut through chalky fields. Soon these little French towns and villages would become household names in Great Britain—and in Germany, too.

The remaining 13 km (8 mls) of front between Montauban and the Somme were held by French troops, who would also take part in the offensive. At Gommecourt and beyond lay General Sir Edmund Allenby's British Third Army, two divisions of which were earmarked to provide a diversion when Rawlinson's main attack went in.

Across No Man's Land, which ranged from a few yards wide in some places to as much as a mile in others, the Germans watched and waited in strongly built defence positions on high ground. Their Commander-in-Chief, General Erich von Falkenhayn, had warned all troops on the Western Front to be on the alert for a counter-offensive, designed to relieve the pressure at Verdun. He thought Alsace-Lorraine the most likely point, but General Fritz von Below, commanding the German Second Army on the Somme, was certain the attack would fall on his men, for intelligence reports indicated a British build-up beyond his wire. Von Below was proved to be right.

After various delays, Rawlinson completed plans for an assault on 29 June. Borrowing from German tactics at Verdun, he proposed to prepare the way with an enormous bombardment lasting for five days. With the number of guns and the vast amounts of ammunition at his disposal, it was to be the biggest artillery operation since the war began.

Rawlinson saw the infantry's task as a virtual walk-over, so confident was he that the storm of shells would pulverize the enemy. Indeed, he ordered his men not to rush yelling at the German trenches in the usual way, but to march steadily and quietly over to them in extended line, rifles at the port. Astonishingly, they were supposed to do this at 7.30, on a summer

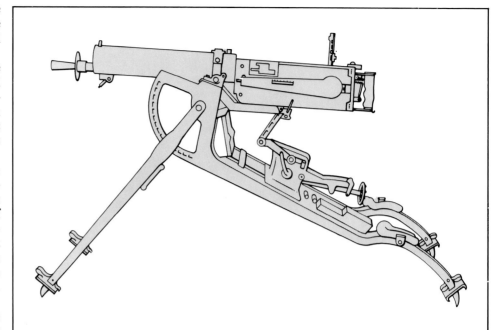

The Maxim '08 was the principal machine-gun used by the German army throughout the First World War. This 7.92 mm water-cooled automatic was capable of firing 450 rounds of belt-fed ammunition a minute; it weighed 32 kg (70 lb 8 oz). The Maxim's effectiveness as a defensive weapon was clearly demonstrated on the first day of the Battle of the Somme, when only a few guns mowed down whole battalions of British infantry in a few minutes.

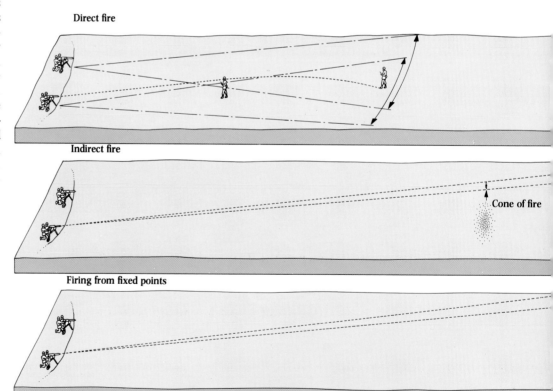

Direct fire

Indirect fire

Cone of fire

Firing from fixed points

Medium machine-guns, as deployed in the trenches during the First World War, produced three distinct patterns of fire. Direct fire was used in defence at short range, when machine-guns were traversed in an arc to spray bullets across lines of attacking troops. At medium range, machine-guns were fired from fixed points and distributed a dense, compact cone of fire, which had an obliterating effect on specific targets. At long range, or where the target could not be

German trenches zigzagged across the high ground in the Somme sector. They were much better constructed and better drained than those of the British, which ran roughly parallel in the plain below. Dug-outs in the narrow, 1.8 m- (6 ft-) deep British trenches were scooped out of the walls and offered little protection against shell fire. At the rear of the trench shown here is the entrance to a German dug-out: a stores and barrack complex built 9 m (30 ft) below ground and lit by electricity.

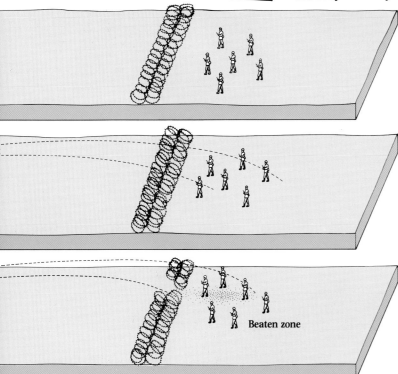

Beaten zone

seen because the gun was behind a ridge, for example, indirect fire was used. For this, machine-guns were fired at a steep elevation so that shots fell over a wide area. All areas subjected to fire are termed 'the beaten zone'.

General Erich von Falkenhayn (1861–1922), Chief of the German General Staff, was certain the Allies would try to weaken his Verdun offensive by launching a full-scale attack elsewhere on the Western Front.

General Fritz von Below (1853–1918), who commanded the German Second Army, held the line in the Somme area. He predicted that his troops would bear the brunt of an enemy offensive, but the staff at Headquarters disagreed with him.

General Sir Douglas Haig (1861–1928), was appointed Commander-in-Chief of the British Expeditionary Force in France in December 1915. He masterminded the Somme offensive.

General Sir Henry Rawlinson (1864–1925), commander of the newly formed British Fourth Army, was ordered to mount a major attack in the Somme sector in the summer of 1916.

The Somme/3

morning, when it would be broad daylight. A dawn attack three hours earlier had been ruled out, to give the artillery better observation in the final stages of their pre-offensive bombardment. This proved to be a disastrous error of judgement.

The guns opened fire on 25 June. The following day it rained, and rain continued to fall heavily throughout the 27th and into the early hours of the 28th. This caused consternation at Fourth Army headquarters, where staff officers foresaw the offensive floundering in waterlogged fields and trenches.

At 11 am, little more than 20 hours before zero, the attack was postponed until 7.30 am on 1 July to let the ground dry out. The artillery had immediately to reduce its rate of fire to spread its ammunition stocks over another three days' unscheduled bombardment. The assault troops already packed in the front line had to be stood down, and those coming up halted. For the thousands of men who had nerved themselves to fight on the 29th, the tedious delay fostered uncertainty and tension.

When the order, 'Stand to,' was passed along the British trenches at dawn on 1 July, the soldiers knew, as they mounted the fire-steps, that it was going to be a fine summer's day. In silence, they watched the sun climb into a clear blue sky, but at 6.25 am precisely, the peace was shattered by a bombardment of terrifying intensity. For exactly one hour and five minutes the guns pounded the German positions.

To add to the enemy's confusion, ten mines had been dug at various points under their front line. The first went up in a great spurt of earth near Beaumont-Hamel at 7.20 am, the others followed at 7.28 am. Two minutes later, the officers blew their whistles, and 66,000 men, each burdened with kit weighing at least 29 kg (65 lb), moved slowly into No Man's Land. One company of the Eighth East Surreys symbolized the 'kick-off' by booting footballs toward the German trenches.

All too soon they discovered that the stroll to unoccupied lines promised in their generals' pep talks was a cruel delusion. The Germans had survived the shelling in deep dug-outs and were now streaming out of them to set up machine-gun posts, while concealed batteries opened a devastating fire on the British forward positions.

Some assault battalions did not even get clear of their own wire before being caught by the Maxims' fatal stutter. Others, who managed to form up and begin their slow advance, were mown down as the German machine-guns traversed back and forth along their lines. Everywhere overloaded British soldiers were falling. Yet still the

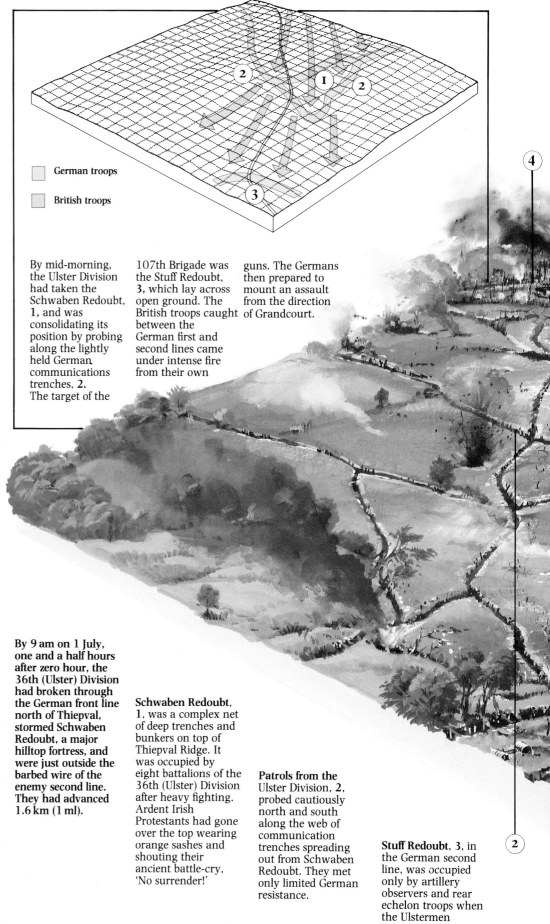

By mid-morning, the Ulster Division had taken the Schwaben Redoubt, 1, and was consolidating its position by probing along the lightly held German communications trenches, 2. The target of the 107th Brigade was the Stuff Redoubt, 3, which lay across open ground. The British troops caught between the German first and second lines came under intense fire from their own guns. The Germans then prepared to mount an assault from the direction of Grandcourt.

☐ German troops

☐ British troops

By 9 am on 1 July, one and a half hours after zero hour, the 36th (Ulster) Division had broken through the German front line north of Thiepval, stormed Schwaben Redoubt, a major hilltop fortress, and were just outside the barbed wire of the enemy second line. They had advanced 1.6 km (1 ml).

Schwaben Redoubt, 1, was a complex net of deep trenches and bunkers on top of Thiepval Ridge. It was occupied by eight battalions of the 36th (Ulster) Division after heavy fighting. Ardent Irish Protestants had gone over the top wearing orange sashes and shouting their ancient battle-cry, 'No surrender!'

Patrols from the Ulster Division, 2, probed cautiously north and south along the web of communication trenches spreading out from Schwaben Redoubt. They met only limited German resistance.

Stuff Redoubt, 3, in the German second line, was occupied only by artillery observers and rear echelon troops when the Ulstermen appeared in front of its barbed wire.

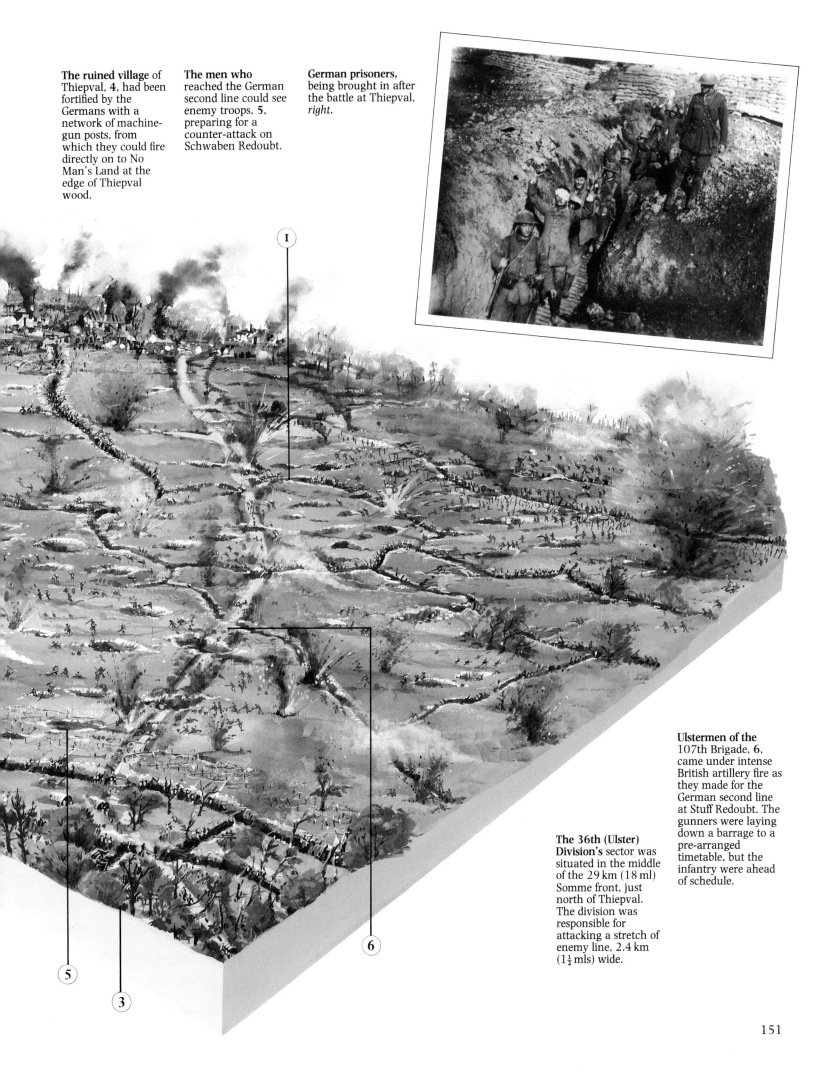

The ruined village of Thiepval, **4**, had been fortified by the Germans with a network of machine-gun posts, from which they could fire directly on to No Man's Land at the edge of Thiepval wood.

The men who reached the German second line could see enemy troops, **5**, preparing for a counter-attack on Schwaben Redoubt.

German prisoners, being brought in after the battle at Thiepval, *right*.

Ulstermen of the 107th Brigade, **6**, came under intense British artillery fire as they made for the German second line at Stuff Redoubt. The gunners were laying down a barrage to a pre-arranged timetable, but the infantry were ahead of schedule.

The 36th (Ulster) Division's sector was situated in the middle of the 29 km (18 ml) Somme front, just north of Thiepval. The division was responsible for attacking a stretch of enemy line, 2.4 km (1½ mls) wide.

waves of khaki-clad men pressed forward at Rawlinson's required pace of 91 m (100 yds) a minute, with a one-minute interval between each successive battalion. The heavily outnumbered Germans were astonished that no effort was made by the attackers to take cover from their deadly fire. One or two machine-gun crews were destroying whole battalions.

Overruling the more cautious Rawlinson, Haig insisted that the objective, on 1 July, of the six divisions attacking north of the main Albert to Bapaume road should include both the first and second German lines, since they were close together on that part of the front. South of the road, Haig's other five divisions, together with part of the French Sixth Army, were to concentrate only on the forward positions because there the enemy's second line was much farther away.

By the end of the first bloody hour, only about 30 per cent of the 84 assaulting battalions were anywhere near where they should have been. The rest were either trapped in exposed pockets in German trenches or had been repulsed.

Rawlinson's right wing and the French were progressing well in their advance toward Montauban, but the assault in the centre of the line—behind which Haig's cavalry reserve was poised to exploit a breakthrough—had come to a halt. North of the River Ancre, toward Beaumont-Hamel, there had been bitter fighting with only isolated successes, and at Gommecourt, the Third Army's diversion was running into difficulties. The least appalling estimate after the dreadful carnage put British losses by 8.30 am at some 30,000 men, that is, 50 per cent of the force employed in the initial attack.

Throughout the long morning Rawlinson fed in more and more men until, by midday, 129 battalions—100,000 soldiers—were engaged in the savage, sprawling battle. News was still good from the right flank. Montauban had fallen to the 30th Division (the only division to capture and hold all its objectives that morning), and the 18th Division was also making significant gains. Elsewhere, apart from the Ulster Division's gallant capture of part of the enemy's second line at Thiepval, it was a grim catalogue of failed assaults and successful German counter-attacks on the short lengths of trench wrested from them earlier in the day.

In the early afternoon, an eerie stillness briefly fell over the field, as if by mutual agreement the combatants had paused to gain their second wind. Then the conflict burst forth again with renewed ferocity. Around Fricourt and Gommecourt, more

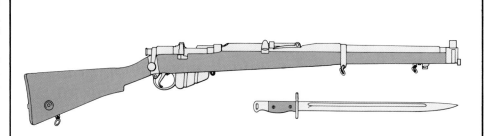

The Short Magazine Lee-Enfield Mk 1 rifle was the standard weapon of the British infantryman in the First World War. It was of .303 calibre, with a bolt action and a 10-round capacity, and was issued with a sword bayonet. The Lee-Enfield, first produced in 1895, was a marriage of the American Lee box magazine and an improved, rifled barrel from the Royal Small Arms Factory at Enfield. During the Boer War, mounted infantry was used extensively, and the soldiers found their long rifles unwieldy when on horseback. It was decided to design a shorter weapon, which could be used with equal facility by infantry and cavalry without sacrificing power. In 1902, the Short Magazine Lee-Enfield was produced: it proved to be one of the best rifles of all time.

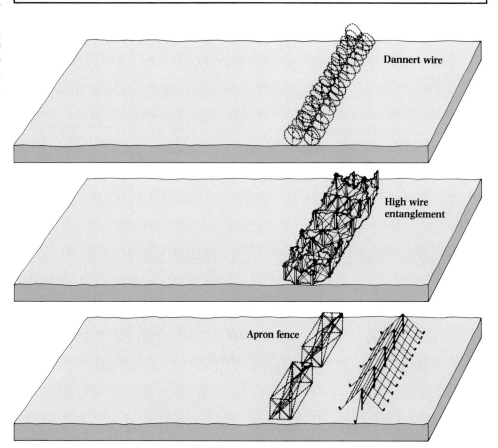

Dannert wire

High wire entanglement

Apron fence

Barbed wire came into its own when the Allies and the Germans began to dig in opposite each other on a 645-km (400-ml) front, stretching from the Channel coast to the Swiss frontier. Both sides protected their trench systems with acres of jagged fences. Coiled, 'dannert', wire was unrolled and then supported by metal posts; some coils were secured to the next with metal clips. High wire entanglements could be constructed by attaching single strands of barbed wire in criss-cross fashion to a maze of wooden posts. Apron fences, with barbed wire in pyramid shape, were supported by corkscrew poles. Both sides sent out wiring parties at night to repair damage.

Before the Somme offensive opened, tunnels were dug beneath ten strongpoints in the German front line and filled with high explosives. The mines were set off just before zero hour. This remarkable picture, taken at Hawthorn Ridge, Beaumont-Hamel, shows the precise moment when 18 tons of dynamite demolished an enemy redoubt just 460 m (500 yds) in front of the British line.

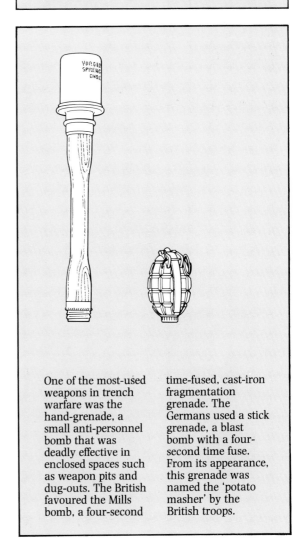

British infantry, *top*, going into battle at Thiepval Ridge. Stretcher bearers, *above*, carrying a wounded comrade out of a trench in Thiepval village.

One of the most-used weapons in trench warfare was the hand-grenade, a small anti-personnel bomb that was deadly effective in enclosed spaces such as weapon pits and dug-outs. The British favoured the Mills bomb, a four-second time-fused, cast-iron fragmentation grenade. The Germans used a stick grenade, a blast bomb with a four-second time fuse. From its appearance, this grenade was named the 'potato masher' by the British troops.

153

British battalions were badly mauled, while at Thiepval the Ulstermen, who had been hanging on to the Schwaben Redoubt since morning, without reinforcements, had to give ground as their ammunition dwindled.

In the south, Rawlinson's right-wing divisions and the French continued to do well. Mametz had now been taken, and for about 9.5 km (6 mls) Allied troops were poised on the edge of open country. The French were keen to push on, but the British stood fast. Their orders called for the capture and consolidation of Montauban on the first day and specifically stated that no serious advance was to be made beyond that until preparations for the second phase of the operation were complete.

Shortly after 3 pm on 1 July, the village of Mametz fell, leaving British and French troops in possession of a 9.5-km (6-ml) stretch of the German front line that ran south as far as the River Somme. Four divisions were poised on the edge of open country. To their dismay, they were ordered to dig in.

Despite French protests that a promising opportunity was being missed, Rawlinson would not relent. The cavalry, which might have proved useful had he agreed to exploit the right's successes, was ordered out of the battle area in mid-afternoon, without having seen any action.

As gathering dusk brought to a close the first terrible day of the Somme offensive, the Fourth Army's commander managed to build up a reasonably comprehensive account of events, despite conflicting reports

After prolonged artillery bombardment and vicious hand-to-hand fighting, at 3 pm the 7th division took what remained of Mametz village, 1. Its capture extended British penetration of the enemy defences on the southern flank to a frontage 4.8 km (3 mls) wide.

Men of the 18th Division, 2, looked out on green fields and trees in leaf behind the German reserve trenches northeast of Montauban, 3. Having gained their objective, they awaited the arrival of support troops to help them exploit their breakthrough. 'Where is the cavalry?', they asked.

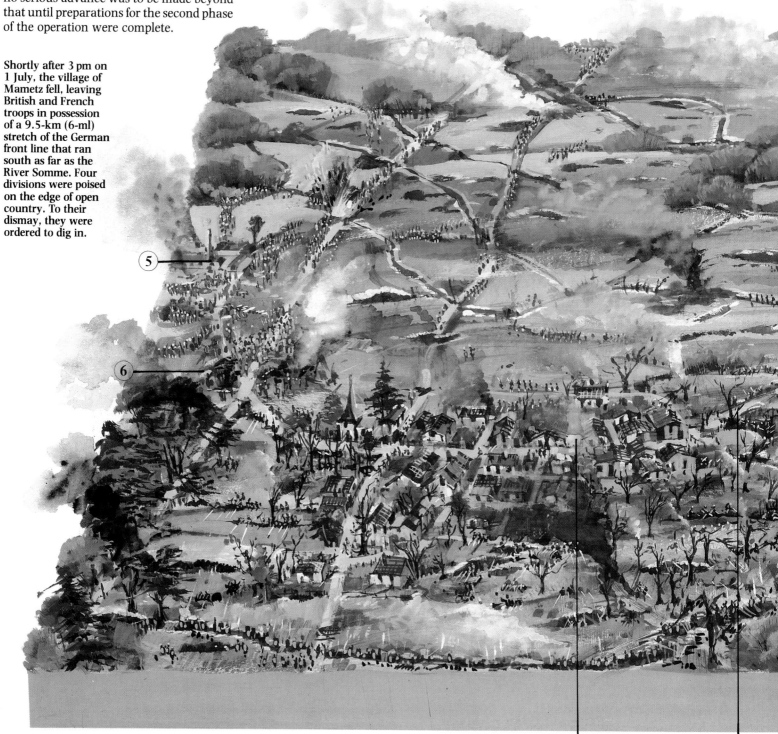

Reserves made their way up to the new British front line. Crossing through the litter of war, 4, which covered the old No Man's Land and the remains of the German trenches, they encountered little enemy fire. One soldier described it as 'a cakewalk'.

The brickyard, 5, now in the hands of the 4th Liverpool Pals Battalion, had been a troublesome enemy strongpoint at the junction of the British and French positions. A swift assault after a bombardment caught the enemy, vulnerable in their dug-outs.

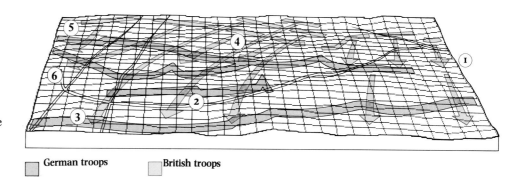

German troops   British troops

Montauban, 3, was the first enemy village to fall into British hands on 1 July. The 30th Division attacked vigorously, taking the German front line, then sweeping on a further 914 m (1,000 yds) to Montauban, which it occupied at 10.30 in the morning.

Elements of the French Sixth Army, 6, formed the right flank of the Somme offensive. With great *élan*, they advanced on a 4.8-km (3-ml) front between Montauban and the river, driving the enemy before them in panic and disorder.

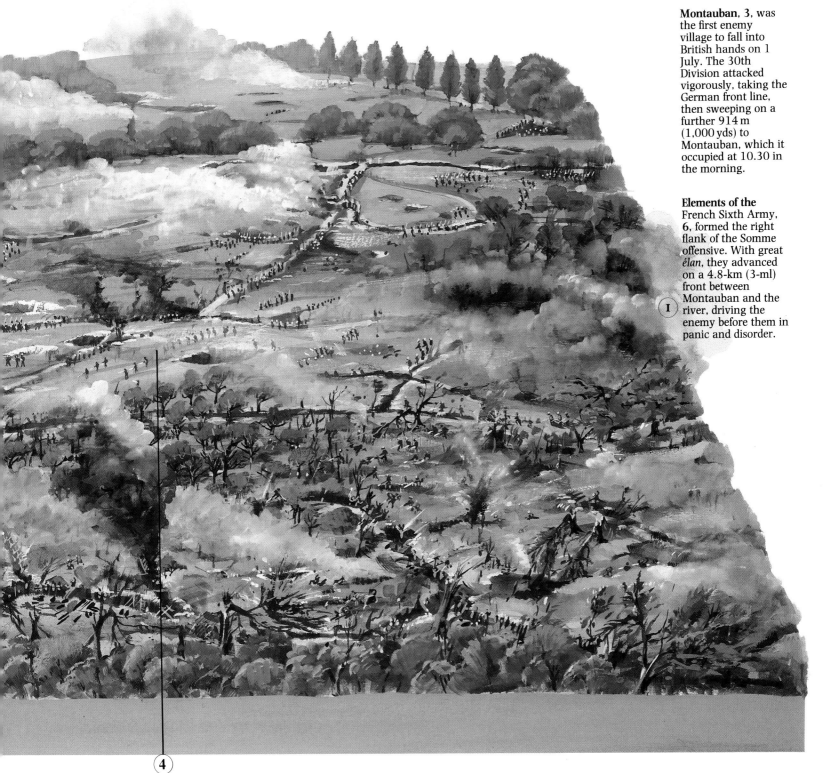

and disrupted communications. His estimate of 16,000 casualties, however, was wildly inaccurate, for, apart from the thousands of corpses, No Man's Land was littered with badly wounded men, some of whom had been lying untended for hours. Behind the front, casualty clearing stations overflowed with wounded, while at the railhead there were not enough ambulance trains available to take the worst cases to base hospitals. What the hard-pressed medical services were trying to do was cope with the British army's blackest day. Losses amounted to a shocking 57,470 men. Of 129 fighting battalions, 32 lost more than 500 men each. Worst hit of all was the 10th West Yorks: 710 men fell.

On the other side of the shell-pocked battlefield, the Germans had not suffered anything like such heavy casualties and were relieved that they had held the greater part of 42 km (26 mls) of trenches.

Their relief was short-lived, for General Haig resolved to sustain the Somme offensive into the autumn, attacking whenever and wherever an opportunity was presented, but never again in the terrible manner of 1 July.

Reinforced and regrouped, the British engaged in a bloody slogging match. For every hundred metres gained, the butcher's bill rose higher and higher; but now the Germans were also experiencing dreadful losses, particularly in their unsuccessful counter-attacks. Haig's men were in the ascendant on the Somme.

In September, a new British invention, the tank, went into action in support of an attack on the heavily-defended villages of Flers and Courcellette. At first the tanks' advance was hugely successful; then some broke down, others became embedded in the mud and the attack foundered.

Throughout the remainder of the autumn, bad weather hampered Haig's operations and, on 19 November, when it was evident that the winter was setting in, he finally shut down the offensive. By then the BEF was astride the ridge occupied by the enemy when the fighting began.

As far as can be ascertained with any degree of accuracy, the British and French between them lost 600,000 men during the four-and-a-half month campaign, the Germans a similar number.

In claiming victory, General Haig rightly stated that his offensive had relieved the beleaguered forces at Verdun, had pinned down German troops which otherwise would have been transferred to the Russian and Italian fronts, and had inflicted damaging losses on the enemy. The achievement of any one of these objectives, he said, would have justified his continued attacks.

Although Britain's latest weapons—armoured vehicles nicknamed 'tanks'—were not used on 1 July, they first saw action during the Somme offensive. On 15 September, at dawn, 32 of the 30-ton monsters rumbled forward at 6 km/h (4 mph) to support an attack on the villages of Flers and Courcellette. As a result of breakdowns, only 18 of the untried giants, each armed with two 6-pounder naval guns, were successful in engaging the surprised Germans. The Mark 1 tanks, which housed a crew of eight inside their diamond-shaped hulls, had started a new era in warfare.

When planning the Somme offensive, General Sir Douglas Haig created a Reserve Army of three cavalry divisions, under Lieutenant-General Sir Hubert Gough, to exploit the hoped-for breakthrough by the infantry of General Rawlinson's Fourth Army. On the morning of 1 July, thousands of troopers were standing to horse just behind the line. As attacks foundered along most of the front, it became apparent that there would be little use for cavalry that day. Only the 2nd Indian Cavalry Division on the right wing could have played a useful part when the infantry reached open country; but Rawlinson would not let them advance.

There can be few more sobering experiences than contemplation of the rows upon rows of graves in the multitude of war cemeteries which dot the now peaceful Picardy landscape. Each represents a young life—British, Commonwealth, French or German— laid down for his country in the most costly battle of the First World War—the Somme. Not all lie in marked plots. A memorial at Thiepval remembers 73,367 British alone, who were never found.

The consequences of the Battle of the Somme are even today in dispute. German losses were heavy, but Haig's planned breakthrough, for which so many lives and so much *matériel* had been expended, had not materialized. The Allied front had been advanced in places, although nowhere for more than 8 km (5 mls). German resistance remained tenacious, and a decision on the Western Front as elusive as ever. There seemed nothing for it but for both sides to face each other entrenched, in a prolonged war of attrition. 'Idealism,' the historian A.J.P. Taylor was later to write, 'perished on the Somme.' No commander yet seemed to appreciate that attack invited disaster. This was not only because attacking troops were exposed to fire while defenders enjoyed the protection of dug-outs, but also because the advent of railways had altered the nature of warfare, for advancing troops were soon ahead of their railheads, and new lines had then to be laid. Retreating troops, meanwhile, fell back on their depots and could be rapidly reinforced. Thus the war in the west was to come to an end only in 1918, when Germany launched a last offensive and—when it was inevitably checked— became exhausted and incapable of further effort.

Tyneside Irish, *top*, advancing in the attack on La Boisselle on 1 July.

Reloading a British 18-pounder, *centre*, near Montauban on 30 July.

The Wiltshire Regiment, *above*, advancing to the attack at Thiepval.

The Ebro/*24 July-18 November, 1938*

The last hope of a Republican victory over General Francisco Franco's Nationalist insurgents in the bitter Spanish Civil War of 1936-9 perished, along with thousands of idealistic young men, in the Battle of the Ebro, a fierce confrontation of 16 weeks' duration. By the summer of 1938, the Nationalists, backed by men, weapons and material supplied by Hitler and Mussolini, had occupied two-thirds of Spain. The Republicans, who had been elected by popular vote in 1931, still resisted in Catalonia in the north and in a large area of the southeast, including the capital, Madrid. They included a strong Communist faction and were supported by Stalin, in much the same way as his fellow-dictators aided Franco. The ranks of the Republican army were also swelled by several thousand anti-Fascist volunteers from abroad, who were formed into International Brigades.

In July 1938, the Nationalists, who had much of the regular Spanish Army at their core and were generally better trained and equipped than their opponents, began to push toward Valencia on the right flank of the Republicans' southeastern stronghold.

Dr Juan Negrin, the Republican Prime Minister of Spain, called for an offensive in the north to relieve pressure on Valencia. His Chief of Staff, General Vincente Rojo, evolved a plan to strike at Nationalist lines of communication beyond the River Ebro and, if practicable, cut a passage to open a direct link with their comrades in Valencia.

For this purpose, the Army of the Ebro was formed under General Guillotto Modesto, a Communist and former woodcutter. It comprised about 80,000 men, who were inadequately supported by artillery and armour but were covered by 100 fighter aircraft sent by the Soviet Union.

On the dark, moonless night of 24 July, Modesto's men and equipment started moving across the river, which was 91 m (100 yds) wide in places, by boat and on pontoon bridges. They took General Juan Yagüe's Army of Africa completely by surprise. Modesto's offensive was launched on a 64-km (40-ml) front from Mequinenza in the north to Amposta in the south, although the main push was concentrated in the centre of the big eastward loop of the Ebro between Fayon and Cherta.

Within 48 hours of the crossing, the 5th Corps, led by General Enrique Lister, a staunch Communist, had captured all the high ground in the loop of the river, taken 4,000 prisoners and penetrated 40 km (25 mls), to the outskirts of Gandesa.

Yagüe's men, having established defensive positions, managed to stem the Republican advance, pending the arrival of reinforcements. Franco, however, did not

The great Republican offensive in northeast Spain in July 1938 was launched against Nationalist positions on the west bank of the River Ebro. The attack was made on a front 64 km (40 mls) wide, from

Mequinenza in the north to Amposta in the south.

Within two days of their surprise attack across the Ebro, on 24 July 1938, the Republicans had advanced 40 km (25 mls) to the outskirts of Gandesa. There they were halted by Nationalist troops on Hill 481. On 1 August, a day of brilliant sunshine, the British battalion of the 15th International Brigade made a final effort to storm the rock-strewn hillside.

Hill 481, **1**, known to the British battalion as 'The Pimple', was a steep, rocky knoll 2 km (1¼ mls) east of Gandesa, which dominated the approach to the town. Nationalists called it, more fittingly, 'the hill of death'.

Nationalist positions, comprising weapon pits and concrete bunkers protected by wire, lined the upper slopes, **2**, of Hill 481. They were held by Moorish troops from General Yagüe's Army of Africa.

Throughout 1 August, the Republicans' British battalion tried to wrest Hill 481 from the Nationalists. Their attacks, **3**, were all repulsed by concentrated close-range small arms fire and a hail of hand-grenades. The losses were heavy.

In the summer of 1936, the Spanish military, restive under the Socialist reforming government that had followed the overthrow of the monarchy, rebelled after a violent clash between the Spanish Foreign Legion and a Communist-led mob in Melilla, Spanish Morocco. The former Chief of Staff, General Francisco Franco, who had been posted to the Canary Islands by the Socialist government to keep him politically inactive, flew to Melilla to assume command. His forces were then flown by German aircraft to Algeciras, in southern Spain. The military garrisons in the northwest declared for Franco and the two forces combined.

During the war, Spain was roughly divided into two regions: the west supported the army (the Nationalists) while the east supported the government (the Republicans). The focal point of the war was Madrid: if Franco could strangle the city's lines of communication, the government would be deprived of support from other areas.

The Nationalist forces, well supplied by Nazi Germany and Fascist Italy, had a marked advantage over the Republicans. Nevertheless, the Soviet Union sent arms and, despite their policy of non-intervention, the United Kingdom and France provided 12 volunteer battalions for the International Brigades.

The Republicans lacked artillery in the battle. A few Russian tanks, **4**, were brought up, but were knocked out early in the fight for Hill 481.

The Nationalists could call down barrages of defensive artillery fire at will, as the shellbursts, **5**, on the slopes of Hill 481 testify.

The Republicans took what cover they could on the rocky, open hillside, **6**. Many sheltered from enemy gunfire behind low, stone barricades, only to be wounded by splinters of rock.

159

intend to counter-attack until he had established artillery and air superiority over the enemy. In the meantime, all the bridges over the Ebro were subjected to bombing raids to disrupt Modesto's supply lines.

On the ground, Lister repeatedly tried to capture Gandesa and, as July turned into August, Republican infantrymen, desperately short of artillery support, were sent up the steep, open, rocky slopes time and again in a futile effort to dislodge the Nationalists. Sometimes they even got within grenade-lobbing distance of Yagüe's positions, which were protected by barbed wire and bristling with machine-gun nests, but they could never break in.

The key to Gandesa was Hill 481, a knoll east of the town. On 1 August, Lister ordered the British battalion of the 15th International Brigade to make an all-out attempt to shift the defenders so that the momentum of the victorious Republican advance could be resumed.

Under a blistering sun, the British courageously attacked again and again. They were driven back with heavy losses by enfilading machine-gun and rifle fire and bombardment from batteries. Their repulse at Hill 481 marked the turning point of the great Republican offensive.

On 6 August, the first Nationalist counter-attacks began, under an umbrella of massed artillery and aerial bombardment: the Republicans lost all their gains between Mequinenza and Fayon in the north. All along its lines, the Army of the Ebro was subjected to incessant bombing and shelling as the Nationalists pressed their attacks. But Lister's men held out tenaciously and, after nearly three months of continuous battering along a 40-km (25-ml) front, fell back 8 km (5 mls).

Franco massed more and more men and guns on the Fayon-Cherta line in preparation for a big push. At dawn on 30 October, his artillery, ranged almost wheel to wheel, opened a three-hour bombardment of First World War proportions, while 100 bomber aircraft joined in the pounding. Infantry and armour moved forward and began to clear the obstinately held heights. By 3 November, the Nationalists' right flank was resting on the Ebro. Eleven days later, Yagüe was poised to oust the remaining Republicans when a heavy snowfall halted operations. On 18 November, however, the last enemy bridgehead across the river was in his hands. The battle was over.

The confrontation on the Ebro degenerated into the biggest, most bloody fight of the war and so drained the Republicans' limited resources that they were never able to mount a big offensive again.

General Juan Yagüe, who commanded the Nationalist Army of Africa on the Ebro front, was an uncompromising officer of much experience. He was known as 'the butcher of Asturias' for the merciless way his African soldiers repressed a workers' uprising in that province in 1934. Franco briefly suspended Yagüe at one point during the war, after he had publicly praised the effectiveness of the Republican Army and described the Germans and Italians as 'beasts of prey'.

General Guillotto Modesto led the Republican army in its initially successful Ebro offensive. A former Andalusian woodcutter, he had been hailed as one of the Republic's best military commanders. Modesto was an ardent Communist who had received his political and military training in Moscow. When Madrid fell in March 1939, he and other Communist commanders fled the country.

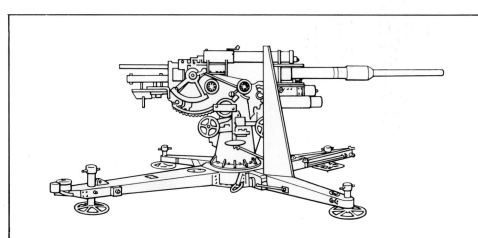

General Franco's Nationalist army received modern equipment and reinforcements from the Fascist dictators, Hitler and Mussolini, who used the war as a testing ground. Nazi Germany sent the Condor Legion, a 5,000-strong combat force equipped with experimental tanks, anti-tank weapons (including the 88 mm gun, *above*, which was to prove so successful in the Second World War) and aircraft. They also supplied Franco with instructors and specialists. Italy provided 75,000 men, many tanks and some 600 bomber and fighter aircraft. The Germans gave the world a grim foretaste of the total war that was soon to be unleashed in Europe, when aircrews from the Condor Legion saturated the undefended town of Guernica on 26 April 1937, reducing it to rubble and causing more than 2,000 casualties.

When the Civil War broke out in Spain in 1936, Stalin pledged Russian aid and encouraged volunteers from all over the world to take up the anti-Fascist cause of the Republicans. By October of that year, the first of the International Brigades were going to the front. Not all of the 35,000 foreigners who went to fight against Franco were Comintern recruits from a working-class background: many were idealistic young intellectuals, *above*, who saw the war as a chance to combat Fascism.

Republican hope of restoring communications between Catalonia and the south faded with the Ebro counter-offensive in the summer of 1938. The end of the war was in sight, for Franco could now advance to seize Madrid and destroy the last Republican bastions in Catalonia. Madrid held out stubbornly but eventually fell in March 1939. The leaders of the Republic's Loyalist Defence Council escaped to France, as later did many of their soldiers. In all, about 700,000 people were killed in the war and a further 30,000 were executed or assassinated after Franco's victory, when tribunals were established to try Republican activists.

European nations had watched the conflict especially closely, and some, notably Germany, learned valuable military lessons. There was one lesson, however, that the Germans did not learn. For 28 months during the Spanish Civil War, Madrid had been besieged and persistently bombed—but without the expected result of wholesale civilian panic. When the Germans tried the same tactic on London a few years later, during the Second World War, the same dogged stoicism was shown by its inhabitants.

During the Spanish Civil War, mounted infantry, *top*, was, surprisingly, still used by both armies. Republican tanks, *above*, were greatly outnumbered by Nationalist armour.

El Alamein/*23 October-4 November, 1942*

Lieutenant-General Bernard Montgomery, having made meticulous plans to ensure victory, retired early to his caravan on the eve of the Battle of El Alamein. His confidence that evening, 23 October 1942, was well founded. Since his arrival in Egypt 10 weeks before to take command of an army which had had a succession of leaders and recently more reverses than successes, he had reorganized, reinforced, re-equipped and retrained the force. Most important of all, he had restored its morale. Montgomery had another advantage over the enemy: Allied Intelligence had broken the Germans' code, and he knew that they were at the end of over-extended supply lines, short of petrol and other vital supplies, and without adequate air cover. It did not follow that they would be easily defeated, but the odds were stacked against them.

The Eighth Army, composed mainly of British and Commonwealth soldiers, was now poised to attempt what the British Prime Minister, Winston Churchill, had been urging for months: 'To take or destroy the German–Italian Army.'

For a time after General Erwin Rommel, the German commander, had brought panzers to North Africa to bolster the flagging Italians, it had looked as if the Axis might reach Cairo. Displaying dash, audacity, tactical brilliance, and often ignoring inhibiting orders from his superiors, Rommel led his tanks and mechanized infantry to a succession of victories against numerically stronger forces. Adolf Hitler promoted him to Field Marshal.

Then Rommel encountered major supply difficulties because many Axis merchant ships were being sunk in the Mediterranean. There was also suspicion in the Afrika Korps that some of the stores earmarked for them were being diverted to the increasing operations on the Eastern Front. Rommel was particularly short of petrol and vehicles. The Afrika Korps became, of necessity, a make-do-and-mend army, even using captured enemy transport until it broke down for want of spares.

Nevertheless the Desert Fox, as he had been dubbed by the British Press, fought on with his customary flair and by the beginning of July 1942 was deep inside Egypt, threatening the Nile delta. By now, however, the supply shortage was critical. Convoys from the main bases at Tripoli and Benghazi took 12 and 7 days respectively to make the round trip along the coastal road, which was under frequent attack from the British Desert Air Force. To add to Rommel's problems, infantry reinforcements were sent without transport, making them 'as good as useless' for desert warfare.

In a concerted attempt to exploit his

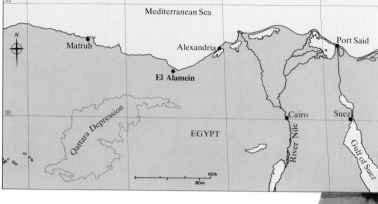

Alexandria, Cairo, and the Suez Canal were Mussolini's objectives, when he advanced eastward from the Italian colony of Libya into Egypt, in September 1940. His plan was to re-establish his prestige by a quick victory after his army's poor showing in southern France.

Great prizes were at stake: control of the southern Mediterranean and the Middle East oilfields, on which the Allies depended for their war effort, and a chance to force a way through Asia Minor to threaten Russia on a second front. By December,

however, the Allies counter-attacked and, though numerically inferior, threw the Italians not only out of Egypt but out of eastern Libya as well. A humiliated Mussolini was obliged to accept help from Hitler's panzer divisions, which were commanded by the brilliant Erwin Rommel.

The war in the desert rolled back and forth for nearly two years after Rommel had captured the area, late in 1940. The lack of a decisive victory was largely attributable to the problems of supply over such great distances and the relative quality of equipment.
At times the British and Commonwealth forces had the better tanks and guns, sometimes the Germans and Italians. Moreover, when either side advanced against the other, those attacking moved farther and farther from their supply base, while those attacked fell back closer and closer to theirs.

By the autumn of 1942, however, the British forces had been heavily reinforced and re-equipped. Rommel knew that time was against him; he must reach the Suez Canal now or the prize would forever elude

him. But between him and the canal lay the Eighth Army, newly self-confident under General Montgomery. The Allies held a strong line, some 64 km (40 mls) long, stretching from the

Qattara Depression— a large, treacherous natural feature in the south—to the small railway junction of El Alamein in the north.

On the night of 24 October, the Allies launched a massive surprise night attack on the German front, across a total of 19 km (12 mls) of mined desert.

The defending German 164th Division, **1**, during frequent flashes of gunfire, could pinpoint the advancing Allies against the night sky. The German machine-gun and mortar fire from both flanks inflicted heavy casualties.

Although one flank of the Italian Trento Division, **2**, was virtually intact after the Allied barrage, the other flank, **3**, was destroyed, after furious hand-to-hand fighting, by the onslaught of the 2nd New Zealand Division, **4**.

Barbed wire, **5**, provided the only protective barriers, apart from minefields, in the featureless desert. The wire was laid down by both sides on a massive scale—hundreds of miles of it—to cover forward positions and hamper the enemy.

Inspired by the skirl of the pipes, the 51st Highland Division, **6**, marched so quickly on the German lines that they were overtaken by their own barrage, as well as hit by enemy fire. But their left flank, **7**, was able to storm the ridge with bayonets and grenades.

At 3 am, a golden, Very light sent up from the Miteiriya ridge, **8**, signalled the success of the 2nd New Zealand Division, **4**. Advancing to level ground, **9**, they dug in to consolidate the line and wait for support.

Misled by faulty intelligence, the 1st South African Division, **10**, was unprepared for the strength of the German defence. Stopped dead in their tracks, they had to ward off a counter-attack by the enemy before moving forward again.

The whole Allied attack, known as 'Operation Lightfoot', was conceived as a series of 'leap-frogging' movements: battalions moved forward in stages, each seizing a strongpoint and providing cover for the next battalion to advance. The Highlanders, **6**, nostalgically named each strongpoint after a Scottish town.

Visibility in the dust and smoke was so poor that the Allied divisions were guided by red and green tracer bullets fired over their heads. Individual battalions followed more precise paths, marked out by masked hurricane lamps and white tape, which led through the labyrinth of the minefields.

Tank support, 11, fell behind, owing to the infantry's rapid advance, and was further slowed down by wrecked vehicles on the paths through the minefield.

163

spectacular gains, Rommel renewed the attack on 30 August at Alam el Halfa. Montgomery had expected this and drove him back beyond the strategically important line from El Alamein, near the Mediterranean coast, to the Qattara Depression, 64 km (40 mls) to the south. With his flanks secure, 'Monty', as his troops called him, organized the Eighth Army to deliver a decisive blow.

Winston Churchill, delighted that the initiative had been seized at Alam el Halfa, wanted the pressure sustained. He urged Montgomery to use the September full-moon period, only a fortnight away, to launch a full-scale attack. Montgomery wisely refused to move until all was in readiness. The time he chose was the eve of the October full moon, when armour and infantry would next be able to operate easily at night. Those seven weeks saw intense activity as he and his staff prepared for 'Operation Lightfoot'. The initial outline of the coming offensive was written by Montgomery himself. As he put it later, a master plan is not a master plan unless the master has written it.

The gravest threat to Montgomery's forces during the massive build-up of men and *matériel* was the desert itself. It was impossible to conceal everything in such featureless terrain, but some deception was achieved by the construction of huge dummy staging areas in the south, far from the point where the main thrust would be made by the Allies.

By mid-October the Eighth Army comprised 195,000 men. Its tank force had increased from 896 to 1,351, including 285 of the latest American Shermans. Artillery, ranging from two-pounder anti-tank guns to medium weapons, numbered 1,900 pieces. On the other side of the minefields, Rommel mustered 100,000 men, 510 tanks, of which 300 were inferior Italian models, and 1,325 guns.

The day before the offensive opened, the men of the Eighth Army were confined to their slit trenches, forbidden to abandon cover for any purpose. This order paid dividends, for the first moment the Axis forces knew that they were to be attacked in strength was at 9.40 pm precisely, on 23 October, when they were enveloped by the biggest artillery barrage since the end of the First World War.

Unfortunately for the Axis, Field Marshal Rommel was on sick leave in Austria at the time. Then, to make matters worse for the Germans, General Stumme, the officer sent to relieve Rommel, died of a heart attack while on reconnaissance at the start of the battle. General von Thoma, commander of the Afrika Korps, assumed responsibility

Lieutenant-General Bernard Montgomery (1887–1976). 'Monty' himself fostered the myth that the austerity of his daily routine extended to his style of command. He stressed the meticulous care with which he planned his battle strategy down to the last detail, yet much of his strength as a leader lay in his flexibility— he might modify his plans at the last minute to suit prevailing conditions.

A veteran of the First World War, he had not seen action since 1940, at Dunkirk, but had spent time in the Home Forces, developing the brand of professionalism that was to transform the whole Eighth Army. He forged diverse units into a cohesive fighting force to dispel the legend of German invincibility.

Field Marshal Erwin Rommel (1891–1944). Rommel's hallmark in battle was a devastating combination of cool judgement and fiery intuition. His inspired talent for turning mistakes into success lay at the heart of many of his victories in Africa.

His distinguished career began in 1910 and he saw much combat in the First World War. He was a full general at the age of only 49. Known as a 'soldier's general', Rommel lived under the same tough conditions as his men; this exacerbated his failing health and led to his absence during the Allied attack.

After his initial successful thrust across Africa, German morale was so high—and the High Command so confident of victory—that the retreat of November 1942 was greeted with incredulity.

General Georg Stumme (1886–1942). Stumme was sent by Hitler to replace Rommel, whose ill-health had forced him temporarily to seek treatment in Austria. His appointment was more political than military, and Rommel, though less than enthusiastic, briefed him fully the moment he arrived in Africa.

Ironically, it was Stumme's determination to stick to the letter of Rommel's instructions which, more than any ineptitude, contributed to the Axis setback under the Allied surprise attacks on 23 and 24 October. Until that moment, Stumme had done much to keep up morale among his troops.

On 24 October, Stumme was reconnoitring the front line when he ran into British infantry. He escaped a bullet but died of a heart attack, which forced Rommel's premature return.

The Sherman tank made its battle début at El Alamein and, from 1943, became the standard Allied medium tank. Its 75 mm gun, mounted in a turret with all-round traverse, vastly improved its fighting effectiveness. And since the gun was hydro-electrically stabilized, it could fire accurately while the tank was moving. Weighing around 30 tons, with a top speed of 40 km/h (25 mph), the Sherman could be assembled from prefabricated parts in 30 minutes. In all, more than 49,000 were built in some 20 different Marks.

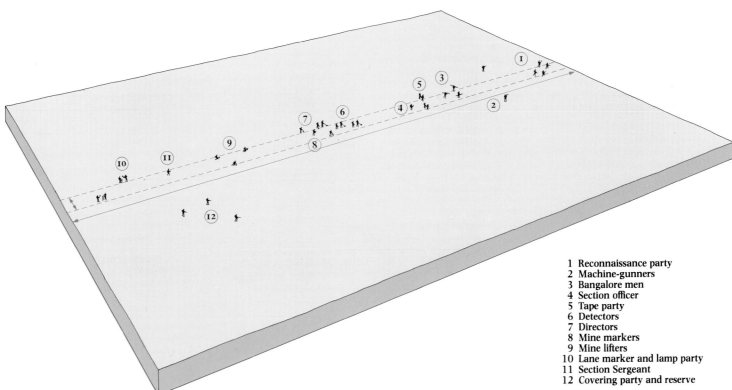

1 Reconnaissance party
2 Machine-gunners
3 Bangalore men
4 Section officer
5 Tape party
6 Detectors
7 Directors
8 Mine markers
9 Mine lifters
10 Lane marker and lamp party
11 Section Sergeant
12 Covering party and reserve

An elaborate team of engineers was needed to clear gaps in the minefields. The old, laborious method of detecting mines by prodding the ground with bayonets was superseded by the new Polish detectors, which signalled the presence of a mine by an electrical impulse, producing a high-pitched whine in the operator's earphones. Once the mines were located and lifted, the safe areas were marked with white tape and a series of poles, from which hurricane lamps were hung, hidden in petrol cans with holes cut in their sides. The lights were changed to green and amber by pieces of coloured glass, indicating the cleared and uncleared areas respectively.

in an extremely confused combat situation. Hitler ordered Rommel to return to Egypt at once.

In two days of heavy fighting, the Eighth Army encountered more extensive minefields and stiffer resistance than had been expected. The casualty list grew, the men were exhausted, and the attack was losing impetus. Montgomery called off attempts to pierce the Axis defence by the 10th Armoured Division in the north and the 7th Armoured Division in the south.

Meanwhile, Rommel had returned to the front and, on the morning of 26 October, German and Italian units fiercely counter-attacked advanced Eighth Army positions around Kidney Ridge. They were repulsed with heavy losses. The following day, they again repeatedly assaulted in that area, with the same punishing results.

The Eighth Army returned to the offensive on the 28th. A concerted thrust was made on the northern flank, spearheaded by the 9th Australian Division, but it made little headway.

A few kilometres across the battle-littered sand, Rommel decided to bring up all German units from the south in readiness for a last-ditch attempt to hold his battered position near the coast road. Such was his despondency that he was already planning a withdrawal to Fuka, 96 km (60 mls) to the west.

There was despondency in Whitehall, as well, where an angry and incredulous Churchill demanded to know why Montgomery's offensive had come to a halt, when he enjoyed such superiority over Rommel. He accused Montgomery of fighting 'a half-hearted battle.'

Undismayed, Montgomery had already decided to abandon the idea of breaking through along the coastal road. He was instead regrouping and planning a new operation, codenamed 'Supercharge', to be launched in the area of Kidney Ridge.

The beginning of the end of this great battle of attrition was marked by the action of the night of 1–2 November. At first the Germans were caught off balance, although resistance soon stiffened. Rommel now knew that he could not hold out much longer. He ordered a withdrawal and informed Hitler of his plans.

After a break in the fighting on 3 November, the Axis forces began to retreat, only to have their orders countermanded by Hitler himself. In a message divorced from reality, Hitler told Rommel: '. . . there can be no other thought but to stand fast, yield not a yard of ground and throw every gun and every man into the battle.'

Next day, while the British 1st Armoured Division and the remnants of the Afrika

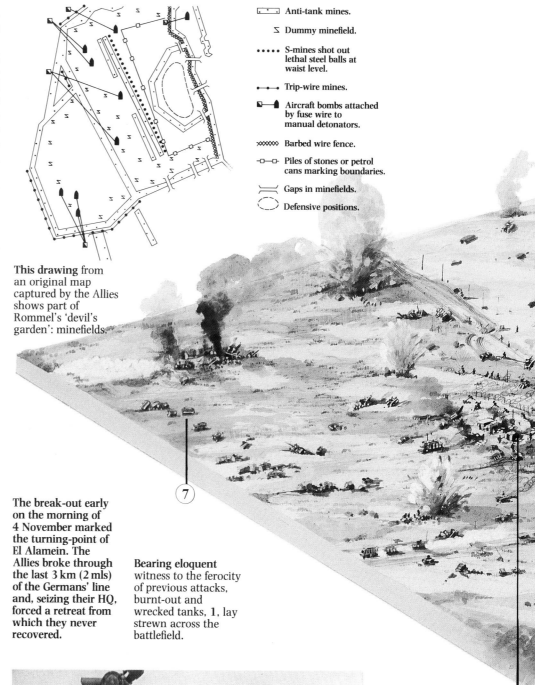

Anti-tank mines.

Dummy minefield.

S-mines shot out lethal steel balls at waist level.

Trip-wire mines.

Aircraft bombs attached by fuse wire to manual detonators.

Barbed wire fence.

Piles of stones or petrol cans marking boundaries.

Gaps in minefields.

Defensive positions.

This drawing from an original map captured by the Allies shows part of Rommel's 'devil's garden': minefields.

The break-out early on the morning of 4 November marked the turning-point of El Alamein. The Allies broke through the last 3 km (2 mls) of the Germans' line and, seizing their HQ, forced a retreat from which they never recovered.

Bearing eloquent witness to the ferocity of previous attacks, burnt-out and wrecked tanks, **1**, lay strewn across the battlefield.

Two Afrika Korps soldiers enduring the miseries of a sandstorm, common in the North African desert. Such storms were known to the British as 'khamseen'; the Germans called them 'ghibli'.

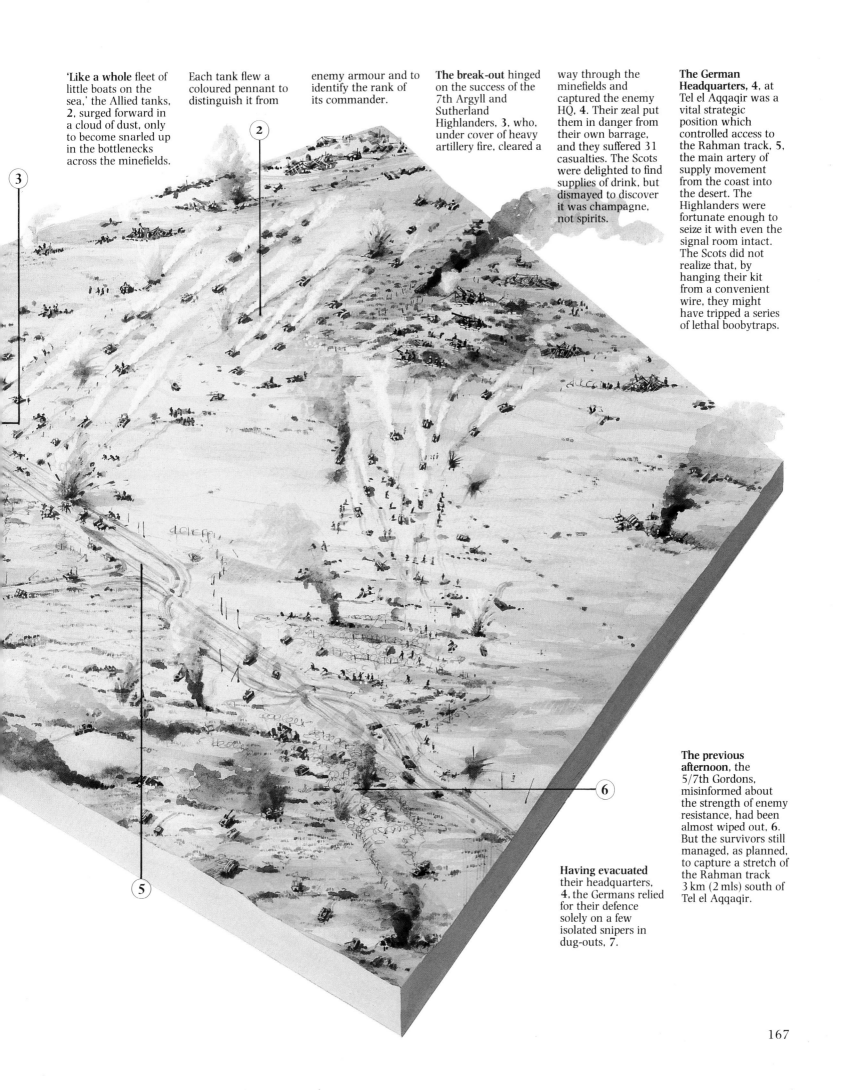

'Like a whole fleet of little boats on the sea,' the Allied tanks, 2, surged forward in a cloud of dust, only to become snarled up in the bottlenecks across the minefields.

Each tank flew a coloured pennant to distinguish it from enemy armour and to identify the rank of its commander.

The break-out hinged on the success of the 7th Argyll and Sutherland Highlanders, 3, who, under cover of heavy artillery fire, cleared a way through the minefields and captured the enemy HQ, 4. Their zeal put them in danger from their own barrage, and they suffered 31 casualties. The Scots were delighted to find supplies of drink, but dismayed to discover it was champagne, not spirits.

The German Headquarters, 4, at Tel el Aqqaqir was a vital strategic position which controlled access to the Rahman track, 5, the main artery of supply movement from the coast into the desert. The Highlanders were fortunate enough to seize it with even the signal room intact. The Scots did not realize that, by hanging their kit from a convenient wire, they might have tripped a series of lethal boobytraps.

The previous afternoon, the 5/7th Gordons, misinformed about the strength of enemy resistance, had been almost wiped out, 6. But the survivors still managed, as planned, to capture a stretch of the Rahman track 3 km (2 mls) south of Tel el Aqqaqir.

Having evacuated their headquarters, 4, the Germans relied for their defence solely on a few isolated snipers in dug-outs, 7.

Korps were engaged in heavy fighting around Tel el Aqqaqir, northwest of Kidney Ridge, Montgomery's longed-for break-out occurred: a few kilometres to the south, New Zealand infantry and the 7th Armoured Division outflanked the Axis right. Fearing encirclement and disaster, Rommel abandoned any hope of standing fast and obtained Hitler's grudging consent for a retreat to Fuka to save as much of the German army as possible.

At daybreak of 5 November, the Eighth Army's armour rolled forward in pursuit. Progress was slow, however, and the only significant portion of Rommel's army to be cut off was the remains of the 20th Mobile Corps. The New Zealanders and the 7th Armoured Division eventually arrived south of Fuka, where they were delayed by a dummy minefield—which was sub-sequently found to have been constructed by the British. Then they ran out of petrol. Rommel, meanwhile, was preparing to fall back a further 128 km (80 mls) along the coast to Mersa Matruh.

A petrol shortage again hindered Allied pusuit, on 6 November. Then, in the after-noon, it rained heavily, and the desert became impassable. All chance of encirc-ling the German army was thus lost. Rommel, who afterwards criticized Mont-gomery for not being bold enough in his pursuit, made good use of the time afforded by the bad weather. He marshalled what was left of his command—the Afrika Korps was reduced to about 20 tanks—and ordered them back along the metalled coast road as fast as possible.

On 7 November, under cover of darkness, Rommel reached Sollum, on the border between Egypt and Libya. There he learned that his enemies were now approaching him on two fronts: 'Operation Torch', an invasion of Morocco and Algeria, had been accomplished by U.S. forces under the com-mand of General Dwight D. Eisenhower. Rommel was trapped.

In the 12-day conflict at El Alamein, Montgomery's Eighth Army inflicted heavy losses on the Germans and Italians. In killed, wounded and prisoners, it is es-timated that they accounted for half of Rommel's 100,000-strong army; more-over, 450 tanks and 1,000 guns were destroyed or captured. Allied losses amoun-ted to 13,500 men; 500 tanks had been immobilized in the fighting, but only 150 were beyond repair; in addition 100 guns had been lost.

Churchill was justly jubilant. To cele-brate the victory at El Alamein he ordered that church bells should be rung through-out Great Britain for the first time since the war began more than three years earlier.

The graves of two fallen Highlanders are temporarily marked by rifles stuck muzzle-first into the sand. The bodies were later removed to a permanent resting place. All wounded were marked in this way for the attention of stretcher-bearers; but, ominously, only the dead or dying had their hats or helmets set on the rifle butts.

Triumphant soldiers of the Black Watch march 258 Germans to a POW cage after the fighting on 28 October. The cairn of stones is one of hundreds erected by British cartographers before the Second World War to serve as map reference points for desert travellers.

British infantrymen apparently surround a dead German, but his British army boots betray him— the picture was set up for propaganda purposes. The absence of water bottles and lack of sand on the guns show that no fighting was taking place at the time.

However, the basic desert kit is clearly shown: khaki drill shirt, Indian-made 'Bombay Bloomer' shorts, full sets of webbing, steel helmets, ration packs, ammunition pouches and bayonets.

Battledress trousers and blouse, woollen cardigans and heavy greatcoats were worn in winter.

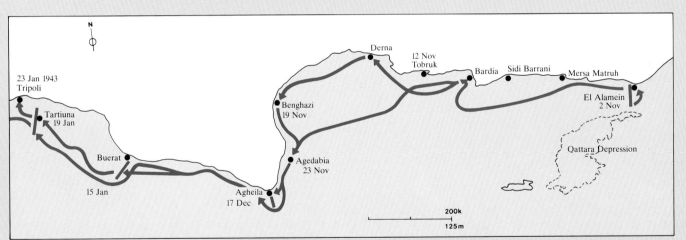

Immediately after the break-out, the retreating Germans were harried by the Allies along the north coast of Africa. In the vanguard of the pursuit was the 7th Armoured Division, whose progress from El Alamein to Tripoli is charted above. Rommel narrowly escaped disaster on several occasions: he was saved by sudden rain storms, which hampered his pursuers, by their petrol shortages and, perhaps above all, by their over-cautiousness—for which Montgomery was to be widely criticized. However, the essential objective—and the turning-point of the war—had already been achieved. As Churchill wrote: 'Before Alamein we never had a victory. After Alamein we never had a defeat.' It was an exaggeration but, in essence, true: the legend of the German army's invincibility was broken.

The European war could not be won or lost in the desert, but for the Germans, the ultimate consequences of British victory were dire. Trapped between the advancing British in the east and the American force, commanded by General Eisenhower, advancing from the west, Rommel had to evacuate North Africa. The way was now open for the Allies to invade Sicily and then Italy. Hitler, when speaking of the First World War, had repeatedly said that Germany must never again fight simultaneously on two fronts. Now he was to have to fight on three: in Russia, in Italy and, after 1944, in western Europe.

Kohima/5-18 April, 1944

In April 1944, during two weeks of desperate fighting, an assorted garrison of 1,500 British and Indian soldiers held off a 15,000-strong Japanese division, which had been ordered to sever the fragile Allied lines of communication at Kohima and then to fortify the area. This move in such unexpected strength was part of a Japanese offensive that was designed to prevent General William Slim from launching his Fourteenth Army in a drive to recover Burma, which had been overrun in 1942.

While fighting had been going on at each end of the 1,125-km (700-ml) long chain of mountains that formed the daunting frontier between India and Burma, Slim had been building up his forces to strike a decisive blow in the centre. The springboard for his assault was the plain of Imphal, the only area suitable for airfields in thousands of square kilometres of rough, mountainous country. Ground communication was limited to one narrow road, which wound 210 km (130 mls) northward through the highlands, crossing the 1,525-m (5,000-ft) high pass at Kohima, before dropping down to terminate at Dimapur, where the Assam railway began.

The plan of Lieutenant-General Renya Mutaguchi's 'Operation U-Go' was for his Fifteenth Army to smash Imphal and create a strong defensive line on the frontier so as to secure Burma for Japan.

Imphal's lines of communication were unusual. The single, vulnerable road ran parallel with the front for more than 129 km (80 mls), but this long, exposed flank did not disturb Slim, for it was considered unlikely that any force larger than a battalion would be able to traverse the 65-odd km (40 mls) of thick jungle that separated the Japanese positions on the Chindwin River from the road. As a result, only one battalion of the Assam Regiment was assigned to cover the eastern approaches to Kohima.

While fierce fighting erupted around Imphal, columns of Japanese troops were reported to be pushing through the jungle in the direction of Kohima. The Allies were now faced with the prospect of their lines of communication being taken, followed by attacks on unprotected Dimapur and the Assam railway. Even a Japanese drive deep into India now seemed possible.

Colonel Hugh Richards was hurriedly dispatched to Kohima to organize its defence. On 23 March, when he reached there, he found that, apart from the Assam Regiment battalion screening the base, a Native State battalion of undetermined efficiency and a few platoons of lightly-armed Assam Rifles, the troops at his disposal comprised an assortment of

On the night of 8 April 1944 the Japanese launched a series of fierce attacks at three different parts of the defences and sustained them next day as well. Some of the heaviest fighting took place in an area no more than 365 m by 274 m (400 yds by 300 yds).

In the spring of 1944, the Japanese decided to mount an offensive from Burma by the Fifteenth Army against the British forces gathering in India. The attack was designed as a preemptive strike to prevent the Allies gathering a force of overwhelming strength against Japan's isolated and under-strength troops in Burma. The position had drastically deteriorated during the early months of 1944, and the Japanese faced the possibility of an attack from both India and China. In conception the plan was sound, but they lacked the forces to make victory likely and allotted only three divisions to the attack. They hoped to advance on Bengal once they had secured the important communication centres of Imphal and Kohima.

The Deputy Commissioner's bungalow, 1, and another one near by, 2, were overrun by the Japanese in the darkness of the early hours of 9 April.

When the garrison was finally relieved on 18 April, all the foliage on the trees in this sector, 10, had been blasted away and the buildings reduced to rubble.

Colonel Richards' positions on Kohima Ridge dominated the main road which linked Imphal with the main supply base at Dimapur.

Shellbursts, around the Japanese positions, 9, testified to the remarkable accuracy of two Indian mountain batteries, firing in support of the defenders from 161st Brigade lines 3.2 km (2 mls) to the north.

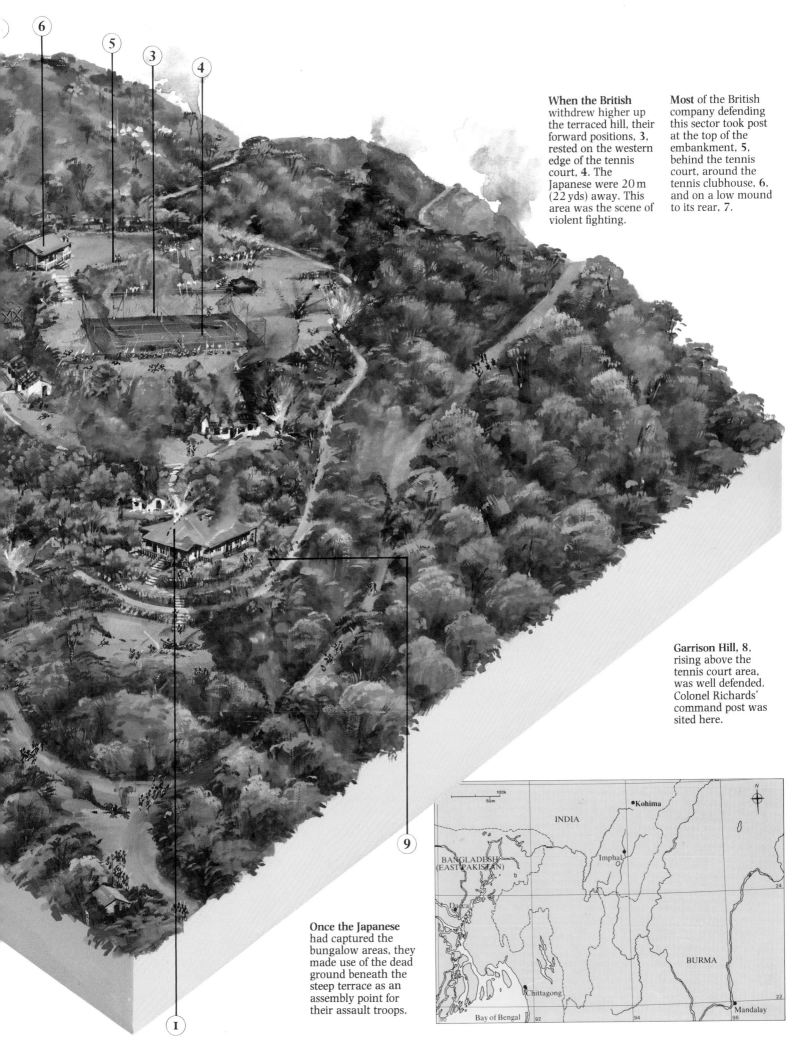

When the British withdrew higher up the terraced hill, their forward positions, **3**, rested on the western edge of the tennis court, **4**. The Japanese were 20 m (22 yds) away. This area was the scene of violent fighting.

Most of the British company defending this sector took post at the top of the embankment, **5**, behind the tennis court, around the tennis clubhouse, **6**, and on a low mound to its rear, **7**.

Garrison Hill, **8**, rising above the tennis court area, was well defended. Colonel Richards' command post was sited here.

Once the Japanese had captured the bungalow areas, they made use of the dead ground beneath the steep terrace as an assembly point for their assault troops.

other units, many of whom had had little or no weapon training.

Richards chose to defend Kohima Ridge, a hilly spur about 1½ km (1 ml) long and 320 m (350 yds) wide, around the base of which the road bent like a hairpin. Then, on 27 March, he learned with dismay that the whole of Lieutenant-General Sato's 31st Division was advancing upon him.

On 5 April, after the Japanese had made contact with the Kohima garrison and most of the Native State battalion had fled, Colonel Richards was relieved to have his motley little force strengthened by a British unit, the 4th Battalion Royal West Kent Regiment, which had been detached from 161st Brigade and sent up to help defend the pass. With the West Kents came the 20th Mountain Battery of the Indian Artillery. Richards now had 1,500 fighting men within his defensive perimeter.

Sato had not only succeeded in moving 15,000 soldiers through the exceptionally rough Assam terrain, but had brought up 75 mm guns to pound the ridge. Day after day he committed fresh troops to attack the gallant defenders. Sheer weight of numbers began to tell, and Richards' perimeter started to shrink as positions were overrun.

On one part of the ridge, the garrison was separated from the Japanese by only the width of the tennis court behind the Deputy Commissioner's bungalow. This was the scene of some of the most bitter close-quarter fighting of the war, as the battle-fatigued defenders grimly beat off all the attacks by Sato's men.

It was also the scene of some remarkable gunnery. Officers of the 20th Mountain Battery directed fire from the remaining guns of 161st Brigade on a hill 3.2 km (2 mls) north of Kohima. There the brigade had been halted by the enemy while on its way to assist Richards. So accurate was the gunnery of the other batteries of the 24th Mountain Regiment that, frequently, they laid a curtain of defensive fire only 13.5 m (15 yds) in front of the garrison's forward positions.

After eight grim days the 'black 13th' dawned. Most of a parachute supply-drop of much-needed water and mortar ammunition fell behind Japanese lines. Enemy artillery found the range of the hospital trenches, which were filled with wounded, and plastered them with shells, while Sato's ferocious infantry attacks continued all day. For Richards' men, the situation was desperate—yet they had to resist for four more dreadful days. When the relief forces arrived on 18 April, they found Richards and his men crowded into a shell-pocked box 320 m (350 yds) square. They had suffered more than 600 casualties.

Colonel Hugh Richards, who commanded the Kohima garrison, was a regular officer of much experience, particularly in jungle warfare. A veteran of the First World War, he had been commanding the 3rd West African Brigade in the Chindit special forces, but was relieved of his command when it was discovered that, at 50, he was ten years over the age limit for this unit.

Lieutenant-General Kotoku Sato, a stubborn but resourceful officer of the Imperial Japanese Army, led the 31st Infantry Division more than 64 km (40 mls) through dense jungle to strike at Kohima. When the assault failed, he lost his nerve and disobeyed orders to link up with other Japanese forces for a last-ditch attack farther south. As a result he was dismissed.

All that remained of the Deputy Commissioner's bungalow after the Japanese had been driven from Kohima Ridge. This view was taken from a terrace overlooking the rear of the building.

Matchstick trees stand where once thick foliage grew on the slopes of bitterly-contested Garrison Hill. A parachute from a supply drop hangs from the tree in the centre.

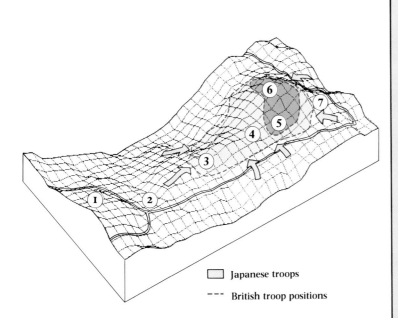

Japanese troops

--- British troop positions

Even when Richards' men had been relieved, the Battle of Kohima was far from over. The Japanese had diverted part of their force to build a fortified line in the pass, which they defended vigorously. Slim ordered relentless pressure to be brought to bear on Sato so that the road link could be reopened as quickly as possible. Even when the monsoon broke at the end of May, the battle continued. Step by muddy step, the Japanese were forced to give ground until, on 22 June, the road was opened once more, and Mutaguchi's battered Fifteenth Army retreated.

In the long term, the Japanese attack played into British hands, because the farther the Japanese advanced, the weaker her forces became and so the Allied advance into the Burmese hinterland became easier to effect.

The Japanese, starving, short of ammunition and in full retreat, still fought stubbornly, even though they were attacked mercilessly both from the ground and from the air. With 65,000 dead, the Fifteenth Army was virtually destroyed as a fighting unit. Kohima–Imphal was the decisive battle of the Burma Campaign and finally turned the tide in the struggle for Southeast Asia.

When the battle opened, on 5 April, Colonel Richards had eight defensive positions organized along 1,983 m (2,000 yds) of Kohima Ridge. These were, from south to north, GPT Ridge (not shown), Jail Hill, 1, DIS Hill, 2, FSD Hill, 3, Kuki Piquet, 4, Garrison Hill, 5, Hospital Ridge, 6, and the Deputy Commissioner's bungalow sector, 7. When the defenders were relieved, on 18 April, their perimeter had shrunk to Garrison Hill, Hospital Ridge and the area behind the tennis court, shaded brown above.

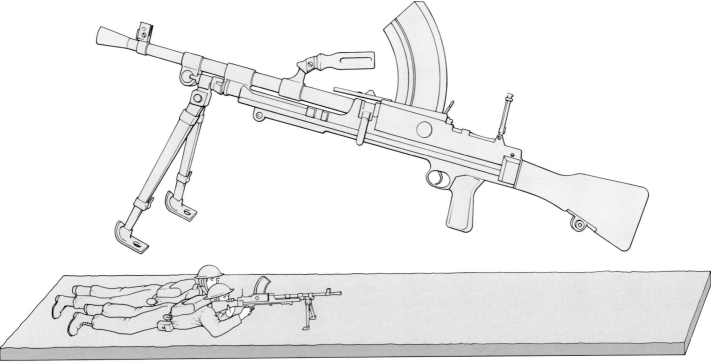

One of the mainstays of the Kohima garrison's gallant defence was the Bren light machine-gun. This .303 in calibre weapon, with its familiar curved 28-round box magazine, was a British development of a Czechoslovakian gun, which came into service in 1938. Every section of every platoon in a rifle company had a two-man Bren group: the No. 1 would aim and fire the gun, while the No. 2 would lie at his left and change magazines, as well as the air-cooled barrel when it became too hot. Each Bren gun was supplied with a spare barrel, a cleaning kit, a spare-parts wallet and 25 magazines. The gun, which was sighted to 1,829 m (2,000 yds), had a cyclic rate of fire of 500 rounds a minute.

Arnhem/*17-25 September, 1944*

Seventeen times in the summer of 1944, the élite British 1st Airborne Division prepared to drop behind enemy lines; on each occasion their mission was cancelled and it seemed as if they were doomed to inactivity. In early September, however, Field Marshal Bernard Montgomery devised a spectacular plan, codenamed 'Operation Market Garden', to beat the Germans by Christmas. The 1st Airborne Division was earmarked for a crucial role.

In that September, Montgomery's Twenty-first Army Group, comprising the Second British and First Canadian Armies, was within 160 km (100 mls) of the Ruhr, one of Germany's most important industrial centres, while General George S. Patton and the U.S. Third Army were within 160 km of the Saar, another industrial area to the south. Both of these colourful commanders had lost the impetus of their armoured thrusts through shortages of fuel and stores, and both knew that whoever gained priority for supplies would gain the honour of being the first onto German soil.

Montgomery went to the Supreme Allied Commander, U.S. General Dwight D. Eisenhower, on 10 September, with a daring plan to defeat Germany by a 'back door' route through the Netherlands, a plan he wanted implemented by the end of that very week.

The Field Marshal needed strong airborne forces to land in eastern occupied Holland, to capture five river and canal bridges on the single main road linking Eindhoven and Arnhem. They must then hold open this 'corridor' of 96 km (60 mls) until spearhead ground troops of the Second Army came up from their positions on the border between Belgium and Holland. From Arnhem, it would be simple to turn the flank of the German frontier defences—the Siegfried Line—and then thrust into the Ruhr.

Eisenhower had some misgivings, but he consented. While the ambitious Patton was still halted at Metz in eastern France, Montgomery ordered intense, detailed planning for the attack, which was scheduled to commence on Sunday 17 September. 'Market' was the codename assigned to the airborne side of the offensive, 'Garden' to the role of the ground forces.

In England, frantic efforts were made to prepare 5,000 assorted aircraft for what was to be the biggest airborne operation ever mounted. Three divisions—the U.S. 101st and 82nd and the British 1st—together with the 1st Polish Parachute Brigade, were to be landed and supplied over three consecutive days because there was not enough time in a single day to

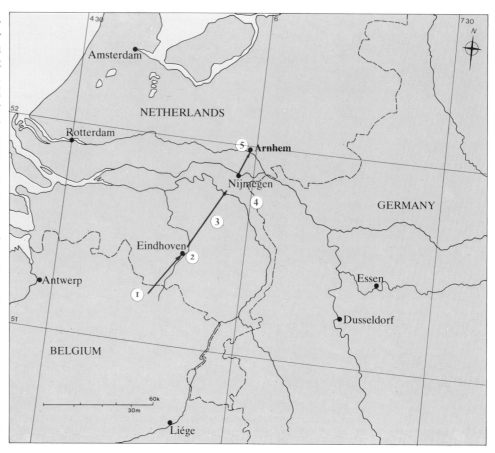

Map showing the area of 'Operation Market Garden'

1. British Second Army
2. 101st U.S. Airborne Division
3. 'The Corridor'
4. 82nd U.S. Airborne Division
5. 1st British Airborne Division

By the late summer of 1944, following the landings in Normandy commencing on 6 June, Allied forces in Western Europe had achieved remarkable successes. The initial landings had been stubbornly contested, but, on 8 August, Field Marshal Gunther von Kluge, then German Commander-in-Chief in the west, told a subordinate general, 'A breakthrough such as we have never seen has occurred south of Caen.' Anglo-American forces were now out in the open, streaming across France toward Germany.

On 15 August, the Allies landed in the south of France; on the 24–25th, Paris was taken; and by early September Allied forces were approaching the Rhine on a wide front. Then a new problem materialized. It was essential to thrust forward in the north to gain a large sea port through which supplies could be ferried in for an eventual attack on the Ruhr.

It was also desirable for U.S. General Patton's Third Army in the east to ad-

vance and combine with forces striking northward, following the successful landings in the south of France. But available resources were not immediately sufficient for both purposes. Field Marshal Montgomery, the ground commander in the north, demanded reinforcements and supplies to enable him to break into the north German plain with his armour. Patton was calling for support to enable him to strike into Germany through the Saar toward Frankfurt. Unable to accommodate both, General Eisenhower adopted a policy whereby neither of the Allied flanks was given priority. The compromise proved disastrous, for German resistance stiffened and both wings shortly ground to a halt.

Montgomery then devised his audacious plan to break this resistance by a series of airborne landings to clear a corridor for the rapid advance of his Second Army through Holland. All depended on British and Polish troops taking the Dutch town of Arnhem.

Shortly before 2 pm, on 17 September 1944, elements of the 1st Parachute Brigade dropped on to open ground at Wolfheze, west of Arnhem. Gliders of the 1st Airlanding Brigade came in at the same time, carrying infantry and heavy equipment.

Parachutes carrying supplies were of bright colours—mostly orange, red or yellow—to identify their contents. Containers were metal cylinders, about 1.5 by 0.6 m (5 by 2 ft) in size, which were painted brown or green.

Not all glider landings were perfect, 1, but even those that were surprised the infantry passengers, for the wheels came splintering up through the floor as the aircraft touched down.

While some paratroopers were unloading supplies and assisting injured comrades, infantry, brought in by gliders, fanned out, 2, to form a defensive perimeter against possible attack.

Battalions formed up at positions, 3, which had been indicated by coloured marker flares. These had been laid by advance parties some 20 minutes before the first landings.

make more than one 480-km (300-ml) round trip.

The 101st was to drop around Eindhoven at the southern end of the corridor, the 82nd in the central area at Nijmegen. Montgomery's main objective, the massive road bridge over the Lower Rhine at Arnhem in the north, was reserved for the 1st Airborne Division and the Poles, both commanded by Major-General Robert Urquhart. He knew that his battle-hungry 'Red Devils' would have to hold out longest and, if the plan went wrong, they would be without support.

Difficulties emerged from the start, but grim reality was obscured by a fever of optimism which brooked no impediment to the 'Market Garden' strategy. Despite reports from Dutch Resistance, identifying German armour near Arnhem (reports supported by R.A.F. reconnaissance photographs), the 1st Airborne Division was briefed to expect minimum opposition from second-rate troops in the 48 hours before the Second Army came up in support.

The first rule of airborne operations— drop as close to the target as possible to ensure surprise—had to be broken because the R.A.F., mistakenly believing the bridge to be ringed with anti-aircraft batteries, was opposed to flying in too close. Urquhart's only other choice was patches of open ground 9–12 km (6–8 mls) west of his objective.

Thus effectively deprived of the advantage of surprise, the first half of the division filed aboard transports and gliders on the morning of Sunday 17 September. Once airborne, they joined a huge migration of British and American aircraft, droning east toward the Dutch coast.

The landings, in the early afternoon, went smoothly and were practically unopposed—but not for long. The old men and boys wishfully thought to be defending Arnhem, turned out to be two veteran divisions of SS Panzers and a Panzer Grenadier battalion equipped with experimental multi-barrelled mortars. The airborne invasion took them by surprise, but they were quick to recover.

While the 1st Airlanding Brigade fought to secure the landing and drop zones for the second wave coming in next morning, the 1st Parachute Brigade's three battalions moved toward the bridge along separate routes. Progress was slowed by throngs of jubilant Dutch, proffering fruit and drinks to the men they believed were their liberators. As the troops probed deeper through wooded and built-up areas, a discovery was made which would have a far-reaching effect on the conduct, and eventual outcome, of the battle: their radios were out of

General George S. Patton (1885–1945), commander of the U.S. Third Army, and **Bernard Montgomery (1887–1976)**, made Field Marshal on 1 September 1944, vied as to whose troops would be first on German soil. Though different in character, both had a flair for publicity: Patton delighted in being photographed in his polished helmet, while Montgomery wore a tank corps beret with two badges or an Australian bush hat.

Major-General Robert Urquhart commanded the 1st Airborne Division and the Polish contingent. R.A.F. alarm about anti-aircraft batteries obliged Urquhart to drop 13 km (8 mls) from Arnhem.

Lieutenant-Colonel John Frost's 2nd Battalion reached the bridge but was cut off. The men fought doggedly for three days, until their positions were finally overrun.

Field Marshal Walther Model, the German commander in East Holland, fled his H.Q. near Arnhem when the landing began because he thought he was the paratroopers' target.

Major-General Stanislaw Sosabowski and his Polish Parachute Brigade were delayed by bad weather. When they finally landed on the third day, the Poles were badly mauled.

This photograph shows gliders massed for take-off on an English airfield. The Airspeed Horsa Mk II, the main British troop-carrying glider, was 20.5 m (67 ft) long and had a wingspan of 26.8 m (88 ft). The Horsa had a crew of two and could carry either 29 infantrymen or bulky equipment such as jeeps, loaded trailers and light artillery.

Paratroopers, their faces blackened, waited at their allotted positions on board the aircraft. Newspaper correspondents accompanying the paratroopers all remarked on their relaxed confidence.

order. Not only were units of the 1st Airborne Division out of touch with each other, in a situation growing more confused by the minute, but they lacked outside contact.

The 1st and 3rd battalions of the Parachute Regiment, advancing along main highways, were soon pinned down by enemy fire. Nevertheless, Lieutenant-Colonel John Frost and his 2nd Battalion made good progress on a secondary road by the river. A railway bridge was destroyed before they could secure it, and a small pontoon bridge farther upstream had been dismantled, but their principal objective—the huge road bridge—was still intact. It was getting dark when they reached it and began to occupy houses overlooking both sides of its long, concrete northern approach ramp.

Gallant attempts to storm the heavily defended southern end of the bridge were driven back by Panzer grenadiers, but the mere presence of the paratroopers on the north side was sufficient to cause serious problems for the commander of the 2nd SS Panzer Corps, Lieutenant-General Wilhelm Bittrich. He could not now, as ordered, move over one of his divisions to help repel Allied attacks at Nijmegen. While he tried, without much success, to get some armour to the south bank via a tiny ferry some miles to the east, he issued terse instructions to clear the bridge at all costs.

Soon Frost's men were engaged in some of the fiercest fighting of the war, as battle-hardened SS troopers tried time and again to dislodge them. In one murderous orgy of fire, the paratroopers destroyed a column of 22 scout cars and half-tracks, which tried to rush them from the south. Everywhere houses were on fire or crumbling under shell fire, and the cellars were filled with dead and wounded.

Not long after the first landings, Major General Urquhart, infuriated by the signals failure, left divisional headquarters in the drop zone and drove in a jeep to ascertain the situation. Eventually he found his deputy, Brigadier Gerald Lathbury, commander of the 1st Parachute Brigade, who was advancing with the 3rd Battalion. A violent and prolonged eruption of street fighting on all sides, however, prevented the two most senior officers in the division from exercising any sort of overall control at a crucial stage of the operation. Lathbury was wounded and was taken prisoner; Urquhart had to hide in an attic for some hours before he managed to return to the British lines.

Learning that divisional headquarters was now at the Hartenstein Hotel in Oosterbeek, 4.8 km (3 mls) west of the town,

This painting by Terence Cuneo depicts Lance-Sergeant John Daniel Baskeyfield, manning, single-handed, a quick-firing 6-pounder MK III at Oosterbeek. This 57 mm calibre weapon discharged a shot weighing 2.8 kg (6¼ lb) and was specially designed to be light for airborne use. Lance-Sergeant Baskeyfield, who was killed at his post, was awarded the Victoria Cross posthumously.

The 2nd Battalion of the British Parachute Regiment was the sole unit to reach the bridge at Arnhem. There, however, they were cut off and subjected to repeated German attacks. One such attack occurred at about 9.30 am on 18 September, when powerful elements of the 9th Panzer Reconnaissance Battalion advanced across the bridge from the German-held south bank.

Twenty-two German vehicles were involved in this attack: a mixture of armoured cars, half-tracks, personnel carriers and some lorries loaded with infantry. To reach the northern ramp, the drivers had to negotiate between smouldering lorries, wrecked during earlier fighting.

The leading vehicles got some way along the northern ramp, 1, before Colonel John Frost's paratroopers, 2, opened fire with anti-tank guns, Piats, grenades, machine-guns and rifles. A massive curtain of fire was laid across the road.

Captain Eric Mackay of the Royal Engineers, with a few sappers and other corps troops, occupied the buildings on the east side of the bridge, 3. He and his men had no anti-tank weapons, only small arms and grenades.

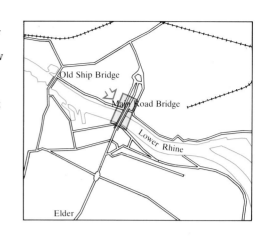

Houses, 4, beside the approach ramp were occupied by the British. Paratroopers were also on the parapet of the bridge, 5, as well as in slit trenches and weapon pits on the embankment at the west side of the road.

Captain Paul Grabner, who was killed in the action, commanded the German assault. Of his 22 vehicles, 12 were destroyed: many of them caught fire, and two half-tracks plunged through the parapet to the road below, 6.

Urquhart commandeered a jeep and drove there under fire. On his return, after an enforced absence of almost 40 hours, he heard that he had been reported captured.

Much had happened during his absence—almost all for the worse. The second wave, bringing the remainder of the 1st Airborne Division, had been delayed by bad weather on the morning of Monday 18 September. When it arrived over Arnhem at 4 pm, the Germans were ready, for they had found a copy of the entire 'Market Garden' plan in a crashed glider. Fierce fighting ensued. There was no coordination between hard-pressed units, scattered over a wide area, which were trying to hold off Panther and Tiger tanks and self-propelled artillery with nothing more than rifles, Sten guns and grenades. Most disappointing of all, nothing had been heard of the Second Army, whose leading element—the Guards Armoured Division—should have been close to Arnhem if the 'Garden' part of the operation were going to plan. The only heartening news was that the 2nd Battalion was still holding the north end of the bridge, but at terrible cost.

Throughout Tuesday the situation deteriorated. All efforts by other battalions to relieve Lieutenant-Colonel Frost's dwindling garrison were halted 1.6 km (1 ml) from the bridge by newly arrived German infantry and armour. Casualties were extremely heavy.

Unknown to Urquhart, the much-needed 1st Polish Parachute Brigade was grounded by bad weather in the English Midlands and could not be flown over that day. Glider-borne elements of the Polish force managed to get away late from airfields in the south but were badly mauled when they descended on their landing ground, which was now in the middle of a battle, and were shot at by both sides.

That day, the division was urgently awaiting vital supplies. Because the drop zones had been taken by the enemy, Urquhart repeatedly transmitted a request for the planes to offload near the Hartenstein Hotel. His radio, however, was still malfunctioning and the messages were never received. R.A.F. pilots flew bravely through blizzards of flak to deliver their precious cargo, which they dropped straight into the hands of the Germans. In all, 390 tons of ammunition, food and medical supplies were dropped, but only 31 tons reached the 1st Airborne Division.

Because his command was fragmented and suffering huge losses, Urquhart came to a painful but unavoidable decision on the night of the 19th: he would have to leave Frost's battalion to fend for itself and pull in the remnants of the 1st Airborne Division

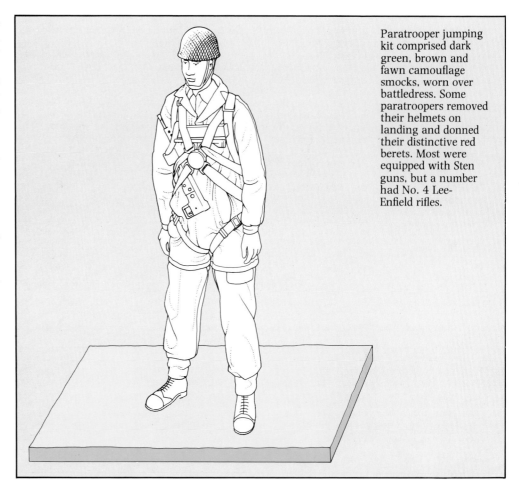

Paratrooper jumping kit comprised dark green, brown and fawn camouflage smocks, worn over battledress. Some paratroopers removed their helmets on landing and donned their distinctive red berets. Most were equipped with Sten guns, but a number had No. 4 Lee-Enfield rifles.

The Sten sub-machine-gun was the most widely used of small arms. This 9 mm calibre weapon weighed 3.5 kg (6½ lb) and had a magazine capacity of 32 rounds. Its maximum effective range was 91 m (100 yds). The gun could fire either single rounds or bursts. In combat, some soldiers would tape together two magazines, ends opposed, for speed of reloading. The Sten gun was at its most effective in house-to-house fighting.

The first two gliders of the Airlanding Brigade crashed into each other on landing; others were badly damaged. This made unloading a more difficult and prolonged operation. Undamaged gliders were opened by removing pins and 'splitting' the fuselage just behind the wings.

The Piat, a British anti-tank weapon, was used by infantry when unsupported by light artillery. It weighed 15.65 kg (34½ lb) and could fire a 1.13 kg (2½ lb) bomb for 105 m (115 yds). The Projector Infantry Anti-Tank weapon was difficult to cock and had a heavy recoil, but was nevertheless a most effective weapon.

A camouflaged Sturmgeschutz assault gun, photographed at Arnhem. Designed by Krupp, this self-propelled armoured vehicle provided supporting fire for infantry. The weapon was 2.1 m (17 ft) long, nearly 3 m (10 ft) wide and weighed 21½ tons. Capable of speeds up to 40 km/h (25 mph), it had 90 mm-thick armour and carried a 75 mm gun and one 7.9 mm machine-gun, an MG 34.

to form a cohesive defensive box around the Hartenstein Hotel. There the survivors would try to hold out until the overdue Second Army arrived. In fact, British tanks were only 16 km (10 mls) away, after a bitter struggle up the narrow road aptly nicknamed 'Hell's Highway'.

When signallers finally had some radio sets working, Urquhart urgently requested that, on 20 September, the Polish drop zone be switched from the planned southern end of the bridge, which remained in enemy hands, to Driel, 8 km (5 mls) west. A hitherto overlooked ferry was still in operation there and could bring the Poles over to 1st Airborne Division's defensive area, part of the perimeter of which ran along the north bank of the river. Continuing bad weather, however, still kept the Polish brigade grounded in England.

In Arnhem, the 'Red Devils' displayed extraordinary courage in the face of overwhelming opposition. At Oosterbeek crossroads, in the centre of Urquhart's defensive box, enemy fire of all calibres was so fierce that his men called it the 'Cauldron'.

Down by the bridge, Colonel Frost, now wounded, and the remains of his 2nd Battalion knew that the end of their magnificent three-day stand was near. By late evening, those who could still fight were down to their last few rounds and their positions were overrun. At dawn on 21 September, the long-delayed Panzers were able to cross the river unmolested to engage the approaching Second Army.

Later that Thursday, the 1,500-strong 1st Polish Parachute Brigade finally dropped into Driel, only to find the ferry out of action and the Germans waiting for them. About 200 men managed to reach Urquhart; the rest dug in and waited.

Early the next morning, 4 days and 18 hours after the first Arnhem drop, a detachment of armoured cars from the Second Army reached Driel by a circuitous route and made the first direct contact with the beleaguered 1st Airborne Division, 365 m (400 yds) away across the river. For all the good it did the paratroopers, it could have been across the English Channel.

While British infantry came up in force on the south bank over Saturday and Sunday, the plight of Urquhart's shattered command grew steadily worse. Supplies were almost exhausted, and all attempts to replenish them failed. When a brave effort by the 4th Dorset Battalion to cross the Lower Rhine and reinforce the defensive box came to nothing on the Sunday night, plans were made for the evacuation of what was left of the 1st Airborne Division. A little after 6 am, on Monday 25 September, Urquhart received the order to withdraw; the timing

Shortly before 10 pm on the night of 25–26 September, the evacuation of 2,500 paratroopers and infantry from the north side of the Lower Rhine began. It was dark and wet, but splashes of light were provided by burning buildings and, less welcome, by enemy flares.

The scene was one of eerie devastation, with abandonded guns, wrecked tanks, and buildings on fire in Oosterbeek village, **1**. Enemy artillery and mortar bursts saturated the embarkation area, **2**, which was illuminated by white flares. Rearguard detachments were still covering the approach roads, **3**.

Troops making for the embarkation points moved along either the eastern, **4**, or the western route, **5**. Small groups were formed up in single file, **6**. Then, with their boots and equipment muffled, they made their way to the river, following white tapes and

getting their bearings from red tracer bullets, **7**, fired from British positions on the south shore.

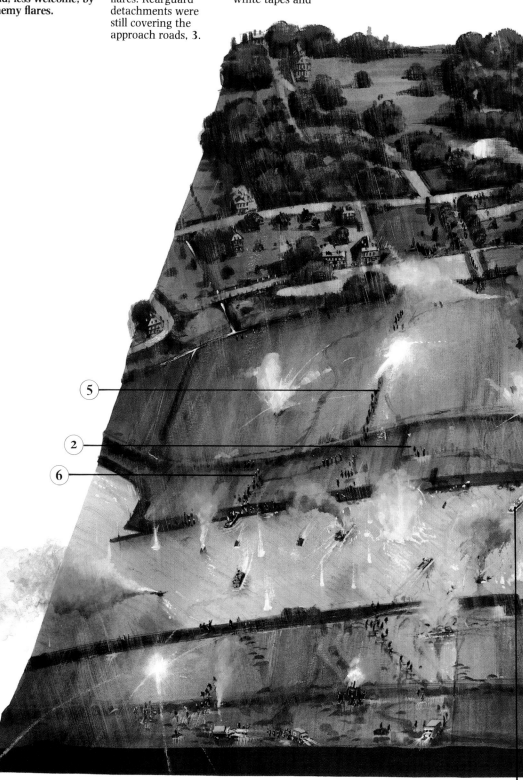

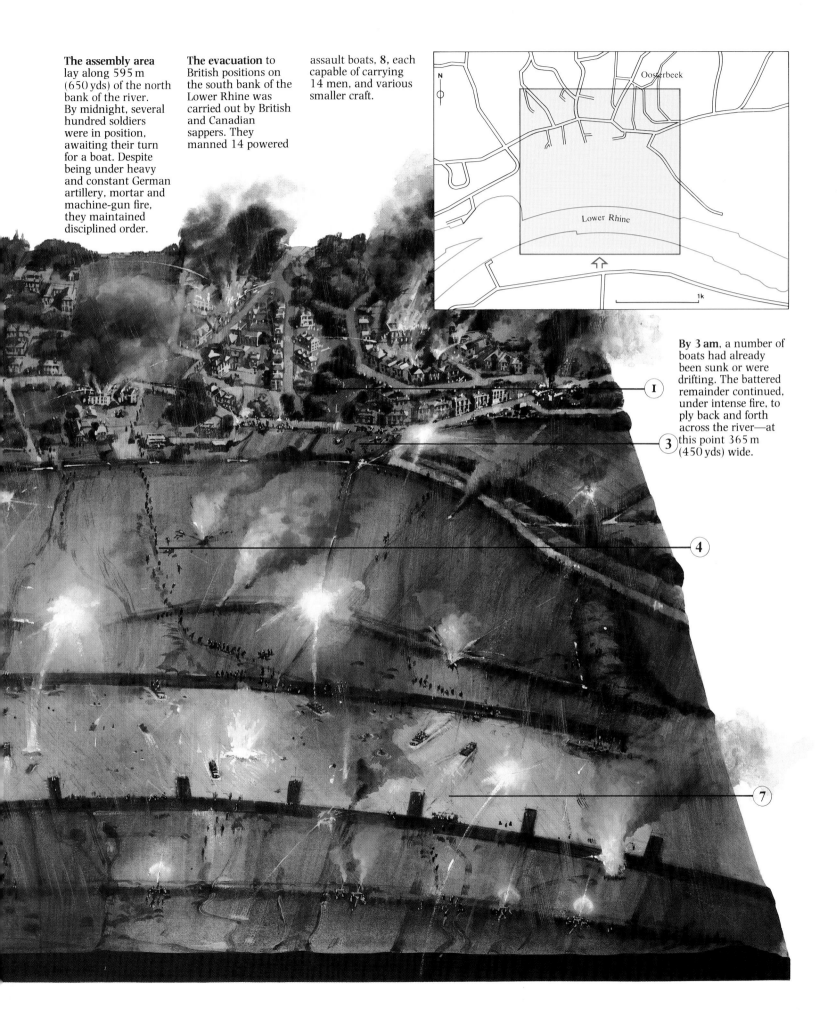

The assembly area lay along 595 m (650 yds) of the north bank of the river. By midnight, several hundred soldiers were in position, awaiting their turn for a boat. Despite being under heavy and constant German artillery, mortar and machine-gun fire, they maintained disciplined order.

The evacuation to British positions on the south bank of the Lower Rhine was carried out by British and Canadian sappers. They manned 14 powered assault boats, **8**, each capable of carrying 14 men, and various smaller craft.

N

Oosterbeek

Lower Rhine

1k

By 3 am, a number of boats had already been sunk or were drifting. The battered remainder continued, under intense fire, to ply back and forth across the river—at this point 365 m (450 yds) wide.

1

3

4

7

183

was left to him. That night, while maintaining an elaborate pretence of manning the perimeter as usual, groups of men made their way quietly down to the river, where a mere handful of boats waited to ferry them across.

There was a final irony: no one had expected so many to get out and there was not enough transport on the other side to cope with them. Exhausted soldiers, who had endured eight days of terrible fighting, were obliged to march the 17 km (11 mls) down to the safety of the Second Army's main positions at Nijmegen. Of the 10,005 men of the 1st Airborne Division, 2,163 reached Driel, together with 160 Poles and 75 of the Dorsetshire Regiment from the abortive relief attempts. They left behind 1,200 dead and 6,642 wounded, captured or missing. The Germans sustained 3,300 casualties, a third of whom were killed.

After the Arnhem disaster, Montgomery's much-vaunted 'Market Garden' plan was abandoned. Denied the bridgehead over the Lower Rhine, all he had to show for the exertions and sacrifices of his troops was a useless strip of Dutch highway. The war would not be over by Christmas after all.

Some of the fiercest house-to-house fighting of the war, *below*, occurred during the Battle of Arnhem; casualties were heavy. Many Dutch men, women and children were killed in the fighting.

A number of the men captured at Arnhem managed to escape, including the four soldiers, *below*, who found a dinghy and rowed down the Rhine to Nijmegen— already in Allied hands.

Hundreds of Allied troops were rounded up by the Germans and interned until the war ended eight months later. Some escaped, while many others, who had evaded capture, were hidden by the Dutch until Allied forces eventually occupied the area. Only some 2,400 men, more fortunate, survived both the grim battle and the hazardous evacuation to safety.

Montgomery sent all survivors of the battle and the evacuation home to England on leave, *left*.

Had the Arnhem operation proved successful, the prize for the Allies would have been inestimable.

Montgomery, in his *Memoirs*, gave four reasons why success was not achieved. First, Supreme Headquarters did not regard the operation as a spearhead to the Ruhr; secondly, the troops were dropped too far from the bridge; thirdly, the weather was unfavourable, and lastly, the 2nd SS Panzer Corps, which was refitting after an earlier defeat, proved unexpectedly resilient. Despite this, he maintained that the operation could have succeeded had it been properly backed and adequately manned and equipped.

As it was, the Allies had still the hazardous, costly task of forcing the mighty River Rhine. Many lives were to be lost and much *matériel* expended before the final victory, which, because of the disaster at Arnhem, was delayed by eight months, until May 1945.

Iwo Jima/*19 February-26 March, 1945*

As the summer of 1944 turned to autumn, the continuing presence of Nipponese army and air force units on Iwo Jima, a small island of volcanic rock in the Pacific Ocean, was seriously disrupting U.S. offensive bombing against Japan.

While the campaign to recapture the Philippines was being completed, regular bombing runs were flown over Iwo Jima to soften up its powerful defences. Reconnaissance revealed more than 600 strongpoints scattered across the arid island; in fact, there were many more, but all skilfully camouflaged.

Between December 1944 and 19 February 1945, when the first of the U.S. troops waded ashore on the island's black volcanic beaches, round-the-clock bombing was maintained, to cause as much damage as possible and to hinder its repair. Then, on 16 February, an American battle fleet steamed into range and began the heaviest pre-landing bombardment of any target in the Pacific. Nearly 40,000 shells, ranging from 5 to 16 inches in calibre, ravaged the landscape. Very little, it was thought, could withstand such a storm of fire; American soldiers would soon discover otherwise.

As the naval shelling reached a crescendo, a great flotilla of 450 ships, carrying General H. M. Smith's assault force—two divisions of the U.S. Marine Corps, with a third in reserve—approached Iwo Jima. There were more than enough men and weapons on board to capture this small island. The only question seemed to be: How long could the Japanese hold out?

Shortly after 9 am on 19 February, the first wave of landing craft and amphibious vehicles nosed toward a broad beach at the southeast corner of the island. The marines who went ashore on a 3,600-m (4,000-yd) front between the main airfield and Mount Suribachi on the southern tip of Iwo Jima, came under concentrated fire from the concealed Japanese positions.

The Japanese commander, General Tadamichi Kuribayashi, who was fanatical

The scene shortly after 9 am on 19 February 1945 shows two U.S. Marine Corps divisions storming the Japanese-held island of Iwo Jima.

Mount Suribachi, 1, dominated the island, which was about 13 km (8 mls) square.

It was heavily fortified by the Japanese and took four days to clear.

Troops of the U.S. Marines' 5th Division, **2,** fought their way across the island. By evening they had isolated Mount Suribachi.

Many American landing craft, **3,** were destroyed on the tide-line by close-range

fire from skilfully concealed enemy mortar batteries.

Braving a hail of fire, the landing craft, **4,** of the marines' second wave headed straight for the beach, which was of soft black volcanic sand.

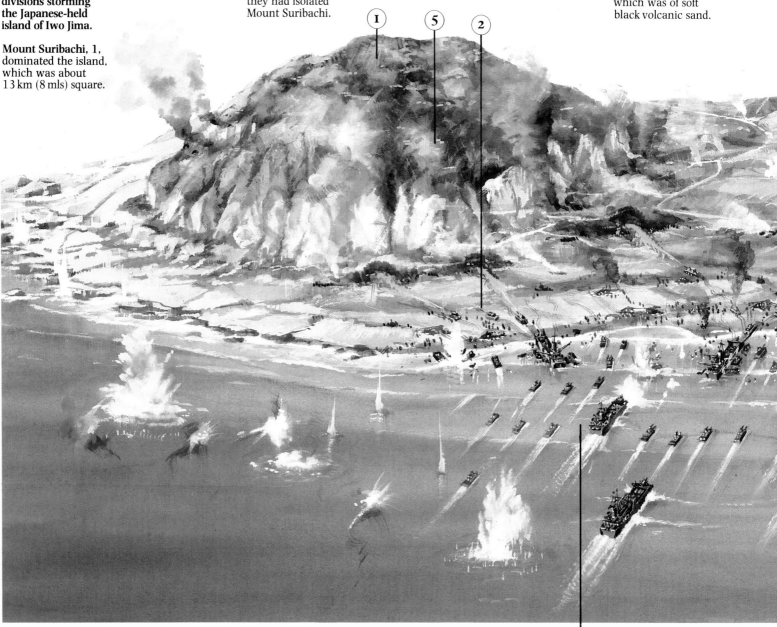

From Iwo Jima, the Japanese were able to track U.S. bomber formations on their way to raid Tokyo and other cities, enabling them to flash early warnings to their compatriots back in Japan. Furthermore, from the island's two airfields—a third was being built—the Japanese flew missions against the bomber streams, as well as attacking B-29 Flying Fortress bases on the Marianas Islands, more than 322 km (200 mls) to the south.

Iwo Jima, which was in effect a heavily protected, static aircraft carrier, had become a major obstacle in the way of American offensive operations in the Pacific theatre and had to be neutralized.

Once taken, the island would provide a convenient forward base from which American fighters could escort their bombers on the long flight to Japan. The island would also be a valuable emergency landing strip for any B-29s crippled on the hazardous 1600-km (1,000-ml) round trip to the heart of enemy territory.

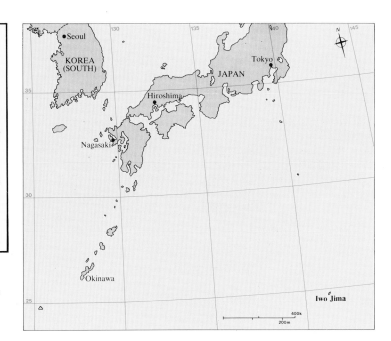

Muzzle flashes, 5, were often the only clue to the position of the Japanese, who had riddled the island with a network of underground bunkers.

Many raids on U.S. bases in the Marianas Islands were flown from the main Japanese airfield, **6**.

Marines of the 4th Division, **7**, went in on the right flank of the landings and struck toward the main airfield.

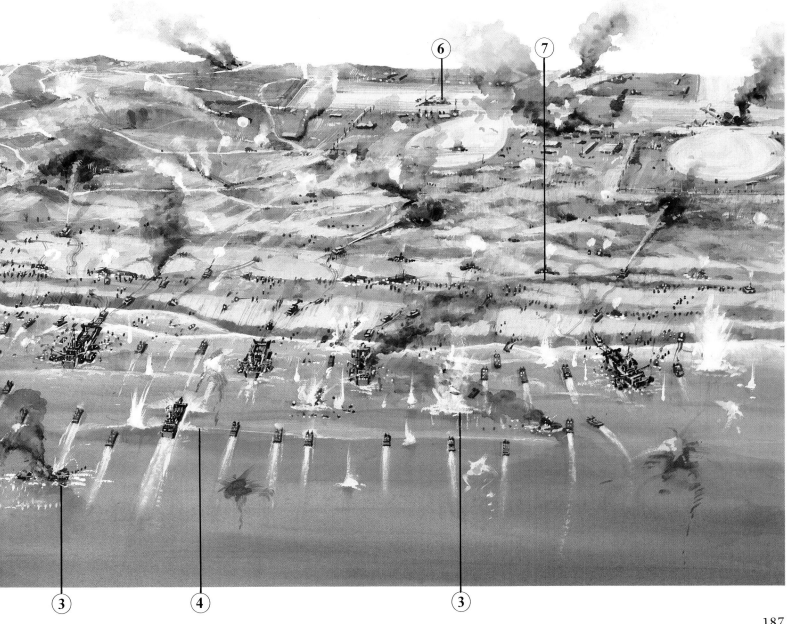

about the defence of this vital base, had laid his plans carefully in the preceding months. His 21,000-strong garrison had riddled the island with a labyrinth of tunnels and strongpoints hewn out of solid rock; almost all had survived prolonged American bombardment intact. Throughout the bombing and shelling, the Japanese had lived a mole-like existence, surrounded by large stocks of ammunition and stores, waiting to repel imminent invasion. Their general had issued a 'fight to the last bullet and last man' order, and his soldiers, imbued with a deep sense of duty and honour, would do so without question.

During the first day of the landings on Iwo Jima, the U.S. 4th and 5th Marine Divisions launched two attacks—one against Mount Suribachi, which dominated their left flank, the other at the biggest airfield, about 0.8 km ($\frac{1}{2}$ ml) inland. Progress was slower than expected, for it was hindered by minefields and stiff opposition; moreover, many vehicles had become immobilized, sinking into the sand on the beach. By 6 pm, the Americans had cut off Mount Suribachi from the rest of the island and had reached the edge of the airstrip. The price was 2,500 casualties.

The marines realized that they would have to fight for every inch of the island and that each one of the hundreds of strongpoints would have to be dealt with individually, using either flame-throwers or high explosives.

After four days of intense fighting, marines from the 5th Division captured the summit of Mount Suribachi. With the island's dominant feature secured, along with the main airfield, General Smith sent in reinforcements from his reserve division to assist in the major task of clearing the northern end of Iwo Jima, a honeycomb of strongpoints, in which the bulk of Kuribayashi's force was entrenched.

The sweep northward began on 24 February, supported by Sherman tanks and assorted artillery, which included rocket launchers; but progress was slow. Fighting was so fierce around Hill 382 in the northeastern area that the marines nicknamed it 'The Meat Grinder'.

By the second week of March, mopping-up operations were being carried out in the hills and gullies and, on the 26th, the last pocket of ferocious resistance was overrun.

The struggle to oust the Japanese from Iwo Jima had been immense and costly—more than 6,800 marines were killed and nearly 15,000 wounded during the 26 days of continuous combat. The Japanese paid a terrible price for their tenacious defence: fewer than 1,000 prisoners were taken out of 21,000 men.

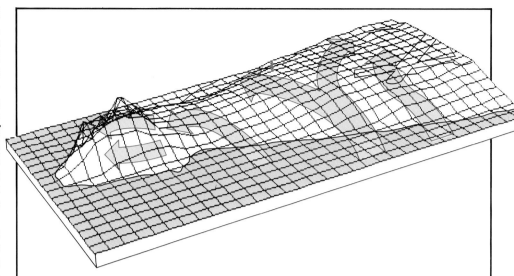

At the end of the first day's fighting on 19 February, the 4th and 5th Divisions of the U.S. Marines had secured a strip 1.6 km (1 ml) wide across the southern end of the island, isolating Mount Suribachi, which fell on 23 February.

The 5th Division began slowly to push northward up the west side of Iwo Jima, while the 4th took the east side. By 24 February, they had captured about half the island, including the main airfield. Next morning, the reserve division, the

3rd, took position between the 4th and 5th, and the reinforced American assault line moved on, their advance contested all the way. The enemy's second airfield was taken and, on 1 March, marines reached the edge of a third strip

being built in the north of the island.

Ten days later, the survivors of the Japanese garrison were penned in the top corner of the island, resisting to the death. It was not until 26 March that the last enemy pocket was overrun.

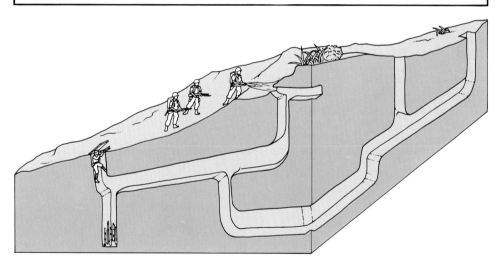

For months before the American invasion of Iwo Jima, the Japanese garrison had been slaving to perfect the island's defences. Although they were not complete when the marines landed, they were nevertheless formidable. Hundreds upon hundreds of

bunkers and weapon pits had been constructed, linked by a labyrinth of subterranean passages; their exits and entrances were most cunningly camouflaged. In some instances, the hills were excavated, then reinforced with concrete to provide

bomb-proof shelter for troops, stores or ammunition.

Once the fighting started, the Japanese were committed to an underground existence, and the Americans found them very difficult to dislodge. A favourite tactic of the defenders was to engage the

marines at close range, pin them down, then withdraw most of their force through their network of tunnels to pop up somewhere else and repeat the process. It was an extremely economical way to use troops and slowed the Americans' advance.

Raising the Stars and Stripes on Iwo Jima, *top*, one of the most famous photographs taken during the Second World War, was captured by Associated Press cameraman Joe Rosenthal on 23 February 1945, as half a dozen battle-weary marines struggled to plant the flag on the summit of Mount Suribachi.

A landing craft, *above*, speeds marines toward the Iwo Jima beach-head and the start of a long, bloody struggle to dislodge 21,000 fanatical Japanese defenders.

If a comparative casualty list of all the Pacific battles were to be tabulated, in proportion to the numbers engaged, the battle for Iwo Jima was the most costly fought by the United States. But the strategic gain was enormous. As General George Marshall, the U.S. Chief of Staff, wrote: 'The Iwo Jima airfields saved hundreds of battle-damaged B-29s unable to make the full return flight to their bases in the Marianas...' In addition, a fighter base was immediately built, enabling the bombers to be escorted *en route* to Japan.

The battle for Iwo Jima also played an important part in the crescendo of strategic bombing unleashed on Japan in the early months of 1945. Cities and large industrial targets were chosen, with the result that, by the summer of that year, 767,000 dwellings had been destroyed in Tokyo and 3,100,000 people had been made homeless. Many of these attacks were made with incendiary bombs, which proved lethal against fragile wooden buildings. 'Nearly 169 square miles were destroyed or damaged in sixty-six cities,' claimed General Arnold, Chief of Staff of the United States Army Air Force, '... with more than 100 square miles burnt out in the five major cities attacked.'

The seizure of Okinawa in April–June 1945, the complete blockade of Japan and the detailed planning that commenced in the summer of 1945 for the final invasion of Japan itself, had left the Japanese reeling under the massive blows of Allied air power. Her days were numbered, and Japanese resistance was rendered pointless, even before the dropping of the two atomic bombs in August 1945.

The Hook/*12-29 May, 1953*

The Korean War began with an act of unprovoked aggression against South Korea. Determined to gain the whole of the divided country, the Communists in the north embarked on a massive arms build-up, aided by the Soviet Union which supplied instructors and weapons. At dawn on 25 June 1950, the North Korean army streamed across the border, the 38th Parallel, destroying half of the South's lightly-armed, 95,000-strong defence force and occupying the whole of the peninsula except for a small area around Pusan.

The recently formed United Nations Organization at first issued an ultimatum to the North, calling for an immediate cease-fire and withdrawal. It was ignored. The U.N. then ordered into the field its first international peace-keeping force. America provided the majority of the troops, with Great Britain and the Commonwealth in strong support.

Under the supreme command of the distinguished United States general, Douglas MacArthur, landings at Inchon on the west coast and a break-out from the Pusan perimeter in the southeast heralded an offensive, which by September had pushed the Communists back across the 38th Parallel and destroyed their air force.

In a bold, though foolhardy, move the U.N. sanctioned pursuit deep into the North. China saw the advance as a threat to her border and promptly entered the war with an army of 180,000 men, becoming the U.N. forces' principal opponent for the duration of hostilities.

The Chinese launched a massive winter assault, which sent the U.N. force into retreat to positions south of Seoul, the South Korean capital. The Chinese forces were driven back, however, and by the spring of 1951, the opposing armies were again facing each other across the 38th Parallel. General MacArthur, who had been insisting that the North should once more be invaded and, if necessary, atomic weapons used, was dismissed by President Harry S. Truman.

After suffering a succession of failed offensives, the Communists agreed to peace talks, which opened on 8 July 1951. This marked the end of the war of movement and the beginning of trench warfare along the 38th Parallel.

Under cover of the protracted armistice negotiations at Panmunjon, the Chinese and North Koreans rebuilt their shattered units. In the spring of 1953, when it seemed that the peace talks might at last lead to some sort of agreement, the Communists attempted to capture key U.N. positions. Possession of these strongpoints would stand them in good stead, regardless

A low, scrub-covered hill in Korea was known to thousands of United Nations soldiers in the early 1950s as 'the bloody Hook'. It dominates the Sami-ch'on valley, the natural invasion route from the north to the south of Korea. Three fierce battles and two smaller actions were fought there, in what has been called 'the forgotten war'; for in Europe and the United States, people seemed barely aware that on the other side of the globe a war was being waged to stem Communist expansion.

Although it did not excite public interest to the extent that other wars had done, the three-year Korean War was a brutal conflict, culminating in the third Battle of the Hook. A Third World War might have erupted, just five years after the end of the Second, but this time it could have included atomic weapons from the start.

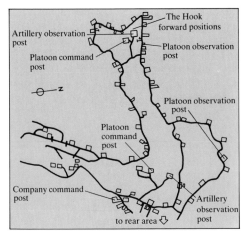

This map shows the web of weapon pits and connecting trenches laid out around the summit of the Hook. The British Duke of Wellington's Regiment held these positions throughout the third and last Battle of the Hook, which culminated on the night of 28–29 May 1953. Intense enemy shelling reduced the trenches to rubble.

The Hook forward positions
Artillery observation post
Platoon observation post
Platoon command post
Platoon observation post
Platoon command post
Company command post
Artillery observation post
to rear area

The main Chinese assault on the men of the Duke of Wellington's Regiment, holding the crest of the Hook, began during a rain shower at dusk on 28 May 1953 and continued in waves well into the night. British operations to clear the enemy from the Hook were not complete until 3.30 am.

Chinese infantry, **1**, swarmed over the Dukes' pulverized front-line positions, **2**, but were eventually repulsed in fierce hand-to-hand fighting.

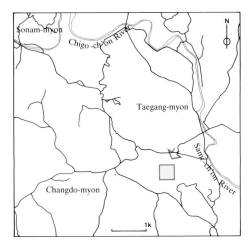

Sonam-myon
Chigo-ch'on River
Taegang-myon
Samji-chron River
Changdo-myon
1k

Many Chinese were caught in the Dukes' barbed wire entanglements, **3**. Their bodies, hanging on the wire, were reminiscent of the First World War.

The Dukes had a defensive fire plan worked out to protect the approaches to their lines. Most Chinese casualties fell to machine-gun, **4**, and artillery fire, **5**, sweeping the forward slopes of the Hook.

Several Chinese carried bags of explosive charges, which they hurled into the entrances of dug-outs, **6**, entombing the occupants.

of whether the negotiations broke down or a demarcation line was agreed and peace in the area restored.

In the middle of the British Commonwealth Division's sector was the Hook, a hill not much above 60 m (200 ft) high, which dominated the Sami-ch'on valley. When Communist activity around the Hook began to intensify, the defences were manned by the First Battalion, the Black Watch, who were experienced in this disputed area, having beaten off the Chinese in the Second Battle of the Hook the previous November. But they were nearing the end of their tour of duty and, on 12 May, were replaced by the First Battalion, the Duke of Wellington's Regiment—the 'Dukes'.

The Dukes, almost two-thirds of whom were conscripted national servicemen not yet out of their teens, filed into the rat-infested trench system on the forward slopes of the Hook and on two other nearby hills, which had been named Sausage and Point 121. In addition to their normal infantry battalion weaponry, they were supported by the guns of Twenty Field Regiment, Royal Artillery, and a troop of Centurion tanks; they could also call down fire from divisional and corps artillery. The British fired 37,000 shells and 10,000 mortar rounds during the third battle.

While the Dukes toiled to make strong positions even stronger, often under heavy fire, a disillusioned Communist soldier walked into their lines and gave himself up. He volunteered more information about the impending attack than all the reports from reconnaissance patrols and radio monitoring combined. The only thing Private Hua Hong did not know was the date of the offensive—but it was imminent.

The deserter predicted that assault companies would creep close to the forward positions under cover of re-entrants, or gulleys, between spurs running off the Hook, named 'Long Finger', 'Warsaw', 'Green Finger' and 'Ronson'. Corroboration of this forecast came quickly, for on successive nights the Chinese began sending strong patrols up each re-entrant to test the defences. All the time their barrages were becoming both more frequent and more intense. It was clear that a major offensive was to be expected.

In mid-morning on 28 May, the Chinese artillery opened a ferocious bombardment, which continued throughout the day and for much of the night, causing havoc in the Dukes' line. United Nations guns replied with a counter-bombardment, creating the greatest artillery duel along a 915-m (1,000-yd) front since the First World War.

Just before 8 pm, a sudden crescendo of shelling, increased Chinese army radio traffic and a whispered 'This is it' from a two-man patrol holed up with a wireless far out in No Man's Land, gave notice that the Dukes would soon be under infantry attack. Light rain was drifting down between the hills when the first enemy assault columns came rushing toward the Hook.

Those Chinese who survived the storm of shells and managed to penetrate the wire found the United Nations frontline trenches pulverized. The Dukes, who had taken shelter from the barrage in tunnels in the hillside, put up a gallant, albeit uncoordinated resistance, but the forward positions had lost their radio and telephone links with command posts in the rear, and there was no longer a connected defensive perimeter. Handfuls of men, often without officers, stood and fought wherever they could amid the débris. Meanwhile, small parties of Chinese, armed with satchels of high explosives, hurled their charges into the mouths of tunnels and bunkers, entombing any occupants.

Reinforcements were hurried to the Hook which, as the eerie light of flares revealed, had completely changed its shape under the earth-moving weight of 10,000 Chinese shells. Toward 9 pm, the Communists launched another attack from the direction of 'Warsaw', only to be halted by concentrated defensive fire. Then two companies tried to take Point 121, and were badly mauled. A little later, opposite Point 146 to the right of the Dukes, the King's Regiment detected a large body of Chinese, and called down a barrage, which in a matter of minutes virtually wiped out a Communist battalion.

It was after midnight when the last big Chinese attack was made across the front of Point 121 and up 'Ronson' toward the Hook. A closely woven pattern of defensive fire caught their infantry as they reached the entanglements. From then onward, support platoons ranged over the Dukes' battered positions, driving out the Chinese. It was not until 3.30 am, however, that they could report with certainty that the Hook had been cleared of the enemy.

At first light, battle-weary soldiers stared in disbelief as the true horror of the devastating attacks became apparent. The British lines were a shambles: weapon pits and trenches 2.4 m (8 ft) deep had been flattened, and men and equipment were buried under tons of earth and rubble. The Dukes suffered 149 casualties in the battle: Chinese losses exceeded 1,000. Mercifully, however, this was to prove the last battle of the Korean War, for on 27 July, an armistice was signed.

Two views of the 'farewell' parade of the 1st Battalion, the Duke of Wellington's Regiment, the last British infantry unit to leave Korea. The regiment won fame through its battles on the Hook.

A **Chinese propaganda** leaflet, calling on their enemy to surrender. Thousands of leaflets such as this were dropped on U.N. lines, but met with no reaction.

A **3-in British mortar**. The bomb is dropped into the barrel and is detonated when it hits a striker at the base of the tube.

After three years of bitter conflict, the Korean War came to an end with the signing of an armistice at Panmunjon on 27 July 1953. Under the terms of the agreement, a demarcation line between the Communists in the north and the Republic of South Korea was established, roughly following the route of the front lines. On both sides of the line, troops were pulled back 2 km (1¼ mls), thus forming a demilitarized zone 4 km (2 ½ mls) wide.

Having successfully defended South Korea's right to exist, the United Nations warned the Communists that any violation of the demilitarized zone or other breach of the armistice terms would be viewed so seriously that resumed hostilities would probably be carried beyond the boundaries of Korea. No peace treaty has been concluded, but an uneasy truce is maintained. North Korea remains an armed camp. South Korea, now a rich and rapidly developing industrial nation, ensures its safety by spending huge sums on its modern, well-equipped army.

2

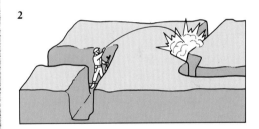

3

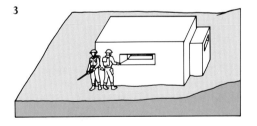

Throughout the Korean War, particularly when fighting became entrenched along the 38th Parallel, both the U.N. forces and the Communists made frequent use of hand-grenades. Both sides employed fragmentation bombs, the detonation of which was regulated by a four-second fuse. British grenades were activated by pulling out a pin; the Chinese type, which was attached to a wooden throwing handle, was ignited by a friction primer. When using a grenade, the thrower had to take cover, **1**, because fragments spread through 360 degrees and extended beyond maximum lobbing range. These grenades were most effective when thrown into enclosed areas, such as trenches, **2**, or concrete bunkers, **3**.

1

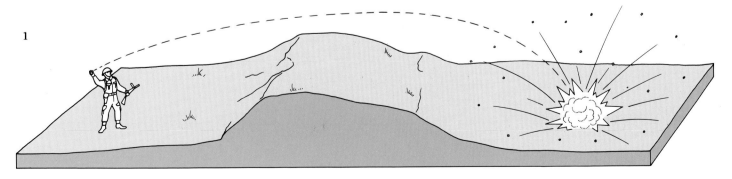

Dien Bien Phu/*20 November, 1953 - 7 May, 1954*

In May 1953, General Henri Navarre assumed command in Vietnam, at a time when French forces were very much on the defensive. He devised a plan to lure the Viet Minh into a pitched battle, in which his supposedly superior firepower would annihilate Giap's guerrillas: in a bold airborne operation, a strong garrison was to be dropped in the heart of enemy territory, where it could not be ignored. The spot Navarre chose was Dien Bien Phu, a village in a small valley nearly 320 km (200 mls) west of Hanoi, the main French base in north Vietnam.

'Operation Castor', as Navarre's plan was codenamed, began on 20 November 1953, when a spearhead force of 1,800 paratroopers descended on Dien Bien Phu and established a strong base. Two airfields were quickly built to ensure a supply link. The garrison, commanded by Colonel Christian de Castries, grew to more than 15,000 men, supported by 60 guns, 10 light M24 Chaffee tanks and 6 napalm-carrying assault aircraft.

Nine defensive boxes, all given women's names, were carefully laid out around the vital airstrips. 'Eliane', which housed de Castries's headquarters, encompassed Dien Bien Phu village east of the main airfield; 'Claudine' guarded the south; 'Huguette' and 'Françoise' the west, and 'Dominique' the north. Farther up the valley, beyond 'Dominique', three smaller strongpoints—'Anne Marie', 'Gabrielle' and 'Beatrice'—formed an outer defence line. South of 'Claudine', 'Isabelle' protected the small satellite airstrip.

The French, confident of their devastating firepower, crouched in their sandbagged weapon pits, waiting for the Viet Minh to attack. Months passed and no attack materialized—but all the while the Viet Minh were making careful preparations to catch the French in their own trap.

Big changes had recently been made in Giap's army, improvements that Navarre failed to appreciate. Efficient training and the acquisition of extensive equipment from China had transformed the guerrillas into a powerful fighting force. Instead of the maximum of two divisions that the French calculated Giap could deploy against Dien Bien Phu, four were moved into the area, together with about 200 guns, some of which were anti-aircraft weapons. Giap's soldiers, masters of tunnelling and camouflage, dug galleries through the range of hills to the east of Dien Bien Phu, overlooking the French defences, and cunningly positioned their guns so that only the tips of the muzzles protruded from the embrasures.

On 13 March 1954, Giap was at last

When the Japanese withdrew from Indo-China at the end of the Second World War, France tried to re-establish control over her old colonies—Laos, Cambodia and Vietnam. Nine years and a humiliating defeat later, the French realized that their days of imperial might were over.

Cambodia and Laos reluctantly accepted self-government within the French Union, but Vietnam was not so pliable. A League for the Independence of Vietnam, known as the Viet Minh, had been established by Communists and Nationalists in 1941, and, when the Second World War ended, they declared their independence. Nevertheless, when the French forces returned, the Vietnamese leader, Ho Chi Minh, grudgingly agreed to Vietnam's being treated as a free state under the protection of France. It was a hostile relationship, however, and open warfare broke out, on 19 December 1946.

In general, the French held the towns and cities, and the Viet Minh guerrillas, under General Giap, dominated the country districts. Giap was content to carry out hit-and-run raids while he built up his forces in the mountain fastnesses of north Vietnam.

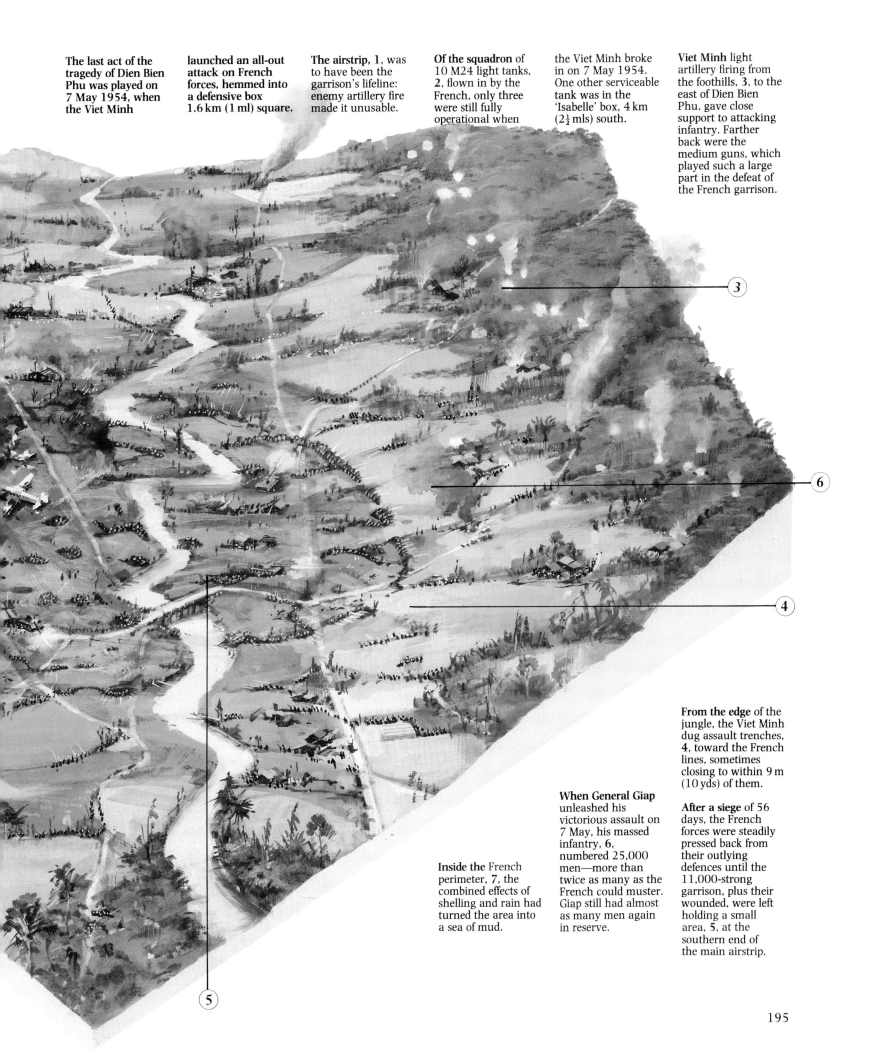

The last act of the tragedy of Dien Bien Phu was played on 7 May 1954, when the Viet Minh launched an all-out attack on French forces, hemmed into a defensive box 1.6 km (1 ml) square.

The airstrip, 1, was to have been the garrison's lifeline: enemy artillery fire made it unusable.

Of the squadron of 10 M24 light tanks, 2, flown in by the French, only three were still fully operational when the Viet Minh broke in on 7 May 1954. One other serviceable tank was in the 'Isabelle' box, 4 km (2½ mls) south.

Viet Minh light artillery firing from the foothills, 3, to the east of Dien Bien Phu, gave close support to attacking infantry. Farther back were the medium guns, which played such a large part in the defeat of the French garrison.

From the edge of the jungle, the Viet Minh dug assault trenches, 4, toward the French lines, sometimes closing to within 9 m (10 yds) of them.

When General Giap unleashed his victorious assault on 7 May, his massed infantry, 6, numbered 25,000 men—more than twice as many as the French could muster. Giap still had almost as many men again in reserve.

Inside the French perimeter, 7, the combined effects of shelling and rain had turned the area into a sea of mud.

After a siege of 56 days, the French forces were steadily pressed back from their outlying defences until the 11,000-strong garrison, plus their wounded, were left holding a small area, 5, at the southern end of the main airstrip.

195

Dien Bien Phu/2

ready to take up Navarre's challenge. Colonel de Castries's men, only lightly protected by foxholes and sandbagged bunkers, were dismayed by the strength and ferocity of the guerrillas' opening bombardment. First, infantry attacks fell on the outer defence line and 'Beatrice' was taken quickly; 'Gabrielle' surrendered two days later and, on 18 March, 'Anne Marie' was also lost. By then, disillusioned by events, Colonel Piroth, the artillery commander, had committed suicide: despite his earlier boasts, his batteries had proved helpless against the hidden might of Giap's guns.

The loss of the outer defences, together with concerted artillery fire and infantry attacks on the remaining strongholds, rendered the main airfield unusable. From that time, all supplies and reinforcements had to be parachuted in. More than 60 aircraft were destroyed during the siege.

The Viet Minh had not bought their early successes lightly, however: it is estimated that 2,500 were killed in the opening attacks and many more wounded. Then, for about 10 days, General Giap resorted to formal siege tactics, but, on 30 March, he reverted to hurricane bombardments, followed immediately by attacks from hordes of screaming infantrymen. In a week of vicious hand-to-hand fighting, the Viet Minh made further inroads: 'Dominique' and 'Françoise' fell, together with a large part of 'Huguette', and sections of 'Claudine' and 'Eliane'. 'Isabelle', out of touch to the south, held out against overwhelming odds. To add to the French soldiers' plight, their unrevetted weapon pits were washed out by the early monsoon.

The guerrillas' losses were enormous, and Giap once more drew back to reinforce and regroup his forces. By 1 May, he had assembled 50,000 men around Dien Bien Phu; these he then unleashed against de Castries's dwindling garrison. The French were obliged to utilize the precious reserves of artillery ammunition that they had kept for an emergency. Although they fought bravely, it was clear they could not hold out for long. A break-out was impossible, and there was no chance of a relief column getting through to help them. Their only hope was a huge air raid on Viet Minh positions by U.S. bombers, operating from aircraft carriers in the South China Sea; or—and the French were serious—the use of a U.S. nuclear weapon. But America, although she had been supplying arms and other aid, would not become directly involved in the struggle. The surrounded French were thus without allies.

Position after position crumbled under massive, reckless attacks and, on 7 May, the last redoubt was overrun.

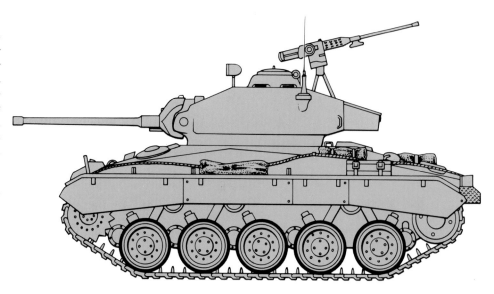

French firepower at Dien Bien Phu, which included heavy and medium artillery and six napalm-armed Bearcat fighters, was further augmented in December 1953 by the arrival of a squadron of 10 light tanks. The American-built M24 Chaffees, each mounting a 75 mm gun and a heavy machine-gun, arrived in 180-piece kit form and were assembled at the side of the runway. The squadron became fully operational on 20 January 1954, and gave sterling service. In the course of the protracted action, each M24 expended, on average, 1,500 rounds of 75mm ammunition. Four tanks remained in service when the Viet Minh opened their offensive. These were deliberately disabled by their crews just before their positions were overrun by the Communists on 7 May.

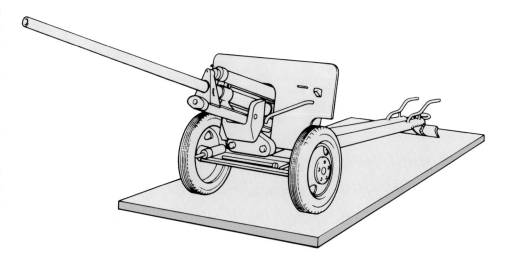

The Viet Minh guerrilla army had been equipped with small arms and little else. But at the end of the Korean War, in July 1953, Communist China began to supply its Viet Minh ally with much more sophisticated weapons—light and medium field artillery, anti-aircraft guns and rocket launchers. It was the deployment of weapons such as the 105 mm gun, *above*, with a range of more than 11 km (7 mls), that took the French by surprise at Dien Bien Phu. These, and many lighter pieces too, had been stripped and carried through the jungle by coolies before being reassembled and positioned in the hills overlooking the French defences—which they proceeded to demolish.

Colonel Christian de Castries, a cavalry officer, commanded the French garrison at Dien Bien Phu. During the siege, in which de Castries did his best against insurmountable odds, he was promoted to brigadier.

General Vo Nguyen Giap had been the military head of the Viet Minh since it was formed in 1941. His guerrilla army first clashed with the French in 1946 and Giap turned it into a formidable force over the next eight years.

By March 1954, Viet Minh artillery fire had destroyed the airstrip, so that all supplies and reinforcements for the French garrison had to be parachuted in, *top*. A column of smoke rises over Dien Bien Phu as French paratroopers, *above*, rush to ward off an enemy attack.

The surrender of the French forces at Dien Bien Phu was a defeat of the first magnitude and, to all intents and purposes, ended French rule in Indo-China. It came as a direct consequence of over-confidence in their ability to dominate a battlefield of their own choosing, coupled with serious underestimation of the guerrillas' strength and capability. France's humiliation did not enhance its position at the Geneva Conference on Far Eastern Affairs called by 19 nations (including Communist China), and co-chaired by Britain and the Soviet Union. This resulted, on 21 July 1954, in the signing of a truce and the division of Vietnam into two states, the North (Communist) and the South (Democratic), as independent nations. The United States accepted the agreements but refused to sign them and reserved its right to take unilaterally whatever steps were necessary in its opinion if the agreements were violated. French troops withdrew from Indo-China, though France retained influence and 'advisers' in the South and also in Laos and Cambodia. The United States took upon itself the burden of providing South Vietnam with military equipment and economic aid and was soon to be sucked into entanglements that were just as disastrous as those that had strangled the French. Americans might well have grimly recalled that, in 1954, President Eisenhower had had the option of coming to the aid of the French, but he rejected the possibility that white troops could defeat native Vietnamese in their own country.

197

BATTLEFIELDS GAZETTEER

Details on how to get to the sites of the battles described in this book and what to see there are listed below. Those sites which are either inaccessible or have no outstanding points of interest have been omitted.

More detailed information may be obtained from a number of institutions, such as the Imperial War Museum and the War Graves Commission in the United Kingdom, the National Parks Service of the United States Department of the Interior in the U.S.A. and, in France, at the Musée de l'Armée, Les Invalides, Paris.

Arnhem

The area of 'The Corridor' and drop zones for 'Operation Market Garden' extended over some 100 km (62 mls) from the Belgian border, north through Eindhoven, St Oedenrode, Veghel, Grave, Nijmegen to Arnhem, and west to Oosterbeek.

The Airborne Museum is housed in the old Hartenstein Hotel, Oosterbeek, which served as Divisional Headquarters for the British First Airborne Division in September 1944. The entire 'Market Garden' operation is described with dioramas and audio-visual presentations, and the museum contains an interesting collection of photographs, as well as weapons and uniforms. The division's cemetery is also in Oosterbeek, together with the Airborne memorial.

The bridge over the Lower Rhine at Arnhem—the target of the operation— was destroyed later in the war. It was rebuilt by the Dutch in 1950 and named the John Frost Bridge, in honour of the commander of the 2nd Battalion, whose men made such a magnificent stand there during the battle.

Austerlitz

Now called Slavkov ü Brno, Austerlitz is on Route 47 to Olmutz, about 8 km (5 mls) east of Brno in Czechoslovakia. The battlefield, which is little altered, is on the south of the road and west of Austerlitz.

Small calvaries mark the graves of the French, Russians and Austrians, who were buried where they fell. In 1912, the Cairn of Peace was erected on the battlefield as a memorial. It contains a chapel and burial crypt, to which any unearthed human remains are transferred. Behind the chapel there is a small museum, with a battle plan and examples of weapons and other relics. There are more mass graves at nearby villages, such as Kobylnice and

Blazkovice. A memorial was erected at Slapanice in 1965 to mark the 160th anniversary of the battle.

Napoleon's headquarters on Zurlan Hill is marked by a diagram of the battlefield carved on a stone cube. At Slavkov Château there are some Napoleonic memorabilia, and Napoleon's victory is commemorated by the Barrow of Peace at Prace. The old posting-station at Požvice, where Napoleon rested after the battle, is also preserved.

Blenheim

The Bavarian village of Blenheim, now called Blindheim, is to the west of the Romantic Road and north of the River Danube. A memorial stone to those killed during the battle is on the edge of the nearby town of Höchstadt, on the Donauwörth road.

The Boyne

This famous Irish battlefield is located on the Drogheda to Slane road, southwest of Oldbridge. The ford at Oldbridge, which no longer exists as a town, ran under the modern iron bridge that now crosses the river. The area over which the Dutch Guards and Irish infantry fought lies in the park of a large house.

Cannae

The ruins of the town of Cannae stand on a small hill between Canosa and Barletta in southern Italy. The changing course of the River Ofanto (formley Aufidus) has led to debate as to the exact location of the battlefield, but it was probably on the right bank of the river. An ancient column commemorating the battle has recently been re-erected. It is inscribed with a quotation from Livy (xxii, 54, 10): 'No other nation could have suffered such tremendous disasters and not been destroyed.'

Colenso

The town of Colenso in South Africa is on the main Durban to Johannesburg road, the N3, about 24 km (15 mls) southeast of Ladysmith. The war cemetery and memorial to the fallen are at Ambleside, about 3.2 km (2 mls) from Colenso on the Winterton road.

Naval Hill, about 3.2 km (2 mls) south of Colenso, is the position from which the British naval guns fired on the Boer entrenchments on the far side of the Tugela River. Hart's Hill, 8 km (5 mls) outside Colenso, is marked at the base by a cairn, near which many of General Hart's Irish Brigade were killed.

The R.E. Stevenson Museum in the

town of Colenso contains mementoes of the Anglo-Boer War and especially of the Battle of Colenso. Near Colenso railway station is a monument to Lt. the Hon. F.H.S. Roberts V.C., who was mortally wounded while trying to recover abandoned guns during the battle.

Winston Churchill's cairn at Colenso marks the place where an armoured train on reconnaisance from Estcourt was attacked and derailed by the Boers on 15 November 1899. Winston Churchill, who was taken prisoner by the Boers, was a war correspondent with the British forces at the time.

Crécy

The town of Crécy-en-Ponthieu is at the junction of the D111, the D10 and the D938 in northern France. From the nearest main town, Abbeville, take the Hesdin to St Omer road for 66 km (41 mls) and 4.8 km (3 mls) before reaching Labroye turn south for Crécy-en-Ponthieu.

Much of the battlefield remains unchanged, except for a factory on the site where the French knights charged through their own Genoese crossbowmen. On Route D111 there is a mound where the windmill, used by Edward III as a command post, once stood. The English lines were directly in front of what is now the D111. An outline map of the entire battle is provided on the site.

Culloden

To reach the battlefield, which is in the care of the National Trust for Scotland, take the A9, Inverness to Perth road, and then turn off on to the B9006.

The Forestry Commission had planted conifers over much of the area, but these have now been cleared and the battlefield restored to its original appearance.

A Visitor Centre, open for part of the year, includes an audio-visual programme. There is a museum nearby, housed in a cottage at Leanach that has survived since the '45 Rebellion. Mass graves of the clans are situated at the eastern end of the battlefield, each clan being marked by a stone. Also worth seeing are the Well of the Dead, the Memorial Cairn and the Cumberland Stone. There is an interesting collection of Jacobite memorabilia at the West Highland Museum, Fort William.

Gettysburg

There are several ways to see the superbly maintained National Military Park at Gettysburg, Pennsylvania: by bus, car, bicycle or on foot. Tape recordings, which direct you across the battlefield and talk you through the action, can be hired. Many splendid regimental memorials have been erected over the battle area.

Do not miss the Visitor Center Museum; the electric map; the cyclorama (a massive circular painting of the battle); General Lee's Headquarters; the Lincoln Room, where the President put the finishing touches to the Gettysburg Address; or the military cemetery, where the Address was delivered.

Much of the old town of Gettysburg remains, and many houses bear bronze plaques with the legend, 'Civil War Building, July 1–3 1863'.

Hastings

The battlefield is south of Abbey Green in the town of Battle, East Sussex, England, which can be reached on the A2100 from London. Battle Abbey was founded by William I to commemorate his victory. The high altar was built over the place where Harold was killed. The Abbey church was destroyed by Henry VIII and the Abbot's house is now a school, but the position of the altar is marked by a Norman Stone in the school's inner garden. The battlefield is open to the public. The course of the action is recorded at several vantage points, and a model shows how the armies were deployed. See, too, the Battle Memorial Hall Museum.

Little Big Horn

The U.S. National Park Service has care of the battlefield, which has been protected since 1940 as the Custer Battlefield National Monument. It is situated in the Crow Indian Reservation in southeastern Montana. The nearest road is the U.S. 87 (1–90), which passes 1.6 km (1 ml) to the west of the battlefield.

There is a Visitor Center and a well-signposted tourist route around the battlefield, giving details of the various stages of the actions fought by Custer and Major Reno.

From Custer Hill, most of the battlefield and the valley with the Indian village may be seen. Fifty-two markers indicate the position of Custer's 'last stand'. Originally the soldiers were buried where they fell, but they were reinterred in 1881 in a common grave beside a memorial. The bodies of 11 officers and 2 civilians had previously been reburied elsewhere at the request of relatives, including that of Custer which was interred at the U.S. Military Academy, West Point, N.Y. on 10 October 1877.

Naseby

To approach Naseby from the south, take the M1 as far as junction 18, turn right for West Haddon and follow the B4036, which passes through the village of Naseby.

Apart from enclosed fields, the battleground at Naseby, Northamptonshire, England, is much as it was in the seventeenth century. Sulby Hedges, where Okey's dragoons were deployed to such good effect, remain as two rows of trees about 18.3 m (20 yds) apart.

There are two monuments: the nineteenth-century Naseby obelisk is about 1.6 km (1 ml) from the battlefield, and about 475 m (500 yds) to the west of Cromwell's charge there is a memorial erected by the Cromwell Association. In Naseby church, there is the table around which some Royalists were sitting when they were captured by Parliamentarian scouts in the village. There is also a broken sword and stirrup iron from the field.

Saratoga

Both battles of Saratoga were fought in the area that is now part of Saratoga National Historical Park. The entrance to the park is 48 km (30 mls) north of Albany, New York on U.S.4. and N.Y.32.

The battlefield is well maintained and a tourist road, 17 km (10½ mls) long, runs through the park. There are several monuments on the field, including the Saratoga National Monument which commemorates the British surrender.

At the Visitor Center, a film about the battle can be seen, on request, before one embarks upon the tour, which has ten stops. At each, aspects of the battle are illustrated with wayside exhibits, walking trails and audio units.

Solferino

The battlefield is located in northern Italy along the Brescia to Mantua highway (N. 236), at a point 6.4 km (4 mls) southeast of Castiglione delle Stiviere. On the site is a memorial to Jean Henri Dunant, who was inspired to found the Red Cross after witnessing the horrors of the battle.

The Somme

Cemeteries abound in the Somme sector of the Western Front in France. The largest war memorial in the world is at Thiepval: it records the names of 73,367 British casualties of the battle. Thiepval, in the centre of the Somme front, is about 8 km (5 mls) northeast of Albert, and may be reached by taking the N29 from Albert to Bapaume until reaching Poziers and then turning left on to the D73 to Thiepval.

There are a number of memorials to various regiments along the front, and some stretches of the trenches can still be seen. Several organized visits to the battlefield take place.

Suvla Bay

The site of the battle at Suvla Bay, on the west coast of the Gallipoli Peninsula in Turkey, can still be identified by trench lines. Memorials to all the soldiers killed during the Gallipoli Campaign are mainly around the Sea of Marmara. British and French war memorials and cemeteries, and a Turkish war memorial, are to be found around Morto Bay. Two further Turkish memorials are at Canakkale and Eceabat on the opposite shore of the Sea of Marmara.

Waterloo

The battlefield is protected by Belgian law and so is little changed. It is situated 20 km (12½ mls) south of Brussels and 3.2 km (2 mls) south of Waterloo, on Route No. 5, the road to Charleroi, via Genappe. There is also access by air, rail and bus and organized trips.

There are a number of monuments on the field, the most imposing being Lion Hill, the Dutch Memorial.

Many buildings associated with the battle are still standing, including La Belle Alliance and La Haye Sainte farm.

There are many places in the United Kingdom connected with the Duke of Wellington, such as Apsley House, the Duke's London home, which is now the Wellington Museum. Stratfield Saye, near Reading, the Duke's country house, was presented to him by the Nation. It may be visited on request. The Guards' museum at Wellington Barracks, London, has a small section devoted to Wellington. In the grounds of Little Dalby Hall at Little Dalby, 4.8 km (3 mls) southwest of Melton Mowbray on the A606 to Oakham, a veteran of Waterloo planted trees to represent the Anglo-Dutch troop positions.

ACKNOWLEDGEMENTS

The publishers of *Great Battlefields of the World* are especially indebted to Mr James Lucas and the staff of the Imperial War Museum, London, for their invaluable assistance. They are also grateful to the staff of the Royal Geographical Society; to Edward Stanford Ltd; to the School of African and Oriental Studies, London, and to Mr Thomas G. DeClaire, of the Geography and Map Division of the Library of Congress, Washington, D.C., for the provision of maps. Military antiques were kindly loaned by Mr C. F. Seidler, Stand 120, Grays Antique Market, 58 Davies Street, London W.1.